China's Intellectuals and the State

Harvard Contemporary China Series: 3

edited by
MERLE GOLDMAN
with TIMOTHY CHEEK
and CAROL LEE HAMRIN

Published by
THE COUNCIL ON EAST ASIAN STUDIES / HARVARD UNIVERSITY
Distributed by the Harvard University Press
Cambridge (Massachusetts) and London 1987

China's Intellectuals and the State

In Search of a
New Relationship

The Council on East Asian Studies at Harvard University publishes a monograph series and,
through the Fairbank Center for East Asian Research and the Reischauer Institute of Japanese
Studies, administers research projects designed to further scholarly understanding of China, Japan,
Korea, Vietnam, Inner Asia, and adjacent areas.

Library of Congress Cataloging in Publication Data

China's intellectuals and the state.

  (Harvard contemporary China series ; 3)
  Bibliography: p.
  Includes index.
    1. China—Intellectual life—1949- . 2. China—
Politics and government—1949- . I. Goldman,
Merle. II. Cheek, Timothy. III. Hamrin, Carol Lee.
IV. Series.
DS777.6.C46 1987   001.1'0951   87-177
ISBN 0-674-11972-X

TIMOTHY CHEEK wrote his Harvard doctoral dissertation (1986) on "Orthodoxy and Dissent in People's China: The Life and Death of Deng Tuo." He is now a visiting professor of Chinese history at Bowdoin College, and is engaged in research on the role of intellectuals and ideology in China. He is a co-editor, with Carol Lee Hamrin of CHINA'S ESTABLISHMENT INTELLECTUALS (Armonk, M. E. Sharpe, 1986).

CLIFFORD G. EDMUNDS, JR., formerly on the faculty of the University of Maryland, is now a political analyst for the United States Government. He is currently interested in the politics of reform in the People's Republic of China, particularly the ideological controversies sparked by recent Dengist policies, and the changing role of the Chinese Communist Party.

JAMES V. FEINERMAN, formerly Administrative Director of Harvard Law School's East Asian Legal Studies Program, is currently Associate Professor of Law at Georgetown University Law Center. In 1979–1980, he was an exchange student at Peking University under the auspices of the U.S. national exchange program administered by the Committee on Scholarly Communication with the People's Republic of China. He returned to Peking University's Law Faculty in 1982–1983 as a Fulbright Lecturer on Law.

JOSHUA A. FOGEL is Associate Professor of History, Harvard University, and the author of POLITICS AND SINOLOGY: THE CASE OF NAITŌ KONAN, 1866–1934 (Council on East Asian Studies, Harvard, 1984). He is now completing an intellectual biography of Nakae Ushikichi (1899–1942) and a translation of the memoirs of Itō Takeo, LIFE ALONG THE SOUTH MANCHURIAN RAILWAY.

MERLE GOLDMAN teaches Chinese History at Boston University. She is the author of several books on the role of the intellectuals in the People's Republic of China, most recently CHINA'S INTELLECTUALS: ADVISE AND DISSENT (Harvard University Press, 1981). She is currently at work on a book about the humanistic elite in post-Mao China.

NINA HALPERN, who formerly taught at Dartmouth College, is now Assistant Professor of Political Science at Stanford University. During 1982–1983, she was at Beijing University, conducting research on the role of Chinese economic specialists in policy-making. Her current investigations concern the way the Chinese government acquires and uses expert advice on science and economics and methods of policy coordination in the Chinese bureaucracy.

CAROL LEE HAMRIN is Research Specialist for China at the Department of State and Professorial Lecturer at the Johns Hopkins School of Advanced International Studies (SAIS) in Washington, D.C. With Timothy Cheek, she is co-editor of CHINA'S ESTABLISHMENT INTELLECTUALS (Armonk, M. E. Sharpe, 1986). She has just completed CHINA AND THE FUTURE (Boulder, Westview Press, forthcoming in 1987) on the relationships among Chinese politics, economic planning, and foreign policy.

DAVID A. KELLY has been engaged in postdoctoral research at the Contemporary China Centre, Australian National University, and as a Fulbright Fellow at the University of Chicago. He has published studies in a number of fields of modern Chinese intellectual history, and is the editor/translator of "Wang Ruoshui: Writings on Human-ism, Alienation, and Philosophy (*Chinese Studies in Philosophy*, Spring 1985). He now lives in Canberra and is at work on a book about humanism and related trends in Chinese Marxism.

KYNA RUBIN, M.A. Chinese Literature, University of British Columbia, spent 1979–1980 at Fudan University studying modern Chinese literature on a grant from the Committee on Scholarly Com-munication with the People's Republic of China (CSCPRC). She now manages the CSCPRC's National Program for Advanced Study and Research in China. Her own work focuses on literary policy in Yan'an in the 1930s and 1940s.

DENIS FRED SIMON is the Ford International Assistant Professor of Management and Technology at the Sloan School, The Massachu-setts Institute of Technology. He is the author of numerous articles on the modernization of science and technology in the PRC and China's use of foreign technology. He recently completed a study of technological innovation in Shanghai's electronics and computer industry.

RUDOLF G. WAGNER is Professor of Sinology at Heidelberg University, and has been engaged for several years in research at the University of California (Berkeley) and Harvard University. His recent book-length studies include THE CONTEMPORARY CHINESE HISTORICAL DRAMA (Berkeley, University of Cali-fornia Press, forthcoming), and REENACTING THE HEAVENLY VISION: THE ROLE OF RELIGION IN THE TAIPING REBEL-LION (Center for Chinese Studies, University of California, Berke-ley, 1984).

LYNN T. WHITE III teaches in the Woodrow Wilson School and Politics Department at Princeton University. He is the author of CAREERS IN SHANGHAI (University of California Press) and various articles about economic and social development in that city. His current research is focused on the mass-group bases during the Cultural Revolution.

CONTENTS

ABBREVIATIONS USED IN THE TEXT AND NOTES

CAS	Chinese Academy of Sciences
CASS	Chinese Academy of Social Sciences
CAST	Chinese Scientific and Technological Association
CR	Cultural Revolution
FBIS	*Foreign Broadcast Information Service*
GLF	Great Leap Forward
GMT	Greenwich Mean Time
JPRS	*Joint Publications Research Service*
LAO	Legal Advisory Office
LDC	less-developed country
NCNA	New China News Agency
NDSTIC	National Defense Science, Technology, and Industries Commission
NPC	National People's Congress
PLA	People's Liberation Army
PRC	People's Republic of China
R&D	Research and Development
RRWT	*Renxing, Rendaozhuyi wente taolunji* (Beijing, Renmin Chuban she, 1983)

RSMC	*Ren shi makesizhuyide chufadian* (Beijing, Renmin Chuban she, 1981)
SSTC	State Science and Technology Commission
S&T	science and technology
SWB	*Summary of World Broadcasts: The Far East*
"WR"	D. A. Kelly, "Wang Ruoshui: Writings on Humanism, Alienation, and Philosophy," *Chinese Studies in Philosophy,* Spring 1985.
ZZZS	Wang Ruoshui, *Zai Zhexue Zhongsheng Shang*
1844 Ms.	Karl Marx, *Economic and Philosophic Manuscripts of 1844*

As this book goes to print, we are watching the dust settle from Hu Yaobang's forced resignation as Party General Secretary, allegedly for promoting "bourgeois liberalization." A number of the intellectuals associated with him and also under attack are covered in this volume. Clearly, this is round two of the unfinished 1983 Campaign Against Spiritual Pollution. Regardless of the immediate outcome, this episode is the most serious in a series of counter-reform episodes since the late 1970s, and it underscores our themes: the continuation of the oscillating treatment of intellectuals between periods of relative relaxation and repression, and the continued dependence of intellectuals on patronage of the top leadership.

China's latest Anti-Rightist Campaign may yet be turned off before too many intellectuals lose their Party cards and jobs, but damage has already been done to the reform program. The Party inner core has suffered a failure of nerve in its self-stated aim of sharing power and influence with a wider range of the elite. Efforts to improve the Party's image and recruit young intellectuals have been undermined. Students overseas will worry about their futures—if they return. And prospects for a smooth succession after Deng Xiaoping have been reduced, because the arbitrary dismissal of a top leader undermines the institutionalization of politics. Overall, this latest conservative backlash suggests that the Chinese leadership is "riding a tiger." Their requests for ideas on political reform—how to democratize a single-Party system—brought them more than they bargained for.

The 1987 Campaign Against Bourgeois Liberalization, which once again links the fate of the intellectuals to leadership politics, highlights the importance of the topic of this book and dictates that our conclusions must necessarily be preliminary. In fact, this volume is only one part of an ongoing intellectual project—to understand how a changing Marxist ideology and political system both reflect and shape the lives of intellectuals. Our joint involvement in this project began, after years of individual research, with a conference panel in 1980. In a companion volume to this one, *China's Establishment Intellectuals* (1986), seven scholars joined Tim Cheek and Carol Hamrin in assessing the motivations and methods for participation in the system by a range of Communist intellectuals who were criticized and purged by Mao in the 1950s and 1960s. Although that book touches on the post-Mao period, its focus is on the reactions of China's intellectual establishment to the failures of the Great Leap Forward (1958–1960) and the roles of these intellectuals in the Cultural Revolution. Merle Goldman's *China's Intellectuals* (1981) also discusses them and the younger, radical intellectuals dominant in the 1970s.

This present work focuses on the post-Mao return of the pre-Cultural Revolution establishment, but it also deals with connections with the Maoist era. Moreover, it moves beyond biography and generational studies to group studies of economists, lawyers, professionals, scientists, writers, and lower-level intellectuals in the People's Republic. To carry out this effort, Merle invited Tim and Carol to bring their proposed conference on "Chinese Intellectuals and the CCP" to the New England China Seminar at Harvard in 1984, and she took charge of the exacting task of finally editing the conference papers.

We should like to express our thanks to all the authors and others who have helped make this book possible and who continue to explore these questions and share their results with us. In particular, we want to acknowledge the helpful comments and insights of the panel commentators at the 1984 Seminar and the input of those authors whose papers could not be included here. Throughout the years of this broader project, the cooperative style of all those involved has been an inspiration and a delight.

Timothy Cheek
Merle Goldman
Carol Lee Hamrin
February 1987

Uncertain Change

MERLE GOLDMAN *and* TIMOTHY CHEEK[1]

Since most literati in traditional China were also bureaucrats, "the cost of their quest for intellectual autonomy was political estrangement," as pointed out by Frederic Wakeman.[2] For those literati who also sought moral autonomy from the state, the cost was even greater. China's intellectuals in the twentieth century have continued to incur this cost whether under Guomindang or Chinese Communist rule and even under the reform leadership of Deng Xiaoping. Although intellectuals in modern times have switched from serving their culture to serving their nation, their service to the nation has severely limited their intellectual and moral autonomy.

Historically, the participation of China's intellectuals in politics has ranged from unquestioning government service through critical remonstrance to total withdrawal from public life. Nevertheless, most of the educated elite since the Song dynasty were closely bound to state service through the examination system, which functioned both to certify their elite status and to recruit them into bureaucratic office. Events of the past century have undermined the traditional links between state and literati, but not the political vocation that made educated Chinese feel responsible for the fate of their country. Three interrelated processes helped transform the previous imperial elite into the intellectuals of today. First, the crisis of legitimacy that followed the fall of the monarchy in 1911 reinforced the elite's consciousness of themselves as autonomous critics of political authority. In this sense, a portion of the elite of the early twentieth century came to resemble a modern alienated intelligentsia. Second, the emergence of modern nationalism made intellectuals aware of their stake in China's survival as a nation, as distinct from the survival of any particular political regime. Third, the development of the Leninist-style political party, both the Guomindang and Chinese Communist Party (CCP), provided new channels for political participation, while at the same time demanding even more exclusive ideological loyalty than had the dynastic system.

China's intellectuals, therefore, have carried within them survivals of the past: the role of the intellectual as servant of the state, and the role as moral critic of the ruler. Between these two deeply internalized roles, China's intellectuals have had to find their place in the modern world. Some of the Chinese intellectuals discussed in this volume are at the same time both high-level intellectuals (*gaoji zhishi fenzi*) and high-level officials (*gaoji ganbu*) in the PRC. Most of the PRC's high-level intellectuals—academics, writers, artists, doctors, scientists, engineers, lawyers, economists, journalists—do not directly staff the Party and government bureaucracy. But they are part of the official establishment, since virtually all institutions in which they work are controlled by the government. At times, they have been denigrated and severely punished, particularly during the Cultural Revolution decade (1966–1976). In the post-Mao period, their rise in prominence and status reflects the political leadership's recognition of their skills as crucial to China's renewed modernization drive. This category of high-level intellectuals corresponds with Edward Shils's analysis of intellectuals who are primarily engaged in intellectual activities that define the "ultimate" or the ideal—issues inseparable from political authority—and have "affirmed, accepted and served the ruling authorities."[3]

In addition to the traditions of Confucianism and Marxism-Leninism, China's intellectuals are also heirs to another tradition—the "enlightenment movement" of the May Fourth period in the 1910s and 1920s. During a period of political disunity and openness to Western culture, many educated Chinese, unattached to any political group, formed strong intellectual and cultural communities and imbibed such Western values as freedom of expression and individual rights.[4] Although they sought to regenerate the Chinese polity, they conceived of their activities as free and independent of political control. Thus, the model of the May Fourth intellectual—politically committed but intellectually autonomous who sought to emancipate themselves from "patriarchal authority" is also an integral part of the culture bequeathed to the present generation.[5] This complex—and contradictory—heritage has produced three major roles for intellectuals in recent decades: ideological spokesmen, professional and academic elite, and critical intellectuals. A number of intellectuals have rotated among these roles at different times in their careers.

IDEOLOGICAL SPOKESMAN

As in traditional China, the overwhelming majority of what today may be called "scholar-cadres" uphold the status quo and go along with official policy, even though they may privately disagree with certain features of it. Within this majority, a small number stand out as the guardians and propagators of the official ideology and values. Ai Siqi, as described by Joshua Fogel, exemplifies this role of faithful functionary in the PRC. He consistently championed the state orthodoxy and provided the authoritative interpretation of the power-holders' views and policies, whatever they were at any given time. The enunciation of dogma and vigorous suppression of views and individuals who questioned dogma put Ai and a small number of like-minded spokesmen into the first rank of official ideologists. Uncritical loyalty to the political leadership, however, created irresolvable difficulties for Ai and the other ideological spokesmen, such as Zhou Yang, in literary policy. To whom were they to give their loyalty when the leader (Mao) and the Party went in separate directions, as they did after the Great Leap Forward?[6]

ACADEMIC AND PROFESSIONAL ELITE

There is a mixed tradition in Chinese culture for an academic and professional elite. John Dardess, in his *Confucianism and Autocracy*, points to the emergence of scholar-officials during the Yuan-Ming transition who developed a set of norms as managers that were relatively independent of state decrees.[7] However, because of their commitment to Confucian morality, which in traditional China overrode commitment to professional standards, they were not truly professional.[8] Nevertheless, not all questions with which scholar-officials dealt had moral or political implications. Some merely required expertise. Benjamin Elman, in *From Philosophy to Philology*, describes the emergence of professionalism among the literati in an academic community in the Jiangnan area of central China during the eighteenth century.[9] These mid-Qing literati stressed "evidential research" in support of their historical analyses, developed a professional academic code, and established institutions of learning relatively independent of state control. Nevertheless, even though they were more concerned with intellectual integrity than with moral integrity, their professionalism was intertwined with their moral commitment to Confucianism, since the texts they corrected were sacred to their beliefs. Thus, China's pre-modern experience provided the educated elite with a tradition for the professions, but not one independent of the overriding state ideology.

The late Qing saw the emergence of a relatively independent class of professionals in a variety of fields—law, medicine, journalism, business, and engineering—whose practitioners generally had little commitment to any state ideology. This development stemmed from training and influences from abroad, specifically the West and Japan, and from the glut of educated elite relative to a static number of official positions in the dynasty. The professionals established their own organizations, professional education, and professional procedures for peer review and promotion.[10] The imperial government of the late Qing, the post-1911 warlord regimes, and the Guomindang tried to manipulate and coopt these professional groups; but, because these governments were weak and their efforts sporadic, professionals achieved some degree of autonomy in the early decades of the twentieth century, even if only by default. Academics also achieved some independence even when living under direct Guomindang rule. John Israel has pointed out that, by the late 1930s, professors at Southwestern United University enjoyed an unprecedented sense of professional self-esteem, secure employment, and freedom to pursue knowledge in their fields.[11]

Except for the writers who allied themselves with the Communist or leftist movements, or a very few on the extreme right, many professionals and academics in Republican China tended to be apolitical; they allied themselves with neither the Guomindang nor the outlawed Communists. When the Chinese Communists came to power in 1949, a small number either left with the defeated Guomindang or expatriated themselves, but the overwhelming majority of academics and professionals stayed in China. In part they were disgusted with the corruption, chaos, and especially the inflation which threatened their salaried lives and for which they held the Guomindang responsible.[12] But, perhaps more important, most of them offered their services to the Communist regime out of a feeling of patriotism. They hoped the Chinese Communist Party would finally unite China and fulfill China's quest for modernization, which, it was assumed, would achieve China's modern goals of wealth and power. These professionals and academics, like most intellectuals in China, acquiesced in the early 1950s in the Party's establishment of political control over their profesional activities and organizations in the belief that their compliance would help China. Nevertheless, tensions soon arose between their patriotic commitment and professional commitment as the Party increasingly identified patriotism with obedience to the Party's own shifting political line and its leaders' often contradictory demands. As James Feinerman says of the lawyers and Denis Simon of the scientists, they defined themselves more on the basis of their professions than in terms of the Party's ideology. Even the economists described by Nina Halpern and the famous historian and President of Beijing University, Jian Bozan, described by Clifford Edmunds, who had allied themselves with the Party before the Revolution, held to standards they refused to compromise, despite political pressure to do so. This contradiction, albeit less acute, continues in China today.

To allay this tension and win better cooperation from professionals and academics needed in its modernization drive, the Party periodically allowed intellectuals to express their views more freely. When this happened, as in the Mao era during the Hundred Flowers of 1956 and the first half of 1957 and again in 1961 and 1962, a significant number of lawyers, scientists, writers, economists, historians, journalists, and other high-level intellectuals demanded the right to practice their professions without political interference. Even though their request to work free of Party intervention in their own areas of expertise stemmed from professional needs and the belief that they would be better able to help their country, the Party regarded their demand as an implicit challenge to its own competence and as a political threat.

Because some academics and professionals, such as economists and scientists, had skills more central to economic modernization than others, they were given more leeway and suffered less repression, at least until the Cultural Revolution. Nina Halpern reveals that there were economists who were allowed to participate in policy-making through established institutions beginning in the late 1950s in the midst of the Great Leap Forward. Since the modernization policies of the Deng Xiaoping leadership in post-Mao China are based on utilizing the technocratic professions, this tendency to give more leeway to scientists and economists than to the nonscientific, humanistic professions has increased dramatically. As Denis Simon and Lynn White point out, they are given special privileges, such as being able to sign consulting contracts with relevant enterprises and to establish think tanks outside direct Party control. A major difference in the Deng era is that the assertion of professional norms has been more welcomed and sustained than in the erratic Mao era.

CRITICAL INTELLECTUALS

China's intellectuals are also heirs to another tradition—the obligation of the literati to remonstrate with tyrannical, arbitrary rulers. This role for the educated elite was more developed than professional roles in traditional China. Although the dynastic system, and indeed the traditional culture, were authoritarian and did not lend themselves to individualism and personal autonomy, they were based on moral values by which the actions even of the ruler and his officials were to be judged. While dedicated to public service and imbued with loyalty to their rulers, true literati were not merely passive implementers of government policies. Within the framework of Confucianism, they saw themselves as a group with a special insight into the established moral norms. They differed from the ideological functionaries in that they were more concerned with political issues than with political status and were unlike professionals in that they were generalists rather than specialists. They saw themselves in the tradition of the Censorate, a state institution originally designed to bring incompetence, corruption, and popular grievances to the attention of the rulers who were then expected to rectify the problems. Their purpose was to improve the relationship between the ruler and the ruled and thereby to improve the functioning of the state. Critical literati advocated and in some cases administered the state-run reform of society, often viewing themselves as "doctors to society."[13]

A small number of intellectuals in the PRC continue to play a role similar to the critical literati. They are more concerned with the philosophical origins and moral consequences of the leadership's failings than with espousing the current Party line or mastering professional skills. As their predecessors were torn between their loyalty to the reigning dynasty and loyalty to their self-professed values, so, too, are critical intellectuals in the PRC torn between their commitment to the state and their commitment to their own interpretation of the ruling orthodoxy, Marxism-Leninism-Mao Zedong Thought. Their views are not only influenced by the pursuit of knowledge and moral improvement inherent in their own tradition, but are also influenced in varying degrees by Western liberal ideas of ideological pluralism, freedom of thought, and representative government, which flowed into China in the early decades of the twentieth century. They were attracted to these concepts, not so much as ends in themselves, but as means to criticize the misdeeds of the leadership in the expectation that the leadership would reform. Thus, like their predecessors, their purpose is to improve the prevailing system, not to replace it. They call for a degree of ideological pluralism and a variety of views, but within the context of the system and its ideological framework. Unlike some dissidents in the USSR, they criticize the shortcomings of the system, but do not criticize the system itself, at least publicly.

Although they are also involved in factional rivalries and opportunistic positioning, when these men and women speak on the basis of their interpretation of the moral principles inherent in the state orthodoxy, they stand at the opposite end of the spectrum from the role of ideological spokesmen for the Party. Their lives exemplify how difficult it has been both to serve the state and maintain loyalty to one's principles. At times, some have been coerced or, worse yet, compelled by their own sense of patriotism, to advocate Party lines inimical to their values. Thus, the chapters to follow sometimes depict individual intellectuals moving between the two ends of the spectrum. Under Mao, those who refused to compromise their principles were publicly disgraced, ostracized, imprisoned, even killed. Under the post-Mao leadership, they have periodically been criticized, even been made the target of a campaign, but shortly thereafter have returned to public life, though sometimes in less exalted positions.

Some were survivors of the May Fourth era, such as the playwright Tian Han, whom Rudolf Wagner describes as using the medium of the traditional historical opera to express his own views. Another survivor, Wang Ruowang, as Kyna Rubin shows, uses the polemical-essay style made famous by Lu Xun to express his moral voice. Rudolf Wagner also discusses a number of writers brought up under the Communist regime, among them the writer-journalist Liu Binyan, influenced by the Soviet investigative reportage of the post-Stalinist thaw, and Wang Meng, influenced by modernist literary techniques. Their works reveal the discrepancies between the ideals espoused by the political leadership and the realities lived by ordinary people. David Kelly analyzes the philosophy of Wang Ruoshui (raised partially in the Communist system), which points to the reality of a nation peopled by the alienated, rather than, as the Party claims, by the enthusiastic supporters of the regime. Unlike the democratic activists of 1978–1979, who were unknowns on the periphery of society,[14] the critical intellectuals, when not under attack, hold high positions in the intellectual establishment with connections to the reform political leadership and with access to the most prestigious publications in China, unless their official patrons are under attack; then they fall along with their patrons.

They represent different generations and different approaches: Some, like Liu Binyan, write highly politicized pieces; others, like Wang Meng and younger writers who emerged after the Cultural Revolution, stress more artistic, less politicized writing. Many other intellectuals may have felt the same sense of moral outrage that critical intellectuals felt about the Anti-Rightist campaign (1957), the Great Leap Forward (1958–1960), and the Cultural Revolution (1966–1969)—movements that became increasingly repressive to intellectuals. But what makes this small number of intellectuals different from their colleagues is their courage to take on the dangerous role of critical intellectuals, to speak out publicly, as did their literati and May Fourth predecessors, against despotic rule, arbitrary officialdom, and the oppression of the people. As Rudolf Wagner observes, they see themselves as intermediaries between the government and the people and as the interpreters to the leadership of the "murmurings" of the people. Lacking a political system in which the people could express themselves directly, these intellectuals have assumed the role of a conduit by which the people's views could reach the political leadership, who were expected to respond to the people's wishes. Therefore, like their literati predecessors, these self-appointed interpreters have sought to strengthen the relationship between rulers and ruled.

Although they did not publicly question the official ideology of Marxism-Leninism-Mao Zedong Thought and did not question the one-Party state, their articulation of grievances and their condemnation of abusive officials implied criticism of the system that allowed such evils. Moreover, their sense of themselves as not mere employees of the state, but as advisors to it, and their conviction that they were more qualified to speak on behalf of "the people" because they were more independent and objective than Party officials, who report back what the Party leadership wants to hear, challenged the Party's claim to represent the people's will.

Until the post-Mao era, critical intellectuals in the PRC, like most of their literati predecessors, failed to question their own assumption that, when they properly informed the leaders of the will of the people, the leaders would respond. Nor did they question that "the people" are an oracle whose wishes are to be interpreted by an elite, whether a group of intellectuals or Party leaders. They claimed to speak on behalf of "the people"—as if there were no differences of opinion or interests among people—or at the very least for the benefit of "the people." But, after the Cultural Revolution, some, such as Wang Ruoshui as interpreted by David Kelly, imply that the very trust in the leadership to respond accordingly may have unwittingly upheld the repressive system.

In addition to the literary and philosophical voices used by the critical intellectuals, a new profession and vocabulary for articulating their concerns is emerging in the social sciences, principally in the

Chinese Academy of Social Sciences (CASS), established in 1978. The disciplines of sociology and anthropology have been revived after twenty years of inactivity. Their practitioners are involved in survey research and opinion polls to ascertain the feelings of the people. They may provide a quantified scientific sample on which the rulers can devise policies responsive to the people's will and from which critical intellectuals can verify their version of the people's murmurings. As explained by Carol Hamrin, social scientists in the Institute of Marxism-Leninism-Mao Zedong Thought in CASS can also provide the information from which the Party itself can revise the official ideology. Whether the social sciences as an independent profession, not to mention as a means of criticism, will be allowed to develop in China from their fragile "sprouts" is by no means certain, but they have the potential for providing a more objective critique of the political system, as well as of the leadership, than has been heard hitherto.

Another change in post-Mao China is the beginning of a shift away from a self-conscious political role among some critical intellectuals. Although a number of them, like their literati predecessors, are still more concerned with issues than with technical skills, some, like former "rightists" Wang Meng and some younger writers, experiment with such modernist literary styles as stream of consciousness and nonrealist imagery. In the post-Mao era, the Party has allowed greater leeway in style than in content and has allowed the depoliticization of what it considers frivolous activities, such as caring for canaries and reading stories of knights errant. Nevertheless, political control of high culture continues. Thus, reformist political leaders inform writers they can write in any style they please as long as their writing assists China's modernization. Even though artistic experiment is more readily tolerated than ideological experiment, it too makes a political statement. To be apolitical in a society that still seeks politicalization of serious literature implies a more general rejection of political intervention. However, as Leo Lee has asked, is it possible to be truly creative by experimenting artistically but conforming ideologically?[15]

THE PARTY'S POLICIES TOWARD INTELLECTUALS

Even though literary inquisitions and persecutions of critical literati have occurred throughout Chinese history, autonomy and variety of viewpoints within a broad ideological framework in public life were generally more tolerated in dynastic times than in the PRC. This was not solely because previous dynasties lacked the muscle and grass-roots organization to enforce their will. After the Qin dynasty (221–206 B.C.), they never demanded the exclusive loyalty that the Party demands. Sometimes, intellectuals did not use this relative freedom to best advantage. Some imposed ideological conformity on their peers in a manner that suggests that the urge to conformity and intolerance in twentieth-century China does not spring solely from the imposition of a strong centralized state.[16] Whatever their limitations, however, many intellectuals during the Republican period spoke out with great courage and insight, castigating social injustice and suggesting alternatives.

With the Communist revolution in 1949, the state finally had the means as well as the will to impose its authority over virtually all areas of intellectual and professional life. Whatever individual, professional, moral, or intellectual autonomy members of China's educated elite had achieved in the past century was circumscribed by the Party's organizational control and periodic thought-reform campaigns. Within the Marxist-Leninist-Maoist framework, there was much less room for alternative views and values than there had been in the Confucian ideological framework and certainly less than in the early decades of the twentieth century.

Nevertheless, in the early years of the regime, the full implications of the Party's policies were not yet clear. Equally important, the majority of intellectuals welcomed or at least complied with the Party's policies. Because of their sense of patriotism, most of the intellectuals went along with the Party even in 1955 when it persecuted the writer Hu Feng and a small number of leftist writers who had criticized the Party's oppressive literary controls. Many intellectuals also acquiesced and even participated in the persecution in 1957–1958 of some 300,000 to 400,000 "rightists" inside and outside the party who had criticized bureaucratic abuses at Mao's behest in the Hundred Flowers campaign in the spring of 1957.[17] In addition to their feelings of patriotism, which justified closing ranks against officially designated scapegoats, there was the omnipresent fear that, if they did not acquiesce, they too would be labeled ideological heretics, political dissidents, and traitors to "the people," which could result in public disgrace, isolation, labor reform, imprisonment, even death.

But, as the regime increasingly equated loyalty to the nation with loyalty to the Party and eventually to Mao himself, the intellectuals became more and more alienated. This tension between their loyalty to their nation and people and their disillusionment with its political leaders has been expressed openly in the post-Mao era. In Bai Hua's controversial scenario, *Unrequited Love*, a prominent artist returns to China from the United States at the time of the Revolution to help his country, only to be persecuted to death by its leaders' policies. Michael Duke points out that Bai Hua uses the word *zuguo* (ancestral land) to describe the artist's patriotism; this implies love of the Chinese people and homeland, not the state, government, or a political party.[18] There is only one departure from this usage and that is in the famous scene in which his daughter asks her father, "You love this nation of ours. . . . But does this nation love you?" In this question she uses the term *guojia*, which means government as well as geographical unit.[19] Thus, Bai Hua distinguishes between one's country and one's government. The intellectual loves his country but, in his story, which speaks for so many, instead of requiting the intellectuals' love, the government has persecuted them. Wang Ruoshui's views on alienation, as David Kelly points out, also suggest that one can be loyal to one's nation while being alienated from one's government. Liu Binyan, at the Fourth Congress of the All China Federation of Literary and Art Circles in September 1979, said that, when he was sent to the countryside for labor reform in the Anti-Rightist Campaign, "I saw that the peasants wanted one thing and the leadership and press something else." When the demands of the people and of the Party contradict each other, Liu advises, "We shall listen to the people; we owe our allegiance to the people," because "the Party is not infallible."[20] Thus, some critical intellectuals in post-Mao China distinguish between commitment to one's country and society and commitment to the political leadership.

Even though Bai Hua was made the target of the 1981 campaign, Wang Ruoshui was a target of the Campaign against Spiritual Pollution launched in the fall of 1983, and Liu Binyan was repeatedly criticized behind closed doors, until the 1987 campaign against "bourgeois liberalization," they continued to publish their criticisms intermittently, unlike the Mao era. Their ability, and that of other critical intellectuals, to express themselves publicly comes from the Party's commitment to modernization. This was true even in the Mao era. Although the Party since 1949 has compelled intellectuals to conform to its shifting political line, it has also sought to stimulate them to work productively and creatively. Since these goals are contradictory, the Party's policy toward intellectuals has oscillated between repression and relative relaxation. Even though each cycle is different, they have a similar dynamic: the Party tightens its control over the intellectuals until the intellectuals appear reluctant to work; then the Party relaxes its control until it appears that its predominance is threatened; then it tightens up again. In the periods of relative relaxation, the Party tolerates and even encourages intellectual debates, and allows outside influences and criticism of officials in order to root out abuses and improve the system. The Party establishes the framework within which, at least in the beginning, intellectuals can express their own views, but it can not fully control the response in which some intellectuals invariably demand a degree of autonomy not only in their own work but also in commenting on broader political issues. To prevent the challenge from critical intellectuals, the Party could simply dispense with periods of relative relaxation, but that would alienate the educated elite who are needed for modernization.

Mao began the first relaxation—the Hundred Flowers Movement—with the expectation that the ideological indoctrination the intellectuals had undergone since the early 1950s would insure that blooming and contending would stay within the limits set by the Party. However, when intellectuals not only criticized officials but the Party itself and demanded more intellectual and political freedoms, Mao no longer sought their cooperation in modernizing China. Although there was another relaxation in the early 1960s, it sprang from increasing factionalism in the Party's leadership and the desire of bureaucratic leaders to work with intellectuals in repairing the damage wrought by the Great Leap Forward. These bureaucratic patrons soon lost power, first bowing to Mao's increasingly negative view of intellectuals and finally suffering with them in indiscriminate and violent persecution from 1966 to Mao's death in 1976. In that trauma, it did not matter if one was an outspoken critic, a professional, or an ideologue who had twisted and turned with every contortion in the political line. All were attacked simply because they worked with their minds and had been influenced by Western civilization or traditional Chinese culture. It was Ai Siqi's good fortune to die in early 1966, just before the Cultural Revolution, because even ideological mouthpieces were swept up in the onslaught, including many of the young, radical ideologues who had joined with Mao, Jiang Qing, and Lin Biao in the power struggle against the Party bureaucracy. Mao came to blame them for the anarchy that ensued when they tried to fulfill his revolutionary exhortations. Whether on the right or on the left, the intellectuals were invariably blamed for the faults of leaders.

The cycles of repression and relaxation continue in the post-Mao period, but with some important differences. Whereas, under Mao, the periods of repression predominated, under the post-Mao leadership periods of relative relaxation predominate. Moreover, the periods of repression are without the ideological fervor, mass coercion, and indiscriminate terror of the Maoist era. Whereas most intellectuals, whether professionals or writers, were treated more or less the same under Mao, different treatment is now meted out to scientists and professionals on the one hand and to literary intellectuals on the other. While the Campaign against Spiritual Pollution in the fall of 1983 was terminated in less than a month against scientists and professionals, it continued well into 1984 against literary intellectuals, particularly those influenced by Western humanist ideas that provoked questioning of the political system. As in the post-Stalinist Soviet Union, the leadership is more willing to accommodate the scientific, professional, and managerial elite, whose skills are directly related to China's economic modernization, than literary intellectuals, whose skills are less clearly relevant.

The Soviet and East European examples have influenced Party policy toward intellectuals. Thus, what George Konrád and Ivan Szelényi say about East European intellectuals may also be appropriate to the Chinese case. They argue that, as the Communist regimes in post-Stalinist Eastern Europe abandoned their revolutionary goals and made concessions to technocrats in order to modernize, an alliance gradually formed between the political leadership and the technocrats; this alliance has not benefited and has even hurt nonscientific intellectuals.[21] The contracts between individual scientists and enterprises, and the establishment of professional think tanks in China, described by Denis Simon and Lynn White, may limit political interference and allow for more diversity in the scientific arena. They may also open the way for depoliticization of scientific and technical activity and increase the wealth, status, and political clout of scientists and technocrats, who understandably would be loath to do without expensive equipment, foreign travel, and membership on important advisory councils. The interests of scientists and technocrats, as Konrád and Szelényi point out, may become identified more with the political leadership than with their fellow intellectuals.

Experience suggests, however, that it is difficult to isolate scientists from the fate of other intellectuals in the PRC. In the Cultural Revolution, Mao tried to protect the scientists from the violence of the Red Guards, but the dynamics of the campaign inevitably swept up the scientists as well. A similar phenomenon has occurred in the Deng era, but in reverse. It is true that the scientists and technocrats have readier access to training, responsibility, study abroad, and even opportunities to influence policies in their areas of expertise than those in the humanities and creative arts, but the split that Konrád and Szelényi describe in Eastern Europe has not yet occurred in China. While the literary intellectuals are still the chief targets of campaigns, the dynamics of the opening to the outside world have affected them as well as scientists. Once the door is open, it is impossible to control what comes in and who is influenced by it. As China discovered in the nineteenth century, Western political and philosophical concepts flow in along with scientific ideas and technological wonders. Li Honglin, an ideological spokesman for the reformers, has pointed out that to isolate the nonscientific realm from foreign influence harms not only that realm but the whole reform effort. He acknowledged that "decadent and degenerate ideology and culture will enter our culture along with science and technology and contaminate the air." But, even if the door were closed somewhat, such "dirty things" would "enter anyway from outside, through cracks in the walls."[22] Thus, relaxation of controls on access of the scientists and technocrats to the outside world inevitably leads to relaxation of controls on the access of humanists too.

Even if the regime should play off the scientists against the humanists, neither group may be willing to play the game. Not only would nonscientific intellectuals like Li Honglin protest, but, more important, the periodic threat of repression and closing off of contact with the outside world, though primarily directed against literary intellectuals, would also frighten the scientific intellectuals. They may be less directly affected, but, as Denis Simon points out, they too are buffeted by shifts in the Party's political configuration and political line. Moreover, they still remember past persecutions in which their attackers made little distinction between writer and scientist. The threat of another Cultural Revolution may unite all intellectuals, as they have never been united before, to resist an attack against any group among them. The famous writer Ba Jin called the Cultural Revolution China's "holocaust" and urged his colleagues to keep its memory alive in order to insure that it will never happen again. "We have a right," he said, "as well as a responsibility to write down what happened to us. Such a record is not merely for our own sake, but for the benefit of others as well as future generations."[23] He points out that what happened was not just the work of the Gang of Four, but of people like himself who allowed it to happen: "It is high time that we all faced the truth of our own complicity; they could not have done it, if we had not let ourselves be taken in."[24] Because of the spectre of another Cultural Revolution, scientists share with nonscientific intellectuals an interest in building institutions and establishing laws that will protect themselves and their autonomy.

TENTATIVE REPRESENTATIVE ASSOCIATIONS

Demands for new laws and institutions were first expressed in the post-Mao era in 1978–1979 by democratic activists, ex-Red Guards who sought to redress the injustices they had perpetuated and suffered in the Cultural Revolution. When they demanded democratic procedures that would have undermined the one-party rule of the Party, their movement was crushed and their leaders imprisoned. Nevertheless, some of their demands were taken up by the critical intellectuals. Evidence that these demands may have had some impact can be seen in the fact that, for the first time in the PRC, professionals began to elect their own officials. In 1981, the Academy of Sciences elected their president and vice-president. At the 4th Congress of the Chinese Writers Association, December 1984–January 1985, writers held a contested election by secret ballot, with General Secretary Hu Yao-bang's sanction. The winners were different from the slate of officers that the Party leadership had presented for approval. Liu Binyan had not been on the Party list, but, because his number of votes in the secret balloting was second only to Ba Jin, he received the post of a vice-chairman of the Writers Association. Party nominees who had participated actively in the campaigns against bourgeois liberalism and Spiritual Pollution were not elected; those who were the targets of those campaigns were voted into official positions. Thus, the participants refused to rubber-stamp the Party's slate and elected their own preferred representatives. Moreover, the Chinese Writers Association was designated at that meeting to be the institution to protect writers' freedom, rights, and opportunities to travel abroad. Although the Chinese Writers Association has no legal power with which to protect writers, it has lobbied on behalf of writers with grievances.

The Chinese Writers Association Conference unleashed a barrage of demands for freedom in other areas, especially in the press, that grew louder in the early months of 1985. Furthermore, other intellectual groups demanded the right to use the same procedures for the election of officers as the writers had. Hu Jiwei, deposed as editor-in-chief of the *People's Daily* in the fall of 1983 for publishing articles on socialist alienation, but subsequently made president of the Federation of Journalists, called for legislation to protect journalists. He asked for a press code to define exactly what is meant when a journalist is accused of "spreading rumors" and "divulging secrets," so as to protect journalists from being accused unfairly of such practices. The vagueness of such terms, he contended, hindered journalists from gathering news freely.

The Chinese Writers Association Conference generated demands the Party was not willing to meet, as indicated by Party General-Secretary Hu Yaobang's speech at an inner-Party meeting of the Secretariat in February 1985 and published in *People's Daily* in April 1985. In it he reasserted that the "press must be the mouthpiece of the Party." Hu Yaobang explained that writers were different from journalists because they were indirect rather than direct mouthpieces of the Party. Thus, writers could write whatever they wanted in any style they wanted; that does not mean, he warned, that they will be published. "Writers can never use their freedom to deprive editorial boards [that is, the Party] of their freedom."[25]

That China's top leaders should rein in demands that went beyond limits they had anticipated in their call for freedom of expression is not new. What is unusual in the post-Mao era is that a few critical intellectuals publicly challenged the top political leadership. Hu Jiwei replied to Hu Yaobang in a "Special Commentator" article in the first issue of the new journal *Xinwen xuekan* (Journalist bulletin). Although associated with the reform political leadership, Hu Jiwei was unwilling to accept their view that journalism can speak with only one voice, the official voice of the Party. He declared that the old rules of journalism used during the revolutionary period were no longer applicable in a period of modernization. In fact, it was such outdated journalistic practices that helped produce disasters like the Great Leap Forward and the Cultural Revolution. He quoted Liu Shaoqi: "Even when [*People's Daily*] advocated wrong things, people believed it pronounced opinions on behalf of the central leadership."[26] Cleverly reinterpreting the regime's claim that writers could write whatever they pleased, Hu Jiwei asserted that, since journalism was also a "branch of learning," it should be allowed "the freedom" accorded other academic subjects. Thus, in journalism seminars and journals, there should be a free atmosphere where journalists can express a variety of viewpoints and freely debate issues.

Demand for a press code and even the opportunity to elect the officials in one's professional association, however tentative, may be a beginning of a democratic process at least among high-level intellectual groups. Yet the question is whether even the most reformist Party leadership will grant the rights and prerogatives that the critical intellectuals are asking for. The process of election by secret ballot has not been repeated in other professional associations. Despite its more benevolent view of intellectuals, the Deng leadership is committed to the Leninist one-party state which allows for no alternative authority. And, as Carol Hamrin suggests in her conclusion, even if the reform leadership wanted to grant intellectuals some legal protections, they would be opposed by more conservative Party leaders still in power.

LIMITED AUTONOMY

Under the Deng Xiaoping leadership, intellectuals have more leeway and more access to the outside than at any other time since 1949. The Deng leadership appears committed to professionalism and expertise. Its reliance on scientists and technocrats in its drive for economic modernization and the fear of another Cultural Revolution may limit the severity of political repression of all intellectuals. Yet, even without the tragic plight of intellectuals under Mao, the intimidating interludes of the Deng era suggest that, while intellectual autonomy has expanded, it is still intermittent and conditional. No matter how enlightened the leaders are or how much freedom they may grant intellectuals at a given time, so long as intellectuals do not have legally protected freedom, leadership can withdraw that "freedom" whenever it believes necessary. Individual expression, in literature or even in science, has not yet been disentangled from political expression. The Party still has the power to prevent the publication of ideas with which it disagrees and to block scientific experiments it considers impractical or not worthwhile. Since China's political structure has not changed fundamentally with Mao's passing, the future of China's intellectuals remains uncertain. Despite the democratic rhetoric, the opening up to the outside world, and increasing forthrightness and courage among critical intellectuals, the Party's periodic repression of intellectuals in the 1980s and the acquiescence of most intellectuals in Party dominance continue, owing to the persistence of a Leninist structure, which implies the political control of intellectuals.

As the enlightenment of the May Fourth era followed disillusionment with the 1911 Revolution, so has the relative liberalization of the Deng era followed the disillusionment with the Cultural Revolution. The May Fourth era evoked criticism of the old orthodoxies; the Deng era has evoked criticism of Marxism-Leninism-Mao Zedong Thought. But will the demands of patriotism, the desire for unity, and the exigencies of economic development inevitably curtail criticism by intellectuals in the Deng era as it eventually did in the May Fourth era? Will the desire for intellectual and moral autonomy continue to mean the political estrangement that Wakeman described for the late traditional period and which characterized the Maoist period? Or will increasing specialization, professionalization, and contact with the outside world gradually change the traditional relationship between intellectuals and the state? Would such a change finally make it possible for China's intellectuals to achieve a degree of intellectual and moral autonomy without political estrangement?

These questions are still unanswered. What is known is that present-day intellectuals are faced with the same dilemmas that faced nineteenth-century intellectuals: How to serve their country and help make it rich, powerful, and modern without compromising their intellectual and moral values. Even though most intellectuals are totally committed to the Party's goal of modernization, some differ as to how it is to be achieved and sometimes differ with the Party's interpretation of the will of the people. The Party has intermittently acknowledged ideologically, but certainly not legally or institutionally, that the views of intellectuals or of an individual may be different from those of the Party. Until that happens, it is likely that intellectuals who seek intellectual and moral autonomy will continue to do so at the price of political estrangement.[27] Even when the price was great, as it was during the traumatic persecutions of the Mao years, a small corps of intellectuals continued the tradition of critical literati and May Fourth intellectuals. There is every reason to believe that, no matter how tense the relationship between the intellectuals and the state may become, there will always be a small number of Chinese intellectuals whose commitment to knowledge and conscience will override their commitment to any particular regime.

PART ONE
Ideological Spokesman

CHAPTER ONE

Ai Siqi: *Professional Philosopher and Establishment Intellectual*

JOSHUA A. FOGEL

One of the assumptions underlying the study of intellectuals in the West has been the tendency to see their interests as defined in opposition to the state. A particularly egregious form of this myopia afflicts our study of contemporary Communist regimes. We call Lech Walesa, Andrei Sakharov, Wei Jingsheng, and many others "intellectuals" because of their opposition to tyranny. At the same time, men such as the Soviet ideologist Mikhail Suslov and the Chinese ideologist Ai Siqi (among countless others) have been seen as the mouthpieces of an oppressive state, lackeys or opportunists in the service of the Party or army. They have clearly not been taken as intellectuals of any stripe, and, in fact, have been regarded as the enemies of intellectuals in their societies.

It is our definition that is flawed. Many men and women with all the proper university degrees or published volumes to their credit, and who serve the state, are indeed intellectuals, although their status as the purveyors and codifiers of accepted and acceptable wisdom has made them, second only to the various security forces in their native states, the very nemesis of intellectuals as we have understood the term till now. For the purposes of clarity, they are best designated as a group as "establishment intellectuals," with the proviso that some members of this group may on occasion criticize the regime (in a friendly way), although the majority, including the subject of this chapter, do not. In late imperial and Guomindang China, and even more so in the PRC, only the most extraordinary figures have been in conflict with the state.

For over a millennium prior to the demise of the Chinese imperial system in the early years of this century, the very definition of intellectual or scholar meant someone who served the state—a person who had passed the imperial examinations and received concomitant rank in the bureaucracy. Service to one's state and society were inextricably linked with one's role as a scholar. One of the cardinal virtues of the dominant Neo-Confucian system of thought was loyalty to one's parents and to one's ruler. This direction did not mean that all scholars prior to the twentieth century were toadies of the imperial institution and its manifold incarnations throughout the empire. It did, though, make the generation of any opposition to a government exceedingly difficult to couch in the proper language acceptable for intellectual discourse.[1]

The People's Republic of China with its new Communist orthodoxy and restructured concept of the central virtue of loyalty has found any number of intellectuals ready to serve its cause in the cultural realms. In the West, however, studies of intellectuals and Chinese communism have focused on the great names (Li Dazhao, Mao Zedong) or on those who have come into conflict with the Party (writers, poets, theater people, human-rights activists). Every discipline in China, every division of government, every avenue of intellectual pursuit has had a well-populated cadre of believers who are neither great nor have come into severe conflict with the ruling powers (with the possible exception of the Cultural Revolution period). In the area of philosophy, particularly Marxist-Leninist philosophy, no one better typified this establishment intellectual than Ai Siqi (1910–1966).

A number of circumstances have made the identification of this second level of intellectuals difficult. First, they have themselves shunned the spotlight, content to live in the shadows of "great men." Second, there is a reluctance, as noted above, to accept such people— purveyors of an often repressive orthodoxy in a wide variety of fields—as intellectuals. Third, in the field of philosophy, China has been willing until recently to admit of only one intellectual, Mao Zedong, and many "philosophical workers."

BACKGROUND

Ai Siqi was born Li Shengxuan in March 1910 in Tengchong county, Yunnan. His family enjoyed a reasonable amount of comfort, sufficient to send him to school and to Japan for several years. His father was well educated and early on joined the Tongmenghui in his native province. Frequently at odds with the local officials or warlords, the senior Mr. Li found himself often on the run. He passed his commitment to reform on to his sons. Ai's elder brother, whom Ai revered, was of a more radical bent and expressed his opinions through the many new newspapers and magazines that mushroomed in the 1910s and 1920s.

After three years of study in Japan and the mastery of several foreign languages, Ai returned to Yunnan, where, by the mid-1920s, there was a well-developed Communist movement, an elaborate underground network, numerous journals, and translations from the master texts of Marxism-Leninism.[2] The immediate cause of his return, as for many Chinese students then in Japan, was the Manchurian Incident of 18 September 1931 and the spectre of Japanese imperialism. Compelled by a righteous sense of patriotism, Ai returned to China with a much firmer knowledge of world literature, Marxism, and philosophy. It was the last of these that would dominate the rest of his intellectual life.

Yunnan, however, seemed excessively backwater to the young firebrand, and he soon proceeded to the center of the leftist movement, Shanghai. There he became involved in many of the most famous intellectual and political debates of the early and mid-1930s. He wrote dozens of essays for the left-wing press in Shanghai under a variety of pen names. After 1933, he primarily used Ai Siqi but also used others over the course of the decade. His philosophical essays from these years combine a relatively sophisticated knowledge of European trends with a vibrant polemical style. His debate with Ye Qing (Ren Zhouxuan, b. 1896), described below, over the issue of science as a panacea (Ye's view) drips with invective.[3]

The principal and lasting achievement of Ai's work in these years was the honing of his ability to explain the complexities of philosophy in a language the common man could understand. This is the hallmark of Ai's written work—the popularization of philosophy, particularly Marxism-Leninism. His first major work, *Zhexue jianghua* (Talks on philosophy), later renamed *Dazhong zhexue* (Philosophy for the masses), was published serially in the semi-monthly *Dushu shenghuo* (Reader's life), a markedly leftist journal, for a year beginning in November 1934. It was reissued as a book in January 1936 and was banned six weeks later. Over the next thirteen years this book went through 32 editions and has been recently reissued in the PRC. The immense popularity of this book and Ai's other writings led one observer to call him "the official thinker of the [Chinese Communist] Party, in view of his positions of service and the success of his books."[4]

MR. AI GOES TO YAN'AN

Shanghai became increasingly difficult as a center for a dedicated Communist propagandist to survive in as the 1930s progressed. Off in Yan'an, where Mao Zedong and Zhu De had led the decimated remains of the Jiangxi Soviet, Mao and his cohorts were finally able to enjoy a brief spell of leisure. Mao spent the time, from late 1935 through September 1937, poring over philosophical texts in preparation for a now famous series of lectures he was to give on Marxism-Leninism. New Soviet texts arrived at this time, works by Deborin, Mitin, Rozental, as well as newly translated classics (such as Engels's *Anti-Dühring*). Among these books was a translation Ai had made in 1935–1936 of the entry under "dialectical materialism" in the *Bol'shaia Sovietskaia Entsiklopediia* (Great Soviet encyclopedia), written under the guidance of Stalin's philosopher, Mark Borisovich Mitin ("the leading Soviet philosopher of the thirties").[5] The Chinese title was *Xin zhexue dagang* (Outline of the new philosophy).

Also among the works Mao reputedly read by an oil lamp in his Yan'an cave was Ai's *Talks on Philosophy.*[6] This popular explanation of the complexities of philosophy showed beyond a shadow of a doubt that the history of philosophy culminated in the scientific creation-discovery of Marxism-Leninism. Mao gathered around himself a cadre of professional philosophers. He was intent on beginning to formulate what the world would later know as Mao Zedong Thought. In 1937, Ai was directed by the Party to move to Yan'an.

Mao needed all the intellectual support he could muster at that time in his debate with Wang Ming over the direction of the Communist movement. According to Wu Liping, Mao exclaimed upon Ai's arrival: "Aha, Ai Siqi, author of *Dazhong zhexue*, has arrived!" In late 1937 or early 1938, Mao gathered together seven or eight people weekly to study Marxism-Leninism. Eventually the group expanded, and in September 1938 the Xin Zhehue Hui (Society for the New Philosophy) was founded under the leadership of Ai and Ho Sijing, another Yan'an philosopher.[7]

Ai held many posts in Yan'an, first as lecturer in philosophy at the Marx-Lenin Academy and at the Anti-Japanese University. Wu Boxiao recalls meeting Ai after a lecture attended by over 1,000 "students" in 1938. Wu approached him, introduced himself, and Ai honored him by writing in his notebook: "Unite the entire country for final victory against Japan and for the struggle to build a free and prosperous democratic republic. Ai Siqi, May 5"–the 120th anniversary of Marx's birth.[8] Ai also wrote for numerous newspapers and magazines and served for a time as editor-in-chief of the Party paper *Jiefang ribao* (Liberation daily). He was also one of the select honored guests in attendance at Mao's talks on art and literature, which laid down the political standards for acceptable creative work. Finally, Ai was centrally involved in the famous Yan'an rectification campaign from 1941 to 1944. He was principally responsible for the translation of the Soviet texts that became the prescribed reading for the rectification.[9]

Throughout nearly a decade in Yan'an, Ai published voluminously–books, articles, and translations from the Russian. He also led the team that produced a selected translation of Mitin's magnum opus, *Dialekticheskii materializm*. The Chinese edition hit the bookstores in March 1939 and was titled *Zhexue xuanji* (Philosophical selections). Its appendixes included a translation of Stalin's "Dialectical and Historical Materialism" and a lengthy, important essay by Ai entitled "Yanjiu tigang" (Outline for study), which appeared in 1940 as a book all its own.[10]

There is no doubt, then, why Mao would have wanted Ai in Yan'an. He was a workaholic, a gold mine of ideology, and, perhaps most important, he had no apparent interest in standing out in the intellectual arena. No one who worked so hard popularizing and translating others' work under a variety of pen names was likely to pose any threat to Mao. If Mao was already in the process of making himself *the* philosopher of Chinese Marxism, the self-abnegating Ai made an excellent helper. From Ai's perspective, tying himself to Mao's rising star required some sharp turns, but it seemed to ensure security and official position.

Ai's writings and translations from this time also played a role in the "creation" of Mao's three philosophical essays of 1937—"On Practice," "On Contradiction," and "Dialectical Materialism," now regarded as the richest flowering of Mao as philosopher.[11] A large number of Soviet works in Chinese translation arrived in the northwest in 1936. Ai's translation *Xin zhexue dagang* was primary among them. Many of these works had been prepared under Stalin's direction. In order to eradicate virulent "Menshevik idealism"—to quote Stalin precisely—and its purported Deborinist carriers, Stalin's house philosopher, Mitin, organized a group of professional philosophers in the Komakademiia to prepare an authoritative textbook on dialectical materialism for the party school. The product, edited by Shirokov and Aizenberg, soon appeared in a Chinese (and Japanese) edition under the title *Bianzhengfa weiwulun jiaocheng* (A textbook in dialectical materialism), translated by Li Da and Lei Zhongjian.[12] Nakajima Mineo demonstrated some time ago that passages from "On Practice" and "On Contradiction" are virtual transcriptions from the Soviet work.[13] Mao's two essays were of course philosophically close to Stalin and his associates in the Komakademiia, and we know that Mao was interested in the ongoing denunciation of Deborin.

"Mao was an ardent student of philosophy," wrote Edgar Snow at the time of his famous interview in 1936. "Once, when I was having some nightly interviews with him on Communist history, a visitor brought him several new books on philosophy, and Mao asked me to postpone our engagements. He consumed these books in three or four nights of intensive reading, during which he seemed oblivious to everything else."[14] Perhaps Ai's *Xin zhexue dagang* was among these "new books." The translation went into its fourth printing in 1937.

Ai's other major translation, selections from the tome *Dialektrcheskii materializm* (edited by Mitin), appeared in its Shanghai edition of 1939 under the title *Zhexue xuanji*. Wittfogel has shown that Mao lifted "sizable passages" from these two works for his own "Dialectical Materialism."[15]

Less of a problem in this regard exists for "On Practice" and "On Contradiction," simply because we remain ignorant of the original texts and must assume, as the Chinese tell us, that the 1950/1952 published forms were much changed. Takeuchi Minoru attempted in 1969 to devise a methodology whereby we might recapture the original "On Contradiction." Although not completely successful, neither was his effort entirely quixotic. It indeed reveals the untapped creative potential for the contemporary China field.

The important, new element Takeuchi introduces into the mix is Ai's appendix, cited above, to *Zhexue xuanji*, entitled "Yanjiu tigang." Despite all the editorial changes it has surely undergone, "On Contradiction" bears an unmistakable similarity to "Yanjiu tigang." In fact, the differences between them may suggest how Mao subsequently changed his earlier essay for publication in light of Ai's work. This supposition is based on the fact that Mao's work, *Bianzhengfa weiwulun (jiangshou tigang)* (Dialectical materialism, lecture outlines), was his original lecture plan of 1937, including a part entitled "On Contradiction."

Takeuchi painstakingly performs a comparative textual analysis of Ai's and Mao's works, in which he points out countless similarities of phraseology, language, and nuance.[16] For example, Section IV of "On Contradiction," entitled "The Principal Contradiction and the Principal Aspect of a Contradiction," is virtually identical to several pages in Ai's work.[17] Although Ai uses the expression *zhudao* for "principal," whereas Mao speaks of *zhuyao*, Mao apparently added little to Ai's work when preparing "On Contradiction" for publication later. All minor inconsistencies and editorial changes aside, the two pieces belong to identical systems of thought.

There are various other possibilities about the relationship between these two texts. Perhaps there was an intermediary text or a parent model on which both were based, such as the Shirokov-Aizenberg textbook on dialectical materialism. Textual evidence indicates that this Soviet work was not the parent model, but some other work may have been. We are now in a position to say that, in terms of the documents, "On Contradiction" was born of a circle of mutually interacting texts: Ai's two translations, his "Yanjiu tigang," and Mao's *Bianzhengfa weiwulun (jiangshou tigang).*[18]

The crucial point here is that, whatever the relationship among all these texts, the non-canonical works used by Mao are exclusively the work of Ai Siqi as translator and interpreter. Although his inability to read foreign languages limited him severely, Mao did have access to other works. Yet, when we examine the language, ideas, and organization of his philosophical essays, the enormous debt to Ai Siqi is obviously borne out. No one in the world knew this better than Ai himself, and he never complained. It was his very lifeline.

YAN'AN AND THEREAFTER: AI AND COMMUNIST CAMPAIGNS

In his role as the epitome of the Party or establishment intellectual, Ai stood in the forefront of CCP policy toward intellectuals. He held a string of important and prestigious positions from the Yan'an period until his death in 1966 in which he exercised a significant, though quiet, control over a large segment of the Chinese intellectual community. Yet, he never rose to any high Party post, nor did his presence and activities ever have the impact one might expect from someone so close to the Chairman—perhaps too close.

In addition to his lecturing at the Anti-Japanese University and the Marx-Lenin Institute in Yan'an, Ai taught for a time at Yan'an University in 1944. He helped establish the North China University in the Communist Shijiazhuang base area in Hebei, and he taught philosophy there.[19] In compliance with a "request" from the central propaganda department, Ai and Wu Liping, another Party intellectual, composed a textbook in 1939 for both party members and others on philosophy of life and world view from a thoroughgoing materialist perspective. It was titled *Weiwu shiguan* (The materialist historical view) in Yan'an and *Kexue lishiguan jiaocheng* (Textbook on the scientific view of history) in Guomindang-controlled areas.[20]

Ai wrote for and edited every Chinese serial publication concerning Marxism-Leninism and philosophy in general. He assumed responsibilities as literary editor of *Jiefang ribao* from Ding Ling when she was forced to step down after being attacked in 1942 for criticisms of the Party. He made the literary bureaucrat Lin Mohan his assistant. He was editor-in-chief of the major theoretical organ of the Party in Yan'an, *Zhongguo wenhua* (Chinese culture), from its inception in February 1940. His article "Lun Zhongguo de teshuxing" (On the particularity of China), arguing the qualities unique to the Chinese (as opposed to other socialist) revolutions, was featured as the second piece in its inaugural issue. The lead article was Mao Zedong's semi-immortal "On New Democracy."[21] Also appearing in this issue were essays by Zhou Yang, Wu Yuzhang, He Sijing, Chen Boda, Xiao San, Hu Qiaomu, and He Qifang—all members of China's future intellectual elite and cultural bureaucracy.

After the founding of the People's Republic, Ai was named vice-chairman of the preparatory committee for the Chinese Philosophical Society in 1949, and he subsequently became the Society's first vice-chairman. He also took over editorship of the CCP's new theoretical journal, *Xuexi* (Study), a position he held until 1958, when it ceased publication. From 1955, he was a member of the philosophy and social sciences departments in the Academy of Sciences in Beijing.

He is remembered by ex-students as a fine teacher of philosophy at the Marx-Lenin Institute from 1949 through the mid-1950s. He lived in a school dormitory with his wife, Wang Danyi, and their son.[22] Lin Mohan contacted him there just after the establishment of the PRC and offered to collect a number of Ai's editorials from the 1940s for a book; Lin was acquainted with Ai's various pen names. The book soon appeared under the title of its lead essay, "*Youdi fangshi*" *ji qita* ("Have target, will shoot arrows" and other essays).[23]

Ai served as a representative from Guizhou to the 1st National People's Congress (NPC) in 1954 and again to the 2nd NPC in 1959. At the 3rd NPC in late 1964, he represented his native Yunnan.[24] These were the highest official government posts he would ever hold.

In addition to these leadership positions and perhaps because of them, Ai was in the forefront of nearly every campaign involving intellectuals. In his mid-1920s in Shanghai, he had directed his pen at several targets. First and foremost was the enormously prolific and equally strident Ye Qing. Ye was particularly odious to Ai and the CCP because he had apostatized from Marxism to a kind of scientific materialism qua human panacea. Eventually he subordinated all of philosophy and even Marxism to scientism. His famous bookstore in

Shanghai published translations of the works of numerous major figures in European philosophy, eighteenth-century materialists, ancient Greeks, and *fin-de-siècle* scientists.[25] Ye's reductionist tendencies proved more than even Ai could tolerate, and the two of them argued in the mid-1930s over this issue of the relationship between science and philosophy. Ai soon rid himself of Ye by labeling him a Deborinite in line with Soviet policy at that time. Ye would, in the years to come, move to Taiwan and write volume after volume on the uniquely inspired brilliance of Sun Yat-sen's *Three Principles of the People*.[26]

Together with Chen Boda, in those years Ai often attacked the group of writers associated with China's preeminent writer, Lu Xun, who were unwilling to accept Party control over literary policy; at the same time Ai would write essays glorifying Lu Xun as a true comrade-in-arms, especially after Lu Xun's death in 1936. Like his close friend (who had sponsored him for membership in the CCP in 1935), the supreme literary bureaucrat, Zhou Yang, Ai never published anything of literary merit save translations from other literatures. Also like Zhou, he wanted literature to serve the greater good as determined by the Party. In the campaigns of the early 1940s, Ai contributed to the criticisms of Ding Ling and her associates, especially the most outspoken critic in Yan'an, the renegade Wang Shiwei.[27]

During the PRC's first decade, Ai appeared most prominently in the highly charged campaigns against Hu Shi and Liang Shuming. He contributed several essays to what was later collected in the multivolume *Hu Shi sixiang pipan* (Critiques of Hu Shi's thought), and he authored a series of attacks on Liang, later collected in his volume *Pipan Liang Shuming de zhexue sixiang* (Criticize the philosophical thought of Liang Shuming).[28] As one of the Party's foremost philosophy cadres, his participation and "philosophical" invective against Hu and Liang were deemed necessary ingredients in the campaigns.

In 1957, when Communist parties around the world were forced to admit the bitter truth of Khrushchev's revelations about the crimes of Stalin, the Chinese trod a middle ground that fell short of Khrushchev's repudiation. Mao of course published his own pamphlet, *On the Correct Handling of Contradictions Among the People*, a critique mainly of bureaucratism. As editor of the Party journal, Ai had the responsibility of breaking with the Stalinist tradition in the field of philosophy. Since his entire intellectual being was profoundly intertwined with Stalinist thought, that task was surely a difficult one, but, as always, he managed to overcome any personal problems and rapidly produced a 230-page volume, *Bianzheng weiwuzhuyi jiangke tigang* (Outline of lectures on dialectical materialism), in March 1957.[29] It was the first Chinese attempt to discuss dialectical materialism systematically in the light of de-Stalinization. Ai also took part in various campaigns not primarily designed for intellectuals, though his role in them often involved dealing with intellectuals. He participated in land reform in Anhui in November 1951.[30]

Ai's only serious brush with trouble, little known until recently, provides an illuminating example of how a Party member who had devotedly followed Party and leader for an entire life coped with the situation in which Party and leader diverge. The occasion was the Anti-Rightist Campaign of 1957, the Party's crackdown on intellectuals that followed the thaw of the Hundred Flowers of 1956–1957. Somehow, "despite his great service to the Party and the people" (as his secretary Wu Bingyuan put it recently), Ai was found wanting and was criticized. After leveling a spate of criticism at Feng Yulan early in 1957, Ai fell sick and was forced to go to Qingdao to recuperate. It was during his convalescence that the attacks against him occurred. The very idea of criticizing someone as conformist as Ai Siqi is baffling unless certain personal scores were being settled or internal jockeying, invisible to the outsider, was underway. A recently published *nianpu* (chronological biography), appended to a volume of his writings, hints that the critics waited until he had repaired to Qingdao before attacking.[31] Perhaps Kang Sheng saw him as a rival in his effort to gain control of the Party school. No one could explicitly label him a "rightist," inasmuch as no "evidence" for it existed. Instead he was attacked for being "dogmatic" in his philosophical writings, particularly the *Talks on Philosophy* (written more than twenty years earlier).

The label "dogmatic," however appropriate it might seem from our perspective, seems ridiculous in the Chinese context of a campaign against "liberal" intellectuals. Clearly, factional politics were at work, as groups competing for the true claim to Mao's spiritual essence went at each other's throats. There are systemic problems reconstructing the details of 1958, because, in post-Cultural Revolution China, Kang Sheng and Chen Boda along with the Gang of Four have been blamed for virtually everything. Ai's secretary from the 1950s, Wu Bingyuan, blames Kang for bringing the Anti-Rightist Campaign into the Central Party School, perhaps in an effort to clear out a goodly number of cadres whose support he felt he could not personally count on. If the reminiscence literature can be believed, Ai willingly accepted the Party's call to be "sent down." He and Wu left for Dengfeng county, Henan, in September 1958.[32] How such a conformist intellectual as Ai found himself in the position of a target at this time must have something to do with factional politics at the Party School. It was no longer sufficient to have a perfect record of Party loyalty; now one had also to demonstrate allegiance of the highest order to Mao himself. Being more Catholic than the Pope is a difficult business indeed.

The contemporary version of Ai's attitude at the time reveals much about the position obedient intellectuals assume in the People's Republic. Those who knew him during his months in Henan recall him as being extremely productive. He instructed local cadres on the necessity of philosophy in everyday life, and explained many complex points of Marxism-Leninism. He even drafted a proposal for the study of philosophy in Henan, which was published locally at that time. If the memoirists can be believed, Ai's ability to use his talents under such adverse conditions reflects his unbending loyalty to the Party. Ai apparently regarded the opportunity as a unique challenge to "learn from the masses" and fortify his own thinking. Indeed, Ai's quintessence was a mighty "party-nature" or *dangxing* (a translation of Lenin's expression *partinost'*). He returned to Beijing in the fall of 1959 as assistant head of the Central Party School for the next year.[33]

The last campaign Ai guided in the philosophical world was against Yang Xianzhen in 1964–1965. The debate involved contradictions and the unity of opposites. Did the two poles of a contradiction merge into one in the formation of a synthesis, as boldly asserted by Yang, or did everything divide into the two sides of the contradiction contained within itself, as Ai righteously maintained? Ai ultimately concluded, dragging out an epithet three decades old, that Yang was a transparent Deborinite,[34] namely that he was excessively intellectual or "idealist" in his perceptions.

Ai confronted another intellectual conundrum in 1964, when Mao announced in his philosophical talks that the second and third laws of dialectical logic (the mutual interaction of quantity and quality, and the negation of negation) were no longer operative.[35] As early as the late 1950s, Ai had begun to accord a greater role to the activist potential of consciousness in transforming the world, though this position was taken in his famous battles with Yang Xianzhen.[36] Ai had codified these laws in popular form as far back as 1935, which was the way most Chinese first learned of them, and again on numerous occasions in his writings over the years. Significantly, Ai wrote no major works between 1964 and his death two years later. If the republication of *Talks on Philosophy* in 1979 means anything, then the three laws of dialectics have been revived as proper Marxism-Leninism, an implicit rejection of Mao's idiosyncratic reformulation of dialectical logic. The superstructure no longer crushes the base.

Ai participated in the 1964–1965 rectification. It remains unclear if he was attacked and underwent reform or simply went again to the countryside as an example to others. All we now can glean from the materials available is that he "participated" in the rectification; indeed, every major unit was sent down during the campaign. In any case, his *dangxing* remained unshaken. He worked for a time in Tong county and in the Dongbeiwang commune of the Haiding region, both near Beijing. His secretary, Lu Guoying, accompanied him on several occasions because of his ill health. For a while they lived together in a "lower-middle peasant household" on a commune. Lu describes, in graphic detail, the vermin and insects with which they cohabited, but Ai persevered. As an example of his indomitable *dangxing,* he recalled for the younger Lu that lice had been a problem in Yan'an too and that comrades then were fond of saying that "without lice there can be no revolution." As if to counterbalance whatever may have been the reason for Ai's trip to Tong county, the authors of his *nianpu* emphasize that, twice during the year 1965, Mao himself sought out Ai's expertise in matters philosophical and that the two men exchanged views on a host of philosophical issues. Mao was particularly curious about the theories of a Japanese scientist named Sakata Shōichi, who had developed some notion of the materialistic verifiability of dialectics at the levels of atomic particles.[37]

Ai died on 22 March 1966 just in time. His funeral was attended by everyone of importance in the Chinese Communist intellectual community, and it was widely reported in the Chinese press. Within several weeks of his death, at least ten members of the funeral party were subjected to criticism and fell from power. The Great Proletarian Cultural Revolution had commenced. Given his proven Maoist record, Ai might have survived the Cultural Revolution; the arbitrariness of politics during that decade makes that estimate uncertain. His "rehabilitation" occurred when Hua Guofeng, Mao's designated heir, was still in control, and it survived the rise of Deng Xiaoping.

THE AI REVIVAL AND THE
ESTABLISHMENT INTELLECTUAL

Ai Siqi's name was hardly mentioned in the Chinese press in the decade following his death. Even after Mao's death and the arrest of the Gang of Four, several years passed before his posthumous reappearance. In 1977 and 1978, several of his works were reprinted, without any new introductory material, almost like feelers in a tenuous political climate. Finally, Wu Boxiao, an old friend of Ai's, broke the ice in the summer of 1978 with a four-page reminiscence. Like so much of the recent remembrance literature, it supplied a wealth of detail about Ai never published before, including Ai's real name and information about his years in Japan. "If Old Comrade Ai," Wu reports Mao to have said, "isn't the greatest guy on earth, then he's the second best."[38]

Then came an avalanche in 1979–1980 when an innocuous letter written by Mao in 1937 to Ai was published three times with fanfare and commentary. Mao wrote:

Comrade Siqi:
Of all your works, your book *Zhexue yu shenghuo* [Philosophy and life] has made a deep impression on me. My reading of it has benefited me greatly. I've copied out a bit of it [19 handwritten pages—JAF] and am sending it along to see if you find anything wrong here. There are several points I have slight doubts about (nothing fundamentally wrong). Please think it over and let me know personally what you think in detail. If you have some spare time soon, I'll drop by [your cave] to see you.

Mao Zedong[39]

Ai's widow, Wang Danyi, described the circumstances surrounding the letter's appearance after forty years. Ai held onto Mao's letter and the accompanying 19 pages for many years. He later gave it to Wang for safe keeping, and, in 1977 with the help of Hu Yaobang, she was able to bring the letter to Hua Guofeng's attention. Hua then passed it along to the Central Committee.[40]

In the same journal, *Zhongguo zhexue* (Chinese philosophy), that

printed Mao's letter appeared a short essay by intellectual cadre Wang
Zuye which repeats the stories of Mao's infatuation with philosophy
in the early Yan'an days and describes how voraciously he consumed
texts. Mao's letter to Ai, Wang notes, provides further proof of Mao's
desire to study and learn Marxist-Leninist philosophy as well as ample
evidence of Ai's important role in this endeavor. "It is important to
study the particularly revealing significance of this letter, now that we
are struggling to restore our Party's glorious tradition."[41]

Why all the hoopla over this 5-line letter? Clearly part of the explanation has to do with a subtle effort to dethrone Mao Zedong not
from the position of an important Marxist-Leninist philosopher but
from the position of Communist China's *only* philosopher. By
demonstrating how much Mao read of others' writings and translations and by stressing how energetically he read them, the canonical
"Mao Zedong Thought" no longer appears *deus ex machina* or, worse
yet, *sui generis*. In other words, the Chinese are not dismissing Mao
or launching a kind of de-Maoization in the philosophical sphere.
They are rehumanizing him by historicizing him. Thus, publishing
Mao's brief note to Ai over and over again (and with Wang Zuye's
injunction to study it) ultimately is meant to tell the readership that
China has had other Marxist-Leninist thinkers beside Mao and that
he learned from them. By the same token it strives to play down the
idiosyncratic elements Mao introduced into Chinese Marxist theory,
such as the elimination of several of Engels's "laws of the dialectic"
and the dominant role of the subject in achieving ends, clearly a return to a more stable, orthodox interpretation of Marxism-Leninism.

Nothing could demonstrate this more clearly than a passage from
one of the articles, by Guo Huaruo, that accompanied the letter
through two of its incarnations. Reminiscing about the late 1930s,
Guo writes:

Chairman Mao had the highest regard for Comrade Ai Siqi. If I asked Chairman
Mao about philosophical issues I didn't understand, he'd tell me to go find Comrade Ai Siqi and chat about it. And that's how I came to know Comrade Ai. The
first time we met, he impressed me as sincere, straightforward, and very bright.
At that time I had only just begun studying philosophy, so my questions were
mere matters of superficiality. Chairman Mao not only respected Comrade Ai
Siqi and had frequent contact with him, but he also respected other philosophers.
For example, Chairman Mao often went to visit Comrade Ho Sijing at his home
to talk over matters.

Guo describes the group of philosophers in Yan'an as a kind of brain trust for Mao. Between them and books written and translated by others—Li Da's *Shehuixue dagang* (Outlines of sociology, 1933) is mentioned by several authors as another of Mao's Yan'an favorites—Mao eventually prepared himself to lecture at the Anti-Japanese University in 1937.[42]

Wang Danyi and her brother-in-law, Li Shengmian, compiled a volume of reminiscence essays about Ai, published by the Yunnan People's Press in 1980. This volume included 32 new essays and a poem dedicated to Ai's memory. Every essay in this beautifully crafted book has a purpose and a message. The more one reads, the more one realizes that the book says much between the lines about Mao and the relationship between Mao and Ai. For example, on page 1, the cultural bureaucrat Liu Baiyu extols Ai and reveals that Ai personally enlightened him and led him on the path to Communism.[43] There would have been nothing odd if Liu had made this point about Mao, but the point is that he makes it not about Mao but about Ai. As a group of ideologists Ai taught briefly in Tianjin in 1952 put it: "We are all students of Ai Siqi . . . In many areas he was a model for us. He taught us our Marxism-Leninism with words; and by his personal example he taught how to be proper Marxist-Leninists, and how to be Communist Party members who would truly pass muster."[44] The entire quotation reads like a parody of earlier litanies to the Chairman.

Guo Huaruo's marvelous essay on Ai also plays on the Mao-Ai relationship in the Yan'an period. He stresses that even Mao had to study and read before he could lecture on the intricacies of dialectical materialism. Guo describes the topics covered in Mao's famous lectures. These are word-for-word the section headings of Mao's *Bian-zhengfa weiwulun (jiangshou tigang)*. We now know that this piece was in fact Mao's lecture notes of 1937 and that an uncut text exists from that time. Wu Liping recently analyzed the juxtaposition of Mao's lectures, Ai's arrival in Yan'an several months later, and their interaction. He notes that "On Practice" and "On Contradiction"—he sacrilegiously calls them the "two ons" (*lianglun*)—circulated in limited numbers in a mimeographed form. Ai, Wu, and other comrades were sent copies by Mao, soliciting suggestions, which were offered and even accepted by Mao for his rewrites.[45] What we see here is the disjunction of Mao from "Mao Zedong Thought." Many have contributed to the latter, including Mao himself, and Ai's role in the creation of the latter is being highly touted.

Before the Chinese leadership was prepared to grant Mao's place among the mortals, admitting such a problematic text as *Bianzhengfa weiwulun (jiangshou tigang)* to be the work of the Chairman was impossible. Guo confirms further that "On Practice" in its present form is a somewhat revised version of Mao's lecture, Part 2.11, while "On Contradiction" derives from Mao's discussion of the laws of contradictions toward the end of the 1937 lecture notes; this time the 1952 edition was greatly revised, probably along the lines suggested by Wu Liping. The most important section expunged from the lecture notes, according to Guo, was "The Laws of Identity in Formal Logic and the Laws of Contradiction in Dialectics."[46] Zheng Yili made this point much more clearly: "If one can in studying the basis of Chairman Mao's 'On Practice' and 'On Contradiction' . . . take another studied look at Ai's *Philosophy for the Masses*, I think it will prove a rewarding" effort.[47]

Thus, Mao received much of his knowledge on contradictions and dialectics directly from the writings of Ai Siqi. The changes, some cited and others hinted at, that Mao made to "On Contradiction" between 1937 and 1952 were considerable. Guo says nothing in this regard, although he does stress that all these changes never harmed the original "spirit" of the lecture, but preserved it and developed it in content and logical structure over time. In other words, Mao learned from others and improved his Marxism-Leninism. No longer is Mao protrayed as the man of superhuman insight and innate philosophic genius, but neither is he dismissed. Slowly but surely Mao is being relativized. With experience, study, and thought (all the things he insisted his cadres engage in), the ideas expressed in his "On Contradiction," according to Guo, improved over time.[48]

Although many have either dismissed Ai as a toady to Chairman Mao or have disregarded him altogether, much of the other reminiscence materials about Ai, including a chronological biography of his life and works, gradually reveal a more complicated, learned, and highly taciturn man. We now know, for instance, that he translated the poetry of Heine from German, a work by Kunikida Doppo from Japanese, Keats's "Ode to a Nightingale" from English, and began work on Bogdanov's *Krasnaia zvezda* (Red star) from Russian. He also prepared early translations of the lyrics of the "Marseillaise," "Song of the Volga Boatmen," and the "Internationale."[49] By citing these pre-viously unknown facts, contemporary authors enhance our image of Ai as a human being and an exceedingly complex one. Here is a man with inordinate linguistic abilities, a student of philosophy, a phe-nomenally prolific writer—over 20 books and nearly 300 articles and published speeches—and, second only to Mao, China's most popular author in the field of philosophy. He was also a dedicated Communist and obedient Party man.

When Leszek Kolakowski remarks that, by European standards, Mao's theoretical writings are so awkward and juvenile that, in com-parison with Stalin, they make Stalin an intellectual giant, we have little basis for argument with him.[50] All the encomiums accompany-ing the publication of Mao's philosophical essays in the early 1950s proved to be more pageant than substance. But, as scholars, we cannot conclude our analysis at this point. Mao's adulators (in China and abroad) and his detractors share a proclivity to see nothing philo-sophically significant beyond him in China.

There was another level of discourse in Marxist-Leninist thought that was usually quiet and always self-effacing. Ai Siqi, like Chen Boda, Zhang Ruxin, and others, was a central figure in this realm of discourse. In fact, it is a testimony to Ai's inordinate self-abnegating nature that, of all the English-language books on Mao and his thought, only Frederic Wakeman's so much as mentions Ai. Ai saw his own role in China not as a great philosopher or innovative thinker, for never did he manifest any urge to stand out, perhaps be-cause of possible political repercussions.

Ai seems to have patterned himself after the major figure in the Soviet ideological second level, Mark Mitin, whose writings he trans-lated. Born of Jewish parentage in the city of Zhitomir (Ukraine) in 1901, Mitin ascended to virtually every position of honor in the Soviet philosophical world. He edited numerous important journals, such as *Pod znamenem marksizma* (Under the banner of Marxism) from 1930 to 1944, and later served as editor of *Voprosi filosofii* (Prob-lems of philosophy) from 1960 until 1967. He was awarded the State Prize of the USSR, two Orders of Lenin, the Order of the October Revolution, and various other prizes. Mitin wrote voluminously on Hegel's dialectics, dialectics and biology, and a multi-volume history of philosophy, to cite several examples. It is likely that none of these would elicit even a passing interest in a serious student of philosophy outside the fold.

Mitin represented the voice of Stalin on matters philosophical. And, he was trotted out to lead campaigns against a variety of evil trends in the Soviet intellectual world, playing a particularly ugly role as Stalin's mouthpiece in the Doctors' Plot affair and more recently as the author of a pamphlet linking Zionism and racism.[51] A large number of his books and articles were translated into Chinese by Ai Siqi and others.[52] One reason Mitin's name evokes no immediate recognition is that he, like Ai in China, never bucked the system. Who knew better than he the consequences of being at odds with the Little Father?

There can be no question that Ai Siqi was an intellectual, as his mentor in the Soviet Union, Mark Mitin, remains to this day. Yet, in neither case do we see so much as an iota of loyalty to the liberal values of the Western academy. In fact, we often witness both men attacking such values as inimical to progress and willing to send their colleagues away for intensive "reeducation" should such tendencies crop up. What we in the West and Japan find so disconcerting about identifying such men as intellectuals is that we do not share the same definition of objectivity. For us, there exists some nebulous, broadly defined scientific approach to research that compels us to collect and test data in certain ways, exchange ideas with colleagues, and ideally accept no dogmatic or arbitrary standards a priori. For Mark Mitin and for Ai Siqi, objectivity always is defined in terms of the Party. Their "Party-nature" has been very strong indeed.

PART TWO

Professional Elite

Economists and Economic Policy-Making in the Early 1960s

NINA HALPERN

In what is now generally thought of as the Dengist era, intellectuals have been accorded unprecedented support from leadership. Efforts to raise the prestige of intellectuals, provide them with better living and working conditions, and enhance their contribution to China's modernization are all rightly considered hallmarks of this era. As a result, much scholarly attention has been devoted to examining the current regime's policies toward intellectuals and the nature of the evolving relationship between intellectuals and government.

Although the current regime's emphasis on increasing the role of intellectuals may be more intense than in the past, it is not new. Our perception of past Chinese policies toward intellectuals is dominated by images of the violent and repressive treatment they received during the Cultural Revolution and the Anti-Rightist Campaign of 1956–1957. Yet those periods were actually major interruptions in the Party's policies toward intellectuals. Most of the 1950s and early 1960s had anti-intellectual features, but there had been fairly steady efforts to increase the use of technological experts' knowhow in policy-making. Past patterns of regime/intellectual interaction should provide insight into the likely evolution of the relationship between the two in this current era. An examination of the role of economists in economic policy-making in the early 1960s provides information on those past patterns of such interaction.

The period of the early 1960s is significant because it has important parallels with the post-Mao era. Both periods were preceded by times in which the economy was badly mismanaged, although the 1958–1960 Great Leap Forward (GLF) was much worse economically than the 1966–1976 Cultural Revolution. In the early 1960s, as in the post-Mao period, China's leaders recognized the need for major organizational and policy changes in both agriculture and industry. And, in both periods, leadership rhetoric stressed the importance of specialists' contribution to policy-making. Even more significant, when the post-Mao leadership began its program of economic reform, it fell back on many of the ideas presented by economists in the early 1960s; indeed, China's most prominent economists in the 1980s were also active then.

Most of the economists who participated in policy-making in the early 1960s were formally outside the government, affiliated with universities or other high-level educational institutions or with research institutes specializing in economic questions. The most important center of economic research in the early 1960s was the Institute of Economics at the Chinese Academy of Sciences, headed by Sun Yefang. Sun was part of the "establishment," in the sense of being a long-time Party member who had worked for some time in the government; but he was also a professional economist. Despite his relative closeness to the establishment, he was quite critical of the leadership's economic policies. While his far-reaching criticisms of the existing economic system had little influence on policy at the time, they nevertheless revealed the degree of autonomy then permitted to professional economists. This autonomy allowed Sun and his colleagues to present ideas that would provide the initial inspiration for the post-Mao reforms.

BACKGROUND: THE GREAT LEAP FORWARD

Economic policy-making in the early 1960s must be viewed in the context of the preceding Great Leap Forward. That movement produced a number of very serious economic problems that China's policy-makers subsequently had to address. During this period, the Party introduced procedures that had important long-term implications for the position of economists in policy-making.

The GLF was an over-ambitious, ill-conceived effort to lift China overnight into the modern world. Its primary aim—to catch up with and overtake Britain in the production of steel and other major industrial products within fifteen years—produced a rapid escalation to impossible levels in industrial targets. Small, uneconomical "backyard" steel furnaces were set up throughout the countryside to smelt more steel. The large-scale transfer of labor from agricultural to industrial pursuits left much of the harvest uncollected. In an attempt to make agriculture keep up with the industrial spurt, peasants were rapidly reorganized into very large-scale collective units called communes, which permitted greater mobilization of labor for productive purposes. Unfortunately, the rapidity and large scale of the reorganization further disrupted normal agricultural activities. It soon became very clear that there were serious problems in the countryside. Peng Dehuai's miscalculated effort to focus more attention on these problems at the July 1959 Lushan Conference was interpreted by Mao as a personal attack on himself; the result was that the problems not only went unaddressed, but were even worsened by a resurgence of radicalism.

The economic problems extended far beyond the agricultural sector. Decentralization measures adopted in November 1957 left more funds with the provinces and also permitted enterprises to retain some profits. This downward transfer of financial resources combined with the general expansionary pressures of the period produced a rapid rise in construction projects, many of them economically irrational.[1] The breakdown in planning at the national level was mirrored in a decline of disciplined procedures within factories. Enterprises rapidly expanded their operations in response to the new unrealistically high targets, and accounting, quality control, and other basic procedures were neglected.

One legacy of the GLF was an economic crisis in industry and agriculture; the GLF also left another legacy of a very different nature. At the very same time that the most destructive policies of the Leap were being implemented, the leadership in 1958 quietly took steps to institutionalize a larger role for economists in policy-making. Although this enlarged role did little at the time to increase economists' influence on policy, it set the precedent for greater reliance on economists in policy-making once the Leap was halted.

This increased role responded to criticisms made during the Hundred Flowers Campaign (from early 1956 to mid-1957) about the exclusion of economists from policy-making. During the campaign, in which the leadership emphasized reliance on intellectuals to promote modernization and encouraged intellectuals to speak out about their problems, some economists pointed out that they had been almost totally excluded from the policy process and prevented from even acquiring statistics that would permit them to understand the economic situation.[2] When the Anti-Rightist Campaign began in the latter half of 1957, those economists making such assertions were criticized. Nevertheless, steps were taken to provide a larger role for economists in policy-making. The most important was a decision taken by the State Council and Party Secretariat in July 1958 to place the Institute of Economics jointly under the Chinese Academy of Sciences (which had always been its superior unit) and the State Planning Commission. The Institute of Economics was also told to establish direct links with the State Economic Commission (the body responsible for annual economic planning) and the State Statistical Bureau. The Institute was given equal rights of access to information on the economic situation as the internal units of the State Planning Commission and State Statistical Bureau.[3] For the first time, economists had formal links to the government and were regarded as potential contributors to economic policy. Although these specific measures applied only to the group of economists at the Academy of Sciences, during the Leap university economists also greatly increased their investigative research and contacts with the bureaucracy.[4] Thus, as the GLF drew to a close in early 1960 changes that were already in place offered economists a better position to help repair the damage of the GLF.

ECONOMIC POLICY-MAKING AFTER THE LEAP

In late 1960, the leadership finally acknowledged an economic crisis. In January 1961, it adopted a new slogan calling for "Readjustment, consolidation, filling out, and raising standards" in the economy. Mao also declared that the failures of the past were due to lack of investigation and declared 1961 an "investigative research year."[5] Investigations undertaken in the winter and spring of 1961 produced many new policy documents, the most important of which were the "Seventy Points on Industry" (Seventy Points) and the "Sixty Points on Agriculture" (Sixty Points). The economists' role in producing these documents reveals much about the attitude of the leadership toward professional economists. The leadership encouraged economists to participate in industrial policy-making, but not in the agricultural sphere.

The Seventy Points on Industry

Aware of serious problems in industrial management, in January 1961 the top leaders took steps to reestablish control over the industrial management system, which had been decentralized during the GLF.[6] In addition, Li Fuchun, head of the State Planning Commission and the member of the Party Secretariat in charge of industry and planning, was asked to draft comprehensive regulations for the industrial sector.[7] In preparing to do so, Li relied both on members of the government economic bureaucracy and academic economists.

In early 1961, Li requested that the Institute carry out its own independent studies of industrial management, asking it to "study in earnest" the question "concerning the portions of power that should be centralized and the rationality of power centralization."[8] The director, Sun Yefang, responded in June with an internal report suggesting fairly radical changes in the management system of state enterprises. Other economists, however, were reluctant to move into this area of research, arguing that the structure of the economic system was a question relating to the superstructure which was outside their province as political economists, who were supposed to study "productive relations."[9] According to Sun, there was a fairly hot debate on this subject. In his June report,[10] he criticized the reluctance of Institute researchers to study aspects of the financial and economic systems. Sun argued that the reason many Chinese economists avoided these subjects was a secret fear that studying the management system and advocating increasing enterprise powers would be considered "revisionism." In addition to this fear identified by Sun, some economists may have been reluctant to participate because of ignorance about the workings of the economic system, due to minimal opportunities in the past to do investigative research; many may have felt more comfortable continuing to write justifications for existing policy rather than going out to do the investigations necessary to make suggestions for change. Thus, not all economists at the Institute of Economics responded to Li Fuchun's request that they study questions of industrial reform. But Sun Yefang certainly did, and he urged others to do so too.

In addition to asking the Institute of Economics to carry out independent studies of the industrial system, Li enlisted economists in an investigative effort that he himself organized.[11] After he was asked to draft the industrial regulations, Li investigated ten factories and other units in Bejing and selected the Beijing First Machine Tool Plant as the focal point of his efforts. He established a nine-man team to conduct a more intensive study there, headed by a deputy director of the State Economic Commission, Ma Hong. The team also included two other members of the State Economic Commission and two from the First Ministry of Machine Building. Nevertheless, academic economists were a strong presence in the group: two members were from the Institute of Economics, one from the East China Textile Academy, and one from the Central Party School.[12]

Other than Ma Hong, the members of this group were not prominent figures, known for their *guanxi* (that is, personal connections) with top leaders. The indications are, therefore, that Li sought a group of relevant specialists from both inside and outside the bureaucracy. The fact that he did not use this opportunity to appoint figures from his own institution, the State Planning Commission, is another indication that he was seeking expertise rather than loyalty from the group. The incorporation of academic economists contrasts rather sharply with what we know of pre-GLF economic policy-making. Thus, it appears to reflect the decisions of 1958 that made those economists legitimate participants in the policy process.

The establishment of this group of specialists was seemingly not a token action. Its three-month investigation was an extensive one, involving interviews and inspections at all levels of the factory. Even though the team reported regularly to Li, supplying him with materials on which he would write comments and make suggestions, he apparently permitted a good deal of autonomy. Although he came often to the factory to inspect different workshops and construction sites, or to hold forums of workers, staff, and cadres, he does not appear to have dominated the investigation or closely monitored the team's activities. A work group of the Beijing Party Committee also took part in the investigation, but there is no indication in the team's final report that the Party Committee determined either the team's object of study or its conclusions. In fact, the report contained rather sharp criticism of the factory's Party branch and its over-involvement in the administration of the factory.

The team's investigation culminated in a long report (almost 300 pages) on its findings. After receiving Li's approval, it was sent to the Beijing Party Committee, which printed and distributed it internally to the relevant top leaders, leading cadres in the economic bureaucracy, and responsible persons in Beijing factories. The report was presumably also used for the actual drafting of the regulations. Because Li Fuchun had acquired other responsibilities, the drafting was supervised by Bo Yibo, head of the State Economic Commission.[13] Bo and a group composed of members of the State Planning Commission and other units, as well as some members of the nine-man team that had done the investigative report, examined many materials and then prepared a draft of the regulations. The draft was revised after consultations with cadres and workers in Harbin and Changchun. The Secretariat then examined and revised the regulations still further. Eventually Mao signed them, and they were carried out on a trial basis at the end of 1961.[14]

Despite the many participants in the process and the repeated revisions of the regulations, a comparison of the draft regulations with the nine-man team's report reveals few differences.[15] The basic thrust of the two was the same: Both emphasized centralized leadership within the factory; responsibility systems; regularization of planning, record-keeping, and equipment management; a larger role for technical personnel; material incentives reflecting the results of work performed; greater economic efficiency; and a larger role for the factory director relative to the Party Committee in administrative work. Many sections of the regulations actually appear to be simplified and condensed versions of the analysis and suggestions presented in the report. Of course, this similarity of the Seventy Points to the advice offered by the economists and bureaucrats who made up Li Fuchun's nine-man team does not prove the influence of economists on policy; it is impossible to judge the extent to which political leaders predetermined the framework within which these individuals carried out their investigations and formulated their proposals. Moreover, one cannot separate the input of the economists from that of the bureaucrats. But economists clearly were formally incorporated in a more than token fashion into the process that produced the regulations.

Finally, economists had another role in implementing industrial reform: They participated in drafting a textbook on industrial management that was intended to provide a detailed theoretical explanation of the Seventy Points for students at universities and academies and cadres at industrial enterprises.[16] In January 1961, when Li Fuchun began organizing investigations for drafting the Seventy Points, investigations and research for this textbook were also begun. Economists from People's University, Hubei and Hunan Universities, and the Northeast Textile Academy carried out investigations in factories and compiled materials for it. Quite possibly, these were among the materials that Bo Yibo used to draft the Seventy Points. In July 1961, the month in which the Secretariat revised the draft of the Seventy Points given to them by Bo Yibo, formal compilation of the textbook began. Both the timing, and the fact that three members of the nine-man team were among the nineteen authors of the textbook, strongly suggest that this book and the Seventy Points were intended to be complementary. Ma Hong was in charge of both the nine-man team and the editing of the textbook; a member of the Institute of Economics, Wei Xiulan, and a number of the Northeast Textile Academy, Tang Ying, participated in both. Altogether, the nineteen authors included Ma Hong, eight researchers at the Institute of Economics, six professors from People's University, and one each from Hubei, Hunan, and Zhejiang Universities and from the Northeast Textile Academy.

The draft textbook, titled *Management of China's Socialist State-Run Industrial Enterprises*, was finished in September 1962. Fairly extensive revisions were then required, probably to render the book acceptable in the newly politicized atmosphere that followed the September 1962 10th Plenum. At that Plenum, Mao again raised the theme of class struggle and demanded a halt to some of the liberal-izing measures being implemented in the countryside, such as the setting of output quotas at the household level. The revisions of the textbook were completed in December 1963, and it was circulated internally, probably meaning that it was available to cadres, but not to the general public. Its main themes were the principles enunciated in the Seventy Points: centralization of management, obeying the plan, accounting, material incentives, and so forth. Yet it also con-tained some language that was quite dissimilar, such as an emphasis on Party leadership in the factories, class struggle, and the dangers of capitalist restoration. By and large, the book maintained the impor-tant ideas of the Seventy Points, but grafted onto them the themes of class struggle and continued revolution as put forward at the 10th Plenum.

Despite the need ultimately to revise the textbook to fit in with new political trends, its initial drafting reveals another facet of econo-mists' participation in the early 1960s. While economists had always been expected to produce writings that justified new policies, this case was somewhat different. The establishment of the new policies and the writing of the textbook to promote these policies this time were interactive processes. Some of the authors of the textbook were members of Li Fuchun's nine-man team and thus were important par-ticipants in the preparations for drafting the regulations. They were, in fact, writing a textbook promoting principles they themselves had suggested. Moreover, they began writing the textbook before the Party Secretariat had produced the final version of the Seventy Points, which suggests that they were not expected simply to write a narrow-ly propagandistic work justifying the Secretariat's decisions.

In sum, economists were incorporated into the industrial policy process of 1961 in three different ways. The Institute of Economics was asked to carry out independent studies of the problem of reform-ing industrial management and to supply advice; a few economists were part of a special group designated to provide input for drafting the new regulations; and a larger group of economists were asked to write a textbook explaining the underlying principles of the regula-tions to a wide audience.

The Sixty Points on Agriculture

The agricultural policy process was quite different. The leadership considered agricultural problems to be even more serious than industrial problems. An August 1960 directive called for agriculture and grain to be stressed above all else and noted that, because of "natural disasters," grain production had decreased and there were inadequate reserves; consequently, in several provinces seeds were being stolen and eaten, out-migration was in progress, and illness and abnormal levels of death were evident.[17] Some efforts were made in 1960 to address these problems. In addition to the directive just mentioned, in November the Central Committee issued an "urgent directive" on the communes (the Twelve Articles) that called for more far-reaching changes. It legalized private plots, family sidelines, and rural markets; required the return of confiscated materials; and called for three levels of ownership with the brigade as the basis to remain unchanged for seven years.[18] Two months later at the 9th Plenum, however, Mao issued his call for a "great investigative wind," arguing that the agricultural situation had still not been fully understood. He thus demanded that comprehensive regulations be drafted for agriculture, as for industry and other economic spheres.

Mao personally oversaw the process of producing the agricultural regulations. Unlike Li Fuchun, who turned to economic bureaucrats and economists, Mao relied primarily on Party cadres from various levels. He first organized three groups to carry out investigations in the countryside; he also called for every provincial Party first secretary to study several communes, factories, and stores. Following his investigations, at a March 1961 conference in Guangzhou, Mao supervised the drafting of the Sixty Points."[19] These regulations reiterated the policies of the Twelve Articles, but provided more specifics and additional measures to ease the burden of the peasants and to make the communes more workable.[20] After the March conference, the draft regulations were disseminated to the Party branches for trial implementation and study. A second work conference was held at the end of May to revise them.[21]

Mao's letters of this period indicate that the participants in the work conference, and the individuals designated to conduct investigations during this period, were all Party figures: specifically, first secretaries of all the Party committees of provincial-level units and the bureaus of the Central Committee.[22] The letters also indicate that some kind of drafting committee was established, but give no information on its membership. Other sources state that the Party Secretariat, under Deng Xiaoping, prepared the initial draft.[23] Another key institution in this process was probably the Party's Rural Work Department.[24]

None of the sources available to us suggest any involvement of specialists from the government bureaucracy, much less any academic economists. The drafting of the major policy statement on agriculture in 1916–1962 was thus monopolized by Party figures, and no effort was made to involve economists in the process, despite the fact that top leaders recognized that agriculture was in crisis. Obviously, economists' roles in the early 1960s varied greatly between the industrial and agricultural spheres.

REASONS FOR THE VARIATION
IN ECONOMISTS' PARTICIPATION

The difference between the agricultural and industrial policy processes described here was not new. A similar pattern had existed before the GLF. Although academic economists were generally excluded from policy-making at that time, government bureaucrats (as opposed to Party generalists) constituted an alternative source of expertise. As Roderick MacFarquhar has described,[25] the major document on agricultural policy of the mid-1950s, the Twelve-Year Plan for Agricultural Development, was a product largely of Mao's interaction with provincial Party secretaries; bureaucrats and other experts were consulted only at the last minute and in a largely formalistic way. Yet Mao's speech on the Ten Major Relationships, which announced significant policy changes in macroeconomic and industrial policy, followed extensive consultations with different segments of the government bureaucracy.[26] Three regulations on reform of the planning, financial, and commercial systems adopted in November 1957 were also based on extensive consultations with the relevant bureaucratic units.[27] Thus, what was new about the policy processes of 1961 was not any new difference between specialist involvement in agricultural and industrial policy-making, but the widening of the group of specialists involved in nonagricultural policy-making to include academic economists.

The question remains of why this pattern emerged. Undoubtedly, both institutional and personal forces were at work. In explaining the difference in specialist involvement in formulating the Twelve-Year Plan for Agricultural Development and the Ten Major Relationships speech, MacFarquhar suggests that it resulted from Mao's sense of his own greater competence in the agricultural than the industrial sphere.[28] This undoubtedly was one factor. Nevertheless, in both cases, Mao consulted with others in deciding policy; however, for agricultural policy he turned to Party figures, while for industry to the government bureaucracy. Thus, the difference must also have reflected his views on where expertise was located in each case.

Mao's views on this had some basis in fact. Agriculture was less subject than industry to bureaucratic planning and management. Large variations in agricultural conditions due to both regional differences and rapidly changing weather conditions meant that the central bureaucrats had less understanding of the agricultural than the industrial situation. Thus, Mao's preference for consultation with local Party figures rather than central bureaucrats in making agricultural policy made some sense. Moreover, even at the central level, agricultural policy-making had always been concentrated on the Party rather than the government side. The Party's Rural Work Department, headed by Deng Zihui, had been far more important in agricultural decision-making than the government's Ministry of Agriculture.

Industry and agriculture therefore differed both in sources of expertise and in the nature of the institutions that were considered responsible for establishing policy. These variations in turn had implications for the role of economists. The primary method adopted in 1958 to enhance economists' involvement in policy-making was increasing their access to the government bureaucracy and to the information that it gathered. Consequently, it is not surprising that where the government bureaucracy was more involved, in industry, there was also more participation by economists. The decision to make the State Planning Commission jointly responsible for directing the Institute of Economics' research was a key aspect of the increased interaction between economists and the bureaucracy; it meant that Li Fuchun, as head of the State Planning Commission, was able to tap the resources at the Institute of Economics when drafting the Seventy Points. This was an important reason why economists were able to participate in industrial policy-making in the early 1960s, where they generally had not before the GLF.

Thus, the involvement of economists in industrial but not agricultural economic policy-making can be attributed both to the greater responsibilities of the government bureaucracy in industrial policy-making and to the 1958 changes that made economists legitimate participants in bureaucratic decision-making. In addition, personal forces were undoubtedly also at work. Li Fuchun is known to have been particularly interested in the contributions of specialists;[29] he was the main force behind the 1958 changes increasing the role of the Institute of Economics. A different individual with responsibility for preparing the industrial regulations might not have involved economists quite so extensively. The 1958 changes obviously established the possibility, but not the necessity for economists to be consulted on policy. Moreover, there are indications that economists at the Institute of Economics were asked in mid-1962 to investigate the effects of liberalizing measures then being adopted in agriculture, such as the extension of rural markets and the setting of production quotas at the household level.[30] Mao certainly was not the one who initiated such studies; he subsequently strongly objected to these policies on ideological grounds. Whichever top leader(s) was interested in these policies (Deng Zihui, Chen Yun, Liu Shaoqi, and Deng Xiaoping all seem strong possibilities) apparently found more utility than had Mao in economists' advice on agricultural policy. In addition to those organizational factors that made economists more likely participants in industrial than agricultural policy-making, therefore, the personal proclivities of the relevant top leader need to be taken into account.

THE SCOPE OF PARTICIPATION: SUN YEFANG

During the early 1960s, the leadership turned to professional economists for help in making economic policy, although not in every sphere. As far as can be judged from available sources, the suggestions that came from the mixed group of bureaucrats and economists composing the nine-man group were quite influential. Like the Seventy Points themselves, however, these suggestions did not call for any radical changes in the system; they were designed to improve the existing economic system without altering it in any fundamental manner. It is probably not surprising that such professional advice was quite acceptable to China's leaders. But not all economists offered such conservative advice. Sun Yefang, instead, sought to convince the leadership of the need for some basic changes in the economic system. He showed himself willing and able to be quite critical of views expressed both by economic bureaucrats and by high-level Party figures. As the storm clouds that eventually produced the Cultural Revolution gathered at the end of 1964, Sun Yefang came under attack for his views, but in the period immediately after the GLF the leadership appeared quite tolerant of his dissent.

Sun obviously was not a typical economist. We have already seen that he had a different concept of political economy than many other members of the Institute. In addition to being more policy-oriented, he had relatively high status as a long-time Party member. He also had much experience working in local and central economic bureaucracies, first in Shanghai, and from 1954 to 1957 as Deputy Director of the State Statistical Bureau.[31] This experience had given him a greater understanding than the average academic economist of the actual working of the economy, and had also allowed him to get to know some important bureaucratic figures, such as Li Fuchun. Consequently, before going to the Institute of Economics he had acquired greater political resources than most economists had. Sun was not a typical economist; his participation nevertheless gives some indication of the limits of dissent permissible during that period.

During 1961–1962, Sun submitted to top leaders three internal reports advocating policy changes. The first was the June 1961 report mentioned earlier, written in response to Li Fuchun's request that the Institute of Economics study the question of centralization and decentralization of the economic system. Where the Seventy Points and the nine-man team's report had focused on the need to centralize authority within the enterprises and for the enterprises to obey the plan, Sun, instead, called for some fundamental changes in the financial and economic systems. Among these were a significant decentralization of authority to the enterprises; a reform of planning methods so that plans would be based on "value" categories (that is, profit) rather than material output; and the allocation of products within the state sector by means of contracts, rather than by administrative fiat. All these suggestions added up to a call for basic change in the planning system.

Sun later said that he did not dare publish this report in *Jingji yanjiu* (the publicly circulated journal of the Institute of Economics) because so many, especially within the bureaucracy, felt that any criticism of the planning and statistical systems imported from the USSR was equivalent to a criticism of socialism. He instead gave the report to Li Fuchun to submit to the central leadership.[32] Sun's actions were consistent with the norms of democratic centralism, according to which individuals are permitted to dissent privately (that is, through internal channels) from existing policies, so long as they continue publicly to uphold them. Obviously, Sun felt that relative freedom was permitted in internal channels. In asking Li to submit the report to the Center on his behalf, however, he apparently sought a sponsor for his controversial views, perhaps for self-protection, or to increase the impact of his suggestions.[33] If he did so for the latter reason, he was unsuccessful, for, like the two reports discussed below, this one had no obvious impact on policy at the time.

A second report that Sun submitted in 1961 was a more direct response to arguments expressed by the economic bureaucrats, and also another attempt to convince the leadership of the need for fundamental changes in planning methods.[34] Sun wrote it in August 1961 in response to discussions held at the July-August Beidaihe planning conference on why the GLF had been such an economic disaster. Sun was concerned because many of the speakers at this conference argued that the primary mistake of the GLF was an excessively high accumulation rate, supporting their position by citing a "law" contained in the Soviet textbook on political economy to the effect that accumulation must not go above 25 percent of national income (during the GLF it had reached 40 percent).

In Sun's view, this was a fundamental misdiagnosis of the source of the GLF problems. Although he agreed that the Leap's major problem was excessive capital construction, he argued that one could not simply pinpoint an arbitrary percentage above which accumulation should not rise. The key question was not the absolute percentage, but whether or not national income and the standard of living were growing enough to support a higher accumulation rate. The real problem during the GLF, Sun argued, was that the expanded capital construction had been premised upon false assumptions about rising national income. And those false assumptions were a result of the type of statistical system China had adopted from the USSR, in which national income was calculated solely on the basis of the amount of taxes and profits handed up to the state by enterprises, agricultural units, and so forth. Sun maintained that these revenues did not necessarily represent a real increase in material wealth. Enterprises might actually be operating at a loss, but could still obtain loans that would give them the ability to hand up their required profits and taxes. This revenue, not backed by material goods, would be "false income."

Thus, Sun sought to shift the analysis of what had gone wrong during the GLF away from policy mistakes to a fundamental reassessment of China's planning and statistical systems. His report, submitted to Li Fuchun, obviously called into question the judgment of the economic bureaucrats as well as some basic features of the Chinese economic system. Nevertheless, Li wrote approving comments on the report, and asked Sun to study the question together with those members of the Ministry of Finance who had attended the planning meeting. Sun did so, but could not persuade them to accept his argument. The bureaucrats insisted that they had long since corrected the defects that Sun pointed out. So, as Sun put it, they "settled the matter by leaving it unsettled."[35] The ability to dissent, albeit in internal channels, was no guarantee of influence, but it does demonstrate that autonomous participation was possible.

A third report, which Sun wrote in 1962, demonstrates that Li Fuchun was not the only recipient of Sun's advice. This was a highly critical response to ideas that Chen Boda (the chief editor of the Party journal, *Red Flag,* who was closely associated with Mao) presented in a 1962 report on current agricultural problems.[36] Sun objected that Chen presented a much more rosy picture of the economy than was justified by the actual economic situation; he also criticized Chen for various theoretical inadequacies, including overemphasizing production problems and ignoring the importance of circulation, and for equating rationing with "planned supply," implying that this was a permanent measure rather than a temporary one to be replaced by free selection as soon as possible.

Sun tells us that Chen responded to his criticisms with praise, but bore a grudge that caused him two years later to denounce Sun as "the biggest revisionist in China," and to mobilize economists to denounce Sun's ideas.[37] Nevertheless, there was no negative reaction at the time to Sun's expression of his views. Sun was not criticized for his ideas until late 1964, when the political situation had changed considerably. In mid-1962, it appears that Sun did have considerable freedom to express his views in internal channels. Moreover, this example demonstrates that he felt able to express disagreement not only with Li Fuchun, who one might argue acted toward him as a sort of patron, but also with Chen Boda, an influential Party figure with whom Sun had no apparent personal ties. Again, however, Sun's views did not prevail. Agricultural policy after this point increasingly contradicted rather than followed Sun's suggestions. The expansion of rural markets was halted, and there was no movement away from rationing. Mao also made clear that, in his view, the economic situation was basically improved, so that attention could turn to political problems.

In sum, during 1961–1962, Sun was able to participate in a meaningful although not influential way in policy deliberations. A key factor permitting this was his access to planning meetings, and consequent ability to learn the nature of policy discussions. This access was apparently a product of the 1958 decision to link the Institute of Economics to the State Planning Commission. Sun's personal connections with Li Fuchun also provided him with an important resource, and he obviously recognized this and made use of it, channeling much of his input to Li. But he did not operate solely within the context of a personal relationship with one individual; he also felt able to offer advice to other top leaders, such as Chen Boda. The nature of Sun's input and the apparent absence of any negative response to his rather far-reaching suggestions and criticisms suggest that the scope of permissible dissent was quite wide at the time.

THE POST-MAO SITUATION

In the period since Mao's death, the new leadership has rediscovered the wisdom of the economists who participated in the policy discussions of the early 1960s. In 1980 and 1981, the nine-man team's report and the textbook on industrial management drafted by Ma Hong et al. were both published openly for the first time. Sun Yefang's articles and reports from the early 1960s — including those circulated only internally — have been published in several volumes. Until his death in 1983, Sun was an active and influential participant in reform discussions; other economists who worked under him at the Institute of Economics in the early 1960s have also become very influential. These have been among the strongest voices calling for reform of the economic system.

The past is also relevant to the current relationship between the state and China's economists in that the institutionalization of links established in the late 1950s between the economists at the Institute of Economics and the government bureaucracy has been revived and furthered with the establishment under the State Council of several economic research centers that draw in both economic bureaucrats and academic economists. These centers provide advice on economic policy to the top leaders. They ensure that the type of participation the economists had in formulating the Seventy Points will occur on a regular basis.

The participation of economists in the post-Mao era has thus become further institutionalized and also more extensive. Many more economists are drawn into policy discussions than before. Nevertheless, certain basic features of the earlier period continue to characterize the relationship between the leadership and economists. The leaders appear seriously interested in obtaining economists' advice; the extent and nature of economic reform since 1978 provides testimony to the receptiveness of the new leaders to economists' ideas. Moreover, they appear willing to tolerate rather far-reaching suggestions for change—such as price reform. Indeed, economists have gone far beyond Sun Yefang in critiquing many aspects of China's Soviet-style economic system. But, although discussion in the open journals is freer than before, as in the early 1960s serious policy discussions and challenges to existing economic policy remain largely restricted to internal channels.[38] The norms of democratic centralism are still very operational. Thus, in the post-Mao era, as in the early 1960s, economists have not been granted the right to involve the public in policy discussions.

Given these basic similarities between the current era and the earlier one, does the experience of that earlier time offer any lessons for viewing the present? The difference we found between industrial and agricultural economic policy-making suggests that the leadership's current commitment to obtaining economists' advice is not likely to produce a uniform reliance on economists in all areas of decision-making. Even though economists today appear to be more often drawn into agricultural policy-making than before, differences in the nature of the policy area, the organization in charge, and the top leader with personal responsibility for a decision undoubtedly will continue to produce variation in the roles of economists. The greater institutionalization of economists' participation only makes it possible for the leaders to obtain economists' advice; it does not guarantee that they will actually do so.

Given past experience, it is not surprising that many of economists' most innovative policy proposals still fall on deaf ears. Sun Yefang's suggestions had little impact on policy in the early 1960s. But this does not mean that such participation does not matter. In the long run, Sun's ideas have been very influential indeed. Thus, a willingness of the leadership to tolerate challenges to its policies, even if only internally, is important. Ideas, once expressed, tend to take on a life of their own. In understanding the real significance of economists' participation, therefore, we should not simply focus on the extent of their influence on current policy. As in the past, their ideas may reappear and be more influential at another time. The willingness of many more economists than in the early 1960s to join in policy discussions, and the liveliness of current economic debates, suggests that further economic reform is likely in the future.

CHAPTER THREE

The Politics of Historiography: Jian Bozan's Historicism*

CLIFFORD EDMUNDS

In September 1978, the prominent Marxist historian Jian Bozan was officially rehabilitated from political disgrace by the CCP's reform coalition under the leadership of Deng Xiaoping. Jian's posthumous rehabilitation occurred in the midst of similar rehabilitations of other noted cultural figures and officials publicly humiliated and purged during the Cultural Revolution.[1] Jian himself had been one of the first victims of "the decade of turmoil," as the Dengists now refer to the period, having been attacked in a public-criticism campaign that began in March 1966 shortly after the first "shots" of the Cultural Revolution were fired at his fellow historian Wu Han. At that time,

---

*The views expressed in this chapter are the author's and are not necessarily those of the United States Government.

Jian was the Chairman of the History Department and Vice-President of Beijing University. He was eventually persecuted to death, taking his own life in a double suicide with his wife in 1968.[2]

The modus vivendi worked out in the early 1950s between China's Marxist historians and the Chinese Communist Party was ruptured by the radical political environment of the Great Leap Forward in 1958. A new generation of more radical Marxist historians, wedded to the Maoist vision of socialist revolution, attacked the historiography of Jian and other establishment scholars of the 1930s generation and challenged their view of the relationship between politics and history. In this environment, Jian was compelled to articulate his own conception of the relationship, and eventually to oppose what he viewed as the excessive politicization of intellectual life.

Jian was one of the most prominent historians in China after 1949, and one of a handful of academic bureaucrats responsible for the political direction and control of academic history. He became Chairman of the History Department at Beijing University in the early 1950s and was appointed Vice-President of the university in 1962. As both an historian and bureaucrat, Jian played an influential role in the organization and development of historical scholarship after 1949. Like other Marxist historians of his academic generation, he was committed to history as a serious scholarly enterprise within the framework established by the regime.

Jian belonged to that generation of leftist intellectuals who established their academic and political reputations in the 1930s, and who became attracted to the CCP as a political alternative to Chiang Kai-shek's Nationalist Party during the same decade. He participated in the great debates in Marxist historical circles during the 1930s that established the basic direction of Marxist historiography for the next three decades.[3] Like other Marxist historians of the 1930s who served as the scholarly establishment in the People's Republic of China after 1949, Jian embraced as the main goal of Marxist historical scholarship the comprehensive rewriting of Chinese history within a Marxist framework, or what he called a Marxist "general history" of China. His own contribution to this goal, the first two volumes of a projected multi-volume work, were published in 1946.[4]

From the time of his first published works in 1929, Jian was well within the Marxist tradition. By the late 1940s, his basic intellectual inclinations were set. He accepted a Marxist teleological conception of history which included universal evolutionary stages and the assertion that economic factors were primary in historical causation. Although he invoked class struggle and the dialectic as analytical categories when engaged in abstract discussions of theory, these concepts were seldom integrated into his specific historical interpretations. As with other nationalistic Marxists, his focus was on "national struggle" rather than class struggle, and he equated the Chinese people as a whole with the oppressed class.[5] Jian supported this broad Marxist framework with an inductive methodology and a strong empirical bias that grounded all generalizations in concrete documentation. He advocated a multi-dimensional approach to history, comprehensive in scope and balanced in judgment, and he valued critical detachment as a companion to theoretical guidance in historical interpretation. As late as 1955, he welcomed criticism of Marxist historiography by Western scholars, because, as he put it, "we are all pursuing truth, and in the presence of truth we shall all unite."[6] Jian had also used history as a vehicle for political criticism. His essays on Song and Ming history during the 1940s were historical allegories commenting on Guomindang strategies and policies.[7]

In the 1950s, political control over professional historians was exercised formally through the institutional structure of the Chinese Academy of Sciences, but, as in other CCP hierarchies, authority was vested as much in key persons as in formal offices, and was exercised informally. In the case of historians, the eminent literary figure, historian, and cultural revolutionary Guo Moruo appears to have been the primary link between professional scholars and the regime. Moreover, in contrast to the early Soviet intellectual establishment, the Marxist historical estabishment in China was dominated by left-wing scholars and political activists like Jian whose intellectual commitments to Marxism and political commitments to the CCP were well established before 1949.[8] Guo Moruo and his colleagues seem to have had considerable flexibility to determine their research priorities within the general strictures of Maoist ideology. The format, agenda, and guidelines that Guo laid down for historical research in 1951 closely paralleled the pre-1949 interests and scholarly work of the leading historian-bureaucrats who had committed their services to the new regime.[9] An implicit relationship between these historians and the political sphere was also established, but never publicly articulated. As committed Marxists, Jian and other academic bureaucrats were not only willing to impose Marxist historiography on their colleagues, but were also willing to defend the regime in theoretical terms to its critics, legitimize it to the Chinese people, and justify to the world the CCP's revolutionary seizure of power. But, while they were willing to serve revolutionary goals in this general sense, they did not view their role as mere propagandists, and they were not willing to subvert academic standards or distort history to serve immediate political ends.

The accommodation worked out between these professional historians of a Marxist persuasion and the CCP was rather effective until the political radicalization of the Great Leap Forward in 1958. The ideological rectification campaigns against "bourgeois" intellectuals earlier in the decade were not directed at historians and there were no major purges of historians until the Anti-Rightist Campaign of 1957. Those purged at that time were associated with the pre-1949 liberal camp and with distinctly non-Marxist approaches to history.[10] Jian supported the regime both in promoting the Hundred Flowers liberalization movement in 1956 and in denouncing the "bourgeois reactionaries" among his non-Marxist colleagues in the Anti-Rightist Campaign that followed in 1957. Thus, although the Anti-Rightist Campaign placed considerable strain on the politically important mediating roles that Jian and other "establishment" historians performed in linking the scholarly community to the party-state, they closed ranks against intellectual critics of the Party and supported the regime.

The politicization of scholarship in the Great Leap destroyed the modus vivendi established between the party and its historians. Radical political leaders demanded that historians, in effect, become little more than propagandists for the radical goals and values of the movement, thus violating Jian's most deeply held values regarding the nature and role of historical knowledge in a Marxist regime, and compelling him to clarify and publicly argue his own point of view. The politicization of history, on the other hand, sharpened a conflict that was emerging between a new version of Marxist history supported by radical younger historians, and the version espoused by the older generation of historians.

The radicals attacked the approach long taken by Jian and others in applying Marxist categories to Chinese history. In the radical view, the historian's primary purpose was to dramatize the moral struggle of class conflict through the ages, to give proper credit to the "laboring masses" rather than to their feudal oppressors for propelling history forward, and to praise heroes and condemn villains according to the single criterion of class affiliation. The most extreme expression of the radical view insisted on expunging all trappings of feudal ruling-class culture from the historical record, including imperial reign titles. The radicals' "anonymous" history, derived from a singular emphasis on impersonal socioeconomic forces, threatened the nationalistic version of Chinese history developed by Jian and others, who had been searching since the 1930s for a framework that permitted the glorification of China's classic civilization and yet remained true to Marxist principles.

Jian's growing dissent from the politics of the Great Leap Forward represented an attempt to redefine and publicly articulate the relationship between historians and political authority in China's Marxist party-state. In effect, Jian was seeking the institutionalization of a limited autonomy from politics for scholarly activity. His dissent in the late 1950s, and his subsequent purge during the Cultural Revolution, centered around his concept of "historicism,"[11] a set of historiographical principles Jian advocated as an antidote to the ideological demands of the radical historians. In the ideological climate of the Great Leap, historicism was both an intellectual perspective and a political weapon. To Jian it constituted a set of interpretive principles and critical standards consistent both with Marxist categories and the goals of nationalistic history. It also served as the justification of Jian's argument regarding the appropriate relationship between historiography and contemporary politics. During the Cultural Revolution, Jian's persecutors seized on historicism, which they alleged to be a bourgeois, anti-class-struggle historical philosophy that he had substituted for Marxism-Leninism-Mao Zedong Thought, to substantiate their charge that he had obstructed the "revolution" in historiography during the Great Leap.

THE GREAT LEAP FORWARD AND THE POLITICIZATION OF ACADEMIC HISTORY

Academic historians were drawn into the nationwide mobilization movements that swept over China in 1958 and 1959, but the Great Leap Forward campaign in academic circles was different in both scale and intensity from previous political campaigns among intellectuals. In part, it aimed at a more thorough implementation of goals that had been established for historians in the early 1950s: eliminating "bourgeois" historiography, replacing the dynasty-centered traditional history of China with a comprehensive "general history" of China written in Marxist categories, and carrying out a thorough ideological remolding of historians. The injunction added in the GLF, to "put history in the service of politics," pointed to a very different set of goals than those of the early 1950s. The major objectives, as described in a Cultural Revolution account, were to bring about a "revolutionization in the ranks of historical-study workers" and a "violent revolutionary movement in the study of history."[12] This call for a revolutionary self-transformation was directed as much at long-standing Marxist scholars, academic bureaucrats, and a new generation of students as at representatives of the bourgeoisie. It was a drive for the total politicization of historical scholarship and the professional life of historians.

Taken at face value, the slogans promulgated for the guidance of academic history after 1958 were simply directives for academic research, but their import was clearly political. They functioned as politically charged metaphors that linked the activities of historians to political mobilization in the larger society and expressed the political goals and values of the new campaign in academic terms. The first slogans announced, "Emphasize the present, deemphasize the past," and "Ancient for the use of the present," were soon followed by three other slogans: "Use the class struggle viewpoint to explain history," "Theory takes command," and "Lead history with theory." These three slogans were intended as academic counterparts to the three major political slogans of the Great Leap, "Never forget class struggle," "Politics takes command," and "Put politics out in front." The proliferation of such slogans after 1958 pointed to the growing pressure on historians to bring their work into line with the goals of the Great Leap Forward and, in particular, with the theme of class struggle. They were to place their scholarship in the direct service of contemporary politics.

This effort to politicize historical scholarship had three major dimensions. First, the range of historical interpretation and debate was greatly reduced, and Marxist historical categories were more narrowly understood and mechanically applied. In addition, the authority of Mao's Thought was given extraordinary emphasis. Second, historical subject matter and interpretation were placed in the service of current political needs, as historians were to become little more than propagandists for the regime. Their responsibility was to write history that not only addressed itself to contemporary issues but also legitimized current policies, mobilized support for the Great Leap, and undermined Mao's political opposition. The third dimension was anti-intellectual in its demand that historians "leave the ivory tower," "learn from the masses," and become directly involved in socialist construction. What this meant in practice was that historians were to go to factories and communes to write their histories. The goal of the movement was to push the Marxist historical establishment in a radical Maoist direction.

This extreme politicization of academic life produced a cleavage between the "establishment" Marxist intellectuals of the generation of the 1930s and a new generation of historians who may be referred to as "radicals."[13] The Great Leap mobilization in history fostered an environment in which historians of a radical persuasion could flourish, or even gain the upper hand, promoting their new conception of the nature of Marxist historiography and its relation to politics. The response of the radical historians to these directives to write history that legitimized current policy and programs triggered a confrontation between themselves and "establishment" Marxist historians like Jian, who held a different set of professional values. This process of politicization, however, ruptured the accommodation that had been reached between the Party-state and its historians.

THE CULTURAL NATIONALISM MOVEMENT

The period from 1959 to 1964 was a time of great ferment within Chinese intellectual circles. In academic history, the diversity of viewpoints and intensity of debate were unparalleled since the social-history debates of the 1930s. The movement to "reevaluate" the role of famous Chinese historical figures, which emerged in 1959 along with a renewed emphasis on the interpretation of peasant rebellions, generated much controversy. In 1960, a heated resurgence of the debate over the "sprouts of capitalism" culminated in the public criticism of the historian Shang Yueh.[14] By 1961, studies on Confucianism and other early philosophical schools flourished, paralleling the "limited cultural renaissance" in all areas of intellectual endeavor. A debate over the problem of "class viewpoint versus historicism," which cut across most of the other themes and issues, attracted much attention in 1963–1964.[15]

While these intellectual activities were greatly influenced by the political atmosphere, they were not simply political by-products of the time, much less politically dictated. They were rooted in the unresolved problems of twentieth-century Chinese intellectual history and Chinese Marxist historiography. The political climate, or various Party factions, may have nurtured, protected, shaped, restricted, or made use of these debates, which in turn may have taken on political purposes of their own, but their basic origins were not political. The major impulse underlying the intellectual ferment of 1961–1964 was a resurgence of cultural nationalism. In the field of history, the cultural-nationalism movement began with the campaign to "reverse judgment" on famous Chinese historical figures, and to reevaluate their roles in the Chinese past. Initiated by Guo Moruo in January 1959, and promoted by Jian Bozan in February, the movement soon won the endorsement of Wu Han and other leading historians and historical playwrights.

Several features of this effort to reevaluate historical figures were significant in light of the intense ideological climate of the time. First, it attracted opinions from all points on the political spectrum, both inside and outside the Marxist tradition. Second, it appears to have been an attempt to go outside of Marxist categories and criteria of judgment in "reopening cases" on China's traditional heroes and villains. It was certainly an effort to redefine Marxist categories in a broader, more flexible manner in order to produce a meaningful nationalist history within a Marxist framework. This approach was opposed by both the radical Marxists and by non-Marxist historians of a more traditional bent. Thus, it was a key element in the emerging debate over fundamental issues of Marxist historiography that divided the "radicals" from the "establishment" Marxist historians. Third, its appearance during the period of peak intensity in the Great Leap mobilization is striking, in light of its basic apolitical or even watered-down Marxist character. Fourth, it coincided with, and provided an academic umbrella for, the publication of subtle attacks on Mao and the party through the allegorical media of historical essays and plays. Most probably, the academic bureaucrats of the Marxist establishment, themselves dissatisfied with the results of their efforts to create a meaningful Marxist version of Chinese history and accommodate nationalist concerns, had thrown their support to, or perhaps even initiated, this important movement in historiography. Its purpose was to broaden the scope of acceptable debate and interpretation on historical questions.

Thus, there were actually two "revolutions among historical-study workers" after 1958: one mounted by Maoist political leaders and "radical" historians, another by scholar-bureaucrats of the pre-1949 Marxist historiographical tradition. While these two "revolutions" probably originated independently of one another, the subsequent development of each was largely a response to the other. The political liberalization of 1961–1962 brought with it official toleration of the cultural nationalist movement and the general intellectual ferment among historians that already enjoyed wide support in the academic community. This movement provided the context within which political critics could write their historical allegories for a limited audience without calling undue attention to themselves. No doubt this dissenting Marxist establishment in history also had political protection or support among high Party leaders. The movement certainly put great strains on Jian Bozan as an academic bureaucrat. At the same time that he was confronted with considerable pressure to comply with the sentiments of his colleagues who resisted the Great Leap politicization, he was also subjected to intense pressure from Maoists to participate in the Great Leap mobilization of historians.

JIAN BOZAN AND THE
GREAT LEAP FORWARD MOBILIZATION

Jian's ambiguous response to the Great Leap mobilization of historians clearly demonstrated his own reservations about the new campaign and the tensions inherent in his role as an academic bureaucrat. On the one hand, by praising the brilliance of Mao's historical analysis and by exhorting historians to intensify the study of Mao's Thought and its application to history, he clearly yielded to the tightening of ideological strictures on historical interpretation. On the other hand, by treating the Great Leap as an extension of the recent Anti-Rightist Campaign against bourgeois historians, rather than as a campaign directed at Marxist scholars, he muted the demand for a radically new political orientation for "establishment" historians.

Whether Jian was fully aware at this point of the political implications for historians of the Great Leap mobilization is difficult to discern, but, by directing his attack primarily at the "poison" of bourgeois history, and by interpreting the new slogans to fit his own intellectual purposes, he created an effective mode of expressing dissent.

Jian's article, "The Struggle of Two Lines on the Historical Science Front," in *People's Daily*, 15 July 1958, issued a call to ideological battle for Marxist historians, but at the same time attempted to interpret the first Great Leap slogans in the field of history—"Emphasize the present, deemphasize the past" and "Ancient for the use of the present"—in a manner compatible with his own point of view. Jian significantly modified the slogans' intended political message by concluding that the question at issue was not the amount of attention devoted to contemporary rather than ancient topics, but the historian's political stand. Having once embraced the correct worldview, he argued, historians could devote even greater efforts to the study of ancient history.

On balance, it was Jian's role as a *red* expert, that is, as a regime spokesman, that was most visible in this article. His exhortation to mount the ramparts of ideological struggle against an entrenched remnant of bourgeois thought dominated the discussion. Yet, an emerging pattern of resistance to the politicization of history was also present in his "intellectualization" of the slogans by transforming them into purely academic issues. It is the professional historian, the red *expert*, rather than the regime spokesman, which can be seen here in his subtle subversion of these political messages. Through his implicit criticism and dissent in interpreting the slogans, he changed their meaning and blunted their political impact.

The radicals had taken a position that linked historiographical issues and standards not only to the ideological requirements of the Great Leap movement, but also to the affirmation of the current party line and to the validation of specific policies. This approach, Jian feared, would lead to the abandonment of critical standards of scholarship as well as to the distortion of both Marxist theory and Chinese history. By transforming political slogans into academic issues he was able to criticize the manner in which they were applied by the radicals. The pattern of resistance Jian created in 1958 took center stage the next year. From early 1959 on, Jian increasingly took the position of an embattled professional protecting his sphere of expertise from the predations of radical politics. His dissent became more explicit as the political climate shifted.

In addition to leading the resistance to the Great Leap politicization of history from 1959 to 1961, Jian was a major figure in the cultural nationalism movement in history, which meant broadening Marxist historiography and developing a meaningful national history. As he resisted the encroachment of radical politics on history he was compelled to articulate a set of methodological and interpretive principles to legitimize his critique. These principles, which he referred to as "historicism" (*lishi zhuyi*), established a theoretical basis for a more satisfying nationalist, Marxist general history of China. "Historicism" was not presented full-blown as a coherent system of thought, but was argued piecemeal between 1958 and 1962 in response to the assault on professional standards and nationalist history on the one hand, and to the resurgence of cultural nationalism on the other. It was employed as an intellectual weapon to attack the former and to legitimize the latter. To Jian, the radicals' simplistic, one-dimensional interpretation of China's past mocked critical scholarship, caricatured the ideal of a comprehensive Marxist history of China, and subverted the proper relationship between politics and history.

HISTORICISM: THE CORE IDEAS

Historicism rested on three core ideas: It recognized the importance of context and empathy in historical interpretations; it stressed the complexity of historical reality, along with objectivity and balance in judging that reality; and it relied primarily on an empirical, inductive methodology. By building on these core values, Chinese historians were able to tie historicism closely to their nationalistic approach to China's past. Furthermore, in developing the notion of historicism, Jian articulated a set of principles that defined the relationship between politics and history.

Context and Empathy

The first core idea of Jian's historicist outlook stressed the primacy of context and empathy in historical understanding. Since all human values and perceptions were historically contingent, each historical period or culture could claim an internal integrity that could be understood only on its own terms. Jian insisted that "one must strictly apply the principles of historicism," and "explain historical events and personalities in terms of the historical conditions of their time."[16] Without such empathy, the historian would be unable to appreciate the historical conditions that shaped a particular world-view and imposed limitations on human consciousness.

The radicals violated these principles in their zeal to "implement policy" in history and to link historiography to contemporary political struggle. In Jian's view, they had indiscriminately equated events, policies, and persons from one time and place with those of another; his first public reference to the concept of "historicism" appeared in his 1958 critique of this practice. The cautionary note accompanying his interpretation of the slogan "Emphasize the present, deemphasize the past" clearly illustrated his emerging opposition to radical historiography. He noted:

Ancient history can serve the present, can serve the class struggle ... but of course this does not mean we can take a non-historicist attitude by indiscriminately dragging events and people into the present and talk nonsense as we please.[17]

As early as March 1959, Jian had differentiated a "class viewpoint" from an "historical viewpoint" and argued against imputing social equality to relations in the past simply because of the egalitarian policies of the current regime. To do so, he pointed out, "is neither appropriate, nor is it necessary . . . This policy has only existed in our day and we cannot ask feudal ruling classes of the past to observe it." This distinction between class viewpoint and historicism was central to his developing understanding of the two concepts as complementary approaches in a unified Marxist framework. He soon applied the distinction to a host of historical issues.[18]

Jian's imperative that history should be understood on its own terms raised fundamental questions of moral valuation that lay at the heart of the conflict between radical Maoist historians and historians of the pre-1949-generation Marxist establishment. The radicals insisted that history should be judged by a single standard—class affiliation—without regard to changing circumstances or historical context. The main task of the historian, in this view, was to eulogize heroes and castigate villains, praise revolutionary struggle and condemn oppression, as expressed in the radicals' formula "All crows under Heaven are black; regardless of time or place, all landlords are evil."

For Jian, on the other hand, historical understanding must be rooted both in an internal standard derived from the moral and cognitive universe of the actors themselves, and in an external standard derived from the universal postulates of Marxist theory as interpreted by Chinese establishment historians. A balanced approach required the application of several criteria of judgment.

The Comprehensive View

The second core idea of "historicism" was what Jian called the "comprehensive view," a balanced view of the past that faithfully recorded and evaluated all relevant data necessary for adequate historical understanding. This "comprehensive view" stressed appreciation of the richness and complexity of historical reality, the uniqueness and variety of historical forms, and the multi-causality of historical processes. The historian's obligation in this regard was to investigate the web of relations among a wide variety of objectively existing phenomena and assess its role in history.

Jian's attack in early 1959 on the radical approach to "smashing the dynastic system" of traditional historiography revealed the basic principles of his "comprehensive view." The campaign against traditional historical scholarship was intensified during the Great Leap mobilization. Its purpose was twofold—to expel the feudal elite from the center stage of history and give the "laboring masses" their due as the true creators of history, and to enshrine class struggle as the central dynamic of Chinese history in place of the dynastic cycle and the "mandate of heaven." It is likely that Jian could have accepted either premise in modified form, but he rejected the extremism of the radicals' interpretation. Their preoccupation with impersonal socio-economic forces led to "anonymous" history; their exclusive concern with the forces of production, class struggle, and the role of the masses tended to obscure, or even deny, the importance of ideas, institutions, individual personalities, and intra-class history.[19] The entire corpus of familiar personalities, events, and stories of traditional Chinese historiography, to which Jian's generation of Marxist historians had a strong emotional attachment, was threatened with attenuation, or even extinction. The most extreme expression of radical opinion advocated expunging from the historical record all concrete manifestations of ruling-class culture. Thus, imperial reign titles, the names and dates of important persons and events, the rise and fall of dynasties, the succession of emperors, court intrigues, and all similar trappings of the "feudal-orthodox view" of the past were to find no place in the new general history.

Jian's "comprehensive view" rejected such single-minded moralism in "smashing the dynastic system." To write a Marxist general history of China was to stress the uniqueness and variety of concrete historical forms and the complex interaction of multiple causal agents in the historical process. Jian had accepted the historical regularities, evolutionary stages, and "motive forces" at the heart of Marxist theory since his first published work in 1929. But to him the richness and complexity of historical reality and the variety of concrete institutions through which the Marxist universal process manifested itself had to be dealt with sympathetically and objectively by the historian. Thus, in this view, the historian's duty was to discover, "from the intricate complexities of historical fact," the "patterns, trends, and regularity in overall historical development." Clearly, the comprehensive viewpoint did not mean that all phenomena would receive equal attention, or that no general patterns existed. "To look at history comprehensively is our principle of writing history, but . . . one must still pass through points of emphasis to reveal history's overall features."[20]

Again, Jian's confrontation with the radicals had raised fundamental questions of interpretation and valuation in Marxist philosophy. What should the "points of emphasis" be? By what criteria was an historian to select and interpret the myriad facts of history? By what standards were historical events and actors to be judged? What concepts and categories would most likely establish a meaningful relationship between the present and the past? Like the first principle of "historicism," Jian's comprehensive view challenged the moral criteria by which the radicals judged history. He rejected the hero-villain dichotomy that condemned or exalted whole categories of events and persons on the basis of narrow ideological considerations or current political demands. If objectivity required a balanced picture of the historical process, it also required a more balanced approach to moral evaluation. "In class society, any bright period has its darkness, and any dark period cannot be without a ray of light." Thus, as Jian put it, "One must use two eyes to look at history, to see both the bright face and the dark face."[21]

Finally, the comprehensive view in Jian's historicism suggested a model for writing a scholarly general history of China that would also contribute to the development of Marxist theory. To "smash the dynastic-system view," Jian urged historians to undertake "deep, detailed research . . . on pivotal questions" and "on this foundation carry out comprehensive, synthetic research on Chinese history." To determine the "social nature" of each period, historians should conduct specialized, "multi-dimensional" research on such topics as the forces of production, class relations, politics, thought, art, "and even religion." Data generated from studies of individual dynasties, combined with "the method and viewpoint of dialectical materialism," could then provide the basis for histories of each stage or period. These histories could, in turn, be synthesized into "a Marxist, scientific general history of China" which would enhance Marxist historiography as a whole. With a comprehensive record of nearly three thousand years of history, Jian asked, "why should we not carry out serious scientific research? If our orientation is correct . . . we can make a definite contribution to Marxist-Leninist historical science."[22]

Empirical Bias

Throughout his career, Jian had attempted to chart a course between Marxist theory and empirical data that did violence to neither, while allowing each its proper contribution to historical knowledge. But at heart he was an inductive thinker who distrusted abstract conceptual schemes and insisted on a solid empirical foundation for all historical generalization. Jian did not explicitly refer to this inductive, empirical methodology as "historicism," but he always discussed it in conjunction with the first two principles, context and comprehensiveness. It constituted the epistemological foundation to historicism.

Jian presented his methodological premises in response to the radicals' interpretation of two of the new slogans for historians, "Theory takes command" and "Lead history with theory." The radicals' interpretation of these slogans not only narrowed the range of historical interpretation and linked historical themes to contemporary political issues but also reinforced the Great Leap trend toward empty recitation of Marxist dogma. Jian feared that history as an intellectual enterprise was moving from one extreme to the other, from what he viewed as the conceptual chaos of bourgeois empiricism to the doctrinaire sterility of formulaic history. As he later chided his colleagues, "We should quote the [Marxist] phrases, but not make them into mere labels; the spiritual essence is more important. We should remember formulas, but not turn them into iron molds to recast history."[23]

Jian by no means ignored the important role of theory in historical analysis. As a Marxist and Party member he was committed to strengthening the ideological understanding of China's historians. Both his personal biases and his political instincts led him to criticize his colleagues for their failure to assimilate and apply Marxist theory. As important as concrete data were, Jian stressed, they acquired meaning only through the mediation of ideological concepts. Yet, the purpose of ideology was to provide an interpretive framework, not to supply specific answers to concrete problems. Thus, "neither Marx, Engels, nor Lenin prepared ready-made conclusions for every concrete question . . . in Chinese history. Even Comrade Mao Zedong taught us only how to study history."[24] In Jian's view, the historian could eventually discern the overall pattern of historical development from the myriad particularistic manifestations of time and place only after careful empirical investigation. Yet, while Jian saw theory as essential to the discovery of patterns, he was ambivalent about the precise role Marxism should play in providing understanding and in giving meaning to history. Although Marxist theory could predict the general direction of history and its basic causal forces, the particular configurations and diverse empirical manifestations of general processes carried an integrity of their own which the historian was bound to acknowledge.

The central problem, as Jian perceived it, was the failure of serious historians to integrate theory properly with data. "When a concrete problem is encountered," Jian complained, "theory and data part company . . . each going its own way without relation to the other."[25] Jian's critique had sharpened considerably by the time of his 1961 *Guangming Daily* article questioning the politically loaded slogan "Theory takes command." The slogan's implicit message for historians conflicted with Jian's epistemological tenets, which rejected preconceived categories and stressed inductive generalization derived from systematically uncovered factual evidence. Moreover, his methodological biases were simply reinforced by the mechanical application of the slogan, which in his view had already caused the quality of historical writing to deteriorate. Fearing that the radicals' interpretation of the slogan was gaining credence in the academic community, his criticism was blunt:

"Theory takes command" is a principle in our writing of history . . . [but it does not mean] to use general principles to encase history, to stuff data into principles to support theory. It is not the use of empty, abstract, general theories . . . to replace concrete history, but is only the use of these theories to analyze concrete history.[26]

Offering an interpretation of the slogan that supported his own views, Jian argued that its true message compelled historians to assimilate data into theory and embody theory in data, thus "enabling viewpoints and facts to unite."

By transforming "Theory takes command" into an historicist principle he used it to attack the very purpose for which it was designed, and created an opportunity to articulate the methodological and epistemological foundations of "historicist Marxism."

HISTORICISM AND NATIONALISM

Jian's battle to retain the content of traditional historiography was motivated as much by nationalist sentiment as by theoretical concerns or scholarly interests. "Nationalism" in this context refers to intense cultural pride and a deep appreciation for the achievements of China's classical tradition and its contribution to world civilization. Like his nationalist contemporaries, Jian wanted to integrate Chinese history into a universal framework, while at the same time preserving the integrity and value of China's historical civilization. The pursuit of this elusive goal had been at the heart of modern Chinese historiography since its inception and had certainly been the key problem for Marxist historians since the great debates of the 1930s. The central objective of Jian and other official historians was the writing of a scholarly general history of China that would satisfy the demands of nationalist sentiment without compromising Marxist theory.

This objective gave special purpose to Jian's defense of critical standards, correct methodology, and particular principles of interpretation. Jian wished to bring a critical perspective to traditional historiography while retaining its substance. In general, he found Marxist historical philosophy compatible with his nationalist motivations. The new interpretive framework and new canons of judgment derived from Marxism could impart new meaning to old material. The stages of historical progression, for example, could well serve as vehicles for accommodating cultural diversity. The peculiarities of each stage, Jian suggested, were shaped by the unique influence of particular cultures just as they were determined by the dynamics of economic change and class conflict. "To overemphasize the special characteristics of China to the point where the general theories of Marx cannot be applied . . . is revisionism," Jian argued, but "to arrange Chinese history according to foreign history . . . is sectarianism. In different national settings, history can assume a different ambience . . . and individual countries can even leap over historical stages."²⁷ Historicism, with its emphasis on context and complexity, with its focus on the varied and unique historical epochs and cultural patterns, and with its appreciation of the roles of individuals in history, was well suited to nationalist historians who wanted to create a new and stimulating interpretation of China's past. To Jian it seemed the perfect complement to Marxism.

The radical approach, by introducing new concepts and topical themes only at the expense of traditional subject matter, threatened the integrity of national history as Jian and other establishment historians envisioned it. Its narrow application of Marxist and Maoist categories, which dwelled exclusively on class repression, peasant rebellions, and the role of the "popular masses," found little value in China's "feudal" past, particularly in its elite culture. Such a position was untenable to Jian. He agreed that to "blindly praise our national history and beautify class society in order to carry out patriotic education" was not necessary. But by the same token, he argued, it was equally unnecessary to "write our national history as empty and colorless, as if it were merely an accumulation of evil in order to meet the demands of class education."²⁸

The issue of the appropriate focus for historical research emerged most clearly in the debate over the role of the ruling classes and individuals in Chinese history. The anonymous and heroic characteristics of radical history dismissed the key individuals and major achievements of China's traditional ruling class as irrelevant, or treated them merely as negative foils to be denounced and vilified.

Jian had no difficulty finding justification in Marxist theory for treating the ruling class as a major topic of historical research or recognizing its progressive role in history. But to go further, to justify in-depth study of all aspects of ruling class culture in the face of the radicals' insistence that the masses alone created history required him to pursue a more eclectic approach. Hence he turned to the imaginative application of various Marxist and Maoist categories, such as "social contradictions" and "non-antagonistic class relations," or his own scientific-sounding concept, "web of causation," to rationalize his position.

Thus, the problem for historians in Jian's camp was not how to justify the study of feudal elites in the abstract, but how to justify the study of specific events and particular persons in Chinese history and how to defend the standards used to judge them. The Marxist dictum that "man makes history," was too general to meet these needs. The questions that divided establishment historians from their radical adversaries were not easily resolved by resorting to general theory. Which "men" created history, emperors or peasant leaders? Which activists were more important, popular masses or Confucian bureaucrats? Which persons responded to historical needs, commanders of imperial troops or leaders of popular rebellions?

The role of individuals in history, long controversial in Marxist thought, was a particularly thorny issue in Chinese Marxist historiography. The difficulty for Chinese historians lay in harmonizing nationalist and Marxist criteria of judgment, that is, in giving adequate recognition to the eminent personalities in traditional historiography while acknowledging that they served oppressive ruling classes. Jian's eclectic approach to this question again reflected the difficulties of establishing canons of judgment that would counter the radicals' criticism and yet satisfy the requirements of nationalist history. Whenever possible, he couched his arguments in terms of formal Marxist theory, but he often simply cited this or that personal view of Marx, Engels, or Lenin. Sometimes he simply relied on commonsense empirical arguments to present his case.

But Jian's criterion of "objective contribution to history" effectively met the radicals' challenge to find a criterion consistent with Marxist categories and yet tailored to the realities of China. When associated with the notion of historical "progress," it carried the ring of Marxist theory, and in some contexts it could be defined strictly in Marxist terms. At the same time, it could incorporate other criteria of judgment when applied to specific Chinese situations. Hence, Jian could neutralize the radical position by praising individuals for their "objective contribution to history," even while condemning them for their class affiliation. The famous fourth-century strategist and statesman, Cao Cao, for example, could be praised and condemned at the same time. For oppressing the people and repressing peasant rebellions he could be roundly denounced, but for unifying China and sponsoring a new genre of poetry he could be praised for contributing to Chinese history and civilization.[29]

In the final analysis, Jian's nationalist criterion was paramount. To him, the achievements of China's traditional elite were a source of deep cultural pride whose value was self-evident. That they "advanced" China's feudal society needed no further demonstration. According to Jian, "every period and dynasty in our national history had eminent figures," from all classes and occupations, including "even emperors, princes, generals, and ministers."

We ought to feel proud of these eminent people, and select some for the general history. We ought to give them the historical position they deserve according to their roles and the size of their contributions. We ought not reject them uniformly on the basis of a simple notion of class status, or, after acknowledging them, immediately reject them.[30]

Jian's category "objective contribution to history" stemmed from his "historicist" approach. It allowed for a balanced judgment of historical actors in the context of their times; it could be linked to Marxist tenets, but was flexible enough to accommodate the specific demands of Chinese national history. To Jian, Marxist "historicism" seemed the ideal synthesis for pursuing nationalist history within a universal framework. It seemed finally to satisfy the long-sought goal of Marxist historians in China.

HISTORICISM AND THE POLITICAL FUNCTION OF HISTORY

Through "historicism," Jian also addressed the issue raised by the radicals of the proper relationship between politics and scholarship, and articulated a set of values that conflicted sharply with those of his antagonists. Although Jian's initial interpretation of the ancient history slogans implicitly rejected the Great Leap imperative to link historical analysis to current policy debate, he did not reject the important political and ideological functions of history in the broader sense. As a Marxist, he accepted the premise that, as social beings, historians were ideologically motivated and politically committed.

Nevertheless, Jian's view of the political role of scholarship diverged sharply from that of the radical historians. For Jian, the historian best served politics through uncovering historical truth and making it available to political leaders for their own ends. Pursuing a line of argument reminiscent of both the "history as a mirror" concept of traditional historical scholarship and the utilitarian approach of early modern Chinese historiography, Jian maintained that historical knowledge derived its political utility from summarizing the moral lessons of the past. The compendium of historical examples discovered by the historian served as an inspiration and guide for the current generation and as a basis for educating the young.

Hence, Jian argued, the new slogans themselves defined the proper political function of history: "Ancient for the use of the present" meant to "summarize all useful experience in history . . . through the historiographical methods of Marxism-Leninism";[31] "Emphasize the present, deemphasize the past" demanded an even greater investment in the study of ancient history in order to learn from the experience of ancient people in production, class struggle, and resistance to foreign aggression; and "Thoroughly implement policy" reminded the historian of those actions in history that were not consistent with the moral basis of current policy, but it did not mean to force feudal emperors to implement policies of the CCP.

Jian's most explicit discussion of the political role of historical scholarship was prompted by the slogan "Thoroughly implement policy." In historical research, Jian asked, should one "firmly implement the spirit of policy," and, "if so, how? This is a problem that has not been solved." The solution, Jian suggested, lay in the historian's understanding of the crucial distinction between policy and theory, and the relevance of each to history. The historian's frame of reference was based on the universality of Marxist theory, not on the particularity of policy with its limitations of time and space. Policy was a framework for action in the "present" of each time and place, thus "Just as we cannot promote China's policies in a foreign country, we also cannot promote current policies in ancient history."[32]

Even while refuting the radicals' simplistic demand for history to serve policy, Jian believed that historians did have a responsibility to the political demands of the time. "If we do not plug current politics into history, can historical study serve politics?" Jian queried. "I think it can," he answered, but not by "finding historical parallels to every contemporary political movement," or by "dragging ancient events and people into the present." The historian "should summarize both the successes and failures in the experiences of production struggle and class struggle and serve politics with these summations." In addition, the historian should "search out the laws of historical development, point out the trends, and serve politics with this knowledge of laws-and-trends." To view the political function of history in this way, Jian concluded, would insure that all historical research was "for the present, for today, for the Great Leap Forward of socialism before our eyes, for a better tomorrow."

Jian's rhetoric could not mask the essential incompatibility between this model of the relationship between politics and scholarship and the model advocated by the radicals. In his view, the scholar's work was independent of any particular policy line. To have political utility, scholarship must first be judged by nonpolitical norms. Although not detached from political values, the scholar was detached from the immediate policy-power arena in a particular regime, except to provide general policy guidelines on the basis of valid historical analogy. It was neither necessary nor legitimate, Jian insisted, for scholars to distort history to justify current policy.

HISTORICISM AND POLITICAL DISSENT: JIAN'S FINAL ASSAULT ON RADICAL HISTORIOGRAPHY

Jian's struggle to balance the imperatives of the radicals' "new history" with the imperatives of sound scholarship, professional integrity, and a flexible, nationalist, Marxist historiography culminated in his June 1962 speech to the Nanjing Historical Society. Departing significantly from his former pattern of dissent, he attacked the slogan "Lead history with theory" directly, rather than simply criticizing the manner in which it had been interpreted. He therefore implicitly impugned the Great Leap mobilization itself and the version of Maoist ideology that rationalized it.

While praising the "great work" and "brilliant accomplishments" of the historical profession since 1949, Jian nevertheless asked, "Are there no deficiencies as we walk on the road of victory? In my view there are . . . [and some] are rather serious." "There was a time," Jian acknowledged, "when the slogan 'Lead history with theory' . . . had a positive function," because it had been a useful tool to "reverse the bourgeois trend of slighting Marxism-Leninism and Chairman Mao's works." But "This slogan has a great one-sidedness and in my personal opinion can even be said to be erroneous."[33]

Anticipating his critics, Jian asked, "How can it be wrong to lead and initiate historical research using the ideas [of Marxism-Leninism and Mao Zedong Thought]?" It was essential to use these ideas as a general guide, he said, but the slogan "Lead history with theory" had come to mean "Replace history with theory." Teachers had abandoned facts, "spoke emptily of principles," imposed "concocted and unfounded conclusions on concrete history" and "molded [it] to fit their subjective notions." They invoked the authors of the Marxist canon simply as "border decorations" or labels. "The emptier the better, the more abstract the better. For a time it seemed as if this had become a kind of fashion."[34]

Jian's critique was relentless as he surveyed the four problem areas he considered basic in confronting the radicals: history and theory, theory and policy, class viewpoint and "historicism," and objective laws and subjective action. Clothing himself in the legitimacy of Mao, Jian assailed China's historians for their failure to adopt Mao's method of combining the universal truth of Marxism-Leninism with concrete conditions. The results, according to Jian, were disastrous. "This even caused the rich and varied content of concrete living history to become a monotonous, dead, dry, and tasteless doctrine, to become a desert."[35]

He concluded with a list of "prominent characteristics of historical research and teaching for the past several years." These were "onesidedness, abstractness, simplification, absolutification, and contemporization." Significantly Jian argued for a division of labor that reflected the distinction between policy and theory. Historians should study theory and general patterns, Jian said, while others should deal with policy.

Thus Jian had explicitly repudiated both the new radical historiography and the politicization of academic history which nourished it. By this action he had placed himself in open opposition to the

Maoist policy for professional historians. During the Cultural Revolution, Jian was accused of causing a "countercurrent" to arise in historical-study circles that "opposed the revolution": With "an old bourgeois lordly attitude, he traveled about lecturing and giving papers, coolly jesting, hotly ridiculing, sarcastically attacking."[36] More important, perhaps, Jian had asserted that book learning was primary in historical research, implicitly rejecting the policy of "leaving the ivory tower" and "learning from the masses" as well as Mao's doctrine that "practice" was the ultimate source of knowledge. Jian had rejected "Lead history with theory" on intellectual grounds, but, on a symbolic level, his message was political. He had challenged the ideology from which both the slogan and the policy were derived.

In the Cultural Revolution, Jian's 1962 speech in Nanjing became the basis for the charge that he rejected the class-struggle viewpoint. Jian's frequent references to Marxism-Leninism and his affirmation of historical materialism were alleged to be a ruse because, his detractors charged, "It is precisely the core of historical materialism which he opposes . . . 'historicism' is a rotten weapon of the bourgeoisie to oppose the theory of class struggle."[37]

In fact, of course, Jian viewed "historicism" as a distinct yet complementary approach to "class viewpoint" within a common Marxist framework. Although he was not always consistent, and there were tensions among the various elements of his approach, he had developed "historicism" within the boundaries of Marxist theory as he understood it. As Jian explained:

To use the proletarian viewpoint to treat any historical problem . . . is a basic demand for a Marxist historian. But in addition to class viewpoint there is historicism. It is necessary to combine class viewpoint and historicism. If one only has class viewpoint . . . it is easy to reject everything one-sidedly; if one only has historicism . . . it is easy to affirm everything one-sidedly. Only by combining the two can one come to complete and fair conclusions about historical facts.[38]

BUREAUCRATIC AUTHORITY
AND PROFESSIONAL HISTORIANS

The political regulation of scholarship in the PRC was exercised through a structure that combined bureaucratic authority with informal networks. Jian's position in that structure, first as prominent intellectual, then as Department Chairman at Beijing University, and finally as Vice-President of the university, was an important factor in his response to the Great Leap Forward and his eventual purge. It gave him public visibility and forced him to make choices he otherwise could have avoided. Jian belonged to that category of mid-level officials selected from among professional peers to implement regime decisions in a particular realm of social activity. While such officials served under top cultural bureaucrats in the Chinese political system, they often held no positions in the government or Party. Occupying a position between policy-making and policy implementation and participating in two well-defined social environments, the academic-professional and the political-bureaucratic, they played a critical and creative role in the political system. Not only did they insure the translation of policy decisions into action, but they also contributed to the less tangible long-run process of political integration. Their roles served the dual political function of structurally integrating different levels of the administrative organization and of binding important social groups into a stable relationship with the ruling elite.

Jian and other incumbents of these mediating or linkage roles had to reconcile the conflicting values and interests of constituencies whose goals and activities were often at cross-purposes. In addition to these external structural pressures, they faced internal psychological and ethical conflicts because of the inherent ambiguities in their roles and the ambivalence of their commitments. Effective performance in these positions required a stable and flexible political environment which allowed for maneuver and compromise. Thus, while there was a dynamic, creative aspect in such roles, there was also high risk and political vulnerability. In times of political polarization or mobilization, the flexibility to accommodate diverse interests was sharply reduced and the incumbents of these roles could no longer perform a mediating function. Eyed with suspicion by both constituencies, academic bureaucrats were compelled to clarify loyalties and take positions. Personal values, the source and intensity of pressures on them, the degree of political unity among top leaders, potential support and protection from various elite factions, and solidarity among professional peers all had a bearing on the choices they made.

The tensions inherent in Jian's bureaucratic role surfaced during the Hundred Flowers and Anti-Rightist movements of 1956–1957, and were clearly revealed in his vacillating response to these movements. He temporarily resolved these tensions by supporting the regime and, to some extent, compromising his academic values. There was still sufficient political unity at the top of the Party structure to insure that dissent could not readily find protection in high places. Moreover, the conditions that encouraged or allowed collective resistance in the academic community to regime policies had not yet emerged.

With the onset of the Great Leap Forward Jian's capacity to reconcile these cross pressures became increasingly limited. The Great Leap mobilization destroyed the accommodation he and other academic bureaucrats had established between the regime and the professional historians and restricted the flexibility and room for maneuver that their mediating roles required. Moreover, this political mobilization coincided with the cultural-nationalism movement, when nationalistic historians pressed for a relaxation of ideological control over historiography. When Jian was compelled to implement a set of directives that were not only offensive to many of his colleagues but violated his own scholarly values and professional integrity, his academic commitments and political loyalties became increasingly incompatible.

In the face of these cross pressures, the ambiguities in his linkage role were exaggerated, while the possibility of reducing tension without abandoning a middle position became increasingly remote. The tensions and conflicts in one arena aggravated those in the other. The sharper the conflict over academic values, the more difficult it was to mediate between political authority and the academic community, but his bureaucratic obligations compelled him publicly to articulate the points of conflict. The liberalized intellectual environment after the Great Leap, and growing political divisions at the top of the Party, generated the conditions, including top level political support, that made Jian's resistance to regime guidelines possible.

From early 1959 to December 1961, Jian increasingly played the role of an embattled professional protecting his sphere of expertise from political expropriation. His dissent became more and more explicit, reaching a peak in his June 1962 speech to the Nanjing Historical Society. In that speech, he explicitly repudiated the Great Leap directives for historiography and implicitly repudiated the whole spirit of political mobilization that prevailed after the Great Leap Forward.

JIAN AND THE QUEST FOR LIMITED
PROFESSIONAL AUTONOMY

As his radical critics charged during the Cultural Revolution, Jian indeed subverted the "revolutionization of historical study workers" in various ways. He interpreted politically charged policy slogans as purely academic guidelines, repudiated the radical historiography that they legitimized, supported academic movements that ran counter to the purposes and spirit of the Great Leap mobilization, and dissented from the view that historians must leave the ivory tower and go among the masses to fulfill their academic and social functions.

Jian, however, did not substitute a bourgeois, anti-class-struggle historical philosophy for Marxism. "Historicism" was a symbol of his response to the changing political and academic environment, a metaphor for a set of historiographical principles and a view of the relationship between scholarship and politics which he had long before integrated into his Marxist philosophy. Jian distinguished "historicism" from class viewpoint, but he viewed the two concepts as complementary approaches within a single Marxist framework. Whatever tensions existed between historical principles and class criteria were either inherent in Marxism itself or a by-product of Jian's nationalist approach to Chinese history.

In effect, then, there were two "revolutions" in historiography generated during the Great Leap Forward mobilization, both of which were committed to developing Marxist history in China in new directions. The politicization of history sharpened and intensified the emerging conflict between a radical new version of Marxist history advocated by younger historians, and a revised version of "establishment" Marxism supported by the pre-1949 generation of historians. "Historicism" was a response to the reemergence of these basic methodological and interpretive questions in Chinese Marxist historiography. It constituted a set of theoretical principles whose purpose was to legitimize one of these approaches and repudiate the other, but it did so within the limits of Marxist philosophy, not in opposition to it. The quest for a resolution to these issues was expressed in the "historicism" versus class viewpoint debates of 1963–1964. Although Jian did not participate in these debates directly, his work was the major target of historicism's opponents.

In 1966 his critics seized on the symbol he himself had supplied, "historicism," to build a case against him of "counterrevolutionary criminal activity." But his actual political crime was his quest for limited professional autonomy in a radical Maoist regime. To pursue this autonomy, and to secure protection for himself and like-minded colleagues from the Great Leap mobilization, he sought support from sympathetic leaders high in the Party. Of course he and other historians and academic bureaucrats had vested interests of their own to protect. Not only was their version of Marxist historiography being challenged by the radicals, but their positions of power and control within the academic hierarchy were being threatened as well.

DENG XIAOPING AND THE HISTORIANS

The Deng regime's reforms in historical scholarship have constituted a "counter cultural revolution" as dramatic as its reforms in other spheres of Chinese life. The relaxation of political control over history-writing and the opportunities for Chinese scholars to communicate with foreign colleagues and to travel abroad are greater than at any previous period in PRC history.

The Party's reform leadership has taken an extraordinary interest in both academic and popular history. It has sponsored a wide range of projects on Party and national history, opened the pages of official Party newspapers and journals to academic debate on historical topics by recognized experts, and regularly published reports on the activities of professional historians. In addition, the regime has rehabilitated prominent historians, editors, and cultural bureaucrats purged during the Cultural Revolution, supported the proliferation of specialized historical journals, established a separate Chinese Academy of Social Sciences which includes history departments, and removed many of the taboos that have long plagued research and publishing in the humanistic sciences. The regime's efforts to foster respect for scholarly history have been matched by an equally vigorous initiative to promote mass education in history as a means of regenerating Chinese national pride and redeeming the Party's popular image in the wake of the Cultural Revolution.

Despite these dramatic steps toward intellectual liberalization and official encouragement of professional history, the regime has failed to answer the most basic question that these reforms have raised: To what extent has there been a fundamental redefinition of the relationship between political authority and professional historians? While the contours of an emerging new relationship are visible, the specific content and structure of the relationship are less clear. The Party's rehabilitation of Jian Bozan in 1978 is very instructive in this regard. Although Party leaders returned Jian to political favor, restored his academic reputation, and legitimized the scholarly norms identified with *historicism,* they used the publicity primarily for political purposes—to discredit their political enemies and enhance their efforts to restore the norms of inner Party political life and refurbish the Party's image.

Jian Bozan was posthumously rehabilitated in 1978 along with the historian Wu Han, former "cultural czar," propaganda chief Zhou Yang, and other prominent intellectuals and cultural officials purged during the Cultural Revolution. Agence France-Presse reported in April of that year that Beijing University wall posters had recently detailed Jian's persecution and death in 1968 and had demanded his official rehabilitation.[39] In September 1978, *People's Daily* published an abridged version of an article in the prestigious history journal *Lishi yanjiu* officially exonerating Jian of all political charges and restoring his good name. The article denounced Jian's critics, justified his criticism of radical historiography, and affirmed the legitimacy of *historicism* as a concept compatible with Marxism.[40]

This publicity surrounding Jian's rehabilitation continued into 1979. In September 1978, China's official New China News Agency reported that Jian's writings were to be republished and declared that Jian was "among the pioneers who made outstanding contributions" to the study of ancient China "from a Marxist viewpoint."[41] In October, *Lishi yanjiu* carried a second article attacking Jian's Cultural Revolution critics, providing details of what it called the "frame-up" against him in 1966.[42] Four months later, NCNA reported that Jian had been honored by a memorial service attended by 500 people at the Babaoshan Cemetery for Revolutionaries in Beijing. Six Politburo members sent wreaths, including Deng Xiaoping and Hu Yaobang, and three Politburo members, including Hu Qiaomu, recently appointed head of the Chinese Academy of Social Sciences, attended the ceremony along with many intellectual luminaries formally associated with Jian. In his eulogy, Zhou Peiyuan, President of Beijing University, acknowledged Jian's contribution to the establishment of Marxist historiography in China and his lifetime dedication to revolution. Zhou reiterated the call to "exonerate him from all ground-less charges and rehabilitate him."[43] Media attention to Jian's life and works has continued intermittently since then, mostly in academic publications.[44]

Although Party leaders restored Jian's political reputation and reaffirmed his professional credentials, the extensive media attention he received was not aimed at addressing the issue of politics and historiography that led to his purge. It virtually ignored the fundamental issue exemplified by his professional life and political persecution—the question of the political role of history in a Leninist party-state. It was designed primarily to discredit Lin Biao and the Gang of Four, and to symbolize the party's efforts to reinstitute democratic centralism, socialist legality, and other orderly processes of party and state life. Such sensitive issues as the historian's political obligations and the relationship between policy and history, which Jian had candidly addressed in his critique of radical history in the early 1960s, were raised only once in the rehabilitation literature, and then only by Jian's son in a specialized journal for historians.[45]

In a tribute to his father's integrity and scholarly contributions, Jian Siping implicitly, but unmistakably, raised the core question which Jian's political rehabilitation had failed to answer. In noting that Jian had expressed views on "some new conditions in history circles" to "sincerely point out incorrect trends," the author was in fact referring obliquely to Jian's polemic against the radical historians and his rejection of their view that historians should be mere mouthpieces for current policy. To make the point clear without violating the unwritten taboo against explicit discussion of the political role of historians, the article recalled that Jian had developed a special interest in the problem of "how to thoroughly implement party policy in writing history." Thus, the author had subtly called attention to the unresolved issue of the relationship between contemporary politics and historiography by quoting the title of Jian's 1962 essay on policy, politics, and history that brought about his political downfall in the Cultural Revolution.

Historicism and the New Historiography

The legitimacy of *historicism* as a concept fully compatible with Marxist historical theory was affirmed by the September 1978 *Lishi yanjiu* article restoring Jian's political reputation. In a strong repudiation of Jian's critics, who had branded historicism as a uniquely bourgeois principle, the scholar and pro-Deng polemicist Li Honglin asserted that historicism and the class-struggle approach constituted a "unity of opposites" within Marxist historical theory. In a detailed critique of the distortions of Jian's ideas by Cultural Revolution radicals, Li reaffirmed the principles of objectivity, faithfulness to evidence and context, and balanced judgment that Jian's interpretation of historicism embodied. Jian was correct, Li said, in rejecting a simplified class viewpoint that "denies everything" and in demanding that historians carry out "concrete analysis" consistent with the conditions of the time; historians should not "judge ancient history by the situation today" or "make demands on ancient people by using the standards of the proletariat." Jian's interpretation of historicism, Li insisted, was in complete agreement with "the principles of Party spirit," since it acknowledged the necessity of "taking a class stand" while at the same time carrying out objective analysis.

Although the term *historicism* had not regained its former status as a major slogan in post-Mao historiography, perhaps because it is still too closely identified with earlier political controversies, the methodological and interpretive principles associated with the concept have been widely advanced. For example, participants in a fall 1979 symposium on historiography convened in Beijing to commemorate the 30th anniversary of the PRC were rather blunt in their repudiation of the radical historiography of the Cultural Revolution and their demands for a new set of standards akin to those represented by historicism. Speakers at the symposium devoted special attention to "the problem of authenticity" in the science of history, and maintained that history could only be written "according to what actually happened." One report on the meeting criticized historical writing "based on dogmas or individual will" and advocated "the unity of scientific character and party spirit." The report repudiated the "'revolutions in historiography' in 1958 and 1966," warning that to continue implementing them would transform Chinese history into "dead learning." In language very similar to Jian's critique of the radicals in the early 1960s, the report criticized the radical slogan "Lead history with theory" for fostering a dogmatism that misinterpreted Marx, and argued that historical science is based on "theory originating from history" through the application of Marxism to the vast storehouse of historical materials. Similarly, the report branded another radical slogan, "Stressing the present more than the past" as "a disruption of the science of history," and blamed an overemphasis on class viewpoint for "replacing concrete analysis with class sentiment." Historical works based on these erroneous ideas, the report concluded, were "devoid of content," "lacking in life," and "completely discard our country's fine tradition in historiography."[46]

Other core historicist ideas have appeared in scholarly discourse without explicit reference to the term. For example, a Chinese scholar writing in an American journal reflected the historicist spirit of the new historiography in a paragraph reminiscent of Jian's discussion of the "comprehensive viewpoint":

Because socio-historical phenomena are complicated . . . we are obliged in our study to take command of source materials in their every detail. And we cannot stop there . . . We have to make an overall investigation of every historical problem connected with it.[47]

Finally, collections of pre-Cultural Revolution methodological essays by Jian and other historians who shared his approach to history have been republished, while lively discussions on the "scientific" nature of history, and a host of other historiographical issues continue to animate the pages of *Guangming Daily* and the specialized academic journals.[48]

This dramatic return to the canons of scholarship associated with historicism has not only been sanctioned, but even encouraged, by official policy. Deng Xiaoping's political dictum of "Seeking truth from facts," when applied to historical scholarship, clearly parallels the empirical, inductive methodology of Jian Bozan's *historicism*. The regime's emphasis on expertise in rejuvenating the ranks of Party and government cadres and its campaign to alter radically the status of intellectuals has fostered an environment in which a more professional approach to history can be cultivated. Most striking, perhaps, is the regime's advocacy of objectivity even in the realm of Party history itself, the most politically sensitive and difficult domain of all. Despite the regime's encouragement of a more professional approach to history, however, and its keen interest in setting the historical record of the Chinese revolution straight, it still does not hesitate to use history in a variety of ways to pursue its own immediate political purposes.[49]

Politics and History

Historians have responded to the new liberal atmosphere by openly repudiating the severe political control of the past and by pushing hard for a more limited role for politics in guiding historical scholarship. The *Guangming Daily* report on the 1979 National Day history forum was no less blunt on this issue than it was on the problem of methodology. Addressing the issue indirectly at first, the report criticized Soviet leaders for "monopolizing not only the right to interpret Marxism-Leninism, but also the right to interpret history and other disciplines." In such a climate, the report complained, social scientists cannot "conduct substantial inquiry and freely express their views." But the report soon adopted a more direct approach to the issue that most concerned Chinese historians: The "more controversial problem" at the conference, it said, was "whether historiography should serve proletarian politics."[50]

Although portrayed as a summary of the diverse views of conference participants, the report's assessment of this question was predominantly negative. While it acknowledged that history "as a social science" should "serve a certain kind of politics," it nevertheless implicitly endorsed those comrades who rejected the dictum "Serve proletarian politics" because of past abuses committed in its name. The report argued for a historiography guided by the slogan "Study history to seek truth," which integrated "scientific character and party spirit," and it proposed that party control be rolled back to allow the open expression of diverse views and the elimination of "forbidden zones" in historical research.

For example, the report cited some comrades who thought that serving proletarian politics "narrowed the road" of history, forced historians "to change with the political wind," and prevented works on historiography from being written. These comrades believed that historians "must take history for its own sake in order to write the historical truth." Yet other comrades, who ostensibly "disagreed" with this analysis, didn't embrace the norm of political service for history any more enthusiastically. They identified the problem as a failure to implement the Hundred Flowers principle, and as a "lack of political democracy and academic freedom." Perhaps emboldened by Politburo member Ye Jianying's tentative reappraisal of Mao in a National Day speech two weeks earlier, one comrade seemed to be arguing that historical analysis should reclaim the political role that it had played in the hands of some historians prior to the Cultural Revolution, that is, criticism of present-day policies. According to the report, he said that "Using the past to disparage the present"—a phrase used by radicals during the Cultural Revolution to accuse historians of attacking Maoism through history—was one form of making the past serve the present.

Finally, the report pressed for a more open review process for scholarly work, and even ventured into the politically dangerous ground of Party history. It argued that, when scholars submitted work for review, "different viewpoints should be allowed" and "too many barriers should not be erected." Even questions of foreign policy in history, the report insisted, are only the scholars' individual viewpoints and "do not represent the views of the government." Addressing the question of Party history, the report acknowledged that "quite a number of comrades" felt there were "too many taboos and commands," and that the time had come to get the facts straight and write authentic history. "To this end," the report declared, "we must dare to speak the truth, and fear neither authority nor power." Implicitly claiming the traditional obligation of Chinese historians to speak truth to power, the report lamented that even feudal society "recognized the virtue of the historian," and "we should be more lofty than they." "Therefore," it concluded, "we should not write history which goes against our conscience."

The issues pursued so directly in this report have continued to spark comment and controversy since then. They were again raised in the midst of a debate over "freedom of creation" triggered by Secretariat member Hu Qili's speech at the 4th Writer's Congress in December 1984. Following the Congress, the journal *Lishi yanjiu* convened a forum in March 1985 for Beijing historians to discuss "how to realize academic freedom under the guidance of Marxism." The forum emphasized "reasoning with facts" rather than "resorting to political power and academic orders to suppress others," and stressed guidance by "basic tenets" rather than the views of individuals. In an implicit but sharp criticism of the ideological manipulation of history promoted by radical historians, the report explained that "basic tenets" did not mean the "application of out-of-context phrases to historical facts." The report also maintained that academic freedom could not be realized without academic equality: The question of "right and wrong" should not be determined "by the status of scholars"; even comrades "in leading posts represent only one of a hundred schools of thought" and should participate in discussions "on an equal footing." The "more truth is debated," the report argued, "the clearer it becomes."[51]

The issue of academic freedom and the proper boundary between the political and academic realms has erupted again in the Party's extraordinary May 1986 celebration of the 30th anniversary of the Hundred Flowers Movement. Veteran historian Hu Sheng, appointed President of CASS in the fall of 1985, argued the new liberal position in the authoritative party theoretical journal *Red Flag* in May. "There are no forbidden zones in academic research," Hu said, and a scholar's individual research "generally speaking" does not "represent the views of the Party and government." In a research body in social science, he continued, "a Party organization must not make any decision on the rights and wrongs of controversial views on an academic issue." Acknowledging that "some problems in social science are likely to touch on political ones," he declared that academic mistakes "should not be elevated to the plane of political mistakes." Furthermore, academic research that "does not involve the conscious application of Marxism," should be allowed. With respect to history, Hu said that "superficially" the study of past events "cannot directly serve current practical problems." It is necessary for historians to understand history first, and "correctly use historical experience."[52]

Other historians applied these principles more directly to history. Writing in *Guangming Daily*, Su Shuangbi stressed that "academic and political problems belong to different categories," and therefore should not be confused. Academic questions, he said, "do not have the nature of a class struggle." Whether one is materialistic or idealistic "does not necessarily have any connection with one's political attitude and position." In addition, a "non-Marxist view in academic discussion is nothing reactionary," and it "should not be confused with an anti-Marxist view." The debates among historians "should be subject to truth only," Su concluded, "and not the maneuvering of experts, people in authority, and power."[53]

In one of the most outspoken attacks on party control over intellectual life since the original Hundred Flowers in 1956, the historian Li Kan delivered a blistering critique of the deleterious effects on historiography of the successive political campaigns that have swept over China since the late 1950s. Arguing a position very close to that of

Jian Bozan in the early 1960s, Li said that "past events can never intervene in or even have direct links with practical politics," but a "comprehensive and thorough study" of history that results in "scientific
understanding" can provide "inspiration and a reference." Defending
Wu Han and other historians criticised during the Cultural Revolution, Li said they had tried to implement Mao's slogan "Make the past
serve the present," out of "goodwill and concern for the cause of the
state and the people." Although Li did not think it intellectually
legitimate to "Use the past to disparage the present" through historical
analogy, he defended the right of historians to do so. "Even if some
people have cited historical facts to 'satirize' the dark side of things,"
he said, this is "a kind of useful criticism." "We must have full confidence that all honest and upright historians who support the Party
and socialism will not vilify their country." Referring to the "depres-
sion and poverty of history," as a result of rigid political control, he
complained that "even now this heavy evil consequence is hindering
the development of our historiography." Calling for "free discussion
and brave exploration," he maintained that there is no need for "any
taboo or 'forbidden zone,'" and that discussion of topics related to
"current or recent politics and policies" should be allowed as long as
"no Party or state secret is touched," or "no domestic or foreign
policy is violated."[54]

Although the regime has clearly fostered a political environment
in which historians can openly press their claims against political
authority, history nevertheless remains highly politicized. Party
leaders have not hesitated to use history in a variety of ways to pursue
their political goals. A cursory glance at the themes of historical essays
appearing in *Guangming Daily,* the academic journals, and in more
politically authoritative media reveals that Chinese historiography is
still driven primarily by contemporary political concerns. Precedents
that justify current policies, albeit reform policies, are consistently
sought through historical analogy. Scarcely veiled debates over contemporary political issues are reflected in historical analysis. Even
while arguing forcefully for more intellectual autonomy, historians
often reaffirm the very boundaries they are trying to expand. The
blunt, sweeping repudiation of Cultural Revolution historiography
and political domination of scholarship expressed in the October
1979 *Guangming Daily* report, for example, was balanced by the
author's simultaneous call to "tighten up criticism in the ideological

realm" in order to eliminate the ideological deviations of such "restoration conspirators" as Lin Biao and the Gang of Four.

One of the more striking efforts by Deng Xiaoping to promote his political goals through history was the appearance, shortly after Mao's death, in *Lishi yanjiu*, of a series of allegorical articles reassessing such Mao-like historical figures as China's first unifier, Qinshihuang, and the Taiping leader Hong Xiuquan.[55] These articles spearheaded Deng's earliest attempts to revise the party's view of Mao Zedong, and foreshadowed the critique of Mao that surfaced openly at the 3rd Plenum of the 11th Central Committee in December 1978. And, of course, Deng's critique of Mao was in turn related to his bid for power and his political struggle with Hua Guofeng. The Qinshihuang discussion closely paralleled the debate in inner Party circles over the role of Mao and the rehabilitation of Deng. The reassessment of Qinshihuang in *Lishi yanjiu* was abruptly stopped when Deng returned to power after working out a political compromise with Hua Guofeng at a Party work conference in March 1977 that evidently included an agreement to back down from criticism of Mao. Hua's ringing affirmation of Mao's status at the 11th Party Congress in August was sharply at odds with the Mao image portrayed by the allegorical articles earlier in the year. Discussions on Qinshihuang reopened in early 1978, however, as Deng again prepared to challenge his political opponents. To legitimize his reinterpretation of Mao Zedong Thought and Mao's political role, and to promote a wider purge of the Party apparatus, Deng initiated a nationwide debate in May on the proposition that "Practice is the sole criterion of truth." Deng's political victory over his opponents at the landmark 3rd Plenum in December included an open critique of Mao that essentially reiterated the themes expressed through historical allegory over the previous two years.[56]

Such perennial historical issues as peasant rebellions, China's opening to the West in the nineteenth century, and prominent reform movements and reformers of the past continue to serve as vehicles for promoting contemporary reform themes, for expressing internal policy debates publicly, and even for allegorically criticizing the policies of top leaders. In 1978–1980, for example, academic controversy on the role of peasant wars in Chinese history, and the nature of motive forces in historical development, paralleled the evolution of party debate over the role of class struggle in socialist society and appeared to mirror current political conflict in historical guise. As the Dengist reformers gradually replaced the Maoist slogan "Take class struggle as the key link" with the call to increase production and pursue the Four Modernizations as the basis of the new party line, historians challenged the orthodox Maoist view that peasant wars—that is, the expression of class struggle in Chinese "feudal" society—constituted the primary "motive force" in premodern Chinese history. They argued instead that the "struggle for production" was the motor driving historical progress.[57]

The discussion on peasant wars and motive forces in history began before the 3rd Plenum of the 11th Central Committee in December 1978 called on the Party to "shift the emphasis of work" away from political conflict and toward socialist modernization. The Plenum's Communiqué declared that "the large-scale turbulent class struggle of a mass character has, in the main, come to an end." Some class struggle was still needed, it said, but should only be directed against the "small handful of counterrevolutionary elements and criminals" still in existence. The debate on peasant wars meanwhile continued to expand during the spring and summer following the Plenum. In his political work report to the 5th National People's Congress in June 1979, shortly before the trials of democracy-wall dissidents Wei Jingsheng and Fu Yuehua began, Hua Guofeng elaborated on the new Party consensus on class struggle. Hu said that the Party must "persevere in the dictatorship of the proletariat and class struggle," but that the latter "was no longer the principal contradiction in Chinese society." Although landlords, rich peasants, and capitalists "have ceased to exist as classes," Hu continued, vigilance must be maintained against those few "class enemies of all descriptions" that still remained. During the period of the trials in the fall, PRC media began a discussion on the nature of class struggle and contradictions in socialist society as the historical controversy over peasant wars and motive forces was reaching its zenith.[58]

More recent examples of present-day political issues appearing in historical guise can be found. A *People's Daily* article on the "hundred days" of reform under the Guangxu Emperor in 1898 seems especially pregnant with implications for contemporary CCP politics. Published in mid-October following the 4th and 5th Plenums of the 12th Central Committee and the rare "National Conference of Party Delegates" convened in September, the article appeared to deal allegorically with high-level political conflict over central leadership appointments and the ideological rationale for Deng's reforms. The author's analysis of the failure of the 1898 reforms contains striking parallels with the direction and consequences of Deng Xiaoping's policies. In particular, the article's treatment of the ideological skepticism expressed by potential allies of the 1898 reformers and its assessment of the political damage resulting from large-scale personnel changes implemented at that time appear to mirror the political problems of Deng's supporters today. Thus, the article may represent the views of those within the Dengist camp who are concerned about the political risks of pushing the reform agenda too far and too fast.[59]

For example, the article seemed implicitly to draw parallels between the sweeping personnel changes carried out during the year—the changes in the Politburo, Secretariat, and Central Committee announced at the September meetings, and the wholesale replacement of provincial leaders prior to that—and the controversy sparked by similar changes implemented by the Guangxu Emperor. Thus, the issue of personnel decisions, according to the article, was particularly contentious among the 1898 reformers, and was a root cause of their failure. By moving too quickly to "reduce redundant personnel," promote new officials, and remove others without cause, the reformers unwittingly mobilized the conservative opposition. The author's description of the conflicting views between the reformer Kang Youwei and his patron the Emperor, suggests allegorical treatment of high-level disagreement over personnel decisions even within the Dengist camp. According to the author, Kang Youwei himself was "profoundly aware" of the political risks involved in acting too quickly to remove older officials, realizing that unless "aged ministers and officials" were "generously provided for" and not removed rashly, they would "rally together to denounce the reforms." Although Kang offered this "wise observation of an experienced person," the Emperor did not heed the advice, and suffered the consequences.

The article's analysis of the ideological difficulties encountered by Kang Youwei in justifying his policies to conservative opponents is equally suggestive of current realities, implicitly inviting comparison with the strategy pursued by Deng Xiaoping in legitimizing current reform policies through reinterpretation of Mao Zedong Thought and classical Marxism. According to the article, Kang's thesis that Confucius was a reformer who justified institutional change on the pretext of imitating the past had not convinced potential supporters of reform. Kang's intention had been to "carry out reforms by paying lip service to Confucius's teachings," and to use Confucius's authority to "shield his reforms, frustrate the conservatives, and reduce resistance to the reforms." However, not only did conservatives oppose his theories, but advocates of Westernization also remained unconvinced. Even supporters of the Emperor, who "sympathized with the reforms politically," rejected Kang's ideas.

These themes of ideological conflict in 1898 are strikingly reminiscent of persistent complaints in the Chinese media that many cadres, including those doing propaganda and theoretical work, have been out of step with the reform agenda since the Party's sweeping resolution on economic reform was adopted at the 3rd Plenum of the 12th Central Committee in October 1984. That document, which claims to be a breakthrough in Marxist theory, has sparked considerable debate over the ideological basis of Chinese modernization. Thus, the author appeared to be warning that the ideological controversy generated by Deng Xiaoping's ideas may be potent enough to defeat them. Summing up his argument, the author rejected the thesis of most historians that the reformers of 1898 failed because they were too timid and unable "to move ahead with big strides." They failed, he said, because the pace of reform was too fast, and the reformers were "too rash and unrealistic." They were "so anxious to bring about good order and prosperity," he concluded, that "their ideals were seriously divorced from reality."

The Deng regime not only uses historical commentary to promote its policy preferences and to appeal for political support from various constituencies, but it also moves quickly to squelch historical discussion that casts doubt on the Party's political legitimacy. A debate on agrarian socialism in the early 1980s, for example, was quickly suppressed because it implied that the liberal Dengist economic reforms ought to go in a more radical direction than the regime was willing to push them. Explaining the Cultural Revolution as the result of moving too rapidly from feudalism to socialism, some participants in the debate implied that a return to the skipped stage of capitalism was necessary in order to move on to genuine socialism. Thus, although the regime claims to support academic autonomy in history, it has consistently used history for its own political purposes.[60]

The Unresolved Questions

The accommodation reached between the present regime and its historians is clearly of a different order than the model of total politicization advocated by the radical Maoists prior to and during the Cultural Revolution. The current liberalization appears broader in scope, deeper in thrust, and longer in duration than any previous such period in PRC history. The Dengist political framework affords new opportunities for historians to pursue their craft in a more professional environment. But even the limited professional autonomy envisioned by Jian Bozan, based on an explicit understanding between the regime and historians and enforced through legitimate institutional mechanisms, seems unlikely in the short term.

Following its practice in other areas of social life, the regime is still groping its way toward an uneasy middle ground in its relations with historians. While tolerating fairly open debate on controversial issues, it silences discussion that threatens its political monopoly. While calling for "concrete analysis" of history as an "objective process," it attacks its critics through historical allegory and promotes public debates on policy through the oblique medium of historical analogy. While tolerating calls for the study of history for its own sake, it demands that historians write "patriotic history" for the moral education of the masses.

Because the Deng leadership uses the Chinese Academy of Social Sciences and its academic journals and forums for political purposes, these preeminent intellectual institutions remain highly politicized. In the tradition of China's past leaders, and consistent with the dictates of the Marxist doctrine it espouses, the regime wants to rest its legitimacy in part on a theory of history and to mold the past to fit the present. It must seek historical interpretations that justify changes in leadership and new policy lines. Thus, the question posed most sharply by Jian and the concept of historicism—where to draw the boundaries between history and politics—remains relevant and unanswered in Dengist China. Perhaps it cannot be answered as long as China remains a Leninist party-state.

To the extent that the regime relies on "experts" to accomplish its purposes in history, there will continue to be tension between the Party and the professional historians, between political norms and profesional standards. The demand for professional autonomy, however limited, will clash with the need for political control. The formal mechanisms established to deal with this inherent tension will be subject to conflicting pressures. The new Dengist academic bureaucrats are professional historians who appear to share the critical standards and resourcefulness of Jian and historians like him. To the extent that these standards are passed on to the next generation of scholars, lively debate will continue to inform academic history and the tension with politics will be strong.

Law and Legal Professionalism
in the People's Republic of China

JAMES V. FEINERMAN

In sharp contrast to the legal tradition of the English-speaking world, premodern China did not encourage the development of an independent and respected legal profession. Even during the Qing dynasty (1644–1911), when Chinese administrative organization was most complex and employed a large number of highly educated special functionaries, legal advisors were relatively few and occupied a low position in society. As one observer of law during this period has noted, articles of the Qing Code officially discouraged the emergence of a legal profession by threatening criminal punishment of those who incited others to undertake litigation or who profited from the management of lawsuits.[1] Men of talent chose to enter the state bureaucracy rather than to risk involvement with this shadowy area of public life.

The last years of the Qing dynasty brought sporadic attempts at reform of traditional administration of justice, among other changes in governmental structures. Along with these reforms, which sought to introduce constitutionalism to China with its separation of powers, hierarchy of courts, and justice in the individual case, came the realization that functional specialization would have to accompany increasing legalization. Magistrates who acted as prosecutors, judges, and juries were replaced by several classes of officials with more strictly delineated powers. Conditions that might have led to the emergence of an independent bar appeared for the first time in China's history.[2]

After the 1911 Revolution, the Chinese Nationalist Government began to institute a modern legal system, borrowing elements from the West and Japan. By the 1930s, a complete set of codified law, along the continental European model, had been adopted. A judicial structure culminating in a Supreme Court was also developed.[3] Yet, the distance between the ideal and the reality was vast; traditional notions died hard, the Nationalist Government never really exercised effective control over most of China, and civil disorder and foreign encroachment gave China's leaders a rationalization for short-circuiting much of the new legal ideology, especially where civil rights were concerned. National unity in the face of adversity provided the excuse for ignoring constitutional protections and procedural niceties whenever cases inconvenient for or embarassing to the government arose.

In the Chinese Communist base areas before 1949 there developed "people's justice," including ad hoc land reform and hastily established on-the-spot people's courts.[4] These proceedings offered little opportunity for the development of a system of legal representation; in fact, their stated purpose was to avoid the complexity of formal courts and to open the legal process to the participation of those without any formal education or training. A few notable legal officials, trained as lawyers, became well known, for example Ma Xiwu; but their fame was largely due to their encouragement of the new Communist people's justice.[5] For a brief period after the founding of the People's Republic until the Anti-Rightist Movement of the middle 1950s, it seemed as though a new type of "people's lawyers" would participate in the administration of a Soviet-style legal system which was beginning to emerge in China.[6] The people's justice of an earlier period, promising accessibility of the system to any ordinary citizen, yielded to pressure for more orderly rule and a minimum of legal guarantees, including the provision of counsel for criminal defendants, which was specifically mentioned in Article 76 of the 1954 Constitution and amplified by the 1956 Organic Law of the People's Courts, Article 7. The purges of 1957–1958 effectively eliminated the practicing bar in China, and it did not reemerge until 1978.

POST-MAO POLICIES
AFFECTING LAW AND LAWYERS

Since the 3rd Plenum of the 11th Chinese Communist Party Congress in 1978, the Chinese legal profession has been reestablished and has grown with surprising rapidity.[7] Despite the paucity of lawyers in both the dynastic and Republican periods and the short life of the organized bar during the early 1950s, the number of lawyers in the PRC has increased markedly in the past five years. Even more impressive than the rising numbers of new lawyers appearing in China has been the penetration of institutions manned by legal professionals into the lowest levels of local government. Such changes, in the face of long-prevailing cultural, political, and institutional attitudes derogating lawyers, require a new examination of the roles played in Chinese society by those with legal training. They also raise a fundamental question: Will increased reliance on legal norms alter the means by which the Chinese leadership exercises control over its people?

This inquiry must begin with some consideration of the state policies implemented since the 3rd Plenum and the legislation resulting from them, especially the 1980 "Lawyers' Law."[8] In addition to these bases for the emergence of a legal profession, contemporaneous social and economic developments in China have also encouraged the profession's growth. In gauging the extent of the influence these legal developments will have on Chinese society, some comparative reflection about the experience of other socialist countries may illuminate current trends in the PRC. Only then can the importance of lawyers and a legal system to a wide-ranging realignment of political power in China, particularly with respect to the position of the Communist Party, be evaluated.

With the downfall of the Gang of Four and the new policy directives that issued from the 3rd Plenum, the Chinese leadership gave priority to socialist democracy and a "strengthening" of the socialist legal system.[9] The rhetoric of the official organs may have originally indicated merely a desire for order after the chaos of the Cultural Revolution and for the stability necessary to achieve economic growth, but events quickly outpaced the stolid development of a new legal order promised by the Plenum. The 2nd Session of the 5th National People's Congress, in July 1979, promulgated seven new laws, including the first criminal code and code of criminal procedure since the founding of the People's Republic of China.[10] Suddenly, a legal system had been created; the clear expectation was that lawyers and others with legal training would administer it. Yet, China's legal educational institutions had been closed for over twenty years, casualties first of the Anti-Rightist Campaign of the late 1950s and then of the Cultural Revolution and subsequent disorder.[11] Anxious that an adequate corps of legal specialists be trained expeditiously to insure the smooth implementation of these new laws, the leadership prodded the educational bureaucracy into expanding the number of places for law students in university-level institutions.[12] A set of regulations outlining the privileges and responsibilities of lawyers was hurriedly prepared.

Many Western observers greeted the news of this reemergent legal profession in China with considerable skepticism. Having followed the experience of Chinese lawyers in the 1950s and the various twists of the Cultural Revolution, they doubted that sufficient status could be accorded to legal professionals to encourage very many of them to be thoughtful, independent lawyers. As one commentator noted:

> The harshness of the penalties for incorrect thought and expression, combined with a long history of political upheaval, make it unlikely that such fearless procurators and judges will soon emerge in the PRC. When the penalty for a politically incorrect judgment may be conviction of the judge himself as a counterrevolutionary or punishment by rehabilitation through labor, the reasons for judicial timidity are self-evident. In 1957, four Supreme Court judges did speak out on how to improve the administration of justice in China, but they were soon declared rightists and have not been heard from since then.[13]

These reservations have been expressed in several forms: Professional expertise was incompatible with Communist ideology; the leading role of the Communist Party offered little room for competing groups that might challenge its dominance; or the Western professional educations of many former lawyers prejudiced the less cosmopolitan Party and state leaders against the whole profession.[14] Years of political turmoil and shifts in policy would have left the Chinese population cynical and reluctant to face the occupational risks of law.

The legal profession that has appeared in the ensuing five years has in part defied these predictions and in part proven them accurate. Lawyers have been trained faster and in greater numbers than might have been imagined in 1980; two specialists who then examined the profession remarked:

[Law] is apparently not a popular choice of candidates for admission to universities; it reportedly often appears as the last preference on the list of departments students include on their applications. Former members of the legal profession or those with legal background are not all convinced of the desirability of returning to what still appears to be a suspect profession.[15]

At a number of leading universities in China today, the law faculties have become among the largest and most popular departments; for example, in 1980, the Law Faculty at Peking University enrolled 570 students in a university of about 8,000 students; when this author taught in that same faculty two years later (1982–1983), enrollment had increased to 1,000 students out of 10,000 in the university.[16]

Furthermore, laws and implementing regulations have been promulgated in various fields with startling rapidity, increasing the demand for scarce legal talent to implement them.[17] Specialization in law has been both fostered and rewarded by central government policies; China's Minister of Justice, Zou Yu, spoke in 1985 of the need for training specialized lawyers who would represent enterprises in particular industries. He pointed out that those who have additional professional qualifications as well as legal training would be "in some way, superior to those who receive exclusive training in the law."[18] Official pronouncements in the press and elsewhere have stressed the importance of law and have attempted to raise the status of the legal profession in the public's esteem.

RESIDUAL PROBLEMS

Still, certain basic problems persist; if left unremedied, they may ultimately prove fatal to the viability of an independent bar in the People's Republic of China. Chief among these threats is the

Communist Party's continued unwillingness to loosen its grip on every institution in Chinese society. Despite the official propaganda stating that no individual or organization can now place itself outside the rule of law,[19] the Party remains largely beyond the constraints the newly established legal system intended to make universal. Proof of this is the continuing tendency to deal with transgressions of law by Party members outside the formal legal system and to punish such violations by Party disciplinary methods. In 1984, *People's Daily* reported a case of a high-ranking official in the Railway Ministry who violated numerous laws by extorting bribes, placing his relatives in foreign universities, and misusing state funds. After an investigation of the Central Discipline Inspection Commission of the Central Committee, he was expelled from the Party. It was only "suggested" (by the Ministry of Railways) that the Ministry of Justice might try him in a criminal case for his violations of the law.[20]

Related to these concerns of the Communist Party is the failure to professionalize the upper reaches of the legal profession over the past few years. State officials involved in the administration of justice, judges at every level, and procurators all lack the necessary training in law to perform their functions as anticipated under the new laws. Short-term special training courses in law have been used to educate newly appointed officials with no previous exposure to law study; in 1980, it was estimated that less than 6 percent of the Chinese judiciary had any formal legal education.[21] In the allocation of assignments to the bench, political dependability has remained far more important than professional competence. Another significant factor militating against increased legalization has been the endurance of an accommodative style of personal relationships based on connections and back-door dealings—throughout Chinese society—which circumvents formal institutions. Official disapproval has not affected this problem appreciably. This reflects traditional Chinese orientation to authority and presents a continuing threat to an individually centered consciousness of civil rights in the face of state and collective pressures.[22]

THE EMERGENCE OF A NEW SYSTEM

Nonetheless, the legal profession has grown in size and influence notwithstanding the obstacles it has faced. A close examination of the roles played by lawyers in China today and the special attention given to certain areas of the law as the new system emerges may explain the profession's current state and future prospects. Among the fields absorbing the professional energies of lawyers in the People's Republic of China at present, three discrete areas provide an overview of lawyers' work: international commercial transactions, the representation of criminal defendants, and management of the domestic economy. These fields do not share equally in the division of legal talent and resources available to the profession, but they all have been singled out for attention in recent years.[23] Each of the fields also has several characteristics, which may explain why certain barriers to the use of law and lawyers have proven surmountable with respect to it. Their development may also suggest the possibility of increasing professionals' responsibility for certain tasks in Chinese society, even at the expense of Party control.

Foreign Investment Law

Since the first of the new laws promulgated in July 1979 to become effective was the law regulating Sino-foreign joint ventures, it is not surprising that Chinese lawyers quickly moved to provide expertise in the area of international business law. For no other reason than mere parity, the Chinese officials negotiating with businessmen from developed countries—accompanied in almost every meeting by legal advisors—would have felt themselves at a disadvantage without their own legal counsel. Taking into consideration the relative unfamiliarity of Chinese trade officials with foreign business practice, the novelty of the Chinese legislation on joint ventures and the vaunted litigiousness of Western businessmen, the perceived need for lawyers was heightened. Furthermore, the appearance of lawyers on the Chinese side of the bargaining table increased the confidence of foreign negotiators (and *their* counsel) in the long-term prospects for observance of agreements reached.

Only a small number of trained legal specialists were available in 1979 to the several state organizations in China which have responsibility for the implementation of the new joint-venture law—the Ministry of Foreign Economic Relations and Trade, the China International Trust and Investment Corporation, and the China Council for the Promotion of International Trade. They have all since established sizable legal departments, each of which includes lawyers trained in law faculties in developed countries. Legal "consulting services" have also appeared; a group called China International Economic Consultants will give legal opinions and advise Chinese entities on foreign practices.[24] Moonlighting law professors from China's most prestigious law faculties have formed special firms to advise foreign clients.

The concession that lawyers were necessary for dealing with foreign business did not present any great change in the attitudes of the Chinese leadership toward the legal profession. Had the role of legally trained professionals in Chinese society remained limited to the foreign-trade context, the creation of a legal profession could have been explained as a response to external considerations not intended to have any important internal ramifications. The initial descriptions of the programs for training new lawyers and the duties they would have seemed to indicate that this might be the case. Indeed, the commentary of several observers in the early 1980s about the Chinese bar anticipated a limited, foreign-oriented profession.[25] The course of legislative activity from 1979 to 1981 further reinforced this hypothesis, since most of the new legislation amplified the joint-venture law or pertained to the newly established special economic zones for foreign investment in Guangdong and Fujian provinces.[26]

Criminal Law

At the same time that the joint-venture law was promulgated, however, the National People's Congress announced both a criminal code and a code of criminal procedure, laws for domestic enforcement, which were to become effective 1 January 1980.[27] In addition to creating a complex legal order for the control and punishment of criminal behavior, these laws mandated, by certain of their provisions, the expansion of the legal profession. Most important, Chapter 4 of the Criminal Procedure Law grants an accused criminal the right to representation by counsel.[28] Despite China's relatively low crime rate and the infrequency of criminal trials, the need for lawyers to represent criminal defendants almost certainly hastened the adoption of the Provisional Regulations for Lawyers in 1980. One of the specifically enumerated tasks for lawyers in the article that outlines their work is defending criminal cases.[29]

The most spectacular early example of China's new-found need for criminal defense counsel was provided by the trial of the so-called Lin-Jiang clique, the group around Lin Biao (reputed to have planned Mao Zedong's assassination in the early 1970s) and the Gang of of Four, including Mao's wife, Jiang Qing.[30] Even though the criminal offenses of which the defendants were accused had occurred long before the promulgation and effective date of the new criminal laws, which were not of retroactive application, the rights to a defense lawyer contained in the code of criminal procedure were extended to the defendants by the Special Procuratorate.[31] Six of the ten defendants availed themselves of this privilege; the provision of defense counsel to the accused in this case was touted by the Chinese government as evidence of the scrupulous fairness with which the trial was conducted.[32] In fact, most independent observers of the proceedings felt the presence of lawyers for the defense was practically irrelevant to the trial; no sincere attempt was made to refute any counts of the government's indictment, and the defendants' guilt was never contested.

Domestic Economic Regulation

Of all the areas into which the Chinese lawyer's responsibilities have expanded, perhaps the most novel has been the new role of law (and lawyers) in managing the domestic economy. This development, somewhat later to emerge than the use of law in foreign business transactions or criminal trials, has proceeded quite swiftly in the three years following the promulgation of the domestically oriented Economic Contract Law.[33] A nationwide reordering of the economic structure, announced in October 1984, has added further impetus to these changes; by bringing the contract-responsibility system, which has produced dramatic results in improving the rural economy, to bear on the urban economy, Chinese leaders hope to invigorate China's industrial system. The reliance upon contracts, governed by recently promulgated law, has required that Chinese peasants and other individuals seek the assistance of lawyers and notaries[34] in the drafting and execution of contracts, among state enterprises and between state entities and collectives. The new law has also encouraged the involvement of legal professionals in the resolution of disputes over contract performance. Recent press accounts have indicated that the work for those trained in civil and economic law has increased dramatically, at every level in Chinese society.[35]

LAWYERS' CONCERNS AND CURRENT STATUS

The extent of the inroads lawyers may have made into each of the areas discussed above must, however, be weighed against the concerns expressed earlier about continuing constraints on the role of the legal profession in the PRC. Communist Party control, lack of opportunities for professional training, and institutional resistance to formal legal process affect the performance of lawyers in China today. For instance, in the foreign economic arena, Chinese efforts to expand foreign investment rapidly have faced numerous obstacles. Inexperienced legal advisors have discounted matters of serious concern to foreign investors when counseling their superiors, leading their ministries and enterprises to make grave mistakes which have retarded the pace of foreign investment in the PRC.[36] Firms of legal consultants established by various Chinese state entities to render advice to foreigners have been ignored by their target audience because of doubts about their ability to provide impartial advice and to represent a foreign client's interests zealously in the face of Party and state pressures to demonstrate loyalty to China and to the principles of socialism.

Similarly, in the work of lawyers as criminal defense counsel, a number of problems have surfaced since 1980. One major debate, so far confined to polite academic exchanges, has concerned the presumption of innocence in criminal law.[37] Although the position of most legal scholars in the PRC has been that Chinese law presumes neither guilt nor innocence before conviction,[38] the general opprobrium which attaches to anyone accused of a crime—even before an appearance in court—makes the job of a Chinese defense lawyer difficult. Without the presumption of innocence, counsel may be understandably reluctant to provide the fullest possible defense for his client, fearing too close an alignment with a presumptive criminal. The role of the defense lawyer has also, in trials open to foreign observation, appeared quite limited, an impression corroborated by published reports of other major cases. In these proceedings, defense counsel is allotted only a few minutes, following both the judge's panel and the prosecuting attorney at the end of the trial, usually to plead mitigating circumstances. Examples of these defenses have included repentance, the defendant's youth and inexperience, presence of accomplices, even the underlying social disorder at the time of the

Cultural Revolution as a precipitating factor.[39] As a result, the full range of defense activities is rather circumscribed by practice.

In domestic economic matters, the role of the lawyer is yet to be fully appreciated. Partly due to their scarcity and partly due to the unfamiliarity of their potential clients with legal procedures, lawyers have not yet begun to have a significant impact on Chinese economic life. The increasing rate at which legislation is being passed should lead to more frequent consultation of legal specialists by actors in the economy, but many longstanding practices will have to be revised first.[40]

Sporadic reports appear in the press suggesting that, even in the Chinese countryside, peasants are now consulting lawyers and others for legal advice; just how widespread these activities are remains a matter of conjecture. For example, a current report in the Chinese press states that "legal-aid offices are mushrooming in China's countryside to help tackle economic tangles brought about by rapid economic development."[41] What these stories do illustrate is the commitment of the Chinese leadership to using legal mechanisms as methods of control for the domestic economy, as illustrated by the contract-responsibility system in the rural economy. Contract disputes have led to the realization that more assistance in drafting and implementation may ease the current demand for judicial personnel to adjudicate disputes. But, at present, many other determinants besides the law play a larger part in controlling the basic industries and agriculture of the People's Republic of China.

REGULATION OF LAWYERS IN THE PRC

As the legal profession has resurfaced in China, the rights and obligations of lawyers—particularly as detailed in the Provisional Regulations on Lawyers—have come under increasing scrutiny. As the basic framework for organizing the profession and describing the functions of lawyers in China, these regulations are an important starting point for understanding the present and potential role that the legal profession may play in Chinese society. It should be kept in mind, however, that these regulations are not the sole control over lawyer's activities. Their legal work must be carried out under the rule of the Communist Party and its policies.

In the first article of the regulations, this basic conundrum appears quite clearly. Article 1 defines lawyers as

legal workers of the state whose duties are to give legal advice to government agencies, enterprises, institutions, public organizations, people's communes and citizens, in order to promote the proper enforcement of the law and safeguard the interests of the state and the collective as well as the legitimate rights and interests of citizens.[42]

In this basic definition, Chinese lawyers are set apart from their peers in other countries (practitioners of an independent profession) by their duties as state legal workers. In ordering priorities for legal work, too, the regulations are clear that lawyers must first guard the interests of the state and the collective and thereafter the rights and interests of citizens.

Further obligations are placed upon lawyers by the requirement in the provisional regulations that "lawyers shall propagate socialist legality throughout their legal practice"[43] and that lawyers "must be loyal to the cause of socialism."[44] While this may be nothing more than the Chinese equivalent of the requirement common in many other countries that lawyers swear to uphold the national constitution and laws, it is significant that this particular formulation—emphasizing the primacy of a political ideology rather than a commitment to particular institutions—has been codified. Two articles of the regulations further enjoin lawyers to "protect the legitimate rights and interests" of their citizens, without providing any guidance as to the standards for judging "legitimacy."[45] These limitations on the Chinese legal profession are troublesome, because they present a means for circumventing the protections of civil rights provided elsewhere in the law. By branding certain actions antisocialist or illegitimate, the Party and state can remove the legal protections for disfavored forms of speech or political activity.

Lawyers' Qualifications

The qualifications for Chinese lawyers described in the Provisional Regulations spell out quite precisely the prevailing standards for professional status in the PRC today, combining political and educational criteria in a precarious balance. A prospective lawyer must be a citizen who "loves the People's Republic of China, supports the socialist system, and has the right to elect and be elected."[46] Such a person may be admitted to the bar as a practicing lawyer after passing a qualifying examination following one of four courses of education and practical experience:

1. graduation from a law faculty with two years' experience in judicial work, teaching law, or research on legal matters;
2. legal training and work as a judge in the people's courts or as a procurator in the people's procuratorates;
3. university education and work in the fields of economics, science, or technology for more than three years and knowledge of law and statutes relevant to those fields as well as some legal training; or
4. a high educational level and legal knowledge and experience equivalent to that specified in (1) or (2) above.[47]

As this article demonstrates, a wide range of people are eligible to become practicing lawyers under Chinese law. The requirements seem to have been purposely broadened to include those who have no formal education in law but who have had long experience in performing legal work, notably judicial and procuratorial workers. In addition, university graduates can enter the legal profession with degrees in fields other than law, if they have some work-related experience with legal matters. As is common in other Chinese legislation,[48] a catch-all provision at the end of the article grants considerable discretion to admit other candidates who do not meet all the applicable requirements but who are nonetheless desirable or necessary additions to the bar.

These standards are a compromise between the dictates of professionalism and the concerns of pragmatism. Although a standard requiring the completion of a rigorous course of legal education is acknowledged by its placement as the first alternative, the other possibilities for admission reflect the paucity of graduate lawyers now available.[49] The flexibility with which various types of educational qualifications will be deemed equivalent in order to maximize the pool of potential lawyers further illustrates this pragmatic attitude. Longstanding notions about the importance of practical experience (and, in some cases, its preferability) are embodied in the provision that would admit to the bar those with practicing qualifications who lack a legal education. Such a provision may have been necessary to insure the acquiescence of the important parties in the smooth functioning of the Chinese legal system.

The Ministry of Justice retains the power to control access to the bar by other articles of the provisional regulations. These require an examination of all who wish to practice law,[50] authorize a period of probationary practice[51] for recent graduates, and empower certain organs under the Ministry to disbar grossly incompetent lawyers.[52] There has been little actual practice thus far, and their wording is quite vague as to particular standards; but they do offer a glimpse of the intended systematization of qualifications for lawyers, suggesting differentiation of those with professional skills.

Lawyers' Employment

The chapter of the provisional regulations entitled "Organs Where Lawyers Work"[53] may be the most illuminating as to the structure of the emerging legal profession in China and the constraints under which it operates. As in the 1950s, lawyers in the PRC today can practice only collectively, in organizations known as "Legal Advisory Offices" (LAOs).[54] These LAOs are set up under the auspices of the Ministry of Justice in various localities, but each is independent of other LAOs.[55] Management of the LAOs, including the assignment of cases, is left to a chief and deputy chief, who are supposed to be elected by their fellow lawyers in each LAO;[56] they direct the work of the office, in addition to doing their own legal work, and report to the judicial organs under which their offices are established. Lawyers' work is assigned by the LAO to each individual lawyer, taking into account the requests of clients who have designated a particular lawyer; accepting an assignment and collecting fees for legal work is done by the LAO on behalf of the lawyers in the office.[57] Lawyers are encouraged to form "bar associations"[58] in addition to the LAOs; these are primarily social organizations with several goals, including the promotion of exchanges between Chinese and foreign lawyers.[59] These groups are often known as "Lawyers' Associations" to distinguish their roles from the business function of the LAOs and from the self-regulatory function of foreign bar associations.

Several problems related to the independence of the bar arise from this chapter's provisions: the force of collective opinion on a lawyer's independent judgment, the financial dependence created by the reimbursement mechanism, and the lack of a direct relationship between attorney and client. Given the many pressures on Chinese lawyers to safeguard the state's interests and to stress the collective rather than the individual's good, the legal profession in the PRC is forced to factor in to a significant extent extra-legal considerations in the determination of legal questions. The characteristic role of the Western lawyer as defender of unpopular ideas and individuals against the tyranny of the majority is far less likely to be played by a Chinese lawyer. The governing ideology has always stressed unity and suppressed dissidence; the collective practice of law will not be conducive to the representation of those who protest the system. In other legal orders, one of the chief assurances that lawyers will zealously represent their clients lies in the client's control of the purse strings; dissatisfied clients soon find other representation. Chinese clients cannot exert such pressure; they must go to a LAO to seek a lawyer and accept the lawyer assigned to their cases. Most important, the relationship between the lawyer and his client always remains one that is mediated by the institution of the LAO. The responsibility of these offices to their establishing authorities (and, ultimately, of the lawyers they employ) creates an ambivalence: Can the Chinese lawyer make his client's interests paramount, or must the lawyer look to the collective employer for final approval?

FUTURE PROSPECTS

The Chinese leadership is faced not only with the challenge of implementing the Provisional Regulations but also with the demands for autonomy and status which a growing sense of professionalism may instill in the Chinese bar. The burgeoning contacts of Chinese lawyers' associations with their counterparts abroad, for example, have shown the Chinese participants in these exchanges a very different world of wealth and prestige enjoyed by foreign lawyers. A number of Chinese students, still far from significant but growing, has been sent to study law in developing countries; the critical method used in law study outside of China and the content of non-socialist legal systems may well influence the thought of the returned student lawyers. Can this be reconciled with the requirements of the Provisional Regulations on Lawyers and of the Party's leading role in Chinese society? As academic legal educations become the rule rather than the exception in the backgrounds of China's practicing lawyers, will the commitment to legalistic norms developed over the course of a legal education result in conflicts with the need to adapt to changing policy consider-ations? Some tentative answers emerge from an examination of prac-tice in the three fields—foreign investment, criminal defense, and domestic economic activities.

Foreign Investment Law

The rapid growth of the sector of the Chinese legal profession work-ing on foreign trade has been notable. From a handful of legal special-ists in 1979, when the Joint-Venture Law was passed, the number has increased to several hundred—perhaps a thousand—today.[60] Of course, one purpose of this expansion has been to serve Chinese entities that need counsel in their dealings with foreign businessmen and their lawyers; however, the Chinese bar has sought to market its services to foreign businesses operating in China as well.[61] Due to the diffi-culty of learning Chinese law, much of it contained in "internal" documents and other publications not generally available, some Chinese lawyers have also found a niche in advising foreign lawyers[62] whose clients are doing business in China. Chinese lawyers also engage in a certain amount of nonlegal consulting business. Reports from foreign clients say that fees charged by Chinese legal profession-als have risen to be commensurate with those of their Western counterparts.[63]

The discontinuities between the Western and Chinese legal profes-sion are manifest in these relationships of Chinese business-oriented lawyers with their clients. Those who advise Chinese enterprises and ministries often display little independent judgment and will not criticize their side's position, whatever the dictates of the law; open criticism of one's client—especially if it is a government entity—might raise questions about a lawyer's willingness to "love the People's Republic of China, support the socialist system . . . ," etc.[64] They may provide some internal guidance, similar to in-house counsel at foreign corporations, but externally they show no will to disagree. Chinese lawyers who advise foreign clients are under suspicion from both their Chinese employing units and their foreign employers because of their divided loyalties—do they "love socialism and the motherland" or will they zealously represent the paying client? Without greater attention to the ideals of professionalism in China it is doubtful that these lawyers will ever be really accepted by either side. Finally, it is often evident to their clients that a lack of legal training in the international business field has left these lawyers ill-prepared for their current work. Many have little practical experience, and they often lack the confidence to deal with new situations flexibly. This may be largely due to the many new roles lawyers are meant to fill in China today. For instance, a recent press announcement[65] of the inauguration of The China Legal Affairs Company stated that not only would it advise both state organs and economic units but that it would also be run as an enterprise bearing responsibility for its profits and losses and conduct an independent economic accounting. Pioneering new forms of enterprise while building a legal order from the very beginnings must put great pressure on these Chinese lawyers. Time and further experience may be the only remedies for their present failings.

Criminal Law

The lawyers who undertake criminal defense work are similarly limited by both tradition and public perception in the scope of their representation. The pattern seems to be well established in Chinese criminal justice that the defense in a criminal case serves only to plead mitigating circumstances and never challenges the substance of a charge or—more provocatively—pleads a client's innocence.[66] Moreover, the right to be represented by a defense lawyer is contained only in the Criminal Procedure Law[67] but does not attach to those who are punished through a regime of informal administrative sanctions, which include the possibility of a three- to four-year term in a labor camp. These have been the more effective sanctions for criminal acts in China, since, even before the adoption of the criminal laws in 1979, Chinese citizens had long been subject to administrative penalties meted out by public security organs and a panoply of local authorities—street committees, comrades' courts, factory and other workplace boards, and Party and Youth League disciplinary committees.[68] Thus, many who transgress the Chinese social order may receive a significant penalty without the opportunity for legal representation. Neither the organized bar in general nor those lawyers who do criminal-defense work perceive themselves as having any obligation to widen the scope of legal protection for the accused.

Twice, in 1981 and 1983, the provisions of the Criminal Law and the Criminal Procedure Law have been relaxed or amended to lessen their restriction on state action to punish crime, resulting in procedural shortcuts and temporarily severer sentences in order to process criminal cases faster and to mete out more punishments.[69] At neither time was there any objection from the defense bar in China. No lawyer in the People's Republic of China saw an obligation—even in the abstract—to argue for the rights of the accused; such concerns, when raised, were dismissed as the worries of only a few Western human-rights organizations. Responding to Amnesty International's 1984 report, *China: Violations of Human Rights*, which protested Chinese treatment of prisoners of conscience and the widespread application of the death penalty, Chinese leaders explained that the nationwide campaigns against crime took precedence. One typical manifestation of official dismissal was an article in *People's Daily:*

> Some foreign bourgeois "humanitarians" object to our condemning those felons to the death penalty, holding that such a practice is "inhumane." However, can it be considered "humane" if we just stop condemning those felons to death but let them continue to kill good people?[70]

Yet, there are encouraging signs that the role of the defense lawyer has begun to be taken more seriously in the Chinese court system recently. Press reports have detailed several instances where judges were punished for abusing the privileges of defense attorneys; editorial comment and letters to the editor have applauded such actions. One example came from Liaoning province, where a county-court judge ordered a bailiff to remove the defendant's counsel from the courtroom because he had raised a legal objection to the judge's conduct.[71] Upon the lawyer's complaint to the higher court, the judge was at first ordered merely to apologize to the lawyer for his conduct, but the outrage of onlookers forced the court to open a more serious inquiry. As a result, the abusive judge was dismissed from his post, and the case was remanded for a new trial.[72] *People's Daily* printed a letter from a famous Chinese economist, Qian Jiaqu, along with its follow-up story, berating the judge for his "Cultural Revolution" mentality and suggesting that he was in line for some legal "reeducation."[73] These instances of concern for the lawyer's independence and status in the face of a state official are heartening evidence that certain fundamental notions are beginning to take root. Whether such attitudes will spread throughout the Chinese polity is difficult to predict, but the supportive article in the Party's chief organ of news and propaganda is a reason for hope.

Domestic Economic Law

The bold steps taken to restructure China's economy, first in agriculture and then in urban industry, have presented a new field for legal representation of ordinary Chinese entities and individuals. Here, as in the area of international business, the situation has been changing rapidly. Since there is no foreign standard against which performance can be judged, nor the problem of split Chinese/foreign allegiances, the official press at least seems to have conceded a role[74] for lawyers in this area. The central importance the leadership has assigned to the economic reforms also presents bright prospects for a more independent, broadly based profession—if the link between economic reform and legalization can be forged and strengthened. The recent state economic reforms have encouraged fresh approaches which may bode well for law.[75] Legal regulation has definitely been targeted as one of the mechanisms to be used to modernize China's economy. The potential for growth is great, since the size of this field—compared to that of international business or criminal law in China—is so vast.

A recent work by a noted specialist on Soviet law[76] suggests that economic applications of law may be the most important function for socialist legal systems. In their attempts to modernize stagnant economies and to maximize the productive capacities of industry and agriculture, Soviet economic planners have turned to jurists to devise legal half-way measures between central controls and enterprise autonomy.[77] In Hazard's analysis, the Soviet planners have concluded that maximization of production depends upon rationalizing managerial structures; this has become the task of economic law specialists. Although this stratagem has yet to yield visible results for the Soviet economy, objective observers seem to agree that it is the only positive direction in which the current economy might move. A similar approach appears to be emerging over the past several years among Chinese planners. Dissatisfied with central planning but unwilling to risk total decontrol, they are searching for a middle road. Clear legal norms, sufficiently detailed to provide guidance in line with state goals, are perceived as the remedy to overly strict central planning. Demarcation of central authority with definite limits, however, raises serious questions about the extent to which the Party and state will be bound by the limits of law. The bargain may be that some rein on their power will be acceptable if law proves it can play an important function in institutionalizing policy and thus promoting political stability.

The proponents of changes in the economic sphere realize that they are not self-executing; there must also be developed a corps of specialists who can introduce, administer, and interpret the new system. A more market-oriented economy, purporting to rely on legal regulation, should certainly require more lawyers[78] to implement the proposed reforms. Whereas there may be enough legally trained individuals in the Soviet Union today to allow the administration of economic reform by legal specialists, the situation in China remains very different. Other priorities were established earlier for the relatively few trained lawyers; it will be quite some time before legal talent sifts down to a significant number of localities all over China. Yet, there is considerable evidence that in China, as has already happened in the Soviet Union, economic planning and the development of law are becoming more closely related.[79] Once in place, such a system would entrench the legal profession in a socialist society in an important way, tying the society's economic success to the quality of its law-making and administration of law. Already, in tiny villages in China, peasants are drawing up contracts, litigating disputes about their performance, and turning to legal advisors for guidance.[80]

Prospects for the future development of the legal profession in China, though difficult to assess at present, are far brighter than at any time since 1949. Traditional attitudes toward law and the lawyers who implement it have changed, if slowly, and bright students are being attracted to the study of law at China's major universities, and even abroad. Certain fundamental changes now underway in the People's Republic, which seem at this writing likely to continue, should reinforce the increasing perception that a strong legal system must underpin Chinese modernization. If these trends do continue, and if the legal profession becomes as well integrated into the administration of China's domestic economy as it has in foreign trade and criminal-justice administration, an independent bar may begin to emerge in China. Chinese lawyers, armed with specialized knowledge and educational credentials to enhance their status, may finally be able to take their place between the citizenry and the Party and state as administrators of law's public role.

China has prided itself on developing a socialist-democratic legal system with Chinese characteristics. Since 1949, the emphasis has decidedly been on the "socialist" part of this formulation, but the legal reforms that began after 1978 have begun to give equal stature to the "democratic." Further development of democracy in the legal system will be encouraged by successful use of law to regulate the domestic economy, to increase the foreign contribution to China's modernization program, and to safeguard legitimate rights of Chinese citizens from official abuse or encroachment. Should legalization proceed at the pace seen over the last five or six years, there is little doubt that the rule of law will be strengthened in the PRC. The legal profession's role will be pivotal, marshaling public opinion in support of law and demonstrating the importance and efficacy of legal norms. The precarious position of the Chinese bar for much of the last thirty-five years has now improved considerably. The Party and state leadership have, for the time being, thrown their support behind the legalization drive. A new respect has been generated for educated professionals throughout China, who are seen as essential to the task of bringing their country into the front ranks of world power and influence. Conditions for the legal's profession's growth and increasing influence are promising; the task for China's lawyers is to make the most of them.

The most pressing problem confronting us is the unified arrangement and proper use of scientific and technical personnel.
    Premier Zhao Ziyang, "Speech on the Work of the Government" to the 6th National People's Congress. 6 June 1983.[1]

CHAPTER FIVE

China's Scientists and Technologists in the Post-Mao Era: A Retrospective and Prospective Glimpse

DENIS FRED SIMON

The training and effective management of high-caliber human resources is considered to be essential to the process of economic development. A pool of qualified individuals is needed to staff administrative offices, to provide advice to government officials, to educate the next generation, and to support industrial and agricultural development through the promotion of advances in science and technology. Harbison and Myers, in their seminal study of manpower and education in developing countries, refer to high-quality manpower as a strategic resource.[2] They note, however, that most LDCs face severe human-resource problems that seriously constrain their prospects for rapid development. These problems include (1) a shortage of persons with the critical skills and knowledge required for effective national development, (2) inadequate or underdeveloped organizations and institutions for mobilizing human resources, and (3) a lack of incentives for persons to engage in particular activities that are vitally important for national development.

More important, the work by Harbison and Myers, as well as the writings of Gunnar Myrdal, Blaugh and others, suggests that the manpower problem is neither just a problem of quantity or quality; also at issue is the creation of an economic and political climate conducive to the effective utilization of the prevailing manpower base whatever its size or capabilities.[3] At present, this lesson holds particular significance for China as it attempts to formulate and implement a series of policies designed to improve the use and productivity of the country's present limited stock of scientists, technicians, and engineers. After over three decades of debate and controversy surrounding the status and role of intellectuals in general, and scientific and technological (S&T) personnel in particular, the leadership in Beijing recognizes that, without an adequate pool of qualified S&T intellectuals and more strategic placement of these individuals, the country's goal of closing the economic and technological gap between itself and the West will be largely unattainable.

Because of the persistence of a host of political problems, the PRC leadership, to a large extent, has been unable to achieve many of its goals regarding the use of scientific and technical personnel. The difficulties that characterize the current program to improve the situation of S&T intellectuals are many and far-reaching. While the leadership from Deng Xiaoping on down has made it clear that "science and technology is a productive force" and that intellectuals "are part of the working class," the status of many intellectuals, including S&T intellectuals, has not improved. Political cadres, many of whom achieved their positions by virtue of the Cultural Revolution and the Gang of Four, continue to obstruct the new reform policies for ideological reasons as well as for reasons of self-interest. Unless China's leadership at both the national and local levels can ensure more effective utilization of S&T intellectuals, the modernization of science and technology will continue to be seriously impeded.

BACKGROUND

Since the formal announcement of the Four Modernizations Program in early 1978, Chinese leaders have paid increasing attention to the role of science and technology in economic development. This focus on S&T has necessitated a close examination of the prevailing status and management of the country's science and technology personnel. Based on a survey of the country's scientists, engineers, and technicians completed in 1983, China's S&T personnel numbered 6.85 million, out of which 320,000 were engaged in full-time scientific research, 1.80 million were engaged in engineering and technical positions, 1.90 million in health and medicine, and 1.38 million were employed in teaching.[4] Faced with the stark reality that China's S&T manpower resources had been decimated by political traumas such as the Cultural Revolution, and that the demand for qualified individuals would continue to greatly outstrip the supply over the next several years, a serious effort has been made to repair the damage to higher education and the environment in which scientists and engineers work. Nonetheless, in spite of these efforts, major bottlenecks continue to constrict the implementation of the reforms for S&T personnel as well as the attempt to give added emphasis to science and technology.

In spite of all the rhetoric about the great changes for science and technology, what is striking about the situation of S&T intellectuals in the post-Mao era is that, when the Chinese press cites problems in this area, they bear a remarkable resemblance to those that existed during the 1950s and 1960s. The dilemma of "red versus expert" may be cast in a different form today, but the essence of the current debate reflects many of the same issues that were important in the earlier years of the Communist regime. Much of our knowledge about the status and employment of S&T intellectuals during this earlier period comes from Leo Orleans's book entitled *Professional Manpower and Education in Communist China.* Written in 1961 in the aftermath of the Great Leap Forward, the book documents a host of "problems" faced by the S&T community: Among the specific difficulties plaguing the S&T community at this time were (1) limited numbers of highly qualified personnel capable of advanced scientific research, (2) over-emphasis in research on its immediate application, (3) excessive centralization of work assignments, (4) the extensive administrative burdens placed on the scientist, (5) too much interference in research planning, and (6) an inadequate infrastructure for research work, specifically insufficient and inferior scientific research equipment, poor libraries, and so forth.

What is even more striking, however, is the apparent persistence of several policy themes that continue to dominate the debate over S&T

modernization today. In spite of the occurrence of several politically inspired ideological campaigns, the 1950s and early 1960s, like the 1980s, was a period in which science and technology were generally held in high esteem and were deemed important to the regime's economic goals.[5] The exception was the Great Leap Forward in the late 1950s. It was also a period in which the leadership was searching for an appropriate formula for the management of scientific and technical personnel. A speech by Premier Zhou Enlai in January 1956 at a Party Central Committee meeting on intellectuals attempted to iron out the correct policy on scientific and technical workers.[6] In his speech, Zhou admitted the existence of "certain irrational features in our present employment and treatment" of intellectuals, citing such problems as bureaucratism, sectarianism, and departmentalism. In pledging to overcome these problems, he promised improvements in working conditions, better incentives and rewards, and more reference materials and equipment.[7] Yet, in spite of the new atmosphere created by Zhou's remarks, the Anti-Rightist Campaign of 1957–1958 quickly changed the prevailing climate. This not only reinforced the political suspicions of many within the S&T community, but it left them once again in a sea of political uncertainty.

Among the important themes, the first and most pervasive was the strong emphasis on the integration of science and production. According to Orleans, "The Party's main aim has been to limit theoretical research and make sure that science concentrates on practical problems which face China in its industrial race."[8] Nie Rongzhen, the director of the country's science planning activities in 1958, noted that "experiences in the development of science in our country during the past few years have proved that only by starting from the standpoint of production and socialist construction can the scientific institutions of our country develop."[9] In spite of the concerns regarding the importance of basic research articulated by members of the scientific establishment as early as the mid-1950s, scientists were constantly admonished to ensure that their research had some practical and immediate applications.[10]

This emphasis on so-called "practical" research had important implications for the position of the Chinese Academy of Sciences, which traditionally had been the country's premier research institution and included China's leading scientific personnel. During the 1950s, the Academy was increasingly viewed as making little practical contribution to the goals of national economic construction. By early 1957, the Academy was replaced in the political hierarchy by a Scientific Planning Committee, an organization that eventually was the precursor to the present-day State Science and Technology Commission.[11] As John Lindbeck notes, the gradual diminution of the CAS in favor of the SSTC was a product of a debate over the nature of scientific activity. The conclusion had long-lasting implications for China's scientific community: The pursuit of new knowledge and understanding for its own sake was to be subordinated to the use of science to support the planned programs of technological and economic achievement specified by the Party and the state.[12]

A second theme highlighted by Orleans is the role of foreign technology and training. "Chinese leaders realize that the gap in the level of scientific and technological development between China and the West is so great that it would be folly to pursue advanced research while the chasm exists—that the quickest and most practical way to raise China's level is to borrow and copy from the advanced nations and adapt what is borrowed to the country's own needs."[13] During the 1950s, an important feature of this policy emphasis was the extensive cooperation in science and technology between Moscow and Beijing. This cooperation provided for the training of Chinese scientific and technical personnel in the USSR as well as the advice and assistance of Soviet technical personnel in China. Estimates are that 11,000 Soviet technicians visited China, while approximately 25,000 Chinese were sent to the USSR for advanced education and technical training. In many of the same ways that the West is influencing China's science and technology establishment today, this interaction shaped, directly and indirectly, China's overall approach to research planning and its management of S&T personnel.[14]

The third theme identified by Orleans is the emphasis placed on the "love of science" and the popularization of science and technology. At the time, however, the lack of adequate numbers of well-trained S&T manpower to meet the country's needs led to a rather broad definition of "science and technology," thereby allowing anyone with or without the appropriate credentials to engage in what might be minimally called research or innovative activities. The attempt to bring science and technology down to the masses during the period led to the ridicule of many of the better-trained S&T personnel. This did not preclude the continuation of more traditional, high-quality research in both the defense sector and the Chinese Academy of Sciences. Nonetheless, the strategy of "walking on two legs" during the Great Leap Forward created a tension between those who prized the scientific endeavor as the purview of an elite segment of society and those who viewed the mental work associated with science and technology as more mundane and subordinate to manual work.

Just as had occurred in the mid-1950s, the early 1960s witnessed a renaissance of sorts in the treatment of S&T personnel and the role of science and technology in Chinese economic development.[15] Under the tutelage of Marshal Nie Rongzhen, the director of the country's overall S&T activities, and others, moves were made to enhance the treatment of scientists, improve the education system, and devote additional resources to the research sector.[16] An article in Red Flag in late 1962 expressed the view that the only way to promote technological advance was to create a "hard core" of research centers staffed by outstanding scientists.[17] This attempt to spark more rapid S&T advance, which was strengthened for a short time with the announcement in 1964 that China had successfully tested an atomic weapon proved, however, short-lived. The onset of the Cultural Revolution in 1965 with its intended attacks on the scientific community proved debilitating to the ranks of the country's scientists, technicians, and engineers.

Among other things, the Cultural Revolution was a manifestation of what Pierre Perrolle has termed "a continuous search for the delicate balance between supporting intellectuals for their contributions to society and dealing with them as obstacles, potential and actual, to social and ideological change."[18] During this period, the dichotomy "red" vs. "expert" surfaced to an even greater degree than in the past, with the former taking clear precedence over the latter.[19] Referring to the attitudes toward Chinese scientists at the time, Lindbeck noted that "they are bearers of ideas and working habits which China's political leaders, hedged by Marxist dogmatic uncertainties, do not appear to comprehend and trust."[20] Although Merle Goldman has shown that, at least initially, actual efforts were made by leaders such as Zhou Enlai to "exempt" and protect the S&T community from political criticism and censure, these were increasingly unsuccessful as the leadership lost control of the Cultural Revolution.[21]

China's scientists became one of the primary targets of the Red

Guards and their political leaders. They were attacked for their elitism, cockiness, ivory-tower mentality, and seeming disregard for the practical needs of the masses. As a result, S&T personnel as well as intellectuals in general were labeled "the stinking ninth category," a designation that not only denoted their low status, but also the perception that they had little to contribute to society. With "politics in command," the scientific endeavor that had long been guarded by the S&T community was completely rebuked.

Unprecedented attacks were launched against scientists during the Cultural Revolution; even those working in high-level defense areas were not exempt from attack. This movement was one of a long series of attempts in Chinese history to come to grips with the role of intellectuals in society and the political system.[22] This dilemma did not begin with the arrival of the Chinese Communists in 1949, but emerged with the start of China's modern history in the late nineteenth century. In an article comparing the scientist and the politician in the West, Roger Revelle suggests that each has little empathy for the other. The scientist is driven by his need to explain, predict, and control phenomena through possession of special knowledge. The politician is motivated by power, often claiming to possess greater insight and access to truth than his scientific colleagues.[23]

In communist regimes, in particular, this tension is exacerbated, as purveyors of the Party doctrine feel threatened by those who can seemingly offer an alternative, more apolitical view of the world that may threaten the credibility and legitimacy of the ruling elite. Studies of the scientific community in the Soviet Union frequently cite this contradiction as the central problem of that country's S&T system since the days of Stalin.[24] The leadership in a socialist system is thus faced with a basic contradiction between the imperatives of innovation and control.[25] On the one hand, it must mobilize the resources necessary to move toward the economic and technological goals it has set for society. As noted earlier, this requires a pool of competent, well-trained individuals who possess needed technical skills. On the other hand, the political cadres in positions of authority cannot afford to allow an overly technocratic view of society to emerge, since such a perspective could make the Party seemingly irrelevant, or at least raise questions about its capacity to govern.

In the Soviet Union, the incorporation of a technocratic group into the ruling elite in the 1960s and 1970s triggered strong criticism from China, which at the time viewed the emerging Soviet leadership as revisionist, bureaucratic, and irreverent from an ideological point of view.[26] In the Soviet case, this incorporation provided many members of the S&T community with special perquisites and extensive benefits which, in effect, coopted them into the system and rendered them less willing to question the system. Whereas, in 1965, Mao's reaction to the increasing technocratic character of the regime was to launch a "cultural revolution" in order to prevent the emergence of a "technocratic leadership," Deng Xiaoping's response in the 1980s has been, in many ways, to move in the Soviet direction and, in some cases, to recast the place of scientific and technical personnel in Chinese society.[27]

S&T PERSONNEL IN THE POST-MAO ERA

Recognizing that the potential success or failure of the Four Modernizations Program depends, to a large extent, on the contributions of scientific and technical personnel, the post-Mao leadership has attempted to relax the political and economic constraints imposed on the country's S&T intellectuals. Current policies include programs to increase the number of technical persons admitted into the ranks of the Communist Party, expand job mobility, improve salaries and living conditions, provide greater financial incentives for important research achievements, and promote more extensive ties with the international scientific community. If these various programs were to be implemented in their entirety, they would alter in a significant fashion the place of S&T intellectuals in the Chinese political and social order. As the record since 1978 indicates, however, major obstacles remain.

Mobilization of S&T personnel takes place within the broader policy context of economic modernization. In March 1978, just one month after the formal announcement of the Four Modernizations Program, the Chinese leadership held a national science conference in Beijing. The conference, which had been in the planning stage for almost two years, involved extensive consultation with the country's top S&T leaders. It served as a forum to promote the rapid and sustained development of science and technology.[28] A comprehensive plan was mapped out listing 8 priority fields, 27 priority research spheres, and 108 key projects.[29] Even though science and technology had been

listed as Number Three in the overall order of the Four Modernizations, Deng recognized that, wihtout significant progress in S&T, the
modernization program could not move ahead.[30]

The crux of the Four Modernizations is the mastery of modern science and technology. Without modern science and technology it is impossible to build modern
agriculture, modern industry, or modern national defense. Without high-speed
development of science and technology, it is impossible to develop the national
economy at high speed.[31]

As with other facets of the modernization drive, the S&T modernization program soon experienced a number of difficulties. As the
program for the economy underwent a period of rethinking and readjustment after the 11th Plenum of the CCP in December 1978, so did
the S&T program. Some of the difficulties were related to sheer
physical constraints. Suttmeier, in his examination of the available
pool of scientists and technicians, notes that the most significant
problem was the shortage of high-quality scientific manpower.[32] In
this context, the leadership soon realized that the damage wrought by
the Cultural Revolution in terms of both research and education had
been far more extensive than originally supposed. At the time, many
Western visitors to the PRC suggested that China's technological capabilities might range from ten to twenty years behind the industrialized
world.[33] Other constraints were associated with the quantity and
quality of laboratory and testing equipment, availability of library
materials, and so forth.

Physical limitations and technical backwardness, while serious,
were overshadowed by more pressing "qualitative" problems associated with the strategic orientation of the S&T modernization program. In essence, there was too much emphasis on basic research and
not enough attention was being given to its application. Part of the
reason that the relations between research and production had not
been well developed was the nature of the command economy and
the fact that factory managers had few incentives to seek out technical
innovations.[34] Under such circumstances, researchers lacked the
appropriate demand from end-users to guide their research. This
problem was further compounded by shortcomings in communication, political attitudes, and the nature of the research environment
in China. These problems relate directly to two primary issues: (1) the
self-perceptions of the scientific community and the relationship

between their collective priorities and those of the economic modernization programs and (2) obstacles to using S&T personnel more effectively, reflecting Deng Xiaoping's belief that "it is not that we do not have talented people, the problem is whether we can better organize them and tap their initiative and use their talents to the full extent."[35]

In an analysis of organizational factors affecting scientific creativity in the United States, Nathan Kaplan cites five critical factors that can significantly affect the potential for innovation and research achievement: (1) receptivity or resistance to new ideas; (2) internal and external pressure to produce; (3) freedom to choose problems and change direction; (4) existence of incentives for creativity; and (5) toleration of novel individuals and their associated work styles.[36] Similar points have been made in other studies of R&D management. These studies point out that the optimal research climate must be one in which leadership behavior supports the norms and values of scientists, especially in terms of professional motivation, self-image, and career ambition.[37] In China, this type of support is just beginning to emerge, though in most cases it is not yet present.

As reports began to reach Beijing concerning all sorts of deviations from stated policy guidelines and continued obstructionism, it became clear that the so-called "leftist" influence in science and technology had not dissipated with the fall of the Gang of Four and the arrival of Deng Xiaoping and his cohorts. As one commentary in Shanghai's *Jiefang Ribao* (Liberation daily) suggested in June 1981, "Leftist errors on the science and technology front are mainly expressed as failure to truly regard science and technology as a productive force; the serious consequences of this are that the subjects and projects for scientific research are incompatible with national economic development and thus are out of joint with it."[38] While the policies being articulated at the center may have reflected a desire for change, the reality at the local level was quite different.

At present there are still many comrades in the Party, including some who are in charge of economic and Party and government leadership, who are insufficiently aware of the importance of science and technology and who do not sufficiently support scientific and technological work. Many Party committees and administrative leadership organs have still failed to put scientific and technical work on their agendas, or pay lip service to its importance, but actually relegate it to a secondary place, so that it loses out when the pressure of work increases.[39]

The effort to promote and popularize science and technology led to all sorts of vulgarizations of Beijing's policies. Some members of the scientific community, anxious to reintegrate themselves within the world scientific community, looked to their colleagues overseas for guidance in selecting research topics and priorities. Others, including stalwarts from the Cultural Revolution, wanting to win favor in Bejing, went through the motions of supporting science and technology, but actually did very little to improve research productivity or the utilization of existing S&T personnel. An article in *Guangming Daily* in January 1981 spelled out some of the more serious manifestations of these two different approaches. The specific problems were reflected in the tendency among many scientists to blindly strive "to catch up and surpass advanced countries" and not paying attention to science and technology work in enterprises or in agriculture and light industry. They were also associated with deficiencies in the management of science and technology resources, frequently resulting in excessive duplication of projects, irrational research plans, mismatches between research tasks and available personnel, and improper use and training of scientific and technically trained individuals.[40]

The fact that, under the reform, experts were still being discriminated against and insufficient importance was attached to science and technology made it difficult, if not impossible, for the leadership to attribute existing problems to "leftist influence." An editorial in *People's Daily* in April 1981 suggested that present problems derived from the fact that (1) no competition was allowed in the system and therefore no attention was paid to economic results and (2) the policy for development of science and technology has never been clear and definite.[41] The general tendency in the aftermath of the Cultural Revolution was to put the S&T system back together the way it had been prior to 1965–1966. Initially, comprehensive reform of the structure and management of the S&T system was not a prime consideration.

It quickly became apparent, however, to key individuals such as Fang Yi, who was, until May 1981, concurrently both the Minister-in-Charge of the State Science and Technology Commission and the President of the Chinese Academy of Sciences, that the centrally orchestrated, plan-oriented Soviet model of science and technology development was inappropriate for addressing all of Chinese needs.

Under the Soviet-style system, there were few incentives for strong links between research and production to materialize.[42] In addition, the vertical structure of the research system promoted compartmentalization rather than cooperation, communication, and coordination. While a highly centralized, task-oriented mode of organization was conducive to accomplishing such major projects as the development of atomic weapons, it was not appropriate for stimulating the type of innovative behavior that leads to new and better-quality products or more efficient production processes.[43] What was needed was not merely a readjustment of existing priorities and management methods, but a complete overhaul of the system, especially with respect to the role and placement of scientists and technical personnel.

THE REFORM OF SCIENCE AND TECHNOLOGY

In spite of the expressed determination to move away from a Soviet-style system, it was not until late 1982 that the government actually began the reform of China's S&T organization and management.[44] In October 1982, Premier Zhao Ziyang used the occasion of the National S&T Awards meeting to point out that China's modernization goals could not be met without improvements in the R&D system.[45] More important, he admonished those who merely paid "lip service" to the call for bringing scientists into fuller play and using S&T to spearhead the modernization drive. His speech was a precursor to the formation of a special leading group for science and technology at the State Council under the supervision of Zhao.[46] In effect, Zhao's decision to take direct charge of the group reflected his desire to put the imprimatur of the premier's office on policies associated with S&T development.

Over the next year or so, a series of policy directives sought a fundamental and far-reaching reform of the science and technology system.[47] These culminated in the March 1985 Central Committee Decision on the Reform of the S&T Management System. The Central Committee document was designed to achieve several objectives. First and foremost, science and technology were to be better coordinated with the economy. While basic research was allowed to continue, the primary focus of research was to be applications in industry, agriculture, or national defense. Consequently, some of the projects favored by the scientific community would be postponed or restructured. The second objective was to promote expanded communication and coordination within the research sector. This was done to avoid excessive duplication, which in some cases had grown quite serious. To achieve this goal, support was given to strengthening the Chinese Scientific and Technological Association (CAST), a semi-government umbrella organization for the more than a hundred professional societies that had reemerged since the fall of the Gang of Four. CAST helped promote academic exchanges, disseminate research results, and provide expertise to government organizations at both the national and local level.

A third objective was to promote expanded transfers of technology in four contexts: from research to production, from the coastal areas to the interior, from the military to the civilian sector, and from abroad to China. In order to facilitate better linkages between research and production, the notion of a contract system was gradually introduced. Under such a system, research units could market their technical capabilities, and enterprises could seek assistance with production-related problems or tasks. The concept that market forces be used to drive the process of technological innovation was one that quickly began to receive attention and support.[48]

The placement of persons with scientific and technical expertise in positions of authority became a priority objective.[49] An earlier example was the replacement in May 1981 of Fang Yi, an administrator by training, as head of the Chinese Academy of Sciences with Lu Jiaxi, a PhD chemist educated in the West. The election of Lu Jiaxi was accompanied by the enlargement of the Scientific Council of the CAS, a 400-person body made up of leading scientists and technical personnel that was responsible for overseeing CAS research planning and evaluation of projects.[50] These changes placed the running of the Academy largely in the hands of scientists. This change in leadership pleased the scientific community, which had long held that only scientifically qualified persons should direct the affairs of this research organization.[51]

The changes at the CAS were merely a first step in the larger attempt to ensure that scientific and technical personnel were moved into decision-making slots in the local and central governments as well as in research institutions and universities.[52] Gradually, the Party's direct role in the research sector began to diminish, as the government directed that at least five-sixths of each scientist's time was to be spent on research-related activities; little, if any, time was left for political study. In early 1982, a "science fund" was created as part of an attempt to introduce the concept of "peer review" into the research-planning process. Proposals are judged by panels of qualified scientists using "objective" criteria for evaluating funding requests for proposed projects.[53]

Scientists, engineers, and technical personnel began to fill positions in municipal and provincial-level agencies. In early 1983, for example, the chief engineer of a chemical company was elected vice-mayor of Tianjin.[54] The case stands out not only because of his research successes in the 1950s, but also because he has had strong family connections with relatives in the United States, a fact that got him into political trouble during the Cultural Revolution. In areas where persons with a technical background were not assigned to formal positions, both individuals and organizations, such as the CAS itself, frequently were requested to provide advice and technical support.

As a result, new impetus was given to the idea of technical consulting. In March 1982, the State Council issued a series of work regulations stating that "units in scientific research, teaching, public health, and industrial and agricultural production may temporarily hire intermediate and high-level scientists and technical personnel as advisers or to teach, give lectures and do scientific research and design work on a part-time basis."[55] These arrangements were institutionalized in January 1983, when a formal consulting organization was established in Beijing in order to provide a mechanism for scientific and technical personnel to offer assistance where needed.[56] According to guidelines provided by Premier Zhao, scientists were to be allowed to offer their services on a part-time basis after they completed their assigned work at their home institution. In return for their services, they were allowed to receive a fee, either on a royalty basis or on a set basis. Once again, organizations as well as individuals were invited to participate. Particular attention was given to the opportunities that such consulting might provide for universities anxious to build up their research capabilities and earn monies for buying needed equipment, and so forth. Shanghai Jiaotong University, for example, was one of the first to take advantage of this situation, earning 1.5 million *yuan* over the space of a year by providing specialized technical assistance to local and ministerial enterprises as well as government organizations.[57]

Underlying the official encouragement of consulting was the desire to deal with the irrational distribution and allocation of S&T personnel that had plagued the research system for many years. A majority of the system's inefficiencies had been due to the overly centralized procedures for assignments. An administrative streamlining, in mid-1981, turned the S&T Cadres Bureau under the State Council over to the Ministry of Labor and Personnel to ensure that future work assignments as well as existing ones would be better managed. It was assumed that the Ministry of Labor and Personnel had a better overview of the country's personnel needs and deficiencies.

One of the more serious problems affecting the S&T personnel structure was the fact that, in some areas, there was an over-concentration of qualified individuals, while in other areas there were inadequate numbers.[58] This problem spanned the range of functional specialization, with some areas, such as Beijing, having an abundance of engineers and others, such as Inner Mongolia, having none or only a limited number.[59] It also spanned the various industrial sectors, with a large concentration of skilled personnel in heavy industry but insufficient numbers in agriculture and light industry. According to *Guangming Daily*, within the industrial ministries, "almost two-thirds of the engineering and technical personnel are concentrated in the two departments of machine-building and metallurgy and all the engineering and technical personnel in light industries combined is less than fifteen percent of the total engineering and technical personnel."[60] In addition, these distribution problems also existed in terms of geography, with the large urban centers, such as Shanghai and Beijing, having more than an adequate supply of S&T personnel and areas within China's interior lacking appreciable numbers of qualified individuals.

Part of the reason for the persistence of these distribution problems was the ideology of departmentalism that pervaded China's S&T establishment, as it does all facets of the bureaucracy. Once a scientist or engineer went to work for a certain ministry or bureau, he literally "belonged" to that unit, thus limiting any real opportunities for job mobility. Another factor that contributed to the situation was the problem of "inbreeding."[61] Many institutions refused to allow their graduates to enter into the work-assignment process, preferring to hoard these people in case of future need. Even though certain types of S&T personnel might have been redundant or underemployed, under the prevailing situation of uncertainty and limited supply it was better to hold on to someone rather than let someone go who might be needed later.

Two other proposals surfaced during the initial discussions concerning reform of the system for S&T personnel. One dealt with salary and living conditions. When asked about their greatest source of dissatisfaction, 82.4 percent of the scientists, engineers, and technical personnel at the Shanghai Laser Research Institute, one of China's premier research units, pointed to problems related to their standard of living. A higher salary was the number-one demand of 34.4 percent.[62] Because of the previous ambivalence about the contribution of their work and their ambiguous political status, intellectuals had been slated to receive very modest wages. In addition, their housing situations had been seriously disrupted because of the Cultural Revolution. In most cases, even in those instances where intellectuals were compensated for their losses after the fall of the Gang of Four, the emphasis on science and technology modernization in Beijing had not translated into better pay and accommodations for the majority of China's scientists and technical personnel. In certain cases, attempts to improve the living conditions of S&T intellectuals were encouraged but, in most instances, were not implemented.

The scientists' financial situation did not improve measurably even with the regime's determined move away from the principle of egalitarianism that had been a major part of the Maoist ethos. The so-called "iron-rice bowl" that allowed individuals to collect their salary irrespective of their accomplishments increasingly gave way to a system of financial rewards for scientific personnel who produce more. In the past, however, because of the tendency of all "to eat from the same big pot," awards received by successful inventors or innovators were divided up within the institute, and at times with other local government organizations. The individual primarily responsible for the research achievement received only a modest financial benefit at best.

The other proposal was to place younger individuals in leading positions with S&T organizations.[63] Due to the existing age structure of the scientific community, many of China's best-trained scientist's are advanced in age. From one perspective, they are still badly needed to ensure that quality standards are maintained within the research system. From another perspective, however, because of their age they cannot handle the heavy administrative and research burdens that are required by the current drive to promote S&T.[64] And, in some cases, because of China's periodic isolation from the mainstream of world S&T affairs over the last three decades, their ideas about research methodology and research priorities reflect training they received many years ago, now badly out of date. Accordingly, one of the dominant themes of the reforms in S&T has been to provide new opportunities for younger scholars and experts. Confronted, however, by the limited number of young individuals with adequate qualifications and the traditional tendency to promote persons primarily on the basis of seniority, this goal has not been easy to accomplish.[65]

Thus, in spite of the sustained pressure on reluctant Party officials and local cadres to pay greater attention to science and technology and the greater authority given to S&T personnel, the reality is that serious implementation problems remain at all levels of society.

Chinese leaders, in their efforts to modernize in a sustained fashion, have linked the reform of the personnel system to the success of the economic reforms announced by Zhao Ziyang at the 3rd Plenary Session of the 12th Central Committee meeting in October 1984. According to Zhao, "In our drive for socialist modernization we must respect knowledge and talented people. We must combat all ideas and practices that belittle science and technology, the cultivation of intellectual resources, and the role of intellectuals. We must take resolute action to redress cases of discrimination against intellectuals which still exist in many localities . . ."[66] As Zhao's speech indicates, ambivalence and mistrust still exist in certain individuals toward intellectuals, including scientists and engineers.

In an effort to ameliorate the relations between officials and S&T intellectuals, the S&T Cadres Bureau was removed in 1984 from the Ministry of Labor and Personnel and placed under the direction of the State Science and Technology Commission. This move recognizes that scientists and technical personnel are somewhat unique and therefore cannot be handled as just another component of the labor force. It represents an explicit attempt to link more closely overall S&T planning with policy-making concerning staffing decisions and the assignment of S&T personnel. At the same time, the Deng leadership introduced additional reforms in the science and technology system.[67] These reforms, announced in a Central Committee document in early March 1985, give official sanction to implementing and broadening many of the proposals that had been introduced during the previous two to three years.[68] They explicitly link the growing emphasis on technology markets and the "commercialization of technology" with the deployment and management of scientists and technical personnel.

Yet, even as momentum builds for pushing ahead with more rapid introduction of reforms, the situation for science and technology remains problematic. The effort to bring more S&T intellectuals into the Party continues to meet sharp resistance. The anti-intellectuals of the Mao era continue to hang on. As one Chinese scholar remarked during a discussion in Beijing in early 1985, "The Cultural Revolution has not been negated." Since 1979, a total of 580,000 "professionals, engineers, and scientists" were admitted into the Party. Yet, according to the Organizational Department of the CCP, only 17.8 percent of the 40.95 million members have received an education above the senior-middle-school level; only 4 percent have received a tertiary education.[69] Some Chinese sources suggest that over 50 percent of the membership is basically illiterate.[70] And, based on statistics in a December 1984 commentary in *Liaowang*, only 22.8 percent of the country's scientific and technical workers belonged to the Party.[71] While this latter figure may seem appreciable, it reflects the ambiguity in the definition of what constitutes an "S&T worker" (a classification sometimes used for marginal S&T personnel) rather than the strong presence of mainstream scientists and engineers in the CCP.

The apparent continued disrespect for scientists is related not only to the make-up of the Party but also to its attitude. According to an article by the Secretary of the Beijing University Party Committee, many people still do not recognize the intellectuals' role in modernization, and even those who do demand higher standards of them than others. Some intellectuals have been considered for Party membership for over ten years, yet, when the membership decision is to be made, certain Party cadres claim "they do not know for sure" and need to continue observing.[72] Similar problems have been encountered by intellectuals in other provinces. In Yunnan, some individuals have applied for membership three to five times but are repeatedly told that "further tests are needed"; in Liaoning, "They regard intellectuals' desire to voice opinions as disrespect toward leaders and their insistence on the correctness of their views as disobedience."[73]

In these cases, the objections to intellectuals are attributed to "the fact that 'leftist' influences have not been totally eliminated." Some "leftist-leaning" cadres view intellectuals as outsiders and feel that "excessive recruitment of new Party members from intellectuals will make the Party degenerate."[74] Or, according to a report by an engineer at the research institute of the Shanxi Electric Power Center, some Party organizations have not even put the recruitment of scientific and technical personnel on their work agenda.[75] An editorial in *People's Daily* in July 1984 identifies seven examples of obstacles due to leftist influences: failure of local party officials to implement the policy on intellectuals; interpreting someone's hard work and dedication as "attempting to climb to the heavens"; being accused of applying for membership under false pretenses; establishing phony criteria in order to find fault, for example, the candidate's voice was too loud; fear of competition; using position and power to sway other members in the direction of one's own prejudice; and introducing bureaucratic bottlenecks as a delaying tactic.[76] In almost each case, the person in question was denied admission; in some cases, they have become so frustrated that they no longer seek admission and, in those few cases where they have gained admission, a number are reconsidering their membership because it appears no longer to hold the attraction and promise it did in the past.

Nonetheless, an increase in the number of scientists and technical personnel who are Party members is seen as a strategic objective of the current leadership. According to an editorial in *People's Daily* in November 1984, "Recruiting large numbers of Party members from among intellectuals who are qualified for Party membership will not impair the Party's nature but is precisely an important measure to raise the overall quality of the vanguard of the working class and to build our Party into a strong core leading socialist modernization."[77] At the present time, the Party is having trouble determining a role for itself and responding to the emphasis being placed on scientific knowledge and technological advance. In July 1983, Hu Qiaomu met with scientists who are Party members of the CAS. At that meeting, Hu specified three goals for these individuals: they should play an exemplary and leading role in scientific research work; they should struggle against all erroneous and reactionary tendencies, and give their support to the Party's directives; and they should strive to be models in Party activities.[78] As the requirements of modernization increase, the Party must have individuals who can play this dual role and serve as models for present and future Party members. Unless the CCP can successfully transform its image and the image of the ideal Party member, there will be little incentive for technically oriented persons to consider membership.

Consistent with and related to this line of thinking is the current attempt to ensure that persons with scientific and technical skills also are placed in leading positions in the military. According to a State Council directive, the central government will successively assign university graduates to various military units to become "military and political leading cadres."[79] In addition, the National Defense Science, Technology, and Industries Commission (NDSTIC), the counterpart to the SSTC, has implemented a series of engineering and technical courses so that the skill levels of defense leaders can be upgraded.[80] Here again, the goal is to develop individuals who possess the technical expertise to serve the country's defense needs while at the same time having the political outlook consistent with the political requirements of the military's party organs—a task not easily accomplished.

Cases where the "leftist" bias toward scientists and technical personnel has been overcome have been given wide publicity in the Chinese press, an indication that, up to the present, these are unusual rather than the norm. At the Nanjing Forest Chemicals Research Institute, 25 of the last 28 persons admitted into the Party were scientists and technicians. And, between 1978 and mid-1984, the proportion of scientists and technicians at this institute who are Party members has risen from 12.5 percent to 26.3 percent.[81] In another case, Bei Zhaohan, the Party Secretary in a Guangzhou pharmaceutical factory, was commended for his role in expanding the use of technically trained individuals.[82] After becoming Party Secretary and Director of the factory, he immediately brought in a technical person to serve as deputy director. In addition, he brought several technicians to his factory and gave them responsible positions, even though they had "bad political labels." In a third case, Wang Hao, a professor of systems engineering and mathematics, was made Party Secretary at the National Defense Science and Technology University. His appointment was cited because he was able to maintain his research activities while performing well in his new administrative post.[83]

The difficulties that S&T intellectuals have experienced in joining the Party reflect the inconsistent implementation of the Party's overall policy toward intellectuals. In many respects, the unevenness derives from a general lack of commitment on the part of local cadres to the modernization of science and technology:

> . . . there are some comrades who neither fully understand the backward state of China's science and technology, nor do they comprehend the reality that the world's science and technology is developing daily. As a result, they simply have little interest in modern S&T, so they lack a sense of urgency for studying and mastering them, or for reforming China's backwardness. To a certain extent, they are still in a fuzzy-minded state, even to the point of consciously or unconsciously setting up obstacles to the development of science and technology."[84]

At times, this situation has prevented the research environment within several institutes from evolving into the type of creative setting described by Kaplan. On other occasions, an unwillingness to listen to scientists and engineers can lead to waste and other inefficiencies. In a Jiangsu province pharmaceuticals plant, for example, an engineer was elected to manage the facility. The Party Secretary, however, failed to follow the advice of the new manager regarding the testing of raw alcohol and used the untested alcohol in making several drugs. Consequently, 80,000 bottles of cough medicine had to be discarded, representing a loss of over 30,000 *yuan*.[85]

In other cases, inaction in implementing the policy toward intellectuals derives from outright prejudice or self-interest. In Xuchang City, located in Henan, strong criticisms appeared in the local newspapers and radio broadcasts concerning "the city's malpractices" toward intellectuals.[86] For example, at the Xuchang City Machine Tools Accessories Factory, officials turned a deaf ear to the new policies—even though they acknowledged their existence and legitimacy. In the city's construction commission, an intellectual consistently was ignored because he reported continued instances of bias and discrimination to higher officials. Consequently, many of the city's scientific and technical personnel petitioned to leave the city. Similar problems exist regarding the treatment of S&T personnel who have returned to China after receiving training abroad. Along with facing problems associated with the absence of specialized equipment, many of the returnees encounter such problems as jealousy and bureaucratic red tape—which ultimately affect their ability to make a contribution.[87] According to a mid-1984 survey by the China Science and Technology Association in Tianjin, 24 of the 52 S&T personnel who have returned from abroad noted that they could not carry out any useful experiments under the prevailing administrative structure, because they are unable to decide on their own research subjects or choose their own assistants.[88]

In certain cases when intellectuals have experienced mistreatment, government officials have taken action to rectify their problems. In Heilongjiang, the Provincial Party Committee dismissed the Party Secretary, the President and one Vice-President of the Provincial Urban Planning and Design Institute for persecuting intellectuals.[89] According to the charges, four of the institute's main technical workers were discriminated against and evaluated mainly on the basis of whether they were obedient or not. When the situation became known to the provincial CCP, they immediately acted to remove the guilty parties. One way in which local and national authorities have begun to respond to these types of situations has been to send investigation teams to various units to inspect their adherence to the policy on intellectuals. The Ministry of Communications, for example, sent an inspection team to one of their enterprises in Hubei after the Party Secretary was accused of "bullying" intellectuals.[90] Though different in their basic orientation, these investigation teams are similar to ones that were sent out during the Maoist era to ensure adherence to Mao's political formula for administration and personnel management.[91]

Several instances have been publicized of officials taking away some or all of the rewards given to scientists and engineers for their expertise. In Guangxi, the renumeration received by an engineer from the Regional Institute of Urban Planning and Design for solving a technical problem for two well-drilling teams was regarded by certain officials as "the proceeds of corruption."[92] In addition, a salary grade hike that had been awarded to the engineer for a regional, first-class technological innovation several months earlier was held back for thirteen months. In a similar case in Sichuan, a junior engineer used his technical expertise to help the Linyang Fertilizer Factory overcome its operating difficulties.[93] According to the contract signed between the engineer and the factory, he would receive 5 percent of the profit earned by the factory if he succeeded or would be charged 5 percent of its losses if the unit continued to lose money. When it turned out that the engineer's work enabled the factory to generate a 240,000-*yuan* profit, he was to be given a 15,000 *yuan* award. Some people, however, suggested that 15,000 was too much for one person to get and that it was unfair. Even though the engineer was eventually awarded the funds by the local Party committee, the dispute most likely raised his apprehension about engaging in future endeavors.

Moreover, the financial benefit and recognition for scientific and technical achievements usually prove less than initially offered. In one case involving the provincial Academy of Agricultural Science in Zhejiang, each time an award was won, each of the actual recipients received as little as 10 percent of the total prize. In most instances, the political and administrative departments took 10 percent, then the service department took 12 percent, the library took 3 percent, the research institute grabbed 15 percent, and the farm took 10 percent.[94] In Beijing, a researcher at the Institute of Posts and Telecommunications had his achievement twice rejected because an envious colleague claimed that it was not really an invention and that he was actually a co-inventor. His accuser marshaled support for his claims from the Institute Party officials, thus delaying recognition of the researcher's accomplishment. Eventually, however, after a thorough evaluation of the product by higher-level officials, the researcher finally received his financial award.[95]

The ongoing efforts to give greater mobility to S&T personnel have also encountered obstacles. At a national forum on the reform of scientific personnel management in July 1984, five measures to promote job mobility among China's scientists and engineers were formally announced.[96] The main objective of the new program is to combine various features of a labor market with the prevailing system of planned assignment. Under this system, outside units can make job offers to selected S&T personnel in other units who can then tender their resignations. The purpose of the plan is to promote the flow of technical expertise to needed areas. It is also designed to facilitate technology transfers through movement of personnel.

Various steps have been taken to implement facets of the program to promote greater mobility. In mid-1986, the State Council issued a circular on "promoting rational transfers of scientists and technicians" to facilitate a more effective job assignment situation.[97] A new system of post-doctoral employment also has been established and put into trial use at the Institute of Theoretical Physics of the CAS. The rules stipulate that anyone who receives a doctorate from the Institute must find a job elsewhere. And persons with degrees from abroad or other Chinese institutions can seek out a position at the Institute by entering into a two-year employment contract.[98] In addition, the former Ministry of Education (now the State Education Commission) has agreed to allow consultations between universities and work units to improve the assignment of college graduates.[99] At a meeting held by the leading group for science and technology under the State Council, various participants from the industrial ministries agreed to transfer 363 S&T personnel from their factories and research units to support 13 major national construction projects.[100] In Guangdong, several engineers at the Huangpu Shipyard were allowed to resign and change jobs.[101] Yet, concerns about possible brain-drain problems from the interior to the coast and particularly the stubborn adherence to departmentalism prevent large-scale job mobility in the immediate future.[102]

According to a report from the National Talent Exchange Consulting Service Center under the Ministry of Labor and Personnel, it has received more than 1,200 requests for job transfers.[103] Out of this number, more than 930 are from persons who are employed in jobs unrelated to their training and more than 240 are from persons who are actually underemployed because their units are overstaffed. These two categories account for 89 percent of the people registered at the center. At the same time, over 180 units have given requests to the center, identifying over 2,100 vacancies. Yet, despite this situation, the number of requests that can be filled is extremely small because of bureaucratic conventions. The exchange center must gain the consent of three parties—the unit in need of personnel, the individual concerned, and the original work unit. In addition, the original units frequently request the return of the transferred workers' housing or they require payment from the receiving unit to cover the cost of training or to compensate for the loss of qualified personnel. In one case, the fee amounted to 2,000 *yuan* in advance.

IMPLICATIONS FOR THE FUTURE

In spite of the concerted and determined efforts underway to improve the status and utilization of scientific and technical personnel, serious obstacles remain. As one source has remarked, "The phenomenon of overstocking, wasting, and misusing scientists and technicians has not been fundamentally eliminated." Some of the bottlenecks are inherent in a Communist regime's relationship to the S&T community.

The Party's claim to legitimate authority rests on the basis of its *scientific* understanding of the laws of socialist development. It must be able to mobilize the country's S&T resources to promote national development, but, at the same time, it must also ensure the political loyalty of the scientific community to give credibility to its "scientific" interpretations.[104] The Party seeks control to achieve these ends; scientific and technical personnel seek autonomy. In China, as in the Soviet Union, the effort to incorporate the scientific and technical community into the policy-making apparatus will most likely alter the character of the Party-S&T relationship and give new definition to the nature of political authority. Yet, the extent and pace of the change will continue to be a source of tension for some years to come.

Other bottlenecks reflect the self-interest and prejudices of political cadres who do not want to relinquish their positions to a new elite. Still others derive from the physical limitations, especially the limited numbers of S&T personnel. While each of these is amenable to some change, the difficulties encountered over the last several years of reforms suggest that a confluence of structural and attitudinal forces existing since 1949 will continue to obstruct effective implementation of the policy toward S&T intellectuals.

Nevertheless, the current attempt to grant more autonomy to the S&T community and to introduce a variety of institutionalized mechanisms for evaluating research proposals and projects, such as the science fund administered by CAS, could alter the relationship between this community and the state. To a certain degree, it will allow the scientific community to be relatively more "independent." The concurrent decision to bring greater market-type forces to bear on the selection and outcome of research will also foster more autonomy for scientists and for the role of science and research in China. Some will clearly oppose putting financial incentives in the forefront of the scientific endeavor. Others will view the contract system as a means to decrease further dependence on the state. While there may be a split among Chinese scientists, with some attached to the ideal concept of pure science and peer review, and others becoming more comfortable with being judged by the market, the bigger split will continue to be between the scientists and the traditional echelons of the bureaucracy.

The ongoing attempt to incorporate more scientific and technical personnel into the leadership ranks at all levels promises to have important implications for the evolving nature of China's political and social system. The possible parallels with the Soviet Union are obvious, but it remains to be seen whether China will look like the Soviet Union in the years ahead. It was suggested early on that Deng may have gone further than the Soviets in his policies toward S&T intellectuals. His willingness to allow computerization to grow in order to facilitate communication among scientists contrasts sharply with similar Soviet approaches toward the use of computers in the past. Deng's objective is not simply to coopt this group, but rather, in some respects, to have them "coopt" the Party, like the literati of old. While Chinese leaders do not want a society run by scientists and engineers, they know that their capacity to achieve the goals set out in the modernization program cannot be attained without the full and sustained support of the country's S&T community and institutions.

In time, Party membership may become subordinate to technical qualifications as the key to upward career mobility. If present trends continue, scientists may look less and less to the Party as a source of prestige. At the same time, they must be sensitive to the demands of modernization and not be taken by catchy themes such as "The third wave" or "The new global technological revolution." The current environment in which S&T intellectuals have slowly begun to flourish is a fair-weather one. Their ability to gain additional freedom and mobility is based on the asumption that the modernization program will move ahead, albeit gradually, without any major problems. In some important respects, the scientific community remains vulnerable to being caught up in a future political struggle if the present levels of political balance and cooperation break down. From the perspectives of both sides, their present alliance with Deng Xiaoping may be one of convenience rather than desire. And, obviously, the newly acquired perquisites of the scientists and technical personnel could be easily taken away should the political winds shift in an unfavorable direction. Barring any major political disruptions, their future may well depend on their "successes" with respect to meeting the needs of the country's industrial, agricultural, and defense sectors.

Despite promising reforms, the position of S&T personnel is still ambiguous. There will always be those who do not trust scientists and technicians. And there are many vested interests that will be upset by efforts to promote S&T intellectuals. In all likelihood, there will be changes at the margins, but it will be some time before China's scientific community can feel comfortably secure in its newly acquired high-status position. This point became particularly clear in late 1986 and early 1987 when several scientists who had become heavily involved in "the movement for democracy" were severely reprimanded by China's political leadership. It will therefore be up to Deng and his successors to ease the apprehensions of the scientific community by ensuring that campaigns such as the one against "spiritual pollution" do not threaten the security and access that China's scientists have obtained over the last several years. Since it will be difficult to provide any guarantees in this respect, there will remain an uneasy tension between China's scientists and the system's political cadres.

Age Distribution of Intellectuals

Age Group	% of Total Number of Intellectuals
60+	4.0
55–59	3.5
50–54	6.4
45–49	12.7
40–44	17.6
35–39	12.9
30–34	9.4
25–29	12.5
20–24	10.9
15–19	10.0
	100.0

Source: *Guangming Daily,* 17 June 1984, p. 2.

Distribution of Intellectuals by Profession

Field	Intellectuals as % of Total Intellectuals	Intellectuals as % of Total Employed in Field
Education	31.9	12.81
Industry	24.6	1.56
State Organs	9.4	7.08
Public Health	8.2	9.50
Scientific Research	6.9	30.60
Construction	4.3	1.77
Agriculture	2.4	0.03
Communications	2.0	1.02
Commerce	1.7	0.63
Culture and Art	1.6	6.45
Management	1.3	9.87
Geology	1.1	6.69
Party Organs	0.9	4.66
Forestry	0.6	0.97
Animal Husbandry	0.1	0.15
	100.0	

Source: *Guangming Daily,* 17 June 1984, p. 2.

PART THREE

Critical Intellectuals

A Spectre is haunting the Chinese intellectual world.
—Wang Ruoshui

CHAPTER   SIX

The Emergence of Humanism: Wang Ruoshui and the Critique of Socialist Alienation

DAVID A. KELLY

Wang Ruoshui, a deputy editor of *People's Daily,* was removed from his position at the outset of the Campaign against Spiritual Pollution in late October 1983. He was closely associated with the discussion of "humanism" and the "theory of socialist alienation" which were primary targets of the campaign. Without naming him, many officially inspired criticisms made direct reference to his views. These had been promoted in the widest political arena by his close ally, Zhou Yang.[1] Zhou's reliance on these ideas in an address to the Marx Centenary conference in March 1983 helped make Wang a byword for heterodoxy, and placed him in the forefront of an intellectual grouping which may be described as China's revisionist counter-elite.[2]

Wang returned to his post on *People's Daily* in late 1984, and was in the interim able to circulate "internally" a reply to the criticisms that had been aimed at him from the highest official level by Hu Qiaomu, Politburo member and ostensibly the leading ideological spokesman among Deng Xiaoping's supporters. Although *People's Daily* returned to an "intellectually emancipated" line, Wang's editorial involvement with it was no longer as visible as it had been. His prestige, high already among young people in particular, was heightened by the way he handled his moment of truth, disdaining to make an about-face or even a self-criticism, as others who were charged with "spiritual pollution" had done.[3]

On the other hand, his outspokenness and intransigence are unlikely to be forgotten in official circles. In June 1985, Hu Yaobang was questioned by Hong Kong journalist Lu Keng (publisher of *Bai Xing*) over the leadership's apparent ostracism of Wang Ruoshui, whom Lu compared favorably with his opponents Secretariat member Deng Liqun and Hu Qiaomu. Hu Yaobang replied that "Comrade Wang Ruoshui has his shortcomings, and you cannot describe him as being perfect." Praised with faint damns in this way, Wang appears to have lived down his official disfavor.[4] Although he was said still to be "in moderate trouble" in 1986, he was retained at *People's Daily*, but without a post and unable to travel abroad.[5]

Born in 1926, a Hunanese, Wang Ruoshui graduated in philosophy from Beijing University around 1948 and went to work in the theoretical department of *People's Daily* in the early post-Liberation period.[6] In the preface to the collection *Zai Zhexue Zhansheng Shang* (On the philosophy front, hereafter cited as *ZZZS*) dated 11 June 1979, Wang divides his writings into five groups. The first consists of critiques of the non-Marxist philosophers Hu Shi and Liang Shuming, which he now admits to be "deficient." The second is of popular articles promoting the Hundred Flowers Campaign. The third group, written between 1957 and 1961, opposes the "'left' and right tendencies of that period." Wang mentions being sent down to the countryside (*xiafang*) in the late 1950s. Returning in 1959, he was involved in controversies with Yang Xianzhen, the Party School Director, philosopher, and proponent of "two combining into one," a slogan in favor of moderation. The fourth group of papers, on the general topic of "(social) being and consciousness," preceded the campaign against Yang Xianzhen in 1964, led by Mao and Ai Siqi.[7] Wang now sees this campaign as "fundamentally mistaken," but polemical exchanges with

Yang have continued down to recent years.[8] The last group of papers, regarded by Wang as his mature work, deals with alienation and human nature.

Wang owed his advancement at *People's Daily* in part, it is said, to Deng Tuo, the journalist-writer who criticized Mao in the early 1960s and was the first victim of the Cultural Revolution.[9] Wang is a Party member and has held high positions, including membership in the Central Committee for Discipline and Inspection (1978–1982), and as delegate to the 5th National People's Congress. Despite criticism in the Spiritual Pollution Campaign, he is a committed Marxist who, in introducing his collected essays, did not neglect to mention the stimulus of Mao Zedong on his development. Yet, shortly before, in February 1979, he had made unusually forthright and widely circulated criticisms of Mao's personality cult at a CCP Central Committee theoretical conference.[10] Attraction toward the thin ice of a conceptual distinction—as implied here, between Mao as a personal source of inspiration and as a symbol of alienated leadership—is perhaps characteristic of Wang.

Wang's criticisms of "modern superstition," as the cult of Mao is abstractly referred to in China, coincided with the movement for intellectual emancipation or "emancipation of the mind" (*sixiang jiefang*) of 1979–1980. The interpretation of this slogan depended on one's place in society. For the new leadership of Deng Xiaoping and Hu Yaobang, it meant emancipation from the thinking of the "whateverists," that is, Hua Guofeng and other remnants of the radical era who obediently followed Mao, whatever his position. It also meant a search for new forms of consensus by responding to popular interests, and reinterpretation of Marxism-Leninism-Mao Zedong thought.[11] For the "lost generation" of political outsiders—youth sent down to the countryside and others who had been denied the chance of betterment in the socialist system—it meant for a time the hope of unprecedented democratic freedoms. Depoliticization promised to remove the stigma of class origin, and to allow the development of a meritocracy based on expertise. For many writers and artists, the emancipation of thinking meant official endorsement of a new diversity of style and subject matter. For intellectuals in general, it was a reaffirmation of their role as arbiters and champions of society's fundamental values and attitudes, and as participants in the state. For some it supported an attempt to shape an ethical consensus arising from the Cultural Revolution in which Deng Xiaoping and many other Party leaders had themselves been victims.

From this attempt a particular grouping arose within the establishment intellectuals which had sympathetic ties with its less advantaged allies, the disenfranchised youth and others frustrated by the Cultural Revolution's aftermath. When the democratic-rights movement was forced underground following Deng Xiaoping's suppression of the movement and consolidation of power in 1979–1980, the alienation movement came to the fore among highly placed intellectuals. They could press for humanist, pluralist values openly and within the system as long as their ideas could be seen as having a Marxist basis. This is the circle that Ding Wang calls the "alienation school" (*yihualun pai*). Ding wrote in 1982:

The main currents of the movement for intellectual enlightenment in China are the "alienation school" and the "tragic-literature school." Their social influence is far beyond that of the "democratic-rights movement." Western critics and scholars have paid attention only to the democratic-rights movement, but disregard or misunderstand the former two, which prevents them from fully appreciating the intellectual-enlightenment movement.[12]

The alienation group resembles the "counter-elites" Ludz described as emerging in East Germany and other socialist states, whose criticism "aimed at the very core of the official ideology, with a certain exegesis, which claims to be true and correct, of the historical heritage."[13] The alienation group in China has attempted to act as the party's conscience, demanding that it recognize its complicity in the personality cult of Chairman Mao. It has made use of the Marxist theory of alienation as a critical weapon in the service of humanist ethical values, and stressed, like Ludz's "counter-elite," Marxism's continuity with the Enlightenment. This group is not merely a temporary faction within the intelligentsia, but one of the most articulate and vocal of the newly distinct intellectual interest groups[14] emerging in the wake of the Cultural Revolution.

PHILOSOPHY AND
INSTITUTIONALIZED REVISIONISM

Wang has used his journalistic position, his name, and the support of powerful patrons to campaign in public, but, to quote the title of his collected writings, these have been campaigns "on the philosophical front." As Tang Tsou puts it, "The real significance of ideological theses in China can be detected only when they are understood both in their theoretical context and in the light of the real situation confronting the political actors and the society."[15] Wang's political survival has depended on the inherent appeal of his position to "enlightened" members of the leadership. But the intellectual interest group he represénts is more than a theoretical front set up by a faction among the political elite. The writings of Wang and his colleagues exceed any "contractual obligations" to a faction. While helping Deng Xiaoping and his supporters make ideology more appropriate to the new political and economic initiatives, Wang and the "alienation school" have opposed a certain drift in the way this has been handled, and have conflicted not merely with "orthodoxy" but sometimes with their erstwhile political allies.

Ludz's frame of reference can be usefully transposed to the Chinese case. He postulates two rival forms of revisionism—one utopian, calling for ethical purism, and one "rational-cognitive," which lays emphasis on modernization of the social system. While both have made attempts to revive Marx's concept of alienation as a critical tool, the latter school of thought often reduces alienation under socialism to "technical" alienation, which will supposedly be abolished by progress and a new order of rationality linked to cybernetics.[16] In China, as in Ludz's examples for Eastern Europe, we find the rediscovery of "alienation" in the aftermath of dogmatic excesses, which threatened to divest the ideology of any transcendental moorings beyond the cult of the leader and party. Severe probings of such pillars of orthodoxy as the dialectics of nature[17] and the epistemological theory of "reflection" are clearly part of the same syndrome. Also similar to Eastern Europe is China's enthusiasm for cybernetics, informatics, futurology, and "science of science," summed up in the idea of the scientific and technological revolution. One would extend this to the proposal by Zhao Ziyang and others of possible leaps to a "Third Wave" of post-industrialization.

The theoretical counter-elite of Wang Ruoshui and the "alienation school," however, do not seek utopia in modern forces of production. Their thrust is in the direction of ethical purism, expressible as the salvation of alienated man. This was signaled at an abstract level by Ru Xin, a Vice-President of the Chinese Academy of Social Sciences (CASS) and philosophical ally of Wang Ruoshui, who wrote in *People's Daily*, in July 1983: "The definition of the overall direction of modernization cannot be solved by any particular scientific discipline, and it is up to philosophy to provide a solution. What is needed is a philosophical guiding thought oriented to overall design."[18]

FORMATION OF THE ALIENATION SCHOOL

One day last year, a famous poet of the older generation told me very seriously, "Having gone through the ten years of turmoil under Lin Biao and the Gang of Four's feudal fascist dictatorship, and having witnessed so many acts of inhuman barbarity dressed up in 'ultrarevolutionary' phrases, I swore to myself that from now on I would not take part in any criticism of humanism."

Recounting this in 1980, Ru Xin remarked, "Such words make one think, and they awakened doubts long submerged in my heart, and forced me to undertake a new consideration of . . . humanism."[19]

There is a double irony in this anecdote. Ru Xin was unable to hold the line against criticism during the Spiritual Pollution Movement three years later. The other irony is that his 1980 statement was itself a recantation. Ru Xin had been a prominent critic of humanism in the early 1960s, when he lambasted the views of the historian and humanist Zhou Gucheng as "a clumsy refurbished version of the bourgeois theory of human nature."[20] Unlike Zhou Gucheng and so many targets of past campaigns against humanism, the advocates of humanism in the post-Mao era are not members of the old bourgeois intelligentsia but trained Marxists who, in many cases, won their spurs as critics of the former group. Thus, Wang Ruoshui figured in criticism of Hu Shi and Liang Shuming in the mid-1950s; Ru Xin in that of Zhou Gucheng; Zhou Yang was officially in charge of many such campaigns. To portray them as blindly seizing on the fads of Western Marxology because of hatred of the radical era is what Hu Qiaomu (see p. 80) has referred to as a caricature, and not a minor one.

Of course, the inner world of the intellectuals associated with Zhou Yang was far from simple at any time. In several cases, criticism campaigns of the Maoist period were handled in such a way as to limit the number of victims, or even to shield some targets from real damage. Ambivalence about the issues at stake in such campaigns can often be detected. Zhou Yang's speech on "Fighting Tasks" (1963) made particular attacks on the revisionists in the socialist world, and the Marxist humanism associated with them. In the process,

he touched on a topic seldom discussed in the PRC, the Marxist theory of aliena-tion. Though he ultimately rejected the validity of this concept, the fact that he alluded to alienation at all suggests that the feeling was palpable in intellectual circles.[21]

It is useful analytically to separate "feelings of alienation" from alienation as an impersonal process,[22] but Goldman's point that the concept was not in universal disfavor is borne out: Wang Ruoshui's 1978 essay "On the Concept of 'Alienation'" was written in 1963–1964 for a theory group under the direction of Zhou Yang.[23] For all its modest disclaimers, it is a solid introduction to the Hegelian and Marxist sources. Taking full note of Marx and Engels's repudiation of the abstract alienation of Bauer, Stirner, and other neo-Hegelians, Wang was already of the view that, "while they expounded the phe-nomenon of alienation under private ownership, Marx and Engels did not hold that alienation came into being only through the appearance of the latter."[24] Though he does not press this point, it indirectly sup-ports the thesis of the reappearance of alienation under socialism. Wang simply says that overcoming alienation entails changing the social system, particularly by developing its productive forces.[25] He argues forcefully that alienation was not phased out of Marx's thought but was placed on a scientific basis (historical materialism) and developed. Wang pointedly closes with a discussion of the nature of individual freedom under communism, taking his text from *The German Ideology:*

The illusory community, in which individuals have up to now combined, always took on an independent existence in relationship to them, and was at the same time, since it was the combination of one class over against another, not only a completely illusory community, but a new fetter as well. In the real community the individuals obtain their freedom in and through their association.[26]

"It is as individuals that individuals participate in it," not as subjects of the state, Marx and Engels had gone on to say of the revolutionary community.

Most of Wang Ruoshui's post-1980 writings are aimed at the general reading public. He has left the hard slogging of textual scholarship to others. His two influential essays of 1980, "Marxism and Intellectual Emancipation" and "Discussing the Alienation Question," appeared in widely circulated journals, whereas "On the Concept of 'Aliena-tion'" had appeared in an esoteric collection of essays.[27]

The article "Marxism and Intellectual Emancipation" is openly polemical, and indicates Wang's determination to resist the re-imposi-tion of dogmatic limits on Marxist interpretation. The central issue is the fallibility of Marxism: its openness to correction and reformula-tion, as opposed to the traditional insistence on infallibility, on a timeless, absolute truth embodied in doctrine. A fallible Marxism had been proposed during the debate over "practice as the sole criterion for testing the truth," notably by Zhou Yang in his role as CASS Vice-President,[28] but the trend had been effectively stopped by the proclamation of the "four basic principles" in 1979–1980 – uphold socialism, the dictatorship of the proletariat, the Communist Party, and Marxism-Leninism-Mao Zedong Thought. Although intellectual emancipation was being wound down, Wang Ruoshui wrote:

> Marxism must constantly be supplemented, revised, developed through testing practice; as soon as it comes to a stop, its life is over; it will be Marxism no longer but dogmatism. Not only is dogma not Marxism, it is the antithesis of Marxism. Originally, Marxism was intellectually emancipated, but in its developmental process it was susceptible to dogmatization at the hands of some people. In this way, the instrument of intellectual emancipation became a fetter constricting the mind. If I may use a somewhat unfamiliar philosophical term, this is the "aliena-tion" of Marxism.[29]

Hence intellectual emancipation is of itself the upholding of Marx-ism, is the requirement of Marxism.

Wang's view of dogmatism as alienated ideology was strongly developed in the celebrated "Discussing the Alienation Question," a month later (June 1980). This paper forms the basic text both of Zhou Yang's Marx Centenary address and of Hu Qiaomu's counterblast. Wang notes the long history of the concept of alienation, its contem-porary importance to studies of Marx in Eastern Europe and else-where, and its denial in the Soviet Union, followed by the reluctant admission that alienation is indeed to be found there. He recalls as well Zhou Yang's 1963 references to these developments. Departing from the technical definition in terms of "subject" and "object," Wang illustrates alienation with a parable of a mother and her renegade son. Not only will he not accept her supervision, he on the contrary supervises her, seeing her as his adversary. She in turn sees him not as a son but as an alien element within the family.

Pursuing the reworking of the concept in Marx's works up to and including *Capital*, Wang notes Marx's belief that alienated labor is the key to all other forms of alienation. But socialism raises the question of whether expunging alienated labor is sufficient as well as necessary.[30] Wang believes that it is not. Despite the socialization of the means of production, alienation is indeed found in at least three main forms—intellectual, political, and economic.

While the expression *alienated Marxism* is not used in the article, dogmatism is still seen as the root of a process of which the personality cult is only the climax. Wang sees the personality cult as a willing transfer to the leader of powers and dignities that rightfully belong to "the people." This is alienation of the leader from the people (much as labor is alienated from the worker under commodity production). The complicity of the people in reversing the true order of dependence is emotionally rooted:

This matter cannot be completely attributed to Lin Biao and the Gang of Four. Many people, including myself, also propagated the superstition, out of adoration then, totally out of adoration then . . . "To summon a spirit is easy, to dispel it is hard."[31]

Hu Qiaomu in the Spiritual Pollution Campaign objected strongly to categorizing as political alienation the transformation of officials, the people's "servants," into their "masters" (*laoye*). Hu's charge that the analysis falls back upon the slogans of the Cultural Revolution seems misplaced. True, Wang refers to Engels's warnings, in his introduction to Marx's *The Civil War in France*, that workers must ensure their ability to recall elected officials who abuse their positions, but the tone is quite restrained, almost tentative: "Nowadays it is of course impracticable to require leading cadres to receive the wages of common workers as in the Paris commune. But we should adopt their spirit, and oppose the extension of privilege." Wang seems unwilling or unable to develop his analysis of power alienation, allowing it to stop short at the level of metaphor.[32]

Economic alienation is traced in its turn to forces for which the ownership system is indifferent. In the formulation taken up verbatim by Zhou Yang in 1983, "There can still be alienation, because man may still have imperfect knowledge of the laws of social development" and hence remain within the toils of commodity production. This view of alienation is not to be confused with alienation under capitalism. Under socialism, there are clear cases of alienated human effort rebounding out of control, in the forms of bureaucratic bungles, environmental spoilage, and massive waste. These become inhuman agencies with lives of their own. This is not the fault of the socialist system, but of particular misapplications of theory—abuses, aberrations, or the results of ignorance.

In September 1980, Wang Ruoshui took up one of the practical consequences of this position in his "Literature and Art and the Alienation of Man," published in the Shanghai daily *Wenhui bao*. The writer or artist should criticize and protest against, rather than affirm and praise, manifestations of alienation in daily life. In replacing social nature with class nature, dogmatic Marxism had made "man" into an abstraction:

A hero in literary works based on the model of an abstract man is only aware of "revolution," "struggle," and being "lofty and perfect." He fails to see his relationships with his family or spouse, completely ignores love and marriage. Such a character often lacks human feelings . . . he can only be the incarnation of concepts of class.[33]

The opposition of "social" and "class" nature used here builds on the remarks on the "illusory community" made in his 1978 essay on alienation. Far from advocating that literature should be devoted to "the expression of alienation," as some critics have implied,[34] Wang points out that official literature produced according to Mao's *Talks on Literature and Art at the Yan'an Forum* had flooded the culture with alienated imagery; there was in fact no shortage of its expression.

Wang again addressed the question of literature in his "Literature, Politics, People" during the nationwide celebration of Mao's *Talks* in spring 1982.[35] Here he challenged outright the principle of "literature serving politics." Whom does literature serve? Serving the people cannot be equated with serving politics; politics is part of the superstructure, whereas the people's material and spiritual needs are not. Literature and politics, as superstructural elements, are equally liable to fall out of alignment with the economic base. There may be occasions on which literature is more accurate a mediator of the people's needs than is political authority. Here Wang is clearly of a mind with Liu Binyan, Wang Ruowang, and other literary intellectuals (see the relevant contributions to this volume). Wang traces the roots of the "literary hells" of the Cultural Revolution to the distortion of politics into an illusory two-line struggle—but this was no error of interpretation due merely to the Gang of Four: "The Cultural Revolution was not a question of a small number of people, it was a problem of the Party, it was a mistake committed by the Party."

THE DEMANDS OF HUMANISM

Wang made two major theoretical statements on humanism: "Man is the Point of Departure of Marxism" (1982) and "A Defense of Humanism" (1983).[36] The changing political situation is reflected in a certain defensiveness; there is more effort to forestall charges of dealing with "abstract" humanity and "ahistorical" alienation.

The first of these articles reverts to academic concern with the interpretation of Marxist texts. It recapitulates the argument that historical materialism does not overturn "man" as the methodological starting point, but places this starting point on a concrete, dialectical footing. Further, holds Wang, the law discerned in *Capital* which illuminated the revolutionary mission of the proletariat is the law of surplus value, which again is a scientific elaboration of the earlier theory of alienated labor. The "Defense of Humanism" opens with a dramatic variation on the first words of the *Communist Manifesto:* "A spectre is haunting the Chinese world—the spectre of man," and closes with

 —A spectre haunts the intellectual world . . .

"Who are you?"

"I am man."

Wang notes the flood of writing about humanism in the previous three years, and sees in this more than a simple reaction to the ten years of disorder. It also reflects the demand for a "highly civilized, highly democratic society." But well-meaning comrades disparage "humanism" as heretical. Wang recapitulates and reinforces many of the earlier arguments against this. Marxism subscribes to the "value of man," which is common to humanism in all its manifestations.

This principle was seen in the revolutionary humanism (*geming rendaozhuyi*) of the liberation war period, an exhortation to display even to the enemy the superior ethical standards of socialism. This slogan somehow survived the Cultural Revolution. Of greater significance in the "Defense of Humanism" are the four concrete demands which translate the "value of man" into political terms:

1. Firmly abandon the "total dictatorship" and cruel struggle of the Cultural Revolution; abandon the personality cult which deifies a human being and degrades the people; uphold the equality of every person before the truth and the law; and uphold the sanctity of personal freedom and dignity.

2. Oppose feudal ranks and concepts of privilege; oppose capitalist money worship and the making of people into commodities or simple tools; demand that people genuinely be seen as people, and assess the individual's worth on the basis of what he is in himself [*cong yige ren benshen*] and not on the basis of origins, position, or wealth.

3. Recognize man as the goal, not only of socialist production but of all work; we must establish and develop mutual respect, mutual loving care, and mutual aid embodying socialist spiritual civilization; oppose callous bureaucracy and extreme individualism which harms others for self-benefit.

4. Stress the human elements in socialist construction; give full play to the spirit of self-mastery and creativity of the working people; stress education, the nurturing of talent, and the overall development of mankind.

Individually, many of these demands conform to the post-Mao political line. Equality before the law, opposition to capitalist money worship and extreme individualism, and so on, have been expressed repeatedly by the authorities. Separating individual worth from "origins" is at odds with views in which class origin is a paramount criterion, but would hardly constitute a heresy in the current climate. What appears as most challenging is the coupling of certain of these demands with others in unorthodox ways. In particular, the third demand associates bureaucracy with extreme individualism, and, in turn, opposes these to making "man" the goal of all work.

In his 1984 encyclical on humanism, Hu Qiaomu reserved special acerbity for the last principle, saying that "the Party also calls on and organizes the people to struggle for their own interests, that is, to serve as a means for themselves."[37] Taking "man as the goal" would lead only to extreme egoism, just the reverse of Wang Ruoshui's conclusion. The difference between the two positions resolves itself in part into divergent convictions about the mediation of popular needs and interests. For Hu Qiaomu, the mediating role is the preserve of the Party. For Wang, on the other hand, there must be a plurality of such mediations (among which are literature and art). This pluralism is characteristic of the school of thought Wang represents.

ZHOU YANG AND THE "ALIENATION SCHOOL"

Zhou Yang, champion of Mao's intellectual policies of the 1950s and early 1960s, is the most important figure directly associated with Wang Ruoshui. His public endorsement of humanism and the theory of socialist alienation at the Marx Centenary of March 1983 posed more of a threat to orthodoxy than anything said previously. Since he had been a target in the Cultural Revolution—accused indeed of having worked behind a revolutionary veneer for the revival of bourgeois humanism—his critics in the Campaign against Spiritual Pollution appeared to be restaging the early days of the Cultural Revolution.[38]

After his rehabilitation he was given some high offices, such as Chairman of the Writers' Federation and as inaugural Vice-President of the Chinese Academy of Social Sciences. Their power did not match the power he had wielded in the past. Lacking a broad base of support, he sought to find a niche for himself as a theoretical spokesmen for those who wished to take "intellectual liberation" quite literally. While bowing to authority when necessary (as during the 1981 Bai Hua affair),[39] he made some unusually frank and independent statements in his official capacity.

Compare, for example, his remarks with those made by Deng Liqun (also an inaugural CASS Vice-President) at a conference held by the Institute of Philosophy in summer 1978.[40] The subject was "Seeking the truth from facts," a slogan then in use against Hua Guofeng. Deng Liqun spoke of the derivation of theories and views from "practice," and hoped that philosophers would look at new issues, and seek to overcome error with reason, not with "clubs" (force) or "caps" (slander). Zhou Yang in his speech complained that some wanted an "absolute authority" for truth. The Gang of Four had gone so far as to make Marxism into an eternally unchanging dogma.

The result was the fencing off of forbidden areas of study, and a stifling of the growth of knowledge. The speech came very close to challenging the infallibility of Marxism, the possibility of its being arbiter of its own truth. There are clear resonances with Wang Ruoshui's later ideas about the alienation of Marxism. Zhou's celebrated speech to the 4th Congress of the Federation of Literary and Art Circles (the first held since 1960) in October and November of 1979 was even more candid.[41] He personally apologized to his former victims, writers like Ding Ling, Wang Meng, and Liu Binyan. He acknowledged that he had oversimplified and vulgarized literature and had used political authority harshly and rudely. He hoped that writers, within certain political limits, would be free to write more faithfully about life, and express a new "truthfulness."

Speaking on Mao's *Talks* on literature and art at a commemorative meeting held by the Federation in May 1982, Zhou displayed a marked convergence with ideas expressed by Wang Ruoshui in his "Literature, Politics, People." China had gone through immense changes since the Talks were given in 1942. It was no longer reasonable to speak, for example, of serving "the people" in a sense that meant only workers, peasants, and soldiers, but excluded intellectuals. Zhou echoed Wang's criticism of the principle of "serving politics," and in passing endorsed humanist Marxism and the critique of alienation. He used a new metaphor, that of the silkworm larva wrapping itself up in its cocoon, to explain the concept of alienation. This metaphor was sharply criticized in an article by a fellow victim of the Cultural Revolution, Lin Mohan, during the Spiritual Pollution Campaign.[42]

The Marx Centenary address ranges much more widely over philosophical issues than any of Zhou's previous ones. Epistemology and cultural criticism are given persuasively "liberal" interpretations. For example, in discussing the handling of cultural criticism, Zhou calls for a revaluation of the key Marxist concept of "supersession" (*yangqi*, deriving from the Hegelian expression *Aufhebung*). The true spirit of supersession requires that succeeding phases of mind or culture retain and assimilate each preceding one as a lower-level component. The unstated political corollary is that a new society cannot be created by violent overthrow of the old; change works with the grain of the old. The legacies of the superseded social order (such as China's "bourgeois" culture) should be accorded the right to function as subordinate parts of the new order. Zhou Yang, following Wang

Ruoshui as usual on a fundamental point of Marxist exegesis, believes that this "preserving negation" should be applied to the inheritance of philosophical and cultural tradition in general.[43]

Turning to the issues of humanism and alienation, Zhou reaffirms the break with his pre-Cultural Revolution views. Echoing Wang Ruoshui's "Defense of Humanism" of two months earlier, he finds that "man is the goal of all our work." Not only have wrongful attacks on humanism led to disaster in the past, but at present only a genuine humanism could counter the seduction of imported bourgeois ideas. Virtually quoting the "Defense" verbatim, Zhou Yang holds that Marxism takes in, but is not reducible to, humanism, a phrase in favor with others of the "alienation school," notably Ru Xin, who was eventually to make a point of repudiating it.[44]

Zhou finds that the concept of alienation played a pivotal role in the young Marx's critical inheritance of the humanism passed down from Feuerbach and the Enlightenment. He uses Wang's 1978 definition of alienation, making more explicit its relevance to socialist society. In his view, "To recognize socialist humanism and to oppose alienation are one and the same thing." Despite the elimination of exploitation, a number of forms of alienation undeniably exist. Examples are taken over from Wang's 1980 "Discussion" without citation, in a passage which gained notoriety in the Spiritual Pollution Campaign:

In the past, we did many stupid things in economic construction due to our lack of experience, and our lack of understanding of socialist construction—this realm of necessity—and in the end we ate our own bitter fruit; this is alienation in the economic realm. Due to the fact that democracy and the legal system were not on a sound basis, the people's servants sometimes made indiscriminate use of the power conferred on them by the people, and turned into their masters; this is alienation in the political realm, also called the alienation of power. As for alienation in the intellectual realm, the classic example is the personality cult, which is similar in some respects to the alienation of religion criticized by Feuerbach. Therefore alienation is an objectively existing phenomenon. It is pointless to be alarmed by the term.

Since thoroughgoing materialists are not afraid to face reality,

it is perfectly possible for us to overcome alienation by working through the socialist system itself. The causes of alienation lie not in the socialist system (*zhidu*) itself, but in problems of our institutional structure (*tizhi*) and elsewhere.[45]

This last distinction is surely crucial for Zhou Yang's argument. On first sight it may appear to be in need of a good deal more elaboration. Can system and structure really be so easily differentiated? It is, however, a commonplace distinction in recent Chinese constitutional theory, and attacking it would seem to offer little critical advantage.[46]

STALEMATE ON THE TEXTUAL FRONT

Despite constant official grumbles, deepening with time, the humanist impulse was propagated all over China with great élan. The theoretical literature devoted to alienation, already huge in 1982, is distinguished by two major trends. There is the "textual front": rival exegeses of key works of Marx and Engels. The other front imaginatively applies the concept of alienation to a variety of topics.

On the textual front, Wang Ruoshui and Ru Xin wrote several long academic papers in the late 1970s, going into the young Marx, classical German philosophy, the French Enlightenment, the young Hegel, and more.[47] This gave them scholarly clout when the movement became more public in 1982 and early 1983. For others, textual interpretation was an exercise in fence-sitting. One could show that Marx had indeed referred to alienation throughout his work without drawing any conclusion, or phrase Marx's use of *alienation* as a critique of capitalism, with no bearing on socialist states.

The application of the "social-effect criterion" (according to which ideas, works of art, and so forth should be judged in terms of their influence on the young and impressionable) to culture in the spring of 1981 brought a clamping-down on articles about alienation.[48] Academic discussion did not cease, but the stiffening opposition led to a greater polarization; fence-sitting became difficult and those like Wang Ruoshui who wanted to continue the debate became noticeably more defensive.

In a selection of excerpts, the *Yearbook of Chinese Philosophy—1983* provides a carefully balanced cross-section of the views prevalent in 1982. One such, that of Yuan Yayu, exemplifies the viewpoint of this broad movement. The concept of alienation is essentially diagnostic; it leads people to recognize certain types of contradiction. The main reason for Marx's frequent recourse to it lay in its ability "to reveal with utmost penetration from a special angle a particular aspect of human social relations, thereby inducing in people a unique self-awakened consciousness."[49]

Xu Ming, another writer mentioned, finds, on the other hand, that alienation was a topic of Marx's immature works, and as such was unscientific. Alienation presupposes a fixed human essence or nature (*ren de benzhi*) from which humanity has become alienated. This in turn implies belief in an archetypal "humanity" (*renxing*); history is thus static, an unvarying alternation of alienation from and return to this nature. If Marx's immature theory were true, claims Xu, alienated humanity would be incapable of returning to its "true nature" even under communism. Rather than being a realm of freedom, new forms of necessity under communism would perpetually impose new alienation phenomena. In the mature Marxist viewpoint, the formation of the human essence is seen as a historical process, rendering the earlier, static theory obsolete. Xu argued that, were the young Marx to be literally interpreted, alienation must constantly recur. Intriguingly, this was also the conclusion of a writer of the opposite camp, who proposed that "humanity advances through the unceasing conquest of alienation."[50]

On the relationship between the earlier and the later Marx, the *Yearbook* finds three contrasting schools of thought. The first, shared by Wang Ruoshui and his colleagues, holds that Marx had essentially completed his reform of the idealist concept of alienation by the time he wrote the *Economic and Philosophic Manuscripts of 1844* (hereafter *1844 Ms*); the later theories continue and develop the earlier notion. An opposing view, held by Tong Xing, finds a sharp break between the earlier and later views. The *1844 Ms* were based on a Feuerbachian ideal humanity, which Marx began to put aside only in *The Holy Family*, written with Engels in 1845. With *The German Ideology* (1845–1846), the original alienation theory had been completely replaced by historical materialism. Alienation had been changed from an omnipotent *explanans* to an *explanandum*.[51]

The third position noted in the *Yearbook* is exemplified in an article by Chen Xianda published in the CASS journal *Social Sciences in China*.[52] Chen finds much more continuity in Marx than did other opponents of the alienation school. The *1844 MS* are accorded some scientific value; indeed, they are regarded as the inception of the entire Marxist system. It was with the *Theses on Feuerbach* that Marx began self-consciously to eliminate Feuerbach's influence. Thus there were two transitions: one from the pre-scientific "alienation" to the scientific "alienated labor" of the *1844 Ms*; and from there to historical materialism after the criticism of Feuerbach had been carried out.

Even in the third, mature stage, Marx still had a theory of alienation. Now, however, its abolition required "a great increase in the development of the productive forces."

Chen's view does not go to the extreme of labeling the alienation theory un-Marxist. It preserves the continuity of Marx's thought and appropriates much of the "alienation school's" grounds of argument. Alienation is reduced to a form of technological under-development. The humanists are merely indulging in escapism:

> The current effort to refer social goals to human nature in China is a reflection of the extreme disgust with the political chaos of the Cultural Revolution. Though fine words of abstract humanism may bring temporary psychic comfort, they cannot increase our strength or heal our wounds.[53]

The upshot on the textual front was that neither side could win an easy victory. Endless variations could be run on the emphasis placed on selected passages of the corpus of material. Use of the original texts tended to be of a token nature, which meant that one usually found what one wanted to find. As Hu Qiaomu had later to admit, discussion restricted to Marx alone looked increasingly artificial.

Those who enthusiastically grasped the concept of "alienation" used it to explore a series of different topics. Perhaps most significant was the use of "alienation" as a key to the explanation of political power. In 1980, Wu Yue suggested that, under socialism, power fetishism replaces money fetishism, since "possession of power or position is then equal to the greater or lesser possession of property."[54] Marx had seen money fetishism as a prime symptom of alienation; Wu implies that under socialism a new range of symptoms is to be recognized, since political power has replaced economic power as a motive. A similar idea informs Liu Pen's "The Cult of Power and its Origins," which argues that "feudal residues" provide no explanation for the continuing attraction that power has for people in daily life under socialism.[55]

Belonging also to this category of exploratory theory are studies of the "alienation of civilization," and of "alienated thought" in traditional Chinese philosophy. On the latter topic, one author found that many key categories of Chinese thought were "theological" and thus involved alienations of the Feuerbachian type. Furthermore, "theological ideas are still far from having been eliminated, and possess the social basis and intellectual roots for survival."[56] Works of this nature testify to the desire for a critique of ideology and society that derives as much from Feuerbach as from (standard) Marxism. Power and ideology are seen to be related by processes that are not purely economic. For these writers, alienation certainly does not reduce merely to technological backwardness. Chen Xianda's criticism of this view indicates a cleavage between humanistic and technological approaches to refunctionalizing the ideology.

This cleavage suggests the direction in which the debate might have evolved had it not been for the Campaign against Spiritual Pollution and the intervention of Hu Qiaomu. There are strong parallels with the philosophical position of Ludz's classic "institutionalized revisionists." Chen's position seems after these events to have been an option prematurely foreclosed by the conservatives, but which may yet prove to be of use. It is deserving of special attention as a clear signal of the cleavage between humanistic and technological approaches referred to above. Furious skirmishing on a personal level between Wang Ruoshui and Hu Qiaomu should not divert us from the possibility that, for the humanists, Chen Xianda's reduction of alienation to technological underdevelopment is the real danger to be faced.

ALIENATION OUT OF BOUNDS: HU QIAOMU'S HUMANISM

The Campaign Against Spiritual Pollution emerged from the 2nd Plenary Session of the 12th CPC Central Committee, held in mid-October 1983. In a keynote report, Deng Xiaoping warned against the spreading of various forms of bourgeois decadence, "spiritual pollution," on the ideological front. Humanism and the theory of alienation, along with "abstract democracy" and modernist literature were cases in point. He traced them back to "weakness and laxity" in the leadership, but sought at the same time to avoid punitive countermeasures like those that had been applied in the past.[57] The campaign quickly ran into serious problems. By mid-December, Deng Liqun, Director of the Propaganda Department at that time, found it necessary to retreat from his strident attacks on the polluters, in the face of public cynicism and serious misgivings in the bureaucracy.[58]

The campaign had made a punitive instrument of Deng Xiaoping's carefully weighted injunctions in a way that he could not publicly support. Far from destroying its credibility, it had made the theory of socialist alienation better known to the public than might otherwise have been the case. Deng Xiaoping himself had experienced this sort of turn of events; his "Three Weeds" (three papers calling attention to major deficiencies in China's economic and technological development) had been the targets of a similar campaign of elimination in the late Mao period, and this eventually helped popularize them.

The Campaign Against Spiritual Pollution wound up in December. Two important documents were published in the lull following the campaign's brief storm. Ru Xin, whose alternating appearances as anti- and pro-humanist have already been noted, took space in three consecutive issues of *People's Daily* to "Criticize bourgeois humanism, and propagate socialist humanism."[59] "In articles I wrote in the past," he confessed, "I not only failed to point out the crucial issues of bourgeois humanism, but, on the contrary, and in an abstract and confused manner, put forward the theory of human dignity and worth." He rejected the "rather popular view," which he had recently supported, that "man is the starting point of Marxism." This "can only be abstract man, because a scientific understanding of man can only be the result of an enquiry into the entire course of development of history and society."

The humanist interpretation of Marx had, in China as elsewhere, paid close attention to the sixth *Thesis on Feuerbach*, which reads: "The human essence is no abstraction inherent in each single individual. In its reality it is the ensemble of social relations."[60] Ru Xin now took the *Sixth Thesis* to confirm the view that "Marx believed that the individual was completely determined by society." Bourgeois humanists believe, to the contrary, that history is created by heroes, and overlook the role of revolutionary collectivism. Consequently, he condemned his former view of Marxism as an "advanced and scientific form of humanism" as erroneous.[61]

In the last of the three articles, Ru Xin revealed that not all of the concessions had been on his side. He called for "vigorously publicizing socialist humanism," not as a *world outlook*, but as a *moral principle* that people ought to follow in dealing with human problems, under the guidance of the *Marxist* world outlook. This formula formed the core of the major speech given by Hu Qiaomu to the Party School on 3 January 1984, and published in *People's Daily* on 27 January.[62] Hu went appreciably further than Ru Xin in finding praiseworthy things in humanism. But finally:

The slogan of respecting "human value" will only encourage all kinds of unrealistic demands for individual well-being and freedom. It will create a false impression that, once the socialist system is established, all personal demands will have been guaranteed and satisfied; otherwise the socialist system would prove "inhumane."

It is not correct to complain that "man is made into a means" or that "man is alienated" just because one is required to serve the interests of the state and the people.[63]

Hu Qiaomu joins Ru Xin in advocating socialist humanism. Socialist humanism is at a higher level of principle than any humanism found in capitalist society. While it is inferior to communist morality, which is the highest moral standard for contemporary people, it represents the critical inheritance of bourgeois thought. Since it can now serve genuinely collective interests, it is free of its former hypocritical character.

Hu Qiaomu reserves his strongest criticism for the theory of alienation associated with Wang Ruoshui and Zhou Yang (who are not named), in which they point out that alienation can occur under socialism because of the cult of personality, irrational economic policies, and political practices in which officials who were "the people's *servants* abused the power invested in them by the people to become the people's *masters*."[64] Fault is found with their definition of the term, with their interpretation of Marx's writings, and their application of the theory to (Chinese) socialist society. The definition, refuted by Hu, is that alienation appears when,

in its process of development, a subject by its own activity creates something which is its opposite, and which then becomes an external, alien force, turning around and opposing or controlling the subject itself.

Instead of treating alienation as an historical phenomenon, limited to a definite, transitional stage of society, Hu charges them with elevating it to an abstract formula. He asserts that:

an account of socialist alienation either refers to the many residual phenomena of the old society and their effects as alienations—which contradicts (the stated) definition; or, conforming to the definition, it is believed that socialism as it develops will inevitably give birth to an alien force that turns round and controls it.[65]

The definition in question, first aired by Wang Ruoshui in 1978, differs only slightly from the one given by Zhou Yang in his celebrated attack on revisionism of 1963.[66] To construct a case against it now smacks of sophistry. Nevertheless, Hu Qiaomu pursues the point vigorously. On the subject of ideological alienation (*sixiang yihua*), which Wang Ruoshui and Zhou Yang viewed in the China context as the personality cult of Mao Zedong, Hu finds that the application of Feuerbach's ideas leads only to a caricature. He allows that the cult was a malignancy, but had developed out of a genuine and natural admiration. The attitude toward Mao had been very complicated, and not on the level of religious belief. Such a caricature failed to explain the "cult"; nor could it account for the Party's success in overcoming the chaos it gave rise to.[67]

Turning to the central issue, the idea of political alienation or "alienated power" under socialism, Hu finds such characterization of the leadership system to be a violation of Marxism. "Any revolutionary party wants not only democracy but also the concentration of power"; to equate this power with alienation is tantamount to anarchism. Indeed the alienation school's image of the people's servants becoming their masters reminds Hu Qiaomu of the slogans of the Cultural Revolution. The founders of Marxism had never referred to adverse factions and trends within the working-class movement as "alienations."

The other applications of the alienation theory, to economic blunders and setbacks for example, betray, in Hu's view, a frivolous attitude. They are generated from pure abstraction. The Wang-Zhou belief that alienation in socialist society would be overcome from within is specious:

Alienation is not like water and fire which can be beneficial as well as harmful. In regard to socialism, it is neither an ordinary defect nor an irrational phenomenon, but a "catastrophe" capable of destroying the socialist system.[68]

Hu Qiaomu's ultimate verdict is that the alienation theory involves a deviation from Marxism. The errors of the alienation school stem from a fruitless attempt to revise the Party's verdict on the Cultural Revolution. The school adopted the bad arguments of Western Marxism, particularly the young Marx's immature thoughts on humanism and alienation. Some thought Marxism would be raised to a higher level in this way, and others took a wait-and-see attitude. In the end, the Central Committee had been forced to take action.

While conceding that Marx left his works in disorder, and may have "used the term *alienation* too much," Hu is intent on pushing Marxism forward, not back. Socialist humanism is a valid ethical standard, but it is of subordinate status. The attempt to give it an independent critical position, in the form of the theory of alienation, has no place in Marxism. Thus rested the official case between 1984 and 1986.

CONCLUSION

We see in the writings of Wang Ruoshui and others an attempt, rooted in moral conviction, to derive from Marx an explanation for the disasters of the radical periods of the Great Leap Forward and the Cultural Revolution and the potential for evil in the present. Wang's perception of the evils is similar to that of the Li Yizhe group and later activists for democratic rights.[69] His diagnosis and his remedy differ, however. Where Li Yizhe bluntly ascribed the evils to a new mode of bourgeois ownership, Wang refers simply to bureaucratic privilege and the difficulties of implementing democracy. His four demands are designed to minimize conflict with the four basic principles, and focus accordingly on values rather than institutions. The "humanity" (*ren*) haunting the Chinese intellectual world is above all the moral conscience of the leadership. If they can confront this apparition, the ethical consensus which can become the basis for eventual institutional reform will be achieved.

The theory of socialist alienation is in an important sense the critical wing of a utopian movement, a movement for values that are held to transcend politics. Such a campaign is political from the outset. For all its apparent theoretical weaknesses, the effects on social consciousness in a broad sense seem from our present vantage point to be considerable. A place for humanism in the official ideology has been won, and the attempt by Hu Qiaomu to confine it to a subordinate status, worthy of a slighting lip-service, has itself come into disrepute. The critical awareness of dehumanizing forces in society will undoubtedly live on, and the critique of alienation will be carried on against new forms arising from the information revolution and other modern technologies.

The movement initiated by Wang Ruoshui and the alienation school was both emotional and rational in its origins. There had been a "limit experience," an existential revaluation, like that of the intellectual Resistance in Europe.[70] There was, as well, knowledge of, and a philosophical engagement with, the movement for socialist humanism and the critique of socialist alienation in the intellectual world of Central and Eastern Europe. The Chinese humanists' overall position closely resembles the ethical purism of Ludz's "refunctionalizing counter-elite." They oppose simple technological utopias and warn against over-optimism while the problems of bureaucracy and individual liberation are still to be addressed. Against this background, one of Wang Ruoshui's most recent and striking public statements is to be understood in its full poignancy:

We have to pay a price for modernization; this is inevitable. Seeking a way without any side effects is utopian. Retreating to the former path exacts an even heavier toll; everyone stays poor. According to Engels, the desire for wealth has been an impetus since the birth of civilization. Promoting the economy will naturally stimulate people's desire for wealth and consumption. Getting rich in a proper way benefits the people and increases the wealth in society. But a minority of people get rich by evil means. To tackle the problem we need a sound legal system that allows no feudal injustice. Capitalist legal rights are more progressive than feudal privileges.[71]

Driven by conviction, the humanists' actions were neither calculating nor entirely naïve. As well as that classical chess game, the interpretation of Marx's alienation theory, they played a poker game, with their own moral integrity as the main stake. The school of philosophy personified by Wang Ruoshui and his spectral "Man" appeared to win, if not the game, at least a round of it. While hostage to the shifting political fortunes of their patrons, their gamble struck a chord that will continue to resonate in Chinese intellectual life.

Postscript

In the last few months, Wang Ruoshui has republished most of the works cited in this chapter in two new collections, *Wei rendaozhuyi bianhu* (In defense of humanism) and *Zhihuide tongku* (The pain of wisdom).

CHAPTER SEVEN

The Chinese Writer in His Own Mirror: Writer, State, and Society—The Literary Evidence

RUDOLF G. WAGNER

The literary arts have been the main testing and battle ground for public political contention ever since the founding of the PRC. In a highly categorized and controlled public sphere the symbolical language of the literary arts has provided some leeway for the articulation of alternative political options. All members of the political class have therefore converged upon this field with their aims, commands, and criticisms. Any book dealing with China's recent political history thus evinces the curious feature of constantly referring to this film, that short story, this opera, or that review as key evidence for top-level political contention.

The legitimate gardeners of this embattled ground are the writers. The political faction in power requires them to educate the "masses" of readers and spectators in the virtues of the latest government line;

dissenters at the top may pressure them to present their criticisms in a veiled literary form; they are looked upon by the people inhabitating the base level of the hierarchy as potential spokesmen articulating their grievances and objections in the face of the powers that be; finally, the writers hold strong views of their own. Through its treatment of the writers the Party communicates to the intelligentsia at large how this class is valued at any given time; the fate of the writer becomes the gauge indicating the pressure exerted upon his technical, managerial, and scholarly peers, and, in both prestige and distress, he most intensely experiences the fate of his class.

Much in the status and role of the intelligentsia in general and the writer in particular reflects the Leninist order of things inherited from the Soviet Union. The Communist experience, with the primordial importance of the public sphere for both the "revolution" and the "counterrevolution," which was dealt with by Lenin and, more systematically, by Gramsci, has led to strict controls over this sphere in socialist states. In China, however, the importance of the literary battlefield is even greater, given the long Chinese tradition of using literature for political ends, and the ensuing deeply ingrained reading habits of the political class.

Operating as the expert in this embattled field, the writer is subject to political pressures and enticements, and is himself no stranger to politics. All participants in the literary debate, however, are unanimous in demanding that the writer should not forfeit the special powers of his craft by simply adding some literary luster to otherwise profane political pronouncements. He is to produce works of great literary quality, if only to enhance their political efficacy.

Thus, the writer becomes the focus of important social conflicts. But in these conflicts he is no passive onlooker; he has his own opinions, he takes sides, and there is always the willing crowd of factional scribblers to tarnish the image of the entire trade. He is under suspicion not only from opposing factions in the leadership but also from his readers. Is he just selling the latest issue of governmental instruction in the more palatable form of literature? Is he telling "the truth" or is he peddling political slogans as the truth? Is he giving in to the pressures of those in power to bend his trade to their interests? Is he yielding to the temptations of being an intellectual with access to the highest leaders of the country and a national readership? It is difficult for him to deal with these matters in a straightforward manner. To establish his credibility and to dissociate himself from the *wenxue tewu*, the literary agents, and other rabble, he has to explain, in detail, what he does and whence comes his legitimacy. Thus, it is mostly the prominent authors who deem it necessary and their duty to define their public role. There is, however, a general hubbub of voices holding forth on the writer's duties and mistakes, in the papers, and at congresses and conferences. Given the volatility of the topic and the stale language of the official cultural discourse, the voice of the main protagonist, the writer himself, is barely audible.

The writer's metier is the writing of fiction, verse, or drama. We may thus expect that he uses his own craft to deal more specifically with the problems of his social role. The difference between his official pronouncements on and his literary treatment of this role is not that between lie and truth. Rather, the literary texts with their symbolical structure give more leeway and can deal with this social role in a much more complex manner. We shall thus study literary texts through which writers deal with their own relationship with the state, Party, and society. They will have to be studied in their own light and logic first before character, plot, and symbolism can be deciphered in their political and social meanings.

THE FATE OF THE *ENGAGÉ* WRITER BEFORE 1949

While there is a long tradition in China of using literature as a political instrument, the modern *engagé* writers emerged only at the end of the Qing dynasty in the foreign enclaves along China's coast. They were neither Confucian literati with their firm station in the hierarchy, nor writers willing to be reduced to mere newspaper scribblers. Imitating mostly French, Russian, Japanese, and English precedents, the late Qing novelists described their role as social investigators and reformers. Liu E, in his *Lao Can's Travels*, depicts himself as Lao Can, an itinerant doctor whose profession brings him into contact with both high and low, and who goes about healing individual physical and social ills.[1] In his dream, Lao Can brings to the junk representing the Chinese state a modern compass which could guide this battered state-ship through the political storms, but the stubborn backwardness and factionalism of his countrymen nearly cost him his life. Lao Can opposes vile bureaucrats, but in no way is he a spokesman for "the people." He is an enlightened modern reformer, a one-man show.

In similar fashion, other writers of the time, like Zeng Pu and Wu Woyao, introduce themselves into their texts,[2] describing the "modern" writer's role in a complex network as that of a social specialist with high ethical standards and patriotic devotion who probes all layers of society with his work, thus establishing communicative links between these otherwise strictly separate segments. There is no vile arch-enemy, no flight of poetic fancy; no writer is battling with his soul and fate. Rather, their role is that of sober observation, moral comment, and, if possible, modest reform. Their style might be termed reform prose.

A second relevant strain of Chinese tradition is the self-perception of the May Fourth writers. Many of them have dealt with their own lives and feelings, but it was Guo Moruo with his *Qu Yuan* who seems to have given the most detailed literary treatment of the role and responsibility of the poet in times of national crisis.[3]

As Laurence Schneider has pointed out, Qu Yuan has been a model for upright and patriotic literary censure ever since the Han dynasty.[4] Qu used his poetry for remonstrance, and his allegories have set the precedent for the reading technique to be applied to this kind of text.[5] Qu lost favor with King Huai of Chu because of a faction of sycophants at court and eventually committed suicide. His predictions, however, came to pass. Some decades after the King had turned down Qu's advice on foreign policy, his kingdom of Chu was swallowed by Qin. May Fourth writers also saw in Qu Yuan a "people's poet" or even a "revolutionary poet."

Guo Moruo's image of Qu Yuan changes with Guo's own self-perception. In Guo's first play on Qu Yuan in the 1920s, Qu Yuan is the poet-hero, the mover of the universe, a person of supreme power, mad in his gigantic dimensions.[6] Ezra Vogel,[7] Leo Ou-fan Lee[8] and especially Yi-tsi Feuerwerker have studied the developments and schools of the writer's self-perception in the May Fourth era and after; Feuerwerker's study on Ding Ling, in fact, argues that "the largest and most significant source for Ding Ling's perception of the writer's role is her fiction," and she shows that, after Ding Ling's "political conversion, the writer is taken down from his pedestal and given a new and humbler role," which also brought out the tension between "literature's assigned position in the overall revolutionary scheme" and "the need to uphold the idea of literature itself."[9] Her sources for the latter points, however, are essays and not fiction.

Guo Moruo's next play on Qu Yuan (1942) provided the first systematic fictional treatment of the writer's relationship with government and society by a May Fourth writer who had by then become a firm partisan of the Communist Party's cause.[10] The play was written and staged under Zhou Enlai's direct supervision some months after the Southern Anhui Incident, during which several thousand Communist troops were killed by their United-Front partner from the Guomindang side. The United Front was in danger of breaking apart. According to Communist charges, the Japanese were intensely lobbying Chiang Kai-shek to switch allegiance to the Axis powers. The political climate in Chongqing, the seat of the Guomindang Government, was repressive, with new censorship laws enacted to silence leftist critics. Guo Moruo, then one of the most prestigious of these critics living in Chongqing, used his position and the time-honored device of the "historical play" to remonstrate with the Guomindang, and to set up, through the historical precedent of Qu Yuan, a model of behavior for himself and others in times of national crisis.

In the play, Qu strongly advises the King to stay with the "United Front" (that is, with the Communists and the Allies) and not to put himself under the sway of aggressive Qin (that is, Japan), a policy advocated by some courtiers and the Queen, prodded by an intermediary from Qin. Guo Moruo, through Qu, claims for himself the stature of Qu as an indomitably upright and patriotic figure, but also his historical vindication. If his warnings are not heeded, Chu will be swallowed by Qin, China will be swallowed by Japan.

The play, set in the 16th year of King Huai's rule—1942 being the 16th year of Chiang Kai-shek's ascent to power (1927)—deals with numerous contemporary issues, including the new censorship laws, preservation of the United Front, popular resentment of Guomindang policies, and even the role of the CC Clique of the Guomindang, whom Guo attacks through his extensive reliance on the very *Zhanguo ci* cherished by this group for the portrayal of the power politics of the Queen (Mme. Chiang) and her confidants.[11]

Guo interprets Qu's "Ode to the Orange Tree" as an attempt by Qu to educate his disciple, Song Yu, in the proper virtues of the writer. The orange tree is firmly rooted in the ground, showing its steadfast purpose, grows free between Heaven and Earth, and bears blossoms and eventually fruit. In the original "Ode to the Orange Tree," Qu

Yuan mentions the fruit's being first green, then yellow; in Guo's play, he adds that it eventually turns "red," symbolizing the politically mature literary fruit of the writer.[12] These fruits are "pure" within, they are *dagong wusi,* all for the public benefit and not for private profit; but at the same time the trees have sharp thorns to protect the "fruit" from unqualified hands and "do not allow you to mistreat [the fruit] at will," that is, censoring the content or forcing literary works to fawn on those in power. Although, within the play, the poem is originally addressed to the intellectuals (including Qu himself), there is in fact little reliance to be placed on them. Zilan is a poet of royal blood, mostly interested in chasing young women. Song Yu is of lower origin but quickly falls for the temptations of a career as a court poet when Qu Yuan is dismissed. Where, then, is the "social base" of Qu Yuan who himself is a member of the King's own clan and thus clearly a member of the upper classes? His intellectual peers leave him in this crisis for their personal profit, but, although Qu is not born among the common people, his heart is with them; he takes up their literary forms and their language and expresses their aspirations. Therefore, they know and love his verse. His relationship to "the people" is presented through Qu's relationship to his young maid-servant, Zhan Juan, a young woman being a stock figure for the "common people of China" or "the Chinese nation" in leftist Chinese drama. Her devotion to Qu is echoed by some supporting characters. But, when Qu's fate turns sour, only Zhan Juan stays loyal to him; she eventually comes to his rescue in prison, drinks the poison prepared for Qu by his enemies at court, and dies with a smile on her face.

The text of the poem to the orange trees has been discarded by Song Yu, for whom it was originally written. It has found its way into the hands of Zhan Juan, who alone deserves the lines

> You are all utmost sincerity, bright as the light of sun and moon;
> I want forever to be your friend to my last day.
> Not bending nor cringing, you battled on for truth to the end;
> Although young in years, you can be taken as the model for this age.

Qu does not set himself or his young intellectual peers up as the model for the age; for his intellectual Chongqing audience he proposes Zhan Juan as the model to follow. Her qualities come out best, however, in her very concern for Qu, the poet-politician. Qu says: "She it is who respects me most; she considers me her father, her master, thinking me more precious than her own life. She it is who can comfort me most. I think of her as my own daughter, as my most dear pupil."[13] The patriotic and pure poet (who, needless to remark, takes no carnal interest in the young woman) remains the "father" and "master" who shows the true way and articulates the truths that the common people then adopt but would not be able to discover themselves.

Qu Yuan, the noble tree rooted in common ground, had described in "Ode to the Orange Tree" the pure literary fruit growing out of him, but he had not dealt with the powers of literature. Near the play's end, Qu, in the diviner's temple which has become his prison, starts by repeating the ecstatic message about the powers of his craft from the texts Guo Moruo wrote during the 1920s, crying:

Wind! Roar, roar! Roar with all your might. In this darkness bereft of Heaven's light when all are asleep, when all have sunk into their dreams, when all are dead, it is the time for you to roar, and to roar with all your might.

This is the time of political darkness; the nation's crisis is exacerbated by the people's being asleep and unaware of it, and even "dead." *Feng,* the wind, also means "airs" and is often used for poetry and literature in general. The first section of the *Book of Songs* is entitled *guofeng,* airs of the states. Now, in this crisis, poetry has to "roar" to awaken the public. But Qu Yuan has learned the lessons of Guo Moruo's own experience. After the ecstatic beginning quoted above Qu reflects more soberly and sadly, still addressing "the wind":

Yet, however you roar, you cannot recall them from their dreams, cannot blow the dead back to life. You cannot blow away the leaden darkness from their eyes. But at least you can blow away some specks of dust, some little gravel, and you might move some grasses and trees to stir. You can rouse the Dongting Lake, the Yangtze River, and the East Sea to come up with mighty waves and to roar in concert with you on the great earth.[14]

The same pattern is repeated in three subsequent metaphorical treatments of literature. The soaring poetic dreams of thunder with its rumbling of wheels might, like a chariot, carry the poet away to the utopian "small islands where there is no intrigue, no filth, no unselfishness, where there are no human beings." But it cannot help with today's problems. The sharp satire of lightning might, like "the sword of my heart," "pierce through the darkness" of the present, but, even then, it would be as if "water is cut for a moment by the dazzling light, and then the waves will close in again."

In his last stance he finally implores light and its element fire, the fiery powers of reason and enlightenment, which are the poet's "self" to "blow up" (baozha) the gods assembled in this superstructure of the diviner's temple. These gods are "the parents of this darkness," and should thus be "blown up" or consumed by the fire of the poet's reason. Rejecting the "rain" of tears, Qu ends his monologue: "Rise up, wind! Roll, thunder! Flash lightning! Destroy all things that slumber in darkness, destroy them utterly!" These verbal threats, however, do not produce any effect. The denouement comes with the King's watchman, a sober military man from "north of the Han River." There, people have learned to cherish the high-sounding poet. The watchman frees Zhan Juan, and, together, the "people" and the practical military man from the north (Yan'an), proceed to liberate Qu, Zhan Juan sacrificing herself in the process. It is the watchman's dagger that kills the administrator of the superstition-ridden superstructure, the man who tried to poison Qu; and it is the flint of this practical man from the north that puts the fire to the edifice of dark beliefs which constitute the temple, a fire which is to be the paean to Zhan Juan's pure virtue. North of the Han River, the watchman tells Qu, people "resist aggression in defense of our country," a none-too-veiled reference to the Communist-held areas around Yan'an. On the level of symbolic action, the Communists (through the watchman) effectively execute what Qu Yuan can only aspire to; they tear down the superstructure of "deception" which leaves people in utter darkness as to their real condition. Qu agrees to go north with this valiant man, a step Guo Moruo, who remained in Chongqing throughout the war, in fact did not take. There is some sad irony in this confrontation between the poet's high-sounding invocation that the powers of his poetry should destroy these gods, and the quick flint in the hands of the watchman. Unable to move the universe on his own, the poet willingly puts himself to the service of the cause. He is "needed" up north. For the time being, only the temple is burnt, while the real power structure remains in place. The King and the Queen still pursue their treacherous policies.

The message of the play was lost on neither friend nor foe. While Zhou Enlai gave guidance and support, the Guomindang literary authorities under Pan Gongzhan organized a conference to criticize the play, and to refute the central allegation. Pan declared: "Our Generalissimo has excelled in leading the war of resistance (against Japan); he has established rich merits and great achievements; we cannot describe the war of resistance entirely in dark colors. Our Generalissimo is not King Huai of Chu."[15]

To sum up, the pre-1949 tradition presents us with two styles of dealing with the writer's social role. In the strain represented by the late Qing novels, the writer is operating in a non-antagonistic environment as a social investigator and reformer. The tone is a moral and moderate reform prose. In the trend presented by Guo Moruo's *Qu Yuan*, the language is battle poetry; the time is that of an immediate crisis. Although the play adheres to the United Front policies, it mostly uses *baozha* (blow-up) language to deal with the conflicts. The national poet may not unhinge the government, but he rises to the occasion by rousing the mighty waves of the people's patriotic fervor. He thus serves the cause, and the watchman without envy lets him play the lead on center stage.

Two options were presented by these two strains. The realistic reform prose implied the role of the writer as loyal critic, while the battle poetry in the form of the historical drama implied the existence of a government oblivious of the vital interests of the nation and so repressive that the historical drama became the only avenue of protest. With all their differences, both strains attributed similar features to the writer's social role—his righteousness, national commitment, engagement for progress, his intermediate station between high and low, the pressures he has to bear. Guo's *Qu Yuan* also marks the demise of a tenet dear to both strains of tradition: His high aspiration and words notwithstanding, the writer's powers are small. The social segment to which he belongs is small and easily bought over. The writer can have a role only if he uses national and popular forms, which at the time of the staging was advocated throughout the Comintern; establishes close links with "the people"; and, most important, joins the endeavour of the watchman from the north. All this modest assessment notwithstanding, Guo as Qu, the national poet, sees himself as the father, the teacher, and the master of the "people," Zhan Juan being Qu's "daughter," "disciple," and, of course, servant. The issue of the relative authority of Qu and the watchman remains undiscussed and unresolved even in a text like Guo Moruo's.

Neither Guo nor his predecessors seem interested in describing the writer as such. His psychic and social life, the intricacies of the creative process that have inspired so many novels in the West remain untouched. Writing, in these texts, deals with political and social issues and is discussed in these terms. The statements, furthermore, are highly personalized. Certain individuals and factions are directly addressed, not the generalities of the political process. In the same manner, the texts deal not with "the writer" per se, but with the social role of the national poet of the type represented by Guo Moruo himself. Writing about the responsibility and role of this figure naturally is the domain of the few authors who have achieved such elevated status.

Both strains were continued in China after 1949; the patterns in which the later depictions were cast were by then well laid out.

THE SELF-PERCEPTION OF THE WRITER IN THE PRC

The "Cog and Screw in the Revolutionary Machinery"

At about the time that Guo wrote *Qu Yuan*, Mao Zedong demanded in Yan'an much more than Qu Yuan had envisaged, namely, that the writer be the "cog and screw in the revolutionary machinery" as directed by the Party, a formula he quoted from Lenin. Writers, Mao demanded, should give up their Shanghai intellectuals' viewpoint, learn about life and people in the area to which they had moved, and write for the cadres among whom literacy was highest. Implicitly, Mao demanded the disappearance of the writer from the literary text. The protagonists were to be workers, peasants, soldiers, and, above all, cadres, and not intellectuals. The perspective was to change from that of a Shanghai leftist city wit to that of the Party leadership and its ideology. What was left of literary refinement, style, and entertainment was to become a "weapon for the education" of the masses and a "weapon" in the struggle. The writer was to disappear into the fulfilment of his assigned task. In Zhou Libo's *Baofeng zouyu* (*The Hurricane*, 1949), this disappearance can be studied.[16]

This novel was written after the Yan'an rectification campaign which prodded writers to "go down" into the countryside and join in the land-reform work there. Zhou, like many of his colleagues, was both a writer of fiction and a journalist. He had translated Sholokhov and Egon Erwin Kisch's *Secret China*.[17] Through these he had become familiar with the new techniques that had entered literature in the 1920s from the medium of film—the cut, the flashback, the spotlight, the close-up. Film stressed the importance of the meaningful visible surface, as did other new media like photography and the literary documentary. Reality was ostensibly meaningful and true; no authorial intrusion or fictionalizing was called for. In *The Hurricane*, the writer operates as a camera held by the land-reform team which enters a north China village; he has neither authorial voice nor a persona in the text. The perspective is determined by the functional association of the "camera" with the team. From the first scene on, we never see the team from the perspective of the village. The narrative approaches and enters the village with the team, and the reader learns about the village gradually as the team proceeds with its investigation and reform. *Shehui diaocha*, social investigation, has to discover who the big landowners are, what links they have with other parts of the population, who the activists are, and who the potential local leaders; the investigation is a part of the struggle, a weapon against the landlords and for the education of potential allies in the Party's endeavor. As the exploration of the family background, economic situation, and political attitudes of each of the villagers proceeds, the members of the team show no individuality and desire beyond their assigned tasks. They have names, but no families, no class background, home province, habits, attitudes, or experiences. Only the slightly ultraleftist intellectual is marked by his "class-wart," the inevitable glasses, indicating that the author has learned the lesson given by Mao, that the Shanghai intellectuals are quite ridiculous. We learn nothing about the team members' attitudes toward land reform except that they fully accept the Party's policies.

In the well-lit center of the stage is the village where everything eventually stands out sharply. The team becomes the instrument of the village's self-analysis, with the writer's camera writing the protocol. The camera is no detached observer. It discovers the very class structure the Party had said prevailed, and this structure determines the villagers' behavior. The close-up is of class struggle; all other elements are rigorously cut. The novel's universe operates on the principle of flat rationality. The camera only has to show. The surface is self-explanatory and coherent; no dark motives or forces lurk beneath.

The Hurricane received a Stalin prize of the second rank, and was handed to cadres together with the land-reform law as study material for their own land-reform work in the "newly liberated areas." The text has gone full circle. It started under proddings from Party leadership and analyzed the village from the perspective of the land-reform directives. It found all their assumptions amply confirmed, and became itself evidence and proof for their correctness, serving for the education of the new land-reform teams. All the functional elements mentioned by Mao are in place, and Zhou made use of a well-established literary tradition from the 1930s to fulfill his assignment.

Although in Yan'an this approach was made mandatory against some opposition, it seems that writers generally went along with it. The immediate needs of the war and their own uneasiness about their backgrounds as city intellectuals favored its acceptance. In Yan'an many categories, including literary categories, were fixed that were to organize the new state after 1949. The constellation in which the "cog and screw" model operated depended on the credibility of the pressing need to fight some imperialist or bourgeois "enemy" and a concomitant willingness among most writers to submit to the leadership's orders and exclude from their works the description of the "dark spots to be found even in the sun itself," that is, the problems of bureaucratism, chauvinism, and privilege-hunting within the Party.

After 1949, as the need to fight the "enemy" faded, the homespun problems of the new society emerged prominently; but literature, for the time being, remained the "cog and screw" in the old, now outdated, machinery. It went on to describe the war; when asked to describe the new society, it came up with only the bland praise reserved for anyone associated with the "progressive" side.

In this, writers followed the trend set in the Soviet Union, where Zhdanov had crushed other, more innovative and critical approaches with his heavy hand. Only after criticism of the "varnishers" had appeared in the Soviet Union after Stalin's death, did Chinese writers dare to take similar steps. Ai Qing, himself criticized in Yan'an for his plea that the Party treat writers with more love and respect, was among the first with his long narrative poem *Heiman* (*Black Eel,*

1954),[18] the hero of which is both an artist and a member of the laboring classes.

Chen Quan is a flute-player and fisherman, stranded on an island ruled by a despot. When Chen played his flute once:

> People who had never shed tears
> Could not understand his music;
> His melodies were low and melancholy
> Sadder than people weeping.

When on a haul under the despot's command the fishermen one evening ask Chen to play for them. He "played three tunes one after the other / First a merry tune, then sad ones." They are overheard by the despot who comes with two guards and assails Chen for his music:

> He came up face to face with Chen Quan,
> His hands folded behind him.
> Looking down on the young man,
> His eyes blazed with anger.
> "From where comes this trumpeter?
> Whose mother has died?
> Who likes such mournful tunes?
> Are you playing my dirge?
> "If you want to leave, get out!
> Don't stay and play such gloomy tunes.
> The rest of you hurry off to sleep,
> Tomorrow we must start back at dawn."

Chen is beaten and falls off the boat but is saved by the fishermen, who stand by him in defiance of the tyrant.

Chen's beloved is Black Eel, the pure daughter of the people, already familiar from *Qu Yuan*. The tyrant demands his *ius primae noctis*, and, when he learns she is already pregnant, he incarcerates the two lovers in the ship's body to let them starve. They, however, set fire to the boat, taking the tyrant, who alone cannot swim, along with them to the bottom of the sea. Although Chen dies, the sound of his flute can still be heard:

> Others say that on a moonlit night
> People can hear the sound of a flute

Magically blending with the singing wind and waves
Fairy music playing ceaselessly through the night.

Since the poem is clearly set "before Liberation," a literary attack against the tyrant is perfectly legitimate. The daughter of the people falls in love with the bard; together they bring down the tyrant and liberate the fishermen from his rule, dying themselves in the process. Chen is a hero, but many of his tunes are sad, and the young woman loves him for them. It is characteristic of the tyrant that he demands optimistic tunes, and beats Chen for playing his "dirge." Through the interaction between Chen and the tyrant, Ai Qing deals with the artist/writer and a ruler who imposes his own cultural policies. The return of an "intellectual" hero in this poem is as surprising as the emphasis on the tyrant's cultural policies. Within the text, Ai Qing does nothing to link the PRC Party and Government in any way with this old tyrant.

As Ai Qing was a nationally known poet with a history of troubles in Yan'an, some official reaction to the poem was to be expected. Indeed, Zhou Yang himself, through his reaction, added a new interpretive layer to the poem. He argued that the poem, with the death of the lovers at the end, was much too morose.[19] Glorious things had just been achieved in Korea; the countryside was being rapidly transformed. Optimism was the mood and should be reflected in literature. Included was an unspoken charge. Had not Hu Feng claimed in 1954 that, under Zhou Yang's administration, Chinese literature had been reduced to saccharine optimism revolting to mouth and eye? Was not Ai Qing in fact echoing Hu Feng's criticisms? When Zhou Yang spoke in 1955, it was the time of the movement against Hu Feng who, for his views, had been thrown into prison for the next thirty years. Zhou's criticism of Ai contained a latent threat. Zhou Yang himself thereby did what Ai Qing did not do within the poem—associate his own cultural policies with those of the tyrant so that the morose spirit permeating the poem indeed reflected the literary mood of the early 1950s.[20]

The poetic medium is not as analytical as prose might be, but Ai Qing uses this narrative poem to counter the official definitions of the poet's duties and the state of literature. Against the mandated optimism that he dismisses as dutiful varnishing, he puts in a melancholy note. Chen as a writer is not a Party-controlled "weapon," "cog," and "screw." He is a fighter, but independently devoted to his people. Instead of educating them, he voices their feelings with his magic flute. Using a historical screen, as Guo Moruo did, Ai Qing seemingly deals with the same sharp contrast between an oppressive government's cultural demands and the aspirations of the people's poet. The text is a statement about PRC cultural policies quite op-posed to the intentions guiding Guo's piece. But Ai Qing saw more continuity than break between the old and the new government's cultural policies. The weakness of his piece, however, is its inability to define the new problems in new terms. This was eventually at-tempted in the analytical reform prose of the Hundred Flowers period.

The Writer as Scout

A new policy emerged in late 1955, as parts of the leadership moved to shift the focus from "class struggle" to "production." This echoed Soviet developments under Khrushchev. The shift dramatically changed the name of the main obstacle from "imperialism" and "bourgeoisie" to "bureaucratism," and it changed the nature of the conflict, in Maoist terms, from "antagonistic" to "non-antagonistic." Within this concept, ratified by the 8th Party Congress in September 1956, the intellectuals ("experts") and youth played an important role as anti-bureaucratic forces propelling China's development forward. The time for reform prose had returned. The notion of the Party as a unified body caved in; the bureaucrats were said to be occupying the Party's middle levels. There was, therefore, a need to think publicly about the writer's role both as an intellectual and as an expert on the public sphere. Since the Youth League (then under Hu Yaobang) harbored both the "young" workers and many of the most active young intellectuals, it may be expected that writers associated with the League would be the first to deal with the bureaucrat and the intellectual's role in combating him. Indeed, the most controversial stories of 1956 were by such writers. For example, Liu Binyan was a journalist with the Youth League paper. His heroes are Youth Leaguers. Wang Meng worked in the League's Beijing Municipal Com-mittee, and the hero in his "A Young Man Who Only Recently Joined the Organization Department" is a very young man who has just transferred from the League to the Party.[21]

In Wang Meng's story, the "young man" from the Youth League combines a variety of the functions associated with intellectuals, and thus stands for more than just a writer. He comes into the organization department which is stagnating under the benevolent but mildly ossified leadership of older cadres. They are not moved by the necessity for action, but by the question of whether "conditions are ripe" for action, meaning whether the climate in the apparatus would permit smooth proceedings. This attitude has led to a severe distortion of the investigative work to be done by the organization department, exemplified in the negative name and actions of Han Changxin, the young intellectual (Han Ever-with-the-Latest Wind). Han is sent to investigate the complaints of factory workers against their director, who passes his time in playing chess instead of organizing production, so that the workers are unable to live up to the high goals of the Leap Forward. Han, however, produces a report varnishing over this dark reality. Thus, the leadership is effectively prevented from getting accurate information. The leadership's policies of accelerating economic development are seen as enlightened, and enthusiastically espoused by the young workers in the factory. But the communication between the enlightened top leadership and the enthusiasts at the base level is clogged by the self-serving complacent distortions of the middle-level bureaucrats. Imperialism and the bourgeoisie have left the literary stage; they are no longer responsible for the ongoing problems in production. The main obstacles are bureaucrats in Party and government.

Enter the young man who takes on a variety of roles in order to solve this problem. First, he carries out a *shehui diaocha*, social investigation, quite in tune with Mao's constant exhortations to get the truth from facts. Although he finds the workers willing to honor the Party leadership's appeal for a speed-up in production, the internal channels of communication are so clogged that he sees no way to move ahead. The young man, as spokesman for the worker's grievances and supporter of the Party's enlightened policies, despairs of achieving anything through his office and goes public. He helps the workers formulate their grievances and sends them to a newspaper, the *Beijing ribao*, which prints the text.

Within the PRC stories, literature and newspapers are mostly used interchangeably, as most writers are also journalists, and as social investigation is considered the basic mode of gathering material for both. Thus, the newspapers and literature, that is the public sphere of the press and public opinion, become the external channels of communication between the enlightened top leadership and the enthusiastic base in their common opposition to middle-level bureaucrats.

Wang Meng thus describes the writer as a part of the new young intelligentsia which is called upon to promote economic and social progress on the basis of factual analysis. The young man is part of the Party's "organization department" in the nation's capital, under direct guidance from Party Central. Thus the writer/intellectual turns up as a Party cadre attached to a high level. The "organization department" is in charge of "general matters," especially Party recruitment. The text calls on the young intellectuals to emulate the young man in his daring new role of critical investigator and agent of social change, and not the opportunism of Han Ever-with-the-Latest Wind. This new role recalls a pattern established under the Han dynasty. Envoys were sent to collect firsthand the people's criticisms expressed in songs and doggerel rhymes. These would become evidence at the annual meeting for the evaluation of the public servants. "Young man" Lin Zhen, whose name means "Thunderstorm Lin," collects grievances and criticisms from the workers in the factory and helps formulate them for publication. In his functions as a writer he subordinates himself to the young activists in industry, merely assisting them in their formulations. Since the status of the intellectual at the time was still ill defined, it was only in this context that the text could permit the young man to articulate his own grievances. In one scene, however, the text goes beyond this limit.

The young man befriends a young married woman from the office who had earlier tried to reform things, but without success. In a scene, whose suggestiveness caught the fancy of many young readers at the time (as well as the ire of many leaders), the young man and young woman sit alone in her apartment, listening to Tschaikovsky, eating water chestnuts and throwing their shells on the floor, while talking about their unsuccessful efforts to get the bureaucracy moving.

A new youth culture emerges here. It finds its expression in a new style of clothing, common musical and literary tastes, romantic dreams about love, and a willingness to be daringly unconventional. It is based on common aspirations to contribute to the progress of the country, on shared frustrations with the bureaucrats, and on an idolization of the Soviet Union where, after Stalin's death, the Thaw had begun and the intellectuals had finally received their due attention. In the story, the young generation of intellectuals reacts in three ways to the problem of buraucratism: opportunistic adaptation (Han); feeble resignation (the young woman); and in the manner of a thunderstorm ("Young Man" Lin). Lin is set up by Wang Meng as the model for emulation.

This becomes clearer when the background of the story is taken into account. Late in 1955, the Youth League Propaganda Department recommended a Soviet work to Youth Leaguers with "a relatively high educational level," Galina Nikolayeva's *The Director of the Machine-Tractor-Station and the Woman Chief Agronomist.*[22] This highly acclaimed Soviet text reflects what might be termed an orthodox line within the Thaw after Stalin's death. The young agronomist heroine, in a similar political constellation as the young man in Wang Meng's text, anticipates and pushes through important changes later advocated by the new top leadership under Khrushchev but blocked by the local leadership. Dutifully, Wang Meng's young man, an intellectual Youth Leaguer, comes to his new assignment with this book in his pocket to "learn from Nastya."[23] In fact, Wang Meng's text is an attempt to adapt the Soviet model to Chinese conditions.

Wang Meng is a cadre writer and does not deal with the technical and managerial intelligentsia. He thus replaces Nastya, whose technical qualificaton eventually secures her success, with a Chinese generalist in a very generalist "organization department." In his text, the problems of production cannot be solved through technical expertise and daring but through the exertion of public pressure on revolutionaries who have turned bureaucratic. There is no engineer or manager joining the young man in his endeavor, which considerably weakens his impact.

Wang Meng wrote the story as a tribute to the 8th Party Congress and its line. Lin Zhen was to be a Chinese Nastya, using literature and the press instead of the iron "laws of science." This intention notwithstanding, the text also catches, perhaps *malgré soi*, glimpses of the mood prevailing among intellectual Youth Leaguers at the time when their first enthusiasm had already been worn thin by some years of experience.

Besides Wang Meng, Liu Binyan wrote the most embattled stories of this period, and he also reflected on the role of the writer/journalist under new conditions. In his first story, "On the Building Site of the Bridge,"[24] which came out in March 1956, some months before Wang Meng's, the narrator is a journalist. He has heard conflicting assessments of a young engineer, Zeng, and visits the site, directed by an old friend, Luo Lizheng, to find out the truth. He goes on his own; no paper sends him. He lacks the institutional Party link of Wang Meng's hero. His sympathies are with the top leadership's call for a Leap Forward and with the Youth League "shock team" under Zeng at the building site. Zeng is a very capable daredevil, loved by the workers, and in tune with the top leadership, but Luo regards him as a nuisance because of his independent mind and challenge to established procedures. Luo never transmits Zeng's proposal to "double the norms" to higher levels; as in Wang Meng's story, the channels are clogged. Although Zeng is successful in the critical test when a flood comes while Luo is not, and, although he is supported by the workers as well as the journalist, the young technical intellectual is no match for the experienced bureaucrats. Zeng is transferred; the writer is as helpless as the workers. The press (and literature) had not yet acquired the new role assigned to it shortly thereafter by Wang Meng. The story ends with the writer's hopeful sigh that the "northern wind" from the Soviet thaw may also blow into Luo's stuffy office and mind.

Some months later, the power relations changed. The helpless young workers and the journalists now move on the offensive in Liu Binyan's "Inside News from Our Paper," published in two parts in June and October 1956 by *Renmin wenxue*. In the "Building Site. . . ," the journalist could only enter as a support character for the production-linked intellectual, the engineer. "Inside news . . ." starts out with Huang Jiaying, the woman journalist, supporting the demands of skilled workers who are kept as an idle reserve force in a factory and want work assigned to them. In the October sequel, the conflict is inside the newspaper offices. Will Huang with her Youth League attitudes be accepted into the Party? By October, the young intellectuals have become literary heroes in their own right.

The paper is run by brigadier Luo's sibling, Chen Lidong, Chen Who-Sets-Himself-Up-as-the-Ridgepole-of-the-Tent, who assumes that without him the paper would instantly collapse. He is hardworking, and used to the military ways of wartime. A gap separates him in politics, work style, and culture from the best of the young journalists. He sees the paper as an instrument to diffuse government pronouncements among the people; Huang and her peers want the paper to be the "voice" and even the "trumpet" of the people. Huang's mentor among the journalists explicitly tells her never to give the impression that the paper is a "government organ." Chen's work style is commandist; the young intellectuals talk and act as peers. Chen is a rigid puritan and lacks any sense of culture; the young intellectuals wear dashing clothes, laugh a lot, are unconventional and, moreover, are in tune with the political weather dominating the story, that is, spring. The political constellation is already familiar. The enlightened top leadership finds an enthusiastic echo among the activists at the base. The connecting channels of communication are clogged, and the Youth League intellectuals lead the battle against the bureaucrats in the middle and establish links in the coalition of progress through literature and the press.

Even more than Wang Meng, Liu Binyan writes under the impact of the Soviet Thaw. He explicitly and directly echoes Valentin Ovechkin when describing the writer/journalist as the "scout" of the Party. Giving him a general assignment to find out the true situation at "the other side," that is, among the non-Party "masses," the leadership has to be sure of the scout's general commitment to its goals. He does not need a *dangxing*, a Party spirit in the sense of blind obedience to each and any Party order, but a *dang de liangxin*, a Party consciousness, which allows for a critical view of reality from the perspective of socialist ideals. This scout, says Liu himself, is to be the "eyes and ears," even "the brain" of the Party. The simile forcefully advocates both the commitment and the independence of the *engagé* writer. The self-respect of the literary Youth League intellectuals has substantially grown from the first through the third of Liu's stories. They eventually emerge as a strong-willed group priding themselves on being the "trumpet" for the people and the investigative organ for the Party. In "Inside News . . . ," they seek power in the media, and acceptance of their reform views in the Party.

Liu Binyan deals mostly with the industrial intelligentsia, Wang Meng with cadres; but at this time both deal with the Youth League challenge. While the texts as originally written differed a great deal in their politics, they had been edited to coincide. Huang fights for the acceptance of her views in the Party. The young man in the end gives a challenging "firm clear knock on the office door" of the district secretary, a symbolical gesture; "He could not just acquiesce in things he thought wrong no matter how many times he was defeated. He would go on until they were put right." This passage, however, has been edited by Qin Zhaoyang, then editor of *People's Daily* and a leading theoretician of the new role to be played by literature. Wang Meng's original young man was quite confident that he would be able "to sway the orientation of the leadership," which implies much less resistance. Wang Meng is more conciliatory toward his bureaucrats. If reminded of their heroic past and confronted with the facts, they change. Liu Binyan's bureaucrats may momentarily adapt to a new power constellation, but they do not change, just lie low awhile to wait for revenge.

To sum up, both Wang and Liu present (and support) a generation of young intellectuals of unquestioned Communist ideals, who emerge under the umbrella of the Youth League and the Party leadership's new policies toward intellectuals and offer a political and cultural challenge to the older generation of leaders. Best represented by young cadres and writers/journalists, this generation sports a freer, more "cultured" lifestyle, akin to that of the Soviet thaw, and demands recognition of its pivotal social importance. The stories show that the old power structure remains intact. The young have made some inroads, but the conflict has just started, and a backlash can be expected at any moment.

Old Battle Lines Redrawn: 1958

By early 1957, attacks against the criticisms and demands encoded in writings like those by Wang Meng and Liu Binyan had started, emanating mostly from the military. By mid-1957, the backlash was on and an Anti-Rightist Campaign unfolded which denounced the young intellectual heroes of the Hundred Flowers period as "bourgeois intellectuals." Fang Ji took it upon himself to denounce his literary colleagues through literary means in his June 1958 short story "The Visitor,"[25] recently acclaimed by some scholars as the secret beginning of a truly "modern" Chinese literature. Fang belongs to the older generation and has retained the skills of his craft from pre-Liberation days.

His story repays in kind what Liu and Wang had said about the bureaucrats. The narrator, a writer, sits in his office at the Writer's Union when a visitor is announced. The visitor's card shows his name as Kang Minfu, the first two characters standing for "Communist," the *fu* for "Mister." This was a fashion during the 1920s, when young

Communist intellectuals sported such outlandish names. Since the scene, however, is in 1958, we know that the visitor is a youth who imitates the intellectual fashions of the 1920s and 1930s, an impression reinforced by his bizarre hairdo, disorderly clothing, and slightly hysterical behavior. Without further introduction, the visitor proceeds to a lengthy confession of his life's tragedy. Having been an assistant to a professor of philosophy he studied philosophy. He fell in love with a woman who had been forced by her stepmother to sing in brothel-like establishments; but, even in these surroundings, she grew up pure, like a lotus in muddy waters. The story takes place at the heyday of the New Folk Song Movement, which raised the popular arts and poetry to new prominence as an antidote to the decadent, morose writings purportedly written by Liu Binyan, Wang Meng, and others, and contrasts the intellectual, Westernized, and urban literature written during the Hundred Flowers with true and lively folk culture.

The Hundred Flowers intelligentsia appear in the story as the visitor, the true popular arts as the young woman. The former extricates the latter from her debased surroundings and they marry. His only intention is to have her all for himself; he blocks her further development and forbids her to sing in public. His professed admiration and support are only a devious way to silence her. The young woman, however, is undaunted, and, though pregnant, eventually leaves the man. She sings again in public, where the concert halls of socialism have replaced the old shady establishments. Freed from the tyrannical, decadent, Westernized, and egotistical control of the intellectual, the lotus blossoms with ever-greater splendor. She decides to keep the baby, absorbing in this symbolical way the best of his bourgeois culture, but keeping it under her own exclusive control. The man breaks down and is saved from utter condemnation only because he turns himself in for labor reform. That resolve is heartily applauded by both the young woman and the writer who listens to his story in his office. In true collegiality, Fang Ji recommends that Hundred Flowers writers follow the example of the "visitor" to atone for the damage they have done and thus be saved from their own destructive urges.[26]

By 1958, the class enemy had again replaced the bureaucrat as the principal adversary. The avenues for reformist-realist prose were closed; its authors were shipped off to the countryside. From the point of view of the intelligentsia, these were times of national crisis. The status of technical and cultural experts was lowest. The Anti-Rightist Movement sent something close to half a million well-qualified people to state farms and villages without either trial or legal redress, and created a climate of fear.

In this crisis, Tian Han, with his honorific Tian Lao nearly on a par with Guo Lao (Guo Moruo), felt called upon to use his status as the head of the Dramatists' Association to come out with a desperate defense of the critical writer's role in the face of a government that had fallen into the hands of villains. He was in charge of the Anti-Rightist Movement in his Association, and thus beyond suspicion. However, he had published, during the Hundred Flowers period, a plea not to waste the actors' youth by all kinds of political meetings, and had later spoken out in favor of one actress branded a rightist. His play extolling the Great Leap Forward, written also in 1958 and dealing with the Ming Tomb Reservoir, eschewed the slanderous language then common in texts dealing with "bourgeois" intellectuals as well as the "anti-rightist" slant. During the Cultural Revolution, Red Guards charged that Zhou Yang had put him in charge of the Anti-Rightist Movement in his association only to prevent it from being carried out there. This charge is not further substantiated.[27] His next play, *Xie Yaohuan*, also a historical play, confirms, I believe, my interpretation of the politics of *Guan Hanqing*, a play which revived the time-honored form for such situations, the historical drama, and used the chance offered by the World Peace Council's decision to commemorate the Yuan playwright Guan Hanqing's 700th anniversary in mid-1958. Tian's play *Guan Hanqing* (May 1958)[28] was thus certain to attract much attention and provided a good platform for a national reconsideration of the role of the writer/intellectual.

The play shows Guan Hanqing writing and staging his *The Injustice Done to Dou E which Moved Heaven and Shook the Earth*, the reaction of the government and the public, and the subsequent fate of the playwright and the actors. *Injustice* is itself a historical play, and Guan uses a story from the Han dynasty to deal with the injustice done to a young woman of his own time. Tian wrote a historical play about an author writing a historical play to deal with contemporary matters. The spectator is thus advised to read Tian Han's *Guan Hanqing* as a historical play dealing with matters contemporary with Tian. Guan Hanqing is forced to resort to this veiled form of criticism by the oppressive controls over the arts established under the leadership of the arch-villain Achmed, the personal favorite of Kublai Khan, the Mongol Emperor of the Yuan dynasty. The form of the historical drama used by Tian Han immediately evokes the situation prevailing in Chongqing where Guo Moruo wrote his *Qu Yuan*.

Guan writes his *Injustice* during a political crisis where Achmed's faction creates a situation of utter lawlessness, visible in the wanton abduction and subjugation of the daughters of the common people by Achmed's henchmen, and in his control over the courts, where corruption and injustice have become the rule. The young women, above all the girl alluded to in the person of Dou E, embody both the high moral qualities and the helplessness of the common people. The avenues of redress are closed; the people don't even dare to weep openly for Achmed's victims. The poet, Guan Hanqing, is of high station, a nobleman and a doctor at the Imperial College. His heart, however, is with the people, symbolized by an unjustly executed young woman. As a doctor, he has contacts both above and below, the image of the writer used since the late Qing. The crisis of the country differs from that prevailing in *Qu Yuan*. There, a foreign power's aggression leads to a national crisis. In *Guan Hanqing*, Tian Han takes care not to utter a single nationalist anti-Mongol word; the Mongols are accepted in this play as the ruling tribe; only Achmed's faction is chastised. The crisis is that of the lawless oppression of the common people, the Han, by a faction of an exclusive and self-perpetuating ruling tribe, the latter suggesting the Communist Party of the present. This also explains why no anti-Mongol sentiments are uttered.

Guan has no official assignment whatsoever to write the *Injustice* play, but is prompted to do so by his own revulsion at the situation, and by the people's submerged voices. They cannot speak, but he in his high station and with the skills of his craft may try to. Tian Han makes it clear that there are situations where nationally prominent writers have to speak up; the present, 1958, is such a time, and he, Tian Han, does his duty with this very play. The detailed description of the conception, writing, and rewriting of *Injustice* in *Guan Hanqing* is a polemic against the situation prevailing in Tian's own time. Guan invites all kinds of *neihang*, professionals concerned with drama, such as actors, writers, and musicians, to join in the discussions and willingly accepts their suggestions. The suggestions of the *wenxue tewu*, the literary agent or spy sent by Achmed, are bluntly rejected as are those of Achmed himself, who wants the play changed. In the face of the constant and direct interference from all government quarters into the creative process and publication decisions at the time *Guan Hanqing* was written, Tian Han extols the collegial solidarity prevailing among the *neihang* people against the political interference of the *waihang*, who are, however, quite capable of understanding the underlying meaning of *Injustice*, and for this very reason want the play changed.

Within Tian Han's play, the strength of literature lies in galvanizing public opinion. True, Guan's *Injustice* cannot prevent the execution of the young woman, nor can Guan prevent Achmed from having the eyes of one of the actresses gouged out, nor is Guan able to protect himself from being thrown into prison. When Guan is distressed about the small powers of his craft compared to the rebels in *Water Margin*, his lead actress and beloved, Zhu Lianxiu, points out to him, that the theatergoers, that is, public opinion, may form something akin to such a band. Achmed is eventually assassinated by an officer who had seen and admired Guan's play. This leads to a major political change. Kublai Khan, when informed about the misdeeds of his favorite, declares the assassination to have been justified, and puts the government into the hands of the "correct" faction under Horikhoson. In times like these, literature is indeed the only available "sword." The poet is back in his national role as the spokesman of the common people, their last refuge, and as the craftman who welds their distraught opinions into a sharp sword.

A year later, Tian Han added a sobering scene. The advent of the new Prime Minister in the original text also solved Guan's own problem; he was released from prison. The new scene shows the new Prime Minister grateful to Guan because it is to Guan that he owes his career. Yet, he is wary because Guan's politics were directed "against authority" and might turn against the new Prime Minister himself. Guan is released from prison, but sent into exile. Ironically, Zhou Enlai's intervention changed the end of the play. Originally, Guan and his beloved were sent to exile together; after Zhou's intervention they were separated.

In tune with the changed climate, *Guan Hanqing* returns to the violent language of battle poetry, which was to become the standard for the historical play, the core genre during the subsequent years.

Compared to the reform prose of the Hundred Flowers period, the pitch of the language is higher, a feature encoded into the genre of the historical play and the historical opera. Here, the vile officials are to be "skinned alive," there is talk about political assassination, the public forms rebel bands, and the work of the writer hits like a "sword." Tian Han does not object to a play's being political and does not advocate a pure literature, but defends the freedoms and the responsibility of a political literature. Compared to the Hundred Flowers texts, the perspective has also changed. There, bureaucratism was attacked as an obstacle to economic progress; here, it is corruption and disregard of the law by a faction in power through the personal favor of the chairman, Kublai Khan. Nevertheless, the continuity of this text with the prose of the Hundred Flowers period is surprising. Tian Han's text eschews the class-struggle approach of Anti-Rightist literature with its restoration of the landlord and the bourgeois intellectual as class enemies. Pointedly, the illegal acts of Achmed are not committed on the basis of his economic strength but of his government position. Second, the intellectual plays the pivotal role in articulating and galvanizing public opinion to bring pressure on the bureaucrats in power. Because of the new developments of the Anti-Rightist Movement, the comparatively mild language of socialist remonstrance used by Liu Binyan and Wang Meng has given way to the much more unambiguous remonstrance based on Confucian values, as befits a historical drama.

Guan Hanqing had many successors on the stage in later historical dramas, like Hai Rui, Xie Yaohuan, and the beloved of Li Huiniang, all of them literati of the old school, who felt compelled to speak out in a time of national crisis and came on stage in a China during the late 1950s and early 1960s when famine was widespread, and the social fabric came apart during the Great Leap Forward. With the exception of *Xie Yaohuan* by Tian Han (1961), where the heroine is a palace lady much resembling the high rank and frail stature of literature, the remonstrance in these plays does not come from the writer but from officials within the administration, an indication of an aggravation of the crisis and growing exasperation even among some bureaucrats.

Tian Han's *Guan Hanqing* was not attacked at the time, but quickly countered by Guo Moruo who by then had become quite a panegyrist for Mao Zedong. Guo's *Cai Wenji* (1959) takes up the fate of a woman poet who had been forced to flee her homeland at the end of the Later Han when China was under the control of various "warlords." Cai (the poet) lived for many years among the Huns, and married there, much as Guo Moruo lived in Japan and married there. The focus of the play, however, is Cao Cao, and Guo explicitly states in the preface that he wants to rehabilitate Cao Cao, who has been much vilified in popular literature like the *Sanguo zhi*. Cao Cao appears as a genius, versed in poetry, strategy, and politics, and bringing about a singular bloom of ravaged China due to his *tuntian* system of "collective agriculture," a none-too-subtle eulogy to Mao Zedong. He forges a friendship with the Huns, and has Cai return to her homeland to contribute to its cultural achievements. After Cai has convinced herself that her apprehensions about Cao are based only on hearsay, she volunteers to write a paean to the new society created by him, although she is saddened by the fact that her new poetry is no match for her earlier lines (which certainly is true for Guo Moruo). The elements described in Tian Han's play as combining to form a crisis of the country are all denounced as rumor and slander in this play. Justice prevails, people are happy to sing the praise of Chairman Cao, the bins are flowing over. It is the duty of the writer to sing the glory of the new, and especially the much calumniated chairman, who by that time was under criticism for his role in the Great Leap Forward. Both during the Hundred Flowers and in the subsequent era, various assessments of the duties and the role of the writer in the given period were available, although works dealing in ever sharper language, ever greater risk, and ever more elusive literary devices with the problem of bureaucratism occupy the center of the stage.

Tian Han's play is not without its weaknesses. Taking up, with explicit references to Qu Yuan, the heroic pose of the poet from the time before 1949, and a plot taken from earlier history, he in effect argues that the old conflicts are still present, all the language about the new society notwithstanding. One might argue, however, that he misjudged the situation. The structure of the polity under the rule of the Communist Party was different from that under the Guomindang or in Imperial China, quite apart from the fact that Tian was a CP member. Given the extent of CP control, the "rebel band" of public opinion was perhaps doomed from the oustet. Tian Han's historical drama was honorable and daring, but it was its weakness that it was a historical drama and failed to account for new circumstances, in terms both of analysis and proposed action.

Dismantling the Model: After the Cultural Revolution

The literary attacks immediately preceding the Cultural Revolution were mostly directed against writers of the older generation, among them Tian Han, who had used the device of the historical drama. Such writers were closer to the center of power than the young writers of the Hundred Flowers period; with them the cultural leadership, including even Zhou Yang, fell. During the Cultural Revolution, the "worker-peasant-soldier" literature predominated, the intellectual as a hero disappeared from the plays and texts, and the writer, if mentioned at all, was the Party journalist on assignment. After the demise of Jiang Qing and her associates, but especially after the 3rd Plenum of the Central Committee in December 1978, which saw the rise to power of Deng Xiaoping, Zhao Ziyang, and Hu Yaobang, the crop of now middle-aged writers who had dominated the Hundred Flowers period was rehabilitated. The strength of the old generation was spent. Its representatives again occupied positions of authority but saw their role mostly as protectors of their younger colleagues, who came back with texts containing the three core elements of their earlier writing, that is, the intellectual hero (the term including the educated cadre, the manager, the scholar, the technician), and the themes of bureaucratism and of love. Some of the underground literature written before 1976 already contained these elements, for example, *The Second Handshake* and "Open Love-Letters."

The intellectual hero and the theme of love already dominated the texts written by the young writers like Liu Xinwu who had grown up during the Cultural Revolution. They had been in one or the other Red Guard faction. By the late 1960s, many had dropped out, having learned that they were pawns in a game where no one knew the rules or goals. They had started reading voraciously, in many cases books borrowed from others or looted from libraries. Between the two active groups, the middle-aged and the young writers, there are significant differences in perception of the writer's role in state and society, which are determined by the publication dates of their texts (attacks on bureaucratism became possible only after the 3rd Plenum in 1978), their political line, and, above all, their generational experience.

Liu Xinwu belongs to the young generation; he was among the first group of writers to take up the pen after 1976. His stories, like "Banzhuren" (Form master), "Suanlaiba didi" (Wake up, Brother), and "Zheli you huangjin" (There's gold here), include reflections on the writer.[30] In the first story, the authorial voice is that of the form master, a party member, who is trying to convince his pupils that they should accept one of the members of the "lost generation" of Cultural Revolution youths, just back from a re-education camp for young criminals. The second story gives the authorial voice to an elder brother who tries to convince his younger brother to muster his enthusiasm for the Four Modernizations and to forget his cynical disdain for the political leadership. The third story's authorial voice is that of a writer, an official at the Writers' Union who is waiting for visitors, to whom he might give advice. Common to all three voices is their being the "elders" of their addressees. They fully support the new Party policies, and they attempt to win over the "younger" ones to the post-1976 political line. The literary text and its authorial voice as a Party- and government- appointed educator, trying to convince the cynical young generation of the merits of the new line is a far cry from the "educative weapon" in Zhou Libo's hands.

Liu's stories, however, are more realistic than the intentions of the author as stated above might suggest. In "Form Master," the authorial voice speaking for the writer has no influence whatsoever on events. The opposition to the admission of the new student came from a girl of working-class origin. She had followed the old Cultural Revolution line as slavishly as she now follows the new line. Emphasis is now laid on rising academic standards; the newcomer would lower their average and create problems in their class; therefore she opposes his admission. Liu, however, has already discovered the new heroes. Here they are represented by an intellectual's daughter. During the Cultural Revolution she had not only had occasion to read many classical Marxist texts in full length (not just quotations), but also works then banned, like Ethel Voynich's *The Gadfly*, and Lu Xun's comments on it. She opts for accepting the young criminal, who is as much a victim of this unique revolution as the worker's daughter with her blind obedience. The pupils of this class thus solve their problems quite alone. The authorial voice of the form master has little to contribute.

The extreme of this good-willed helplessness of the authorial voice is reached in "There's Gold Here," published in late 1979. Here the voice is explicitly that of a writer. This middle-aged man passively and with apprehension waits for visitors in his office at the Writers' Union. The text recalls Fang Ji's 1958 denunciation, and may be read as a response.

The first visitor is the pampered son of a high-ranking cadre, who offers a Japanese cassette-recorder in exchange for the writer's support for getting one of his pieces published. The second is the son of a lower cadre. His father had been branded a "rightist" in 1957 and had committed suicide. The son fled to Xinjiang where no one asks for papers, lives with a common-law wife—amazingly, for an intellectual cadre's son, a peasant woman—and has hitchhiked from Xijiang to the capital with a fat manuscript under his arm and the intention of tell-ing the narrator that the latter "had not always been telling the truth completely." Perhaps Liu Xinwu comments in this scene on the selec-tive truthfulness of his own earlier stories. The writer's control over events as well as his moral influence are at their lowest in this story. Even when offered the bribe, he does not consider reporting this to the authorities, but meekly hopes that the young man will not re-turn. The same is true for the other young man; even though the narrator hopes the fat manuscript will be published, he does nothing to help him. In giving the narrative voice to a writer and indicating his helplessness, not only vis-à-vis the young men, but also the Party, Liu, for the first time, puts a little distance between himself and the educative purpose of the Party. Again, the young people manage quite well without a strong and influential educator. The plot in part con-tradicts the words of this text, showing the demise of the role tradi-tionally given to literature by the Party. In literary terms, this seems to be a promising dead-end road. The texts reflect the progressive loss of their own purpose and function.

Soon after his return to the literary stage in 1979, Wang Meng offered his reflections about his social role in a widely read story, "Youyou cuncaoxin" ("The loyal heart," sometimes rendered "The barber's tale").[31] The barber's shop in the story is an easily recognized analogue for a literary salon. The mirrors of reflection theory are on the wall, the purpose is *titou*, cutting the hair, a proverbial expression for mild and good-willed criticism, the salon is filled with the chatter of the trade, and the perfumes of the various essences used to beautify the customers, which indicates the second function of this craft. The mirrors have been smashed during the Cultural Revolution, when, as the charge goes, literature stopped reflecting reality. The Red Guards took over, and the propaganda loudspeaker they mounted on the roof of the barbershop indicated the then new functions of literature in Wang Meng's eyes—blaring propaganda. The only leftovers from this period the barber finds upon his return are clubs (the familiar instrument of literary criticism of this revolution) and a small heap of human feces complete with worms (a rather vindictive assessment of the quality of the literary products left behind by the writers of that time). The story is a highly allusive reflection on the functions of literature and the writer in the new circumstances.

The barber's shop is situated within the premises of the guest house of the provincial government, and described as a *fuwu hangye,* a "service trade," true to literature's mandated functions of *wei zhengzhi fuwu* "serving politics." Thus, literature is institutionally under the control and in the service of the top leadership. This barber is a Party member, even the secretary of the branch. During the Cultural Revolution he has saved the life of a high cadre, who then was, like the present leadership, under criticism. The barber thus has befriended the "true" Party during a critical time, and saved the life of its representative. After Mao's death, his new friend is restored to power. Being himself of lowly station, but having this friend in the leadership, the barber assumes the intermediary position already familiar from both the Hundred Flowers texts, and Tian Han's *Guan Hanqing.* But these are only the relics of an old structure. In fact, Wang Meng's barber faces the debris of his old world. Like Wang Meng himself, the barber has come of age. The social base of the coalition of reform of the Hundred Flowers period, that is, the youthful activists among workers and intellectuals, has vanished. Two youths are present in the story, the barber's son, and the chauffeur of the guest house, who had earlier refused to transport the "counter-revolutionary" high cadre to the hospital. The two youths represent the extremes of the predominant attitudes among this generation as seen by Wang Meng. The chauffeur is the opportunist; he refuses first aid to a sick man when he is out of power, and is quick to use the barber's connection with the now rehabilitated official to get back-door privileges for himself. Wang Meng refuses to see him as a victim of the Cultural Revolution as Liu Xinwu had depicted the pupil of working-class origin. For Wang, the chauffeur is intrinsically bad.

The barber's son might stand for the very young generation of writers. He has only contempt for the higher-ups and sees all of them, old and new, as self-serving bureaucrats. When the barber leaves to visit his high friend, the son accuses him of "spinning threads to those higher-ups." The base has vanished, and the leadership has deteriorated. In "Newcomer" the line of the top leadership was utterly correct. In the new story, though the barber's friend develops a reform program to eliminate "ultra-leftists" and restore human rights even for prisoners, he forgets most of these reforms once he is back in power. In 1956, the "young man" battled against the bureaucrats; the barber, in 1979, bereft of his social base, sets his hopes on the bureaucrats.

The barber himself has to find a new moral base. The socialist idealism of 1956 has been washed out by his long experience. What is left is a strong humanitarian impulse, a commitment to the values of honesty and friendship, and a sense of social responsibility. His loyalty to the new leadership arises from the absence of a credible alternative. He has no illusions about his high friend. True, on occasion, that friend dons simple clothes to do incognito investigations in the manner of the "correct" officials of olden times, and he is credited with some organizational talent, but he also is vengeful, conceited, arrogant, and avid for luxuries.

The growing cynicism around him, however, warns the barber that a new social cataclysm is in the offing. To prevent a recurrence of the Cultural Revolution, the barber sets out to keep the channels of communication between high and low open. He proffers the criticisms of the common people, including his own, to his high friend, and defends the friend among the common folk with the argument that the new leadership certainly is not ideal but better than the Gang of Four. This mediation is a demanding job, bringing neither pleasure nor prestige.

The institutional place for its exertion, the barber's shop, has now lost its usefulness. Where, during the 1950s, high and low easily communicated, the public is now excluded, since the shop is situated within the premises of the provincial leadership, and high walls have been erected around them. The barber has to use his spare time to gather material, and his own money to pay for the trip to the reinstalled cadre. His role as a critic and propagandist has become his private commitment, not the exercise of his profession. In his new role, he is completely alone. Both sides between whom he tries to mediate, misinterpret his motives. The youth and his colleagues in the service trade think he suddenly has the "knack" of getting contacts with higher-ups, and try to use him to procure their share of the desired backdoor goodies; or, like his son, they reject him for this very reason. When the barber, intending a criticism, refers to the goods sold at discount prices to cadres joining a conference organized by his high friend, the latter assumes that the barber wants his share and hands him a voucher.

Wang Meng is no longer talking about "writers," "youth," and "intellectuals." His barber is a loner; his "responsible attitude" is misunderstood by all sides. It is certainly not far-fetched to assume that Wang Meng is trying to describe, explain, and defend his own social role to both his readers and the leadership.

In Liu Binyan's new writings, we find similar developments. Two texts deal specifically with the new situation of the writer/journalist, "The Fifth Man in the Overcoat," and "Between People and Monsters."[32] The first deals with a journalist recently reinstalled after having been sent away as a rightist in 1957. He is greeted in the office upon his return by the very person who had then denounced him. He asks to be assigned to the section dealing with readers' letters, in most socialist states an exceedingly important section, since the reader's letter provides one of the few avenues of redress for injustice suffered. As in Wang Meng's story, however, he cannot follow up and act on the complaints within the institution of the paper. His private home becomes a secret address for those who have been unable to redress their grievances by direct appeal to the authorities, especially people wronged in 1957. The journalist's role of a social investigator and articulator of popular grievances is incompatible, Liu's story argues, with the political set-up of the paper, even in post-Mao China. True, the top leadership has already made the correct decision to rehabilitate the rightists, but there is much resistance against this in the middle levels of the bureaucracy, who in fact make most of the specific decisions. In the story, the journalist/writer sets himself up as an independent social institution, gaining the people's trust through honesty and courage, and making good use of the little leeway accorded him as a journalist. The writer assumes a moral and humanist stance, having suffered enough to disregard the possibly dismal consequences of his actions for himself.

In "Between People and Monsters," the writer intervenes only occasionally. Two common workers, not the journalist/writer, have investigated the network of corruption woven by Wang Shouxin.

They have taken their fate into their own hands, suffering grue-somely. Nonetheless, they are not the "beautiful heroes" of the 1956 stories. One of them, an elderly worker, is outright obnoxious, with his bluntness offending even his own friends. This stubborn character is supported by another worker, who has the curious idea of setting himself up as a one-man branch of the Sociology Department of the Chinese Academy of Social Sciences, and proceeds in a manner both meticulous and satirical. He defines what must be seen as the purpose of Liu's story in a wall poster entitled "A Satellite for the Social Sciences," which reads in part:

In the eighth decade of the twentieth century, several leaders of the Bin county Party Committee successfully launched an experiment on social bourgeoisie for our social sciences. This experiment not only provides the Chinese Academy of Social Sciences with valuable scientific material, but, in my opinion, presents study materials for all socialist states in the world. . . . It seems to me that the rise and career of Wang Shouxin corresponds to certain scientific principles; other-wise her existence would not be possible. Therefore her dissection and analysis will help to promote the development of human society and of the social sciences.

The two men together seem to operate as the persona of the author, combining a nearly sectarian combativeness with analytical acumen. The story is a sociological study of the career of Wang Shouxin and of the conditions in socialist states that made her rise to power possible. The text goes on in great detail describing the social and economic processes through which this new "social bourgeoisie," as exemplified by Wang Shouxin, forms itself into a class with enough cohesion to survive even the demise of Wang Shouxin herself. The writer in the story is but the secretary and mouthpiece of the people's sociologists, who turn their "sociological" insights into instruments of battle against this new class; the readers are enabled to discover similar structures in their own surroundings. The voices of the two men remain unheard; the truth is known, but the leadership listens only to the smooth talk of the local bureaucrats. In fact, Liu's story "intervened in life" in the old sense, by making the results of the two men's investigations nationally known and putting pressure on the government to handle the case properly. Wang Shouxin was shot, and some charged Liu had shot her with his pen.

In terms of communication, the channels are hopelessly clogged. The intellectual here has abdicated his prominent role of 1956, but the two workers face the same problem confronting Wang Meng's barber. There is no socialist idealism left; they cherish conservative and traditional moral values like incorruptibility, honesty, and truthfulness. Although Liu treats the "social bourgeoisie" much more harshly than Wang Meng, both men have passed through similar experiences and have evolved in a similar direction, seeing themselves as lonely and misunderstood voices in the wilderness, while the leadership as well as the common people go about their messy lives. Both retain the self-righteous pathos without a hint of the self-irony so characteristic of the modern Chinese writer. The socialist scout has turned into a free-lance sociologist motivated by traditional values.

Members of the youngest generation of writers not only changed the traditional functional model of the purpose of literature; they proceeded to dismantle it altogether. The "cog and screw" function is here flatly rejected. In some of the texts by younger writers, the writer no longer appears as the journalist on assignment but as a poet or a painter, whose craft seems less politicized.

In his story "Feng" (Maple), published in February 1979, Zheng Yi describes the process of disillusionment that results in the writer's or artist's retreat from his traditional political role.[33] The "I" is an art teacher, acting as the author's persona. His language bears vivid testimony to his profession, emphasizing color, perspective, and emotion. The action takes place in the early phase of the Cultural Revolution. The faction to which the teacher loosely belongs sends him to sketch the military set-up of the opposing faction in a school building under the guise of painting the maple trees surrounding the school. The maple leaves are glowing red after the first frost, an image of the revolutionary fervor surrounding the educational world at the time. The teacher is to use his craft as an instrument in "class struggle" by gathering intelligence about the "enemy." He is caught by a patrol led by one of his former students. She respects art, and decides to let him run away, her suspicions notwithstanding. Furthermore, her boyfriend is with the teacher's faction, and she sends him a letter via the teacher. In the middle of this turmoil, only art and love are not completely subordinated to factional discipline. The art teacher, however, ends his flight in the basement of the very school where the battle is about to begin. When one of his friends is killed, he quite literally exchanges the brush for the gun, and becomes a "soldier in the class struggle." The purpose of this battle eludes all participants, it being part of the political intrigues in the Center. Eventually the two lovers confront each other on the roof of the building, arms in hand, and the young woman jumps to her death to avoid being taken prisoner by her boyfriend. Later, when power shifts again, her boyfriend is accused of having forced her to jump, and is executed. Things have come to the ultimate in senselessness. The artist does not even go to witness the execution. He walks through a land where the maple leaves are red again, but now their revolutionary fire is the color of blood oozing from a wound.

The experience of the Cultural Revolution has made the heroic stance of the "cog and screw" artist questionable, even ridiculous. After thirty years the naive enthusiasm of a Zhou Libo has become impossible because of historical developments. The artist in "Feng" became for a while a "cog and screw," but has failed in his mission. Eventually, he withdraws, and joins the *xiaoyaopai*, the faction of those who "roam freely around" without joining any faction. Given the mandates of the time, the refusal to take a political posture becomes itself a political statement.

WAITING FOR THE NEW CLASS TO FORM

The texts studied hitherto in which the writer does not disappear in the fulfilment of his function present him as an individual, not as a representative of a self-conscious class of intellectuals, which would include the technical, scholarly, and managerial specialists as well. Tian Han's *Guan Hanqing* and Wang Meng's 1979 story deal with the interaction among their heroes' peers. But, in the first case, they are all related to the theater world; in the second, they are in other service trades. Only Liu Binyan, with his radical modernism and strong class analytical bent, indicates links between the various sectors of the intelligentsia. As a journalist/writer, he lobbies for the technical and managerial heroes in industry who are suppressed by the bureaucrats, and on occasion, as in "At the Building Site," the authorial voice of the journalist explicitly sympathizes with the engineer and supports him.

The fragmentation of the intelligentsia in most of these texts could be read as a reflection of a real fragmentation. However, reading this as a blunt reflection of reality would be simplistic, since literature is also subject to internalist forces, like traditions. Indeed, the topos of

the writer as the heroic articulator of the mute people's secret grievances is such a tradition, as is the fast-moving, "modern" journalist
clearing the way for the engineers and specialists, the latter of Soviet
origin.

The reform policies announced in China since 1979, with their
strong emphasis on the role of the intelligentsia in the Four Modernizations and the concomitant dramatic decrease in the Party's
prestige and credibility, have combined to form a new awareness that
the intelligentsia are rising to the status of a class, whose members
would join to defend modernization along the lines of the reform
program which not only represented their own interests but those of
the entire people. This new awareness, which challenges the inherited
wisdom about classes in the PRC, is visible in some texts.

Bai Hua's "Unrequited Love,"[34] appeared first as a story in June
1979 and was later made into a filmscript, *Kulian.* The film was shot,
and then banned after Deng Xiaoping and Hu Yaobang intervened.

The main protagonist, Ling Chenguang (Light of the Dawn), is a
painter. His mentors are a painter of popular kites, a Buddhist monk,
and a scientist. He thus absorbs the popular, the religious, and the
scientific traditions. During the Civil War, he paints propaganda
posters denouncing the Guomindang and is forced to flee the country.
He becomes a famous painter in the United States. The voice of the
motherland reaches him through a poor fisherman's daughter who
saved him once, and he returns to China during the McCarthy years.
He marries the lowly daughter of the Chinese earth, and not the
Westernized daughter of the scientist, a conscious choice. Soon after
his return, political oppression sets in, and Lin is moved to a minute
windowless apartment.

Even in this hole, he goes on painting. In April 1976, he joins the
Tiananmen rally against the Gang of Four and puts up a painting
showing Qu Yuan lifting his arms to heaven, with the text of Qu
Yuan's "Tianwen" (Questions to heaven) in the background. He has
to flee the police, and hides in the marshes, the traditional refuge of
the dispossessed and of rebels. There he meets an old fisherman, who
turns out to be a well-known professor of history but who now lives
by fishing and stealing for his moderate needs. The two are discovered
by a river patrol, and, in a flashback, Ling is shown dodging the
Guomindang police, as now he dodges the Communist police. In the
end, a large party of people, including Ling's daughter (who has left

the country to marry an overseas Chinese), the history professor, and Ling's wife, come to find the painter. Politics have changed, the professor's book has been published, Ling is to be restored to honor. But he flees into the depths of the marshes, and dies on a large patch of bare land. From the helicopter that discovers him, a huge question mark is sighted, which he engraved in the snow with his last strength. His body is curled up to form the dot, and his hand is lifted to heaven in a frozen reminder of Qu Yuan's gesture.

Through stories of secondary figures Bai Hua indicates that the painter suffers the fate of the intelligentsia at large, including the scientist, and the professor. The ideal of the intelligentsia is represented by a recurring symbol, a flock of wild geese forming in the sky the Chinese character *ren* (man). The flock of geese is a familiar metaphor for the idealized relationship among intellectuals. They are untrammeled and free, equal, sharing each other's company in solidarity. Their forming the word for *man* is a modern observation, making them into the endlessly repeated stock symbol for *rendaozhuyi*, humanism.

The filmscript starts with a quotation from Qu Yuan, and Qu Yuan is constantly referred to. The meaning of this symbol, however, has drastically changed. In Guo Moruo's play, Qu spoke for the nation, challenging the authorities. Bai Hua's painter does nothing of the sort; he demands only the right to survive and to paint the beauties of his motherland. This is reinforced by another symbol, the marshlands to which he flees. It is the symbolic area of opposition, appearing in this form even in Tian Han's historical play *Xie Yaohuan* (1961); it is where the rebels against the Great Leap policies gather. Here the marshes are only a place to hide and survive. The artist's only challenge is the question mark. The question is put to heaven and to fate, not to the government, the Party, or Marxism-Leninism; no answer can be expected from those quarters.

The military propaganda department under Liu Baiyu came out against the film, and it was banned because it contradicted the propaganda efforts of the government among overseas Chinese. Shortly thereafter, however, Bai Hua was awarded a national prize for his poetry, and Liu Baiyu conceded that he had gone too far in attacking the film as "unpatriotic."[35]

The new leaders made concessions to and imposed restrictions on both ends of the political spectrum, trying to calm things down. Given the signal function of the treatment of this case for the entire intellectual community, two writers shouldered the task to probe into the leadership's motives in handling the case.

"Lishi jiang zhengming" (History will prove) was written by Ke Yunlu and Xue Ke in autumn 1981, and published two years later in the midst of the Campaign against Spiritual Pollution.[36] The title is taken from the statement of a European history professor and columnist who challenged his Chinese visitor: "In the sixty years since the success of the October Revolution led by Lenin, Communist governments have never been able to maintain harmonious cooperation with intellectuals for any longer period of time. Stalin did not achieve this, and after him Mao Zedong also failed in this point, as do all present socialist states. History will prove that the contradictions between intellectuals and the Communist parties in power cannot be solved by any leader of a Communist regime by any means."

The visitor, Fang Zhiyuan, the newly installed Party Secretary of the Chinese province of S, takes on the challenge, promising that the new Chinese leadership will find such a solution. Upon his return, he learns that the Cultural Affairs Bureau of his province has banned the play *The Death of a Poet Before Daybreak*. *Daybreak* refers to the events in October 1976 when Jiang Qing and her associates were removed and to the name of Bai Hua's hero. The play was then renamed *Tragedy of Our Times*, or, briefly, *Tragedy*.

Reviews of "History will Prove" openly mention the story's link to the *Kulian* case.[37] *Kulian* starts with the symbolical image of the hero, a solitary reed standing up to a hard wind, obstinately refusing to be thrown to the ground. The only scene from *Tragedy* quoted in "History will Prove" refers to this passage from *Kulian*. "A solitary island is besieged by the wild waves of the sea, trembling under their impact. Under the onslaught of a fierce storm a single pine tree time and again struggles to lift its crown, but is finally uprooted."[38] Although the reed in the beginning of *Kulian* is not broken, the painter dies in the end; in "History will Prove," the pine tree is eventually uprooted, but not broken. The double symbol in "History will Prove" of the solitary island with the single tree would seem to point at the embattled place of the intelligentsia at large, and the heroic individual intellectual on it. The characters are introduced with telling names. The provincial secretary is Fang Zhiyuan, Fang Who-Sets-His-Mind-on-Long-Term-Prospects. His opponent, the writer, is Lu

Ye, He-Whose-Way-Is-in-the-Wilderness, a man confused about the proper direction to choose.

For Fang, the affair has "great general importance," and the discussions within the Party about the play are "the concentrated reflection of the contradictions" in society at large. Through the medium of deciding the fate of the play, much broader issues are addressed. Fang gives a surprising assessment of the political potential of the intelligentsia. The head of the Cultural Affairs Bureau may be unhappy about their "cockiness' (*qiaoweiba*) and "obstinate refusal to submit" to Party orders. He may be astonished at their daring to criticize the Party, since only the Party can criticize itself, the new top leaders knowing more than the middle-level bureaucrats. The view down from the plane carrying him back from Europe gives Fang a broader perspective:

Ten years of "Holy War" to deprive the intelligentsia of their social status have only proved more clearly the key position they have with regard to the prosperity or demise of material production as well as civilization and culture. Eventually, this has strengthened their social status. But the clearer understanding of their social status and their awakening political consciousness have begun to form them into a much more mature and also much more self-confident social force. In their minds and eyes no Party leader will ever again wear any kind of halo. They view the political situation and specific policies with a probing look. Indeed, they certainly will not submit and worship easily. . . . On what does the authority of the rulers of socialist states rest? Do they have nothing but (crude) power at their disposal?[39]

The intelligentsia know that the Four Modernizations are impossible without their cooperation, and refuse docile submission. The play is banned on the instigation of a senior critic who teaches at the provincial Party school. This school stands next to military headquarters, indicating the link between the Party dogmatists and the military. Protests against the ban come from writers and readers; students stage the play "for reference" and write up a questionnaire to gauge public opinion; the university journal prints articles to defend the play after it has been banned; and students from different faculties organize a public discussion. The list of these faculties is used by the authors to point out those groups of the young intelligentsia most fervently supporting the liberal reforms and Lu Ye, the writer. They are Chinese Literature, Philosophy, Law, International Politics, and Economics.[40]

(Curiously, the hard sciences and technical professions are absent.) The "pressure" (*yali*) resulting from these combined efforts, to which "small-character posters" are added, is intensely felt in the leadership and balances the pressure of the hard-liners.[41]

Within the provincial Standing Committee of the Party, the opponents of the play are "extremely dissatisfied with some of the things going on in literary circles, but, in their minds, the lessons of ten years of chaos, the present social situation, and some pressures from public opinion lead them toward making efforts to control themselves and refrain from adopting big-gun measures. They are in constant conflict between their feelings and their intellect, and time and again they are balancing the two."[42]

The supporters of the play are as ambivalent. Lu Ye refuses to attend a public meeting organized by the students; he declines the role of dissident. The student leader, Fang Pingping, none other than Fang Zhiyuan's daughter, reviles Lu as a weakling, but secretly has second thoughts. Her belief system collapsed during the Cultural Revolution, and today it rests on one single pillar—democracy.

But based on whom would democracy advance? Perhaps based on the intelligentsia which had the strongest demand for and awareness of democracy, especially the younger generation? Was this young generation at the core of a future Chinese "modern culture"? Looking with cool eyes over the agitated head of other people, she had once read piece after piece of the big-character posters at the Democracy Wall outside the government quarters [in Beijing], read one [unofficially printed] "Forum" after the other. But these proclaimed "thinkers of the new age" . . . did not even reach the level their older brothers and sisters had attained by 1971. They were too wild, and too inexperienced. They had not really lived through the Cultural Revolution, and they did not understand a thing about Chinese politics, the situation of the country, or people's minds. They were without any base . . . However, in her criticism of the young "democrats," she suddenly discovered that they also were critical of her! What did she have in common with them? Where were the differences? She discovered that she ended up by returning to (or indeed always having maintained) a position which in theory she seemed unwilling to acknowledge: All progress in China's social culture remained visionary hope without the force of the Communist Party! What they called "relying on the strength of the people's masses" to promote the development of democracy—did that not mean a return into the rut of the Cultural Revolution? Would not anarchism and utopian socialism again run rampant? Thereupon a thought flashed through her mind: Democracy is a political form that is inseparable from a certain political base.—But this ostensibly was an orthodox Marxist viewpoint![43]

Her father with the long perspective intervenes: "We will only be able to convince you when China has achieved economic development and cultural efflorescence. But you must give us some time."[44] In the same manner, he tells the Party school critic Liang Feng (Liang-the-Wasp) to "make a more thorough study of Marxism-Leninism." To prevent a recurrence of the popular turmoil of the Cultural Revolution, the two sides have to be "disengaged."

The play is banned, and so is the criticism of the play. Both right and left "get fifty strokes." And both sides are placated. Fang visits Liang-the-Wasp at home and acknowledges his good intentions; he allows Lu Ye, who refuses to rewrite his play, to receive the history professor from Europe who had challenged socialism's ability to handle the question of the intellectuals, and Lu is permitted to go on a speaking tour abroad. These acts quite accurately reflect Hu Yao-bang's attempts to diffuse the issues both of *Kulian* and a similar case, Sha Yexin's *Jiaru woshi zhende* (If I were real). Fang Zhiyuan, standing for the new leadership, preserves the social fabric. In the logic of the story, any "excess" of democracy would only bring about counter-excesses on the right. The new revolution comes slowly from the top, and those most interested in its success, the intelligentsia, better lie low until the "material conditions" for more democracy have come about. In the end, Lu Ye has not changed his name, but his opinions. He is thinking about joining the Communist Party. This is the time of transition, with everyone *mosuo* (groping in the dark). Fang does not see what contribution muddle-headed writers could make. They only obstruct the smooth development of the revolution from above.

Apart from its evident propagandistic purpose, "History Will Prove" gives an account of the logic underlying the new leadership's treatment of the writer. Friend and foe are haunted by the same spectre, the Cultural Revolution. The story appeals to the critical intelligentsia to submit to the new leadership for the time being until reforms have strengthened the intelligentsia's role and weakened the dogmatists' standing enough to permit more leeway for the intelligentsia.

CONCLUSIONS

There is a substantial body of modern Chinese literary texts showing directly or symbolically the writer's perception of his own role in the state and in society. These texts engage in a dialogue with each other, rejecting assumptions of texts with a different role model, reexamining earlier assumptions in the light of new experience, and linking up with earlier literary texts and traditions detailing the writer's social stature. These texts form the core medium through which the literary community in today's China discusses itself. The greater subtext potential of literary texts with their silent verbiage encoded into plot, proportion, emphasis, omission, character, and symbol makes them the most refined and the only possible instrument of such a discussion in a public sphere dominated by rigidly defined and ruthlessly enforced categories.

The texts written in the realistic manner purport to reflect reality honestly and directly. The historical drama follows the same rule, but reflects the present on the screen of the past. The illusion of reality created by the text is produced by means of fictional techniques. Therefore, the surface of the text cannot be used as "sociological" raw material. The texts are best read as fictional constructs, as "artifacts," where each element is loaded with meaning.

Two basic metaphors for the writer's role confront each other, each having its own time and logic. One sees him as a "cog and screw" or a "weapon" in the revolutionary machinery controlled by the Party, a completely functional subordination to confront a mighty enemy against whom all forces have to be mustered. After the victory of the Revolution, "imperialism" and "bourgeoisie" cease in fact to be the main obstacles. Groups within the Party that lack the qualifications for leadership in the new phase maintain the old construct, the logic of which then predominantly becomes one of legitimizing the ongoing exertion of absolute control. The second metaphor is that of the writer as a professional (a journalist, scout, doctor, sociologist, eye, ear, and brain) committed to the great general goals of economic and social advance, but operating on his own responsibility. The basic commitment here is not to the Party machinery, but to the "people," who are as often and as much idealized as the cadres within the first model, in a time of a well-organized, profesional-led economic and social policy guided by a more or less enlightened leadership, supported by the common people, and obstructed by bureaucrats. The writer acts as the "trumpet" and spokesman of the "people," trying to forge a link between high and low through the outside channels of the public sphere, the press and literature. Seen in long-term perspective, the first model loses out because of the decreasing credibility of its basic premises. Within the literary community, a lively literary polemic as in "Maple" has contributed to and reflected this demise.

Two literary traditions before 1949 describe the writer's role in a rapidly changing China, both associated with a stylistic pose. The reform prose of the late Qing soberly describes social ills, often adding evaluative moral comment from the authorial voice. The writer functions, as in *The Travels of Lao Can*, as investigator and social doctor. The ecstatic language described here as battle poetry raises the poet to heroic dimensions determining the fate of his nation and the universe, with the darkest possible colors reserved for those in authority. The second style found both its apogee and demise in Guo Moruo's *Qu Yuan*. The "scout" literature and its derivatives mostly use the reform prose, reinforced by a similar stylistic and political pose in writings from the Soviet thaw. However, in a daring and well-calculated move, Tian Han returns to the high pitch of the battle poetry in his *Guan Hanqing* to denounce the bureaucrats, not as a complacent and self-serving group in the administration's middle level, but as the faction effectively holding the reins of power and subjecting the "people" to their lawless tyranny, the Anti-Rightist Movement seen as the present-day equivalent. In a similar manner, Bai Hua adopts this stylistic pose in *Kulian* to describe a history of the intelligentsia in the People's Republic of China, ending his life as a question mark. Guo Moruo and Tian Han, despite their fundamental differences remain bound within the same model. Wang Meng and Liu Binyan, despite their traumatic experiences, change only within the same pattern. History and experiences are not enough to change the basic premises; a new generation has to arrive.

The writers operating within the "scout" model try to combine a commitment to the Party's ultimate goals with the role of advocate and spokesman for the common people. As nearly all are Communists, this would seem to be based as much on their personal beliefs as on tactical considerations. At both ends of the spectrum, however, they are under suspicion, as potential dissidents on the one end, and badly disguised government propagandists on the other. Their credibility in their relatively independent position depends on their ability to allay both kinds of suspicion. The texts that have been mentioned are thus a part of the writers' efforts to project their public image. For this reason, many tactical considerations enter in. Tian Han does not criticize Kublai Khan; Wang Meng's loyal barber goes into great detail about the backdoor privileges arrogated by the new leadership; Bai Hua's painter is overflowing with patriotic feelings. The hypothesis that these texts operate in the above context is confirmed by their omission of the intrinsically artistic aspects of the creative process.

Within the texts belonging to the anti-bureaucratic school, the writer/journalist occupies a unique social position. He is the only person with access to both high and low, familiar with the machinations of those in power, and the rumors and ruminations among the voiceless masses. He knows the line, and the facts, becoming the only instrument of social self-investigation in a society structured to preclude access to hard and sober facts. Objectively, the writer most intensely experiences the fate of the intelligentsia as a whole, but in most texts he has but few links to the technical, economic, and scientific parts of the intelligentsia. He patterns himself in the mold of the old *ermuguan* (ear-and-eye officials), the censors, who were to acquire first-hand evidence on the middle-level officials for the court, or of Qu Yuan. But, with the exception of Liu Binyan, he does not operate as part of a city-based modernist professional elite with a stake in their greater say within a modernist political concept.[45] The ubiquitous social access of the writer is reinforced by his unique geographical mobility from "Lao Can's Travels" to the constantly traveling protagonists in Wang Men, Liu Binyan, and others. In a country where rigid rules govern travel and access to institutions, sources, and individuals, the geographical freedom of the writer becomes a vivid symbol.

The self-perception of the writer's role has not been static. The older May Fourth authors had trouble subscribing to the "cog-and-screw" theory, but they also felt ill at ease with the Soviet imports from the Hundred Flowers period. Tian Han in 1958 goes back to the pathos of the Qu Yuan model, adapting it to fit the new form of crisis and the new responsibility laid on the shoulder of the nationally prominent writer. Wang Meng and Liu Binyan lost most of the props of their 1956 model after twenty years of often bitter experiences. But, although their personae are now quite lonely, even isolated, although their values have taken on a more traditional color, and although the dashing scout has given way to the sober, elderly sociologist, they retain the basic pattern when describing their roles.

Some writers of the young generation have started an active dismantling of the dominant models, all of which give a strong political role to the writer.

Were the argument true that the ambiguous role of the writer was determined by Leninist state structure, we should have to find similar methods of self-depiction, and similar models for self-description in the other socialist states; this should not only be true for the 1950s when links were close within the socialist world, but should result from similar structures even after the dissolution of the socialist camp. A comparison in this case is no frivolous enterprise but will help elucidate the specificity of the Chinese texts within this structural family. A glance through the literature of other socialist states confirms the basic assumption. Writers from Lev Kassil,[46] Tvardovsky,[47] Tertz/Sinjavski[48] in the 1940s and 1950s in the Soviet Union to Heinar Kipphardt,[49] Stefan Heym,[50] Christa Wolf,[51] Tadeucz Konwicki,[52] Kundera,[53] and George Konrád[54] in East Germany, Poland, Czechoslovakia, and Hungary have all used fiction to describe the writer's social role to both government and public. The structural similarities are stunning. First there is the social station giving access to high and low. Kassil's mirror-maker is himself a simple craftsman, but of such national prominence that the king of windbags wants to employ him in his service, and marry his daughter. Inversely, Christa Wolf's Cassandra, the seer, though Priam's daughter and a high priestess, eventually links up with the lowly women down at the river's banks. Tertz's hero receives his orders from the Master (Stalin) himself. Konrad's "Loser" as well as his "caseworker" have access (sometimes involuntarily) to both the top and the bottom of society. Heym's Ethan, the historian, interviews King David's wife as well as simple soldiers from his band, and he is to write under King Solomon's orders. The only person in all these texts to cross the sharply drawn borders separating various segments of society, especially the border between leadership and people, is the persona of the writer. The writer's original basic commitment is to the welfare of the common people, not to directives from above. This welfare is best served by an unadorned and public recognition of the facts, giving rise to the images of the "historian" and the "sociologist."

The texts reflect, sometimes describe, historical experiences. Cassandra originally comes up with the "proper" visions demanded by the politics of her father, but later, as the war proceeds, she withdraws to the "temple district" of literature, and ends speaking the truth but being believed by no one. Her own father imprisons her, and the Greeks kill her because she is Priam's daughter. Christa Wolf here reflects her own role and its changes up to the present where she sees a new European war brewing. Konrád, also writing after many decades of socialism, describes the career of his hero from partisan to propagandist, from propagandist to Communist rebel in the 1956 Hungarian uprising, from rebel to sociologist, and from sociologist to dissident. In the end he gives up even this last political role, and enters a madhouse where it is only "us madmen against you idiots." Generally, the historical experiences follow the same trend as in China.

The writers see their role as immediately social and political, not mediated by their being members of the intelligentsia, the other parts of which rarely play any role. They do not speak for themselves or an interest group, but for truth, the nation, the people. They make it clear that writers are a weak and embattled crowd, and the hero is often set off against the government propagandist like Zadok, Solomon's high priest, or Cassandra's brother Helenus, if the hero of the story is not from the very outset the satirical inversion of the (absent) true hero in Tertz's *The Trial Begins*, and Kundera's *La Plaisanterie*. In the Chinese texts these negative figures appear in *Qu Yuan* as well as in *Guan Hanqing*, in Wang Meng's and in Liu Binyan's stories.

In the light of elements common to these texts from the socialist camp, the features characteristic of Chinese texts stand out more sharply. The Chinese texts maintain a very high moral pitch marked by a stunning self-righteousness of the writer's persona, emphasized by a complete absence of self-irony. Neither self-irony nor compassion suit the self-righteousness of the Chinese writer, perhaps indicating the greater stress that accompanies a critical stance under Chinese conditions.

The illumination at the top is characteristic only of the Chinese texts. The others do not see the necessity of affirming their basic commitment to the latest government line. It seems that both stronger commitments to a national political role and stronger pressures from the leadership to affirm loyalty are responsible. As these features indicate, leeway for the critical writer has been consistently smaller in China than in most other socialist states. Wang Meng's toned-down version of Nikolayeva's story—which in the Soviet Union was attacked for "embellishing reality"—triggered an "earthquake" in China. The tighter controls imposed on writers by the government—at least until early 1985—also attest to the fact that the Chinese leadership appreciates the power of literature more than do leaders of other socialist states.

Besides official publications, most socialist countries have a grey zone of nonofficial periodicals and publishing houses. In some countries, like Poland and Hungary, the literary standards of the country are in effect set by these publications, and even the officially accepted writers will try to match such standards and to be well-received in this nonofficial community. Konwicki's "A Minor Apocalypse" deals with a writer and a group of "dissidents" to whom he has loose contacts; Konrad's *The Loser* engages in a debate with this community with which again he is loosely linked; Collin in Heym's novel of that name[55] secretly vies for the praise of Pollock, a figure with unclear political contours indicating "political problems" of the kind associated with dissidents. Literary quality has been greatly enhanced by this contact and competition. In China, too, such unofficial literature has existed. There has, however, been little fiction and poetry, and the official authors have been careful not to become associated with this current. They have neither encouraged nor supported these sprouts. The weakness of the unofficial realm of Chinese culture diminishes the overall quality of contemporary Chinese writing.

The experience of the critical Chinese writers during the last decades has certainly not been encouraging. Writers like Wang Meng and Liu Binyan owe their return and ascension to prominence to a political faction for parts of which the Cultural Revolution has become an obsession. Each stirring of the public mind or critical text that otherwise might be subsumed under "democracy" can instantly be interpreted as a return to the forms of contention practiced more than a decade ago. This is a serious concern, but there are also tactical uses of this concern to silence critics. "History Will Prove" would seem to be such a tactical construct.

After the experience of the last decades, writers' confidence about the dynamics of the Chinese polity has been reduced to the ultimate gesture of Bai Hua's painter. It is the time of *mosuo*, of groping in the dark, as Fang with-the-Long-Perspective admits. As the writers'

Congress in January 1985 indicates, a part of the leadership is willing to remove some of the literary and thematic barriers to have the writers join in the *mosuo*. And the events in January 1986, with Liu Binyan's eviction from the Communist Party, show that there are powerful others who view this type of writer-personality as incompatible with party membership and unsuitable for the governing elite of the country.

CHAPTER EIGHT

Keeper of the Flame: Wang Ruowang as Moral Critic of the State

KYNA RUBIN

"The artist," said Wang Shiwei in 1942, "is primarily the instigator of the spiritual force of the revolution. While the statesman often is a sober and cool-headed person good at carrying out the actual struggle to eliminate filth and darkness and to realize purity and brightness, the artist is often more passionate and sensitive, good at exposing filth and darkness and so, from a spiritual level, replenishing the Revolution's fighting power . . . The work of the statesman and the work of the artist are mutually supplementary and independent."[1] This statement from Wang Shiwei's "Statesmen and Artists" provided the theoretical foundation among a number of well-known revolutionary writers for the division of labor between the political official and the artist/intellectual and the rationale for writers to "expose filth and darkness" wherever they found it, even, or especially, among statesmen. With this justification Wang Shiwei also brought forth his famous article "Wild Lily," which criticized the Yan'an establishment in 1942. With a similar theory and rationale, the writer Wang Ruowang, four decades later, also advocated the distance between politics and art, and the right of writers to check on practices and policies they regard as unethical and incorrect. Wang stated in 1980 that "literature must never serve as retainer and slave to politics but instead should be its relative and comrade-in-arms!"[2] Leaders should "make suggestions to writers only in their capacity as ordinary members of an audience, that is all."[3] In 1942, Wang Shiwei employed the wild lily to symbolize criticism of the Communist leadership when he wrote that the "wild lilies" of the Yan'an countryside, though "the most beautiful of the wild flowers . . . are said to be slightly bitter to the taste, and of greater medicinal value."[4] In late 1979, Wang Ruowang, berating the term *poisonous weed* used by the CCP to damn politically unfit literature, asserted that "numerous plants are indeed poisonous, but, after pharmacological research and refinement, is it not true that it is precisely the poisonous element of many of these plants that is found effective against cancer, arthritis, and other diseases?"[5]

Wang Ruowang also views literature as an equal "comrade" of politics, echoing Wang Shiwei's vision of the artist's work as complementary to that of the political official. Both would hold that the artist's task is to assist the statesman in pointing out the darkness in society so that the statesman can design means to eliminate the evil and rectify the incorrect, the unethical, and the immoral. When statesmen lose sight of the people's needs, the writer, in good Confucian tradition, has the responsibility to intercede. His sometimes adversarial position within the state is justified by his principled loyalty to the neglected voices of his countrymen. This is the basis of the tacit agreement between writers and the state assumed by Wang Shiwei forty years ago and by Wang Ruowang today.

This common view of their roles vis-à-vis the state links Wang Shiwei, the long-deceased first victim of the Party's first literary purge in Yan'an in the early 1940s,[6] and Wang Ruowang, very much alive in the 1980s. The tie, a strong one, binds many of China's contemporary social critics to a moral tradition of protest among Chinese intellectuals who were steeped in the Confucian value system and Western liberal ideas introduced into China in the early decades of the twentieth century. They believe in speaking the truth even when it does not always agree with those in power, because ultimately assertion of the truth and only the truth can save the nation when its statesmen waver from the correct and moral path.

Wang Shiwei's dissent within the system through his *zawen* was only one example of the collective reaction of many Yan'an writers to what they perceived as the inequality and hypocrisy of some leaders and policies in the Communist capital. The articulation of this group reaction in the literature pages of the Party organ *Jiefang ribao*, edited by Ding Ling, led to an effort to rein writers in, as seen in Mao's famous "Talks at the Yan'an Forum on Literature and Art."[7] Yan'an in 1942 set the course for the strained relationship between artists and statesmen for years to come.

The underlying conflict between the self-righteous voices of writers claiming to speak for the people and the equally self-righteous government authorities hoping to present a smooth exterior to the outside world lives on four decades later. Wang Ruowang in the early 1980s is a relatively visible example of a number of contemporary authors, particularly young writers, whose romantic vision of themselves as defenders of "truth" has brought them into conflict with the present leadership, especially during the Anti-Spiritual Pollution Campaign of late 1983.[8]

Wang Ruowang, born in Jiangsu in 1918, entered the Communist Youth League and the League of Left-Wing Writers in Shanghai in 1933, where he was an underground Party organizer in a factory. His first organized rebellion against authority took the form of what he calls "toilet literature" (*cesuo wenxue*). The factory workers could safely air their views in their own latrines, since factory management used separate facilities. He went on to write satire of Chiang Kai-shek and was arrested by the Guomindang. While in prison for three years, he smuggled out leftist poems in Latinized script to get past his jailers, who apparently could not read *luomazi*. He went to Yan'an as a youth in his early twenties and entered the CCP in 1937. He was very much influenced by events there and carried on the writers' Yan'an tradition in the PRC. In 1955, he became co-editor of *Wenyi yuebao*, predecessor to *Shanghai wenxue*, where he is co-editor today, though technically retired.[9]

"What were you doing in those days in Yan'an?" I asked him at his home in Shanghai during one of a series of interviews conducted with him in 1980. "You won't see my name in the history books, but I was there," he assured me. He was very much there, editing a wall newspaper that became a prominent scourge to Yan'an leaders for its incisive attacks against them and life at the base.[10] The wall paper, called *Qingqidui* (Light cavalry), which included *zawen* of Wang Shiwei, was started in April 1941, six months before Ding Ling's provocative literature page in *Jiefang ribao*.[11] The very name of the paper illustrates its link to Lu Xun, the idolized fighter of darkness. "Light cavalry" had been used by Lu Xun to refer to the use of *zawen* in battle against the enemy. The wall paper became so popular that it was soon distributed in mimeographed form to units and leaders all over Yan'an.[12] Kang Sheng closed it down in 1942, labeling it "anti-Party," and all those involved with it were criticized.[13]

Wang Ruowang also became suspect in Yan'an because Kang Sheng grew suspicious of the political loyalty of some of the young people Wang had recommended to come to the Red base from Xi'an. Kang Sheng sent him to a post in Shandong, where he discovered upon arrival that there was no post, no living subsidy, and no ration coupons for food. He stayed in the Shandong countryside for two years, studied traditional Chinese medicine, and became a "barefoot doctor" before they were known as such. He survived, he told me, because of the kindness of the peasants. Some called him the Wang Shiwei of Shandong. At the end of the war, after his stint in Shandong as persona non grata, he was rehabilitated by Kang Sheng.[14]

How has Wang been able to continue the tradition in the PRC? He is imbued with a sense of mission that might be called religious in its intensity. All through his life, much of which has been spent in jail and disfavor, Wang has rarely questioned his own values. He was an anti-authority figure from his teen years, first under the Guomindang, and then in his own Communist Party. His moral obligation as he views it since the late 1970s is to speak up for those who can't because they're dead[15] and for those other survivors who won't because they're tired and afraid. Since he has rarely sacrificed his calling to the whims of the times, perhaps he has not faced the confusion of values that so many other intellectuals have. Wang's criticisms are not limited to speaking for the victims of past political persecutions. He also aims his wit and satire at the post-Cultural Revolution leadership, especially the bureaucrats controlling literary policy.

His targets are not the socialist system or Communist Party but those who implement the system. In answer to the question of whether or not there should be Party leadership of literature, he writes, "Of course we do [want it]. The point is that we no longer want the type of leadership that arrogantly rides high over us and lectures and attacks us . . . we don't wish to eliminate Party leadership but to soundly change the Party's style of leadership."[16]

Despite his sense of mission, Wang is a relatively unthreatening quantity. He is a well-known figure among Shanghai intellectuals, who remember well his bold *zawen* of the Hundred Flowers, and he is a hero among many youths, a feisty personality not unlike Xiao Jun in the 1930s and 1940s, whose obdurateness some found offensive.[17] While Wang's popularity, coupled with a limited amount of protection from friends among the leadership, may grant him some immunity to censure, his brash style seems to turn many people off, thus lessening his threat in the eyes of the Party. "Wang Ruowang?" said a Chinese friend in Shanghai in 1980, "He just likes to shoot off his mouth." Her reaction to Wang's often pugnacious style has not been uncommon among Chinese intellectuals, even those who support his idea of writers checking up on Party incompetence and misdirection. His nonconformity does not wear well in China's conformist society.[18] One might tentatively assume that Wang's following, though substantial, is not broad enough to threaten the leadership he so often satirizes. Wang's familiarity might act in his favor. Having revived the wild lily several times in the PRC when given the opportunity to do so, Wang is a known quantity among Party literary bureaucrats, a tolerated gadfly whose targets of amusement and scorn have not changed through the years. He is predictable, and this might make him semi-acceptable. Furthermore, China after Mao was more willing to accept a limited number of relatively innocuous voices of dissent because they provide an outlet for general hostility that might otherwise be expressed in a more dangerous form to the state. A crucial indication of how the leadership presents and legitimizes Wang's dissent to the outside world, and perhaps to itself, is found in the short introduction to *Wang Ruowang's Selected Zawen*, scheduled for publication in early 1986 by Anhui Xinshutu:

Wang Ruowang's *zawen* contain obscure talk but never false or formulaic talk. They also contain incorrect and excessive talk, *but they never betray the four basic principles* [emphasis added]. Readers can make their own judgments after reading this collection.

The key here is that Wang is presented to the public as a writer who, while provocative, is nevertheless acceptable because he remains within the political boundaries set by Deng Xiaoping's "four basic principles" of upholding the principles of Marxism-Leninism and Mao Zedong Thought, socialism, the leadership of the CCP, and the dictatorship of the proletariat. Wang himself, when asked why he is tolerated, has replied that he knows well the boundaries and stays just within them.[19]

In his daily life, Wang has also made certain concessions in his relations with the Party, though when placed in the context of the traditional scholar-intellectual (*wenren*), they appear less like concessions than a way of life. He writes at home rather than attending to the affairs of his office at *Shanghai wenxue*, a move recommended to him in 1981 when he was implicated in the anti-Bai Hua affair. His retirement (known as *lixiu* rather than *tuixiu*), entitled him to a salary higher than the one he received while working, and is generally awarded only to veteran revolutionaries. His low profile at work and "exile" to home might well be seen as one price he pays for being outspoken, but he interprets or rationalizes retreat from daily duties at the magazine as a welcome opportunity to devote more time to his personal writing, especially his autobiography. He spends most time on these activities during periods of disfavor, when he is unable to publish, as happened from September 1985 to April 1986.[20] He also publishes innocuous writings, such as reviews of traditional theatre and books, eulogies to old comrades, and anti-feudal commentaries on love and marriage.[21] Like the retreat to his own thoughts at home, this kind of writing is not anathema to the traditional Chinese intellectual. It is not surprising, then, that daily compromises such as these have left Wang's moral integrity intact. There may be other more damaging compromises, but in his work and conversations he appears as a man at peace with himself, as evidenced from the title of his autobiography, *Feeling Good* (*Ziwo ganjue lianghao*). Without this good feeling about himself and what he has done in his life, he has stated he "would have jumped out of a six-story building long ago."[22]

Within the daily boundaries where he must work, however, Wang has admitted to a strategy often practiced by intellectuals throughout persecution, that of "practicing *qigong* while being made to do the 'jet plane.'"[23] This refers to an attempt to create a positive, healthy experience (practicing an ancient breathing technique called *qigong*) out of an unhealthy one. Victims under attack during the Cultural Revolution were often forced to hold their arms high behind their backs while bending over in a "jet plane" position. This coping technique so succinctly articulated by Wang has been used, figuratively of course, by Chinese intellectuals throughout history, and indeed reflects a general Chinese philosophical means of dealing with adversity.

DISSENT IN THE HUNDRED FLOWERS
AND EARLY 1960S

Wang's spate of some ten *zawen* criticizing Party dogmatism and excessive literary control in response to the Hundred Flowers call was quintessential Wang Ruowang. In his usual direct manner, he lashed out against what he saw as the hypocrisy and elitism of Party members, their bureaucratic and dogmatic methods of rule, distrust of non-Party intellectuals, and lack of concern for the suffering of the common people.[24] The titles of some of his *zawen* bring home his point: "Creating Barriers Step by Step," "A Partition Apart," and "Something Amiss." The words *barriers* and *partitions* described the gap between the leaders and led. He also castigated the Party for its blind faith in the Soviet Union.[25]

In "A Partition Apart," he described a wall that "is sometimes invisible and not able to be touched . . . sometimes you tear down one wall only to discover another behind it and you feel as though you· are entering the Forbidden City. This wall is not made of bricks, stones, or cement, but is a product of the mind, like conceit, arrogance, mutual suspicion, tacit understandings, and the like."[26] Wang here addressed the frustrations of non-Party intellectuals who want to contribute to socialism but are blocked by this wall from participating in Party affairs. He accused the Party of responding to the concerns of intellectuals hypocritically by attributing their separation from the Party to special treatment to be enjoyed, when, in fact, according to Wang, this is a ploy to keep non-Party talent from joining the inner ranks. In another *zawen* of spring 1957 entitled "On 'Backward Elements,'" Wang wrote, "We cannot use only political standards to measure a person's progressiveness or backwardness . . . For example, some people actively speak out at meetings, are never absent from political study sessions, and do whatever their superiors ask them to do. This kind of activist is very visible. But then there is the type of person whose political progressiveness does not show on the outside. He buries himself in his work, loves his career, but is not good at writing up work reports and records of his accomplishments. If he can't figure something out he says so . . . but many comrades can't see him because he can be discovered only by delving deeply into the work of the masses."[27] Wang implied here that the Party was not informed on what goes on below it. The more one uses political criteria to label people, concluded Wang, "the more the Party will alienate itself from the masses."[28] Wang struck a chord dangerously sensitive to Party leaders in 1957, and he became an early victim of the Anti-Rightist Campaign.[29]

Soon after the Party removed his "rightist" label in 1962, Wang criticized the leadership once again. This time his target was Great Leap Forward policies in a story called "Yi kou daguo de lishi" (History of a caldron).[30] The story follows the fate of a caldron from 1946 to 1961. Once belonging to a landlord, during land reform it falls into the hands of a poor peasant, who uses it creatively for the public good. After the Great Leap Forward the peasant is forced to sell his treasured possession to the authorities, who are insensitive to the importance of the caldron to the peasant and who will most certainly, it is implied, use it stupidly and inefficiently. The story ends on this sad note. One day in October 1962, Wang's wife, who had had a history of nervous breakdowns since his purge of 1957, came stumbling home with two words— "We're finished." By chance she had sat in on a meeting of Shanghai city officials that turned into a fierce denunciation of Wang for his latest short story.[31] Leader of the attack against him was Ke Qingshi, Shanghai Party boss.[32] The wife's mental state deteriorated rapidly. She died in 1964.[33] "*This* was too high a price to pay" Wang has said of the 1962 episode.[34] Needless to say, he spent most of the Cultural Revolution in prison as a "counterrevolutionary."

DISSENT IN THE POST-MAO ERA

Wang was silent until early 1979, when full rehabilitation allowed him access again to a public forum.[35] Unlike writers of "literature of the wounded"[36] who shot their arrows at the officially accepted targets, primarily the Cultural Revolution leaders, Wang aimed his attack at the post-Cultural Revolution leadership and the system that allowed the likes of the Gang of Four to assume authority. He, Liu Binyan, and others, shared a common cause in those few relaxed years for writers following 1978.

In the five years after his 1979 comeback he produced almost as many *zawen*, articles, and short stories as he did over the three-decade span between 1933 and 1962.[37] In this way he feverishly delivered himself of the anger many in his generation had borne in silence for so many years. He published in almost all of the leading literary journals and culturally oriented newspapers, including the Party organs *People's Daily* and *Red Flag*. In the mid-1980s, his articles began appearing in more general publications, such as economic newspapers and family magazines, as his interests broadened to include economic reform, love, and family.[38] The law, or lack thereof, in China became an issue of acute concern for him in the early and mid-1980s. A piece he wrote in *Democracy and Law* deplored public executions and the public photo displays of criminals, so prevalent all over China. The same article lobbied for the creation of a legal system independent of any one faction in power.[39] Another article published in the same journal exhorted leaders to provide safeguards for intellectuals who dare to speak their minds. The absence of laws to protect intellectuals was responsible, he said, for the tragedies of Peng Dehuai and Zhang Zhixin. He illustrated his point with an anecdote about the foreigner (with whom Wang clearly identifies) who is impressed by Chinese doctors' ability to rejoin severed hands but wonders why safety precautions are not taken at the factories to prevent such accidents in the first place.[40]

Wang responded immediately to articles and editorials that smacked of bureaucratic, uninformed attitudes toward writers and literary creativity. Not everything he wrote got published, but he has said that the catharsis gained merely from the very act of writing was essential to him.[41]

In the freer atmosphere of 1979 and 1980, Wang's writings were especially daring. Four months after returning to work after virtually a 22-year absence, he fought, three years after the Cultural Revolution, against a new threat to writers. In June 1979, *Hebei wenyi* printed a scathing attack upon writers who refused to "praise virtue," that is, extol the deeds of workers, peasants, and soldiers and sing the glories of the Four Modernizations. The article, called "'Gede' yu 'quede'" (Praising virtue and lacking virtue),[42] accused writers of "lacking virtue" because they dwelled on only the dark aspects of contemporary life. It referred to those writers who believe that literature and art transcend class boundaries as "worms and maggots feeding on the corpses of revisionist masters on the trash heap of history."[43] Putting himself on the line right after his comeback, just as he'd done in 1962, Wang responded swiftly to the *Hebei wenyi* challenge in *Guangming Daily*. His reply, entitled "A Gust of Cold Wind in Spring" (Chuntian li de yigu lengfeng),[44] alerted the intellectual community to the fact that prejudices against them held over from the Cultural Revolution were not to be underestimated and that vigilance was needed to fight those in power who still viewed intellectuals as enemies "lacking virtue." Wang, as he and other intellectuals usually do, quoted current Party speeches to legitimize his case. The exchange drew quite a bit of attention, was joined by others, and Wang appeared to win out. The autumn months of 1979 proved to be an unprecedented spring-time, albeit short-lived, for writers in China.

During those months, Wang put forward the idea that is central to his Wang Shiwei-like conception of the relationship between politi-cians and artists, a stunning request to the Party to "govern through inaction" (*wuwei er zhi*), in the Taoist mode of passive, benevolent leadership. He made this request in no less an authoritive Party jour-nal than *Red Flag*.[45] His models for "passive" leadership of the arts are Zhou Enlai and Chen Yi, who in 1962 admitted that some sectors were better left to the experts themselves. Wang writes, "This is like the saying 'When you are careful to grow flowers the flowers won't come up, but if you accidently throw a willow seed on the ground it will grow by itself.'" Willow trees are tough and don't demand much, he told the leadership, just sunshine and earth. All literature needs, insisted Wang, was the sunshine of Party "concern" and a stable political state. The Chinese people would be its earth. Yet, he writes, "some leaders in the literary world . . . treat writers and artists like kindergarteners . . . who are incapable of even crossing the street without Auntie's help."[46] He urged leaders to let writers "think inde-pendently" and create on their own, and to go down to the masses in their own way, not as in the past like a "flock of ducks."[47] Like Wang Shiwei, he was telling the leadership to mind its own shop and allow writers to do the same. This particular essay was criticized in 1981 and again in late 1983 for rejecting Party control of literature. It has been a continuous target of controversy since Wang wrote it in 1979.[48]

In 1980, he criticized the "feudalistic" thinking of "high officials" who maintained that the 1979 demands for literary freedom and democracy had "gone too far." His essay "Analysis of a Stage Line"[49] starts out explaining that stage characters often reveal the essence of their personalities through one characteristic statement. The characteristic line he analyzes is: "There are people writing about artistic democracy and opposition to the 'will of high officials' and some have gone too far; what they're really after is usurping power." Wang determines the date of its origin and the social position and level of paranoia of the speaker. "The use of the term *usurping power* by this person on stage illustrates the heartfelt feelings he has for his newly acquired power. At the least stir of a blade of grass he is terrified he will lose his power . . . From this we can see that it is easy to talk about realizing artistic democracy in China, but, in trying to carry it out, the very first obstacle one meets is certain 'leading cadres.'"[50] Wang denies that he rejects the leadership of the Party, distinguishing between "Party leadership," which he views as acceptable, and "the will of high officials," which he sees as arbitrary. Wang does not limit the suppression of artistic expression to the Gang of Four era alone, but claims that it stretches back "several decades."[51] This statement sets him apart with a small number of outspoken contemporaries who have attributed the suppression of intellectual freedom to Party excesses both before and after, not just during, the Cultural Revolution. Wang ends his essay with a word of warning to those officials who think they can scare intellectuals into silence with accusations that they are trying to "usurp power." "Oh, my high officials," he sighs, "do not be so naive!"[52]

In 1980, he wrote an article called "Literature is Not Subordinate to Politics,"[53] which, like the "governing-through-inaction" idea, echoed Wang Shiwei's "Statesmen and Artists" line. Here he uses the Marxist concept of structure and superstructure to illustrate that politics and literature are equal comrades-in-arms, which, alongside philosophy, ethics, and religion, make up part of the superstructure. All, he states, *equally* reflect the economic structure. Literature and politics as complementary interests was precisely Wang Shiwei's tenet in "Statesmen and Artists." Wang Ruowang goes even farther at one point to emphasize that politics is only the "little brother" to literature and art, which are its "older brothers." He compares literature to the pine trees on Huangshan, which, though crushed by large rocks, always manage to survive in the end.[54] Wang cites the Chinese novels *Dream of the Red Chamber, Tales of the Marshes,* and *Journey to the West,* which are great, he asserts, because their authors were not burdened with the chore of delivering the political message of the day.

The modern playwright Cao Yu, says Wang, was never, after 1949, able to produce plays on a par with his pre-Liberation masterpieces *Leiyu* and *Richu*. Wang criticizes Cao Yu's 1978 play *Wang Zhaojun:* "Although the papers printed a lot of praise for it, many audiences found it hard to swallow. The problem with it is probably that the playwright paid attention only to catering to present policies. In promulgating the friendly coexistence and great unity among ethnic groups, he betrayed historical facts."[55] Wang adds, "Whoever forces writers to portray politics alone and reduces literature and art to a tool of class struggle will inevitably lead literature and art to a dead end."[56]

Toward the conclusion of the article, Wang refers to a 1927 speech by Lu Xun, "The Divergence of Literature and Politics," to reinforce his argument. This speech, which Wang asserts Party Lu Xun experts would like to ignore, claims that dissatisfaction with the status quo is the common denominator for both literature and revolution. But politicians, says Lu Xun, can't stand people who think and speak out, and this is where politics and literature become opposing forces. Once the revolutionaries gain power, claims Lu Xun, they no longer tolerate a "revolutionary" literature. Wang Ruowang, like Wang Shiwei, Ding Ling, and the other outspoken Yan'an writers, relied on the CCP-accepted hero Lu Xun to lend credibility to his cause.[57]

The defense of controversial plays has been a particular interest of Wang Ruowang's since 1979. An ardent fan of traditional opera, he objected to the application of transitory political standards to historical scripts.[58] He defended an extremely controversial contemporary play called *If I Were Real*, staged in 1979 before being banned from the theaters.[59] Based on a true story whose protagonist became a cause célèbre and folk hero for Chinese youth, this hilarious satire exposes the corruption of China's Party elite by recounting the successful adventures of a smart-alecky youth who enjoys all sorts of perquisites by pretending to be the son of a senior military commander. Wang, at the 4th National Writers and Artists Conference in November 1979, articulated loudly and clearly his support of the play, a stand that did not endear him to literary officials, but one that was fairly predictable, considering his taste for controversy and freedom of expression. "Could it be that the nation will come to ruin with the performance of one play?" joked Wang about *If I Were Real*.[60]

Although Wang Ruowang, since 1979, has written more *zawen* than fiction, two fictional works stand out as calls for intellectual freedom.[61] One is an indictment of literary suppression, not during the Gang era, but since the Cultural Revolution. The other, more autobiography than fiction, is a grueling account of his experiences in Chinese prisons, in which the CCP jail of the Cultural Revolution and the entire experience of that period is painted in a much darker light than that under Guomindang rule.

The first, "'Shangxingou' daixu" or "By Way of a Preface to 'The Sad Canal,'"[62] is a short story narrated by a conscientious editor from Shanghai, supposedly Wang, who relates his visit to a nearby county in search of the author of an exposé sent by mail to his editorial office. The editor decides the story, though awkwardly written, deserves special attention because a messenger from the author's commune has been sent to Shanghai to retrieve the manuscript in order to prevent its being published. When he goes to the commune, the editor discovers that the author, a young teacher, has been "temporarily transferred" away "for his own safety." Why? Because the exposé he submitted for publication uncovered the corruption and ineptitude of commune leaders and their gross exploitation of local peasants. The title of the manuscript, "The Sad Canal," refers to a long ditch leading to nowhere, built at the expense of the peasants despite advice against it from engineers. Peasant homes along the waterway were demolished for the project and no new adequate housing has been provided as promised. The editor, as *deus ex machina*, convinces the commune Party secretary to admit his mistakes to commune members, allow the young writer to return home, and fill in the canal.

Wang portrays the commune officials as arrogant and cold-hearted toward the peasants but obsequious to the Shanghai editor because of their fear that he will publish the true story of their canal debacle. He paints a touching picture of the fears of the young teacher's wife. But, at the same time, he introduces a gray zone in the person of the Party secretary. Wang, who was accused in 1979 of presenting all veteran cadres in an unfavorable light, might have been responding to his critics, because he depicts the Party secretary as well-meaning, but a victim of his own poor judgment. The Party secretary is presented as a hapless cog in a monstrous machine in which he is compelled to operate. While Wang's portrayal of the Party secretary seems magnanimous, his detailed description of the inherent corruption of the system is not. By probing the Party's administrative structure Wang makes it known that his target, like Liu Binyan's in "Renyao zhijian" (Between man and monster),[63] is not the remnants of Gang-of-Four thinking, but the very political framework that permits such an inhuman, bureaucratic administration to thrive. Lest he be accused of equating post-Cultural Revolution policies with the excessive policies of the Gang period, Wang has the Party secretary explain that, if this were still the Gang of Four era, the young teacher would have been thrown in jail directly rather than just transferred away.[64] It may all be relative, Wang is telling us here, but such assurances are hardly comforting.

In the end, the editor saves the young teacher by striking a deal with the Party secretary not to publish the story until a certain date, after which the commune's chances of winning a "Dazhai award of merit" will not be put in jeopardy. Ending with a note of caution, the editor concludes his account of the affair with a letter from the young teacher saying that there's no longer anything to prevent his story from being published, but that he feels "very concerned that our policies change so often. You can't guarantee that what is sanctioned today will not be taboo tomorrow."[65]

The second and most prominent of Wang's works since 1979 is his very personal novella, Hunger Trilogy, published in 1980.[66] This is a gripping record of Wang's survival through three struggles against hunger—the first during a hunger strike in a Guomindang jail in the 1930s, the second while lost in the bush in Shandong fleeing from the Japanese in 1942, and the third, and most difficult, in a Communist jail during the Cultural Revolution. The trilogy is a tale of hunger and survival, survival in both the literal and spiritual sense, from one inhumanitarian regime to another. Wang's graphic, painful account of the lives and deaths of leading Chinese intellectuals in a Cultural Revolution prison in Shanghai towers above other writing about that dark period by its sheer personal force and the degree to which Wang brings into focus man's inhumanity to man. Beneath the indictment of universal cruelty is the implication that the Communist jails of the 1960s and 1970s were more beastly than those of the Guomindang in the 1930s.

Indeed, Wang interlaces the third part of Hunger Trilogy with comparisons between the CCP prison and the Nationalist prison of his youth. While the food in this jail is no worse than that in the Nationalist prison, there is not as much of it. While leftist prisoners in the 1930s were permitted to receive food and medicine from family members the "counterrevolutionary" inmates of the 1970s were not.[67] As for reading material, Wang writes:

The range of permissible books allowed prisoners included only *Mao's Selected Works* and the *Little Red Book*. We had read this book I don't know how many times and had it down pat, so it no longer aroused our interest. I recalled how I had obtained my education. I am a primary school graduate and entered the factory after just half a year of middle school. Yet while in the Guomindang jail I had had the opportunity to read many books. I read several hundred of the "Universal Library" series published by Commercial Press and studied Japanese with Comrade Xu Yushu. It would not be inaccurate to say that prison had been "my university." Yet, under the name of "military rule," public security jails permitted prisoners to study only one course. This course was called "hunger."[68]

Early on in his later prison stay, Wang is taken into an interrogation room for questioning. He discovers that every detail of the room, down to the chair with the restraining leather straps, matches that of the room in which he was interrogated for his Communist activities in 1934. In fact, he is sure this is the identical room, with one difference—the portrait of Mao hanging on the far wall.[69] The stark assertion is that, after forty years, the scene has not changed at all, only the aegis under which dissenters are suppressed. What a cruel irony of history, laments Wang in prison, that the very system for which he risked his life as a youth is now responsible for unspeakable atrocities![70]

Wang contemplates organizing a hunger strike in the CCP jail, as his older cellmates had done in 1934. He was 16 then, and everything seemed possible. But now he is 48 years old, the oldest in his cell rather than the youngest. He realizes that a hunger strike to demand more and better food would be a futile, lethal exercise—first, because his fellow inmates are not as unified in philosophy and purpose as his 1934 comrades and would not easily agree to a hunger strike, and, second, because the CCP jailers would like nothing better than for their charges to die of starvation, making fewer "ants to feed," as Wang puts it. Wang implies that the Guomindang warden was compelled to give in to prisoners' demands because of United Front policies at the time, policies lacking in the PRC during the Cultural Revolution.[71]

Not only were the physical abuses suffered in the CCP prison much more severe, but Wang maintains that the mental anguish, too, was much worse. In the Nationalist prison it was easier to persevere because one knew who the enemy was. In the 1970s, emotional and intellectual confusion compounded the physical hardships because no one understood who the enemy really was. In the trilogy, Wang begs to know when the world will be set right side up again and when the "counterfeit"[72] Communist Party will be overthrown. In retrospect, it is simple for Wang to recognize his jailers as "counterfeit Party" people. But the reality of unanswered questions and unexplained phenomena that plagued the victims of the Cultural Revolution at the time affected Wang, too, as seen in his efforts to discourage a young man in the CCP jail from committing suicide. He urged him to believe in the "New China." But he says himself, "Actually I felt as insecure as he did."[73] Wang's uncertainties and anger are voiced through a character with whom he very much sympathizes, a doctor trained in America who returned to China full of hopes and dreams of serving the motherland. This Dr. Gu, a cellmate of Wang's, one day remarks to Wang despondently, "Is it possible that the motherland my wife and I sought after is this savage and lawless nation? Ah! I was blind, like a moth attracted to a lamp, I threw myself at the light only to destroy my whole life!"[74]

Wang also speaks directly in his own words of bewilderment and anguish over the horror the Cultural Revolution evoked in veteran revolutionaries like himself: "Motherland, plagued by heavy disasters, seventeen years after revolutionary victory, how could you have the heart to throw your loyal sons and daughters once again into a hellish pool of blood? I've already been through two devastating bouts with hunger; could it be that this great land for which I struggled with blood and sweat could torture its beloved son so savagely?"[75] Wang reflects on the great irony of his experience of serving six years in a CCP prison: "The Guomindang reactionaries [in 1934] had sentenced me to ten years but I was freed after serving only three and a half. I had always rejoiced over my great good fortune. Who would have thought that, after the Revolution succeeded, I'd have to pay off for that free time I got through sheer luck [by serving time in a CCP prison]? Was this predetermined by my personal destiny or was it just the tragedy of the times?"[76]

Wang's poignant portrayal of the patriotic intellectual returned from a life of comfort abroad only to be rejected and betrayed by his government is very similar to Bai Hua's protagonist in *Kulian*, for which Bai was made target of an "anti-bourgeois liberalism" campaign in 1981.[77] Wang was also singled out for criticism in 1981 together with Bai Hua, but his life and work were not particularly affected, though he retreated to his home to write.[78] In 1983, he rejected the leadership's lectures to him on the need to conform to the

Anti-Spiritual Pollution Campaign and responded by offering more calls to "plead for the people."[79] That same year, People's Literature Publishing House issued a small collection of his short stories written between 1940 and 1980, including some former "poisonous weeds."[80] In August 1985, Wang was again criticized by the leadership and was unable to publish until April 1986.[81] In 1986, a collection of his *zawen* and fictional works written between 1980 and 1986 was due to appear under the title *Banfengyuetan.* He now continues to write, but most of his energy is devoted to his autobiography. The autobiography will cover sixty years of his life to 1977, the time of his rehabilitation. The first part, spanning his first ten years, appeared in 1982.[82]

The spirit of the wild lily is still very much alive in Wang Ruowang. While other intellecuals of his age and idealistic bent have traded their independent voices for the safety of Party officialdom, Wang's record shows him unlikely to betray the moral code by which he has lived and on some occasions nearly starved. The artist in Wang Ruowang has always dominated the statesmen who have tried to rule him.

Postscript

On 14 January 1987, Wang Ruowang was expelled from the CCP in the wake of pro-democracy student demonstrations, a catalyst to a new movement against "bourgeois liberalization." The expulsion of Wang, together with scientist Fang Lizhi and fellow-writer Liu Bin-yan, was a signal to Chinese young people and intellectuals of the power the CCP still wields over those within its ranks who cross the ever-changing boundary of criticism acceptable to the Party.

Wang's expulsion is a prime example of how the party definition of "acceptable" can shift in line with current political demands. Wang's criticism of the Party did not seem to grow more pronounced in 1986 than it had been; but present political dynamics among the leadership appear to have narrowed the boundaries in which intellectual critics are permitted to operate. Furthermore, some CCP leaders have undoubtedly been trying to silence Wang for a long time and needed the "cover" of a new movement to do so.

The crimes with which Wang is charged by the Shanghai Municipal CCP Discipline Inspection Commission seem to be limited to ideas he advocated in speeches he is said to have delivered at universities and at meetings in the Shanghai area in 1985 and 1986. The CCP largely restricted its criticisms of Wang to a lack of party discipline, that is, to a trespassing of the Four Basic Principles. Since the quotations attributed to Wang came from talks rather than published writings, it is difficult to ascertain the veracity of the charges. The accusation that he violated the Four Basic Principles is particularly ironic in light of statements to the contrary in the preface to *Wang Ruowang's Selected Zawen* (p. 237 above). This never appeared in 1986 as scheduled—a hint of things to follow.

The CCP justified Wang's expulsion on the basis of his betrayal of the oath of a CCP member by "attacking and defaming the socialist system while advocating the capitalist road; vilifying and negating CCP leadership; and opposing and distorting the Party's current policies under the cover of advocating 'reforms.'" Furthermore, he "openly called himself 'the founder of bourgeois liberalization' and encouraged college students and other young people to 'follow the road of liberalization.'"

Wang's personality was continually alluded to. Deng Xiaoping is reported to consider Wang "conceited"; the Shanghai Writers Association, of which he was a member, "patiently criticized and educated him on many occasions, but he refused to mend his ways and resorted to double-faced tactics. Instead of showing signs of repentance, he asserted that he would fight to the end."

Wang is experienced in weathering political storms, and is reported to be unafraid. But he surely cannot escape the irony of being a victim of the same remnants of "leftist" forces about which he has warned fellow intellectuals since 1979.

At this writing, the Party is trying to prevent panic among intellectuals that any repetition of large political movements of the past is about to ensue; Party representatives across China are told that this attack against "bourgeois liberalization" should be limited to "a few big shots," that local areas should not "grab small local Fang Lizhi's." There is no indication that Wang Ruowang will be jailed or sent into exile. He is reported to have been present at an early February Chinese New Year celebration sponsored by the Shanghai Writers Association, a sign that he has not been entirely ostracized. But the renewal of serious attacks against intellectuals in China cannot help but bear out Wang's own hesitancy concerning creative freedom in China, expressed to this writer in spring 1986—"only the future will tell."

PART FOUR

The Party's Policies toward Intellectuals

CHAPTER NINE

Thought Workers in Deng's Time

LYNN T. WHITE III

China's intellectuals have a distinctive history over the past half century. Those who were educated from the mid-1930s to 1949, during years of foreign attack and civil war, naturally wanted to strengthen and unify China. Above all, they were patriots. Many opposed the Guomindang on nationalist grounds, when it failed to stop Japan's invasion in the 1930s—but many intellectuals by the late 1940s also hoped they could act as a "loyal opposition" under a socialist regime.[1] The pre-1949 background of most Chinese intellectuals—teachers and technicians, as well as artists and scientists—involved sharp early nationalism and sharp political frustration.

After 1949, patriotism spurred by the Korean War enabled the Party to recruit a broader spectrum of urban intellectuals to its cause than it had reached before.[2] Their will to aid China and help the new regime was largely overwhelmed, however, by a 1955 campaign against the writer Hu Feng, by the 1957 Anti-Rightist Movement, by the early 1960s loyalty tests after Great Leap economic failures, and above all by the Cultural Revolution.[3] During this largest trauma of the late 1960s and early 1970s, intellectuals became the "stinking old ninth" (*chou lao liu*) category among "class enemies."

Although CCP policies toward intellectuals have fluctuated since Mao's death in 1976, the Party's general aim has been to rekindle the enthusiasm of intellectuals, so that they might help the country modernize. Hesitancies in implementing this goal have been many. The old hope of the regime's early years—that useful thinkers could also be loyal Communists—saw a renaissance after Mao died. Party policies toward this end have involved several steps. First, the "right-ist" labels that stigmatized many intellectuals have been removed, in most cases; this has been a prerequisite to any other Party approaches to thinkers. Second, official concern has recently been expressed about intellectuals' living conditions, housing, and income; their difficulties in the practical aspects of life have at least been publicized. Third, jobs are now given to some intellectuals in ways that are new for the PRC; some recent publications even refer tentatively to an "academic freedom" that intellectuals need in order to do their work.[4]

THE INTELLECTUALS' STIGMA

Removing rightist labels has, since 1957, been an essential part of any CCP policy aimed at remobilizing intellectuals—but there is evidence that many mid-level Party bureaucrats still feel threatened by having ex- "rightist" intellectuals in the same units. Deng Xiaoping tried to send signals to these bureaucrats at the first session of an "All-China Science Conference" on 18 March 1978. He said that "the modernization of science and technology is the key to the Four Modernizations." He averred that the only difference between brain workers and hand workers was the different labor roles assigned to them. Therefore the intellectuals "were becoming" part of the proletariat, and some were already ordinary workers.[5]

The removal of labels from most—though not all—"rightists" accompanied this effort. The portion of intellectuals who needed such labels erased was large, but the Party was very slow to publish any procedures.[6] All 63 rightist cadres in the Ministry of Public

Security were rehabilitated early,[7] before the procedures were published. In 35 ministries, committees, and institutes of the State Council, which employed half of all "high-level intellectuals in state organs at Peking," over 90 percent of the rightists were able, by 1982, to remove their noxious labels.[8] In this same group, 241 husband-wife couples were reunited, and 2,300 intellectuals received better housing. Surprisingly few (244 of a non-reported total) in this group had joined the Party by 1982,[9] but 28 percent of the "high-level scientific and technical personnel" were admitted to "leadership groups" (*lingdao banzi*).

Over half the 2,000 intellectuals in the Chinese Academy of Social Sciences had run into political trouble during the Anti-Rightist Movement and the Cultural Revolution. By the middle of 1979, 800 of them were rehabilitated. Relatively few (45) rightists from the Academy were still employed there—some had died, and many had been sent to farms and then to work outside the Academy. Of the few who remained, almost all (44) were absolved.[10]

Interview information indicates the label-removal process had several features, some of them problematic. The most obvious difficulty was that many rightists died before the late-1970s absolutions, sometimes for causes related to the political attacks against them. Their families were helped by the new procedures, but the victims themselves were in no position to benefit.

For the living, the official papers on an ex-victim's "rightism" were returned to him or her, usually from the files (*dang'an*) of the work unit's public security branch. The ex- "rightist" would receive a "resolution" (*jielun*) indicating several points: It stated that the victim had been incorrectly classified as a rightist, and it assured that the pre-conviction salary level would be restored. Many 1979 resolutions also provided that the previous job could be resumed (provided the person was not beyond retirement age)—but later resolutions omitted this clause, because the police were reluctant to restore urban household registrations (*hukou*) of rightists who had spent decades in rural villages. In many cases where the local unit's Party bureaucrats had not been changed since 1957, the resolution contained a sentence to the effect that the ex-victim had said or done some wrong things, even though he or she could not be called a "rightist" for these mistakes. The local bureaucrats badly needed such a clause, lest their own earlier action in classifying the rightist be used against them.

Because of the inclusion of this item, some presumed ex-rightists refused to sign the documents removing their labels. Taking old papers from personnel files did not completely solve the problem anyway—since the resolutions were always placed in the dossiers.[11] Intellectuals and their offspring could never be sure that these certifications of previous stigma would not be held against them if the political winds changed.

Party members who had been declared rightist, practically all of them intellectuals, were treated more leniently than non-Party thinkers. Their CCP memberships were restored. Often their wages had been reduced in 1957, but, unlike non-Party rightists, they received salary reimbursements (*bufa gongci*) to cover the years of the incorrect classification. This windfall, in most cases considerable, followed the precedent of reimbursement for bureaucrats who had suffered salary cuts during the Cultural Revolution. It allowed CCP ex-rightists and their families to live in high style; and it caused resentment among many rehabilitated non-Party rightists.[12]

Although some high cadres think that "repressing academic talent is a crime" and a "system for controlling the repression of talent" is needed,[13] others think differently. Vice-Premier Bo Yibo declared in a prominent speech that "Some leading cadres" still "do not trust" (*bu xinren*) scientists and technicians.[14] By 1982, the State Council and CCP Central Committee had resolved that central Party and state cadres should all go to study under famous specialists.[15] In 1980, for example, "central leading comrades" from the CCP Secretariat and State Council were required to attend lectures on ten set topics, including "Modernization and Environmental Protection," "Space Technology and the Modernization of the National Defense," "The Role of Mathematics in Modern Construction," "The Scientific Control of Population," and "Resources and their Rational Use."[16] One stated goal was to make the cadres into intellectuals (*zhishi hua*)—but the enthusiasm of most mid-level and some high cadres for this transformation remained a serious question.[17]

Another effort to enhance the prestige of intellectuals involved giving them leadership jobs. The Party's theoretical journal, *Red Flag*, urged the bureaucracy to "select excellent talents from among intellectuals boldly."[18] The leadership was said to need a "rational structure of intelligence" (*heli de zhili jiegou*) in terms of specialties, ages, educational levels, and general ability and character.[19] A few intellectuals, such as Liu Daoyu, who became President of Wuhan University at the age of 48 (still in his cradle, by PRC standards for such posts), were made models.[20] The loud public ado that greeted "young" President Liu's inauguration should lay to rest any notion that the tradition of geriatric leadership, nurtured now by both the Communist and Confucian traditions in China, is in any danger of dying. But at least Liu is a scholar, not just a Party figure.

At lower levels, the evidence suggests that intellectuals lost their stigma less readily, because local cadres can still discriminate against teachers. Reporters in Beijing continue to hear anecdotes such as the following from the summer of 1983:

Liu Zhonghou was in the middle of giving a zoology lesson, when the door to her classroom swung open. The young Sichuan teacher found herself under attack from seven people wielding whips, knives, and sticks. After bludgeoning her unconscious, her assailants fled. Despite the seriousness of the attack, Mrs. Liu's story was ignored by the police because the local judicial official had made it clear that he was not interested in the "problems" of intellectuals.[21]

This case came to the attention of the national newspaper for intellectuals, the *Guangming Daily.* Yet just one of the assailants was tried. When three women teachers were beaten up in Huairou county near Peking, the Education Minister held an interview to make clear this was a despicable but not isolated event: "The destruction of school property and the insulting and beating of school employees are phenomena that still come up all the time. . . . Some leading departments still don't completely pay attention to the problem; there are even some who wink at (*zongrong*) or support such bad people."[22]

When Hebei earthquake expert Liu Bingliang was declared "anti-leadership" by the leaders of his local unit, he appealed to higher levels several times. Only after much red tape was he relieved of this label.[23] From 21 June to 23 July 1982, *Guangming Daily* received 100 letters to the editor, detailing similar cases of maltreatment.[24] A directive in *People's Daily* ordered the "conscientious solution of problems in investigating work with intellectuals."[25] Each local jurisdiction was given the outline of a report it should submit, concerning these matters. The need for such rules only highlights the continuing stigma that many local CCP cadres still attached to intellectuals.

DEGREES, TITLES, RANKS,
AND PARTY MEMBERSHIPS

The slow restoration of PRC universities in the 1970s was not thoroughgoing until 1978, when the entrance-examination system was restored. "Key-point" universities and schools were designated, as they had been in the 1950s, and they were even to some slight extent financed. "Teaching research groups" were established to write new textbooks. Curricula included more science and less politics.[26]

For the first time since its founding, the PRC government in 1980 authorized the granting of graduate degrees. Before 1949, Chinese universities had done this, and many old intellectuals took degrees at foreign universities. No PhDs or MAs were granted in China during the 1950s, however, despite extensive discussion of the possibility.[27] The 1980 policy creating a degree system had to be resolved by the Standing Committee of the National People's Congress (as if government had some obvious competence to rank thinkers).[28] Details of the procedure for granting degrees were not public until mid-1981[29] when the PRC granted its first doctorates. But this event was not celebrated until a year later, because only then had the number of new PhDs become noticeable—18 in the whole country. At the same time, 15,000 students received MA degrees, and 320,000 became baccalaureates.[30]

In late 1979, China's State Council also passed temporary regulations on the proper titles of engineering and technical cadres.[31] Elaborate accompanying documents gave the criteria for evaluations and promotions.[32] For scientists, the first steps toward creating similar classifications were taken in mid-1980.[33] Such measures were put on the books for professors and teachers, medical doctors, journalists, agricultural technicians, and even social researchers. *People's Daily* printed tables to relate titles from diverse professions. It was decided, for example, that a "high-level correspondent" (*gaoji jizhe*) outranks a "master in economics" (*jingji shi*), whereas an editor (*bianji*) has to give way before the correspondent, but not before the economist.[34] Such protocol was not left to chance.

The Party also began to recruit more intellectuals. After most rectification movements, it had been possible for some intellectuals to enter the Party, especially if their class backgrounds were favorable or their skills impressive. At other times, especially during major political campaigns, CCP membership had been very difficult for intellectuals to obtain. By 1978–1979, the Party was relatively open. Some high leaders, including Hu Yaobang, were concerned that the Cultural Revolution had done too much damage to intellectuals' lives; offering CCP membership was one way to make amends. Yet *People's Daily* reported that certain intellectuals who had suffered during the late 1960s and early 1970s received their Party memberships too late— "only after they had made their contributions and had died."[35]

Because Party admission is a prolonged process involving consultations between at least three layers of bureaucracy, mid-level functionaries who disliked particular intellectuals, or had past conflicts with them, could often "blackball" their applications for admission. As *People's Daily* commented in 1983:

The Party's policy on admitting intellectuals is far from being realized. The reality is that many intellectuals are applying for admission into the Party, and they are being refused. Under the sway of "leftism" some Party members even fear that more intellectuals in the Party will change its nature. They stubbornly hold to the view that intellectuals are working hard only for their fame and profit, and they are applying for admission into the Party out of ulterior motives.[36]

Although it has been claimed that 36 percent of intellectuals are Party members,[37] evidence suggests that most of these are schoolteachers and that the portion among "high intellectuals" is considerably less than 10 percent.[38] Even if Hu Yaobang or other Peking leaders wish to change this, they seem unable to do so.

INTELLECTUALS' LIVELIHOODS AND CONDITIONS OF WORK

As early as 1977, "investigation groups" were launched to look into the living conditions of intellectuals, apparently as part of the official effort to reforge links with them after the Cultural Revolution. One group, investigating Peking secondary school teachers, found that their wages averaged only about 50 *yuan* per month (about US$30, plus slight supplementary benefits). At one school, teachers who had completed their own educations in the early 1960s still averaged only 42 *yuan*. These were all state schools; at private "people-run" (*minban*) institutions, the salaries are lower. This investigation group also found that teachers' housing conditions in 20 percent of the cases were "totally difficult" (*shifen kunnan*)—and as many more were classed "ordinarily difficult" (*yiban kunnan*). Ten percent of the teachers were married but could find no housing to start their new families.[39]

Problems of this kind were especially severe for "middle-age intellectuals" (*zhongnian zhishi fenzi*). If they were educated during the Great Leap or Cultural Revolution, their qualifications for work were often less good than those of older or younger cohorts. Funds to upgrade their training were generally not available.[40] Here is the report of a large survey of middle-aged intellectuals in East China: "First, their salaries are low," and they usually have to support either parents or children in the same household. In Shanghai, for example, many such families have to spend 30 or 40 *yuan* each month on food alone. "Second, their housing is inadequate." Husband, wife, and children all must use one table—and teachers cannot begin to prepare lessons until everyone else has gone to sleep.[41] "Third, their health situation is generally not good." Fourth, they have no opportunity for further training. A spokesman said that, even in Shanghai, China's most cosmopolitan city, 70 percent of the 350,000 "employed intellectuals" suffered such conditions.[42]

Even among high intellectuals, the situation was not much better. Some recreational facilities, formerly restricted to senior cadres, were opened to intellectuals shortly after Mao's death, and bonuses and prizes were established for academic research.[43] A 1982 survey of a number of prestigious institutions including Qinghua University, however, still found many difficulties for middle-aged intellectuals. At that University, where 64 percent of the 2,300 instructors were between the ages of 40 and 55, their income and housing were comparable to those of secondary-school teachers. Moreover, these intellectuals had to spend more hours "washing clothes, shopping for food, and cooking" than the optimal use of their time for society would indicate. The report gave a sad picture of the intellectual's life, even under a sympathetic regime:

Because the burdens of middle-aged intellectuals are heavy and their means of livelihood are deficient, they become exhausted and diseased so that their level of health deteriorates. In many units, the death rate (*siwang lü*) of middle-aged intellectuals even equals or exceeds the alarming level among old people.[44]

Short of a major change in official budgeting to benefit intellectuals, the means to solve these problems are not obvious. A recent reform, allowing scientists to consult outside their main work organizations on a private basis for extra pay, could increase their incomes. When the Minister of Labor was asked, however, why experts did not do much consulting despite this legalization of "scientific and technical work outside employment" (*yeyu keji laodong*), he said that bureaucrats in regular work units wrongly stopped wages or discriminated against their employees receiving extra money. Once again, there is conflict between intellectuals and Party bosses in local units—and the central government admits an inability to prevent it.

"Contract" or "responsibility" systems, now used by peasants, became available to some intellectuals in 1983–1984. Arts troupes were especially encouraged to make contracts (*hetong*) with schools, factories, or other institutions, to provide performances. Among the expected benefits, the Minister of Culture did not hesitate to mention that, "since state subsidies are down, individual incomes can be up."[45] He also said the responsibility system would "develop the activism of performers" and would give them more incentives to act.

Contracts also reached academic institutions. Professors and researchers at Shanghai's Jiaotong University were encouraged to hire themselves out to factories, whenever possible.[46] But by no means did all the revenue from such activity accrue to the individuals who did the work. Jiaotong charged a hefty overhead of 60 percent on research contracts (and scientists probably have a universal dislike of such charges). Factory technicians could also engage in consulting on the side. Spare-time jobs are encouraged, by high bureaucrats if not by middle officials.[47]

Work-time cross appointments have been criticized. A survey of institutes in the Shanghai branch of the Chinese Academy of Sciences during 1979 gathered information on the cross appointments of 205 scientists. One third of them (67) had posts in five or more of the institutes. These double-job (*jianzhi*) cadres concentrated in the higher echelons, especially among institute heads or deputy heads—more than half of whom had appointments at ten or more institutes.[48] One problem with this arrangement was that too much time was spent at meetings, too little at research. This last problem will be so familiar to scholars in other countries, it needs no elaboration.

Practically all the reforms for intellectuals—increased incomes, encouragement of spare-time work, slight budgetary improvements for educational institutions, awards, titles, and the airing of complaints about intellectuals' bad living conditions—were déjà vu. These items can all be found in the policies of 1956–1957.[49] A characteristic of campaigns is that they end. Some recent movements (notably the birth-control campaign)[50] have restrained intellectuals less than most Chinese. Yet, as in the past, a shift of political winds might lead to a sudden deterioration in their status. They could once again lose their "role" or "use" (*zuoyong*), as the policy statements put it.

As in the 1950s, livelihood benefits to intellectuals come at a price. The state, especially through university and school placement offices, still allocates all graduates to jobs. There is no guarantee that a work assignment will be located where the graduate cares to live. This practice was also a feature of the 1956 liberalization,[51] when "democratic parties" were especially charged to organize the "send-down" (*xiafang*) of intellectuals in their membership. By 1982, there were again special efforts to encourage their rustication to distant provinces.[52] By 1983, the State Council approved a resolution on sending intellectuals to poor and border areas.[53] But most sent-down intellectuals, in the early 1980s,[54] as in the 1950s,[55] went to rural areas or smaller cities less far away.

Some intellectuals were also sent to help in factories. As one report makes clear, they were not always accorded a warm reception by the managers there:

Some leading comrades acknowledge the slogan that intellectuals are part of the working class, but their deep thoughts take intellectuals to be "aliens," and always unreliable ones at that. . . . They even take the real virtues of some intellectuals to be faults.[56]

By 1984, schools such as Shanghai's Jiaotong University became models for sending not just graduates but also staff to other institutions. In a five-year campaign of "management reform," Jiaotong sent more than 500 professors and instructors to other places—firing them in a very non-traditional way, if they were selected but did not agree to go.[57] There was no pretense, in this movement, that the intellectuals had volunteered to move. They were given a maximum of three months' salary at Jiaotong and an offer of a job at a single other place. Then their employment was ended.

By 1984, the send-down rules tightened for graduates also. *People's Daily* reported openly that, by March of that year, 162 university graduates in Shanghai had refused to go to jobs outside the city. Since the pretense of voluntarism had long since disappeared, the bureaucrats took steps. They assured that the refusers would never receive help in finding any other jobs. They forwarded the household registrations to neighborhood committees. They published a list of refusers among state enterprises and asked that none be hired for a period of five years.[58] Finally, they noted that "the comrades of the Higher Education Bureau hope that the units where the graduates' heads of household are employed will help do ideological work among the heads of households thoroughly, and thus support obedience to the state allocation."[59]

The renewed emphasis on official job allocation for intellectuals contradicted another trend of the early 1980s: a revival of procedures by which educated people can apply for jobs on their own. In 1981, the national CCP newspaper allowed that various "personnel departments can explore the establishment of organs such as 'talent companies' (*rencai gongsi*) and 'employment reception stations.'"[60]

Since officials who knew nothing about the fields to which they assigned intellectuals had caused obvious inefficiencies, Party newspapers suggested that either each leading cadre get an education, or experts be given power in such decisions.[61] The alternative option—a free market in which people themselves could search for jobs—increased in legitimacy because of real uncertainty that the bureaucrats could handle their task. There were, of course, restrictions on this policy. Intellectuals were not free to move from small cities to larger ones; in fact, they were encouraged to move to towns.[62] The restriction on joint employment (*jianzhi*) still applied to some job-searchers, but the presumption against working in multiple units was relaxed, if technicians could transfer information from one to another.[63]

Pervasive conflicts between intellectuals and Party men increased the emphasis on transfers and the allowance of job applications. Since Party cadres were usually not removable from their fiefs, but intellectuals with whom they had long histories of tension could not serve productively there, moving the technical experts elsewhere was sensible administration. Lin Mu, Chief of the Scientific and Technical Cadres Bureau of the Labor Ministry, wrote a *Guangming Daily* article enthusiastically praising any means to bring "rational movement" of his charges from job to job.[64] If this could be accomplished under the "state plan," he approved it. But if free applications, decentralized hiring agencies, and even personal initiatives were necessary, they were allowed. High-level official enthusiasm for job circulation was often expressed in terms of its value for technical information exchange. But long-term personal rivals who were intellectuals and bureaucrats in the same unit often spent too much time thinking about each other, rather than their work.[65]

INTELLECTUALS' ACADEMIC FREEDOM

Although housing and income are important to Chinese intellectuals after so many years of neglect, the degree to which they can express what they think is even more important. Freedom of expression is almost a prerequisite to freedom of thought, because intellectuals give each other ideas over time, if they can communicate. During and after the "democracy period," November 1978 to March 1979, even official newspapers admitted this much. The *Peking Daily* carried an article claiming that "a socialist state cannot have 'thought crimes.'" This article quoted the PRC Constitution—not just the clause about freedom of speech, but also an article that prohibits certain "activities" as counterrevolutionary:[66]

The key, here, is that we must distinguish between the expression of thought (*sixiang yanlun*) and activity (*xingwei*). There is a difference between thought and activity. To explore problems, express opinions, and hold views are among the basic rights of citizens, protected by the Constitution; there is not a bit of similarity between exercising these rights and committing a crime. "Speech is the sound of the heart" (*yan wei xin sheng*),[67] and speech and writing represent forms of thought.

Although this view was published officially, it was contradicted by top leaders. As early as March 1979, an unnamed *Red Flag* "Commentator" laid down four principles he considered necessary to China's modernization: supporting the socialist road, the dictatorship of the proletariat, the leadership of the Communist Party, and Marx-Leninism/Mao Zedong Thought.[68] This more restrictive set of principles was linked to the main campaign of the hour, the modernization drive, whereas the more liberal set was in the Constitution. Would the law or the campaign prevail when they conflicted? Intellectuals could only guess.

Intellectuals are especially interested in freedom to pursue and publish their professional ideas. Lin Mohan, who was purged as a counterrevolutionary in 1967 and now reappeared a decade later as the Vice-Minister of Culture,[69] raised three haunting questions: "First, are some themes not permitted to be written? Second, are some personalities, for example, 'middle characters' (*zhongjian renwu*, that is, neither heroes nor villains), not to be described? Third, are some artistic styles, for example tragedy, not to be used?"[70] Lin answered that all these things should be permitted.

Even into 1980, after the 1978–1979 democratic movement was suppressed, defenses of scientific freedom appeared in print. "Rights of hypothesis" (*jiashuo quan*) were essential to the development of natural science. Social scientists therefore asked why the same epistemology should not apply to human knowledge.[71] If one group of thinkers can make "mistakes" that later prove fruitful, then why not another? Anemic professional discussions in China, especially among middle-aged researchers, were contrasted even in the Party's theoretical journal, *Red Flag*, with livelier debates that Chinese noticed in other countries.[72]

When the Chinese Academy of Sciences established a "Science Foundation" (Kexue Jijin) awarding grants for research, it needed criteria to evaluate the competing proposals. Since most applications were for natural-science projects, the published standards could be unspecific with respect to political principles—but they were linked to modernization; so Deng's four strictures must have applied.

The Foundation undertakes to support projects that: (1) are relevant to modernization, (2) promise basic research, (3) may benefit various fields, (4) develop and apply new techniques, and (5) use current equipment efficiently and promote cooperation among units.[73] The list is general. It is assumed that the main investigator's salary is paid by his or her work unit. Previously acquired equipment cannot be charged against a grant. All in all, the formal rules are similar to those in other countries.

Projects outside the natural sciences run into more problems. Two policies are in conflict. One of them urges "seeking truth from facts" (*shishi qiushi*), and this requires academic freedom. But Deng adds another: obedience to the Party, which means bureaucrats, and to Marxism, which in China still officially includes Mao Zedong Thought. Free research must thus follow a pre-set truth. This "contradiction" becomes like a mystery in the ecclesiastical sense, as editorialists try to explain it. One of them, after identifying the antinomy clearly, affirms: "We certainly must unify these two things. We certainly can unify them."[74] Protesting too much suggests consciousness of the difficulty.

For research projects, decisions about allowable methods depend on the personalities of the cadres in charge. More intellectuals have now been appointed to head research units.[75] But, overall, work is still coordinated in ways similar to the 1950s. A "science and technology responsibility system" (*keji ceren zhi*) establishes the following principles. (1) Each unit—indeed, each research group and individual—has a definite research plan, to be finished with a specific time period. (2) The quantity and quality of results are to be measured and reported to the bureaucracy. (3) Further work is approved mainly if its results can be used in factories or other institutions. (4) Research groups may engage in contracts and share some of the income. This system is designed to control more than to liberate thinking. Especially when applied to humanistic and social studies, it most resembles the Soviet system.

THE PARTY RESOLUTION
AND THE INTELLECTUALS

The CCP policy toward intellectuals in the post-Mao era is ambiguous. The policy pendulum has swung from relative tolerance to relative intolerance at various times during the past half decade—but, on a constant basis, the Party has tried both to mobilize and to control thinkers, even though these two goals are in deep conflict.

The "Resolution on Certain Questions in the History of Our Party since the Founding of the PRC," adopted by the 6th Plenary of the 11th Central Committee of the Party in mid-1981, does not condemn the repression of intellectuals unequivocally. It calls the Rectification Movement of 1942 "a tremendous success," without detailing why.[76] It says that the Hundred Flowers line of 1957 was a "correct policy regarding intellectuals," but also that, in 1957, "a handful of bourgeois rightists seized the opportunity . . . to mount a wild attack against the Party."

But the scope of this struggle [against rightists] was made far too broad, and a number of intellectuals, patriotic people, and Party cadres were unjustifiably labeled "rightists," with unfortunate consequences.[77]

The Party still views the Anti-Rightist Movement as having been proper, even though it went too far—yet the new Resolution's statement on this watershed experience offers no criterion to explain how far would have been far enough.

The Resolution claims that many rightists had their labels removed by the early 1960s;[78] but, in September 1962, "Mao Zedong widened and absolutized the class struggle, which exists *only within certain limits* [emphasis added] in socialist society. . . ." The proper extent of those limits is never described.

The Resolution says that, by "the latter half of 1964, and early in 1965 . . . a number of literary and art works and schools of thought, and a number of representative personages in artistic, literary, and academic circles were subjected to unwarranted and inordinate political criticism."[79] Here again, the Resolution makes no attempt to define what degree of political criticism was really warranted: none or much, even though less than occurred.

As regards the Cultural Revolution, the 1981 Central Committee at first seems to be more forthright:[80]

The criticism of the so-called reactionary academic authorities in the Cultural Revolution, during which so many capable and accomplished intellectuals were attacked and persecuted, also badly muddled up the distinction between the people and the enemy.

But the Resolution is far less clear whether any "enemy" with power really existed in the PRC by 1967. It says the Cultural Revolution was "divorced from both the Party organizations and from the masses"—but this assertion is dubious, in light of evidence that conservative Red Guards defending Party cadres in many units recruited members of those units' Youth Leagues and those cadres' families. There is also evidence that the most radical anti-cadre Red Guard groups contained some members with intellectual backgrounds, whose access to schools and jobs had been hindered by the Party's affirmative-action programs in the early 1960s. These data suggest the CR was not "divorced" either from Party organizations or from anti-cadre masses.

The Resolution says, "Most of the intellectuals . . . who had been wronged and persecuted did not waiver in their love for the motherland and in their support for the Party and socialism."[81] Yet the

Anti-Rightist Movement of 1957 had made clear that sanctions on critics of the Party would be severe. In the post-Mao era, many intellectuals, especially old ones, undoubtedly censored their expressions of dissent, while others, especially young students, adopted the mixed view that bad Party cadres should be attacked, even if the abstract symbols of the Party and its Chair were sacred.[82]

To its credit, the Resolution does not wholly blame the Cultural Revolution on "Comrade Mao Zedong's mistake in leadership." It at least claims to seek broader "social and historical causes." It offers two such: (1) "Class struggle" had been the Party's watchword during its previous periods of political success, and (2) international tension with the USSR encouraged Chinese protests against domestic "revisionism."[83] The first of these suggestions is debatable, in view of evidence for the importance of peasant nationalism in the Party's rise.[84] The second ignores what was happening in Vietnam at that time; and it may overemphasize the potential of any foreign influence in the politics of this gigantic, inward-looking country.

The Resolution is more persuasive when it generalizes from Mao's main fault—"he began to get arrogant"[85]—to the central problem in many Party units:

It remains difficult to eliminate the evil ideological and political influence of centuries of feudal autocracy. And for various historical reasons, we failed to institutionalize and legalize inner-Party democracy and democracy in the political and social life of the country, or we drew up the relevant laws but they lacked due authority. This meant that conditions were present for the over-concentration of Party power in individuals and for the development of arbitrary individual rule and the personality cult in the Party.

The 1981 Resolution reaffirmed a 1978 "principle that neither democracy nor centralism can be practiced at each other's expense." It "pointed out the basic fact that, although the exploiters had been eliminated as classes, class struggle continues to exist within certain limits."[86] This assertion is designed to recruit intellectuals' talent and to retain the loyalties of Party men who dislike them, rather than to be clear. The proper limits of "class struggle" remain undefined. The unification of "democracy" and "centralism" is a mystical, useful tenet of CCP faith.

The Resolution concludes with the warning, "Any word or deed that denies or undermines these four principles [socialism, dictatorship, the Party, or Marxism-Leninism/Mao Zedong Thought] cannot be tolerated."[87] That moralistic position is likely to prevail over legal ones for years, although CCP leaders seem less sure lately that they have inside information on the future and the right.

The clearest recent example of the Party's continued wariness of intellectuals was the Campaign to Eliminate Spiritual Pollution (*jinshen wuran*).[88] This movement, begun in October 1983 at the 2nd Plenary of the 12th Party Congress, had four "tasks": to unify thought, purify work style, strengthen discipline, and cleanse organization (*tongyi sixiang, zhengdun zuofeng, jiaqiang jilü, chunjie zuzhi*). These are all abstract; the campaign had few concrete, programmatic goals. It involved the criticism of some artists,[89] but it was mostly a propaganda movement. Formally, two main spiritual faults were the targets: the notion that capitalist practices can help China, and the notion that any proper Marxist analysis can show "alienation" between the Party and Chinese society.[90]

Yet, these two premises underlie many concurrent Party policies in the Four Modernizations Campaign (largely a matter of borrowing pointers from capitalism) and in CCP efforts to restore links with people—notably intellectuals—whom the Party has obviously alienated. The gist of the Spiritual Pollution Campaign is that, although quasi-capitalist and anti-alienation policies are needed, no one must think of these policies *as* capitalist, or as aimed at preventing alienation. No matter what people knew, they were supposed to think in socialist terms.

Many such study materials, however, warned against carrying the Spiritual Pollution Campaign too far. They claimed this new "spiritual" movement for "socialist civilization" was different from the anti-pluralist hunts of the 1950s and 1960s, especially the Cultural Revolution. As *People's Daily* said:

Don't take just any question and make it a matter of spiritual pollution. Don't take things which you haven't seen or dislike, and make them into spiritual pollution without analysis. Don't resemble some comrades, who think "Spiritual pollution is a basket (*kuang*), and anything can be packed into it."[91]

The Party's problem, in the Spiritual Pollution Campaign, was to instill more Communist discipline among intellectuals—just what the Gang of Four had tried to do—while dissociating itself from the recent history of repression. This was the Party's only hope of laying a claim on intellectuals' talents, but it is a hard trick to turn. The upshot of the new campaign was not that socialist morals should be understood, but that discussion of them should be kept within public bounds set by the Party. Independence in "searching truth from facts" would subvert the official monopoly on moralizing.

A NEW RELATIONSHIP BETWEEN
STATE AND INTELLECTUALS?

Under Deng Xiaoping, there have been tentative improvements in living and working conditions for Chinese intellectuals. The importance of this group for China's future development is now a policy slogan. Deng himself has addressed many audiences on this topic, and those speeches have been published in an obvious effort to persuade intellectuals that the regime favors them at last. In particular, since July 1977, Deng has excoriated the "two whatevers" (liangge fanshi) view of Hua Guofeng, who preferred a continuation of all Mao's policies. He has also castigated the "two assessments" (liangge guji), from a 1971 document, which claimed that, before 1966, all China's schools and universities had been dominated by the bourgeoisie, and that the great majority of China's intellectuals were bourgeois.[92]

Deng has not been alone in these efforts. Premier Zhao Ziyang chose personally to head the State Council's "Science and Technology Leadership Group."[93] Hu Yaobang, General Secretary of the Party is, according to Communists and dissidents alike, the highest leader with a relatively steady concern for intellectuals.[94] Old generals Nie Rongzhen and Wang Zhen, who have some history of interest in technology, deliver similar speeches.[95] Even the likes of Deng Liqun, Director of the Party Propaganda Department and a leader of the Spiritual Pollution Campaign, regularly deliver positive, abstract affirmation of the importance of intellectuals.[96] Economic cadres and Central Committee members do the same.[97] Even though they pushed the Spiritual Pollution Campaign, Li Xiannian, Peng Zhen, Song Renqiong, Chen Yun, Hu Qiaomu, and other high Party leaders periodically contribute nice, formalistic sentences about intellectuals. Even Marshal Ye Jianying, who may be the leader most threatening to quasi-liberal policies,[98] has been heard to say positive things.[99] Dozens of articles cite praises from dead leaders about intellectuals—more credibly from Zhou Enlai, more inconsistently from Mao Zedong.[100]

If words were not enough, there are models too. Ding Shengshu, a linguist at the Chinese Academy of Social Sciences who died in 1983, is to be studied for his "high loyalty to the Party, the motherland, the people, socialism, and the Communist cause."[101] Less was said in the euology about his work with language reform, but he completed every task he was assigned by the Party. Another model intellectual is Zhou Qiumin, Associate Professor at the South-Central School of Mines and an expert in electrical machines, who also died before canonization. As *People's Daily* says in a long article, he participated from the age of 15 in underground Shanghai Party organizations. He was sent to study at M.I.T. for four years after 1979.[102] Jiang Zhuying, a middle-aged optics expert, died from working too hard. He was a "perpetual-motion machine" (*yondong ji*) because of his constant, nervous, enthusiastic efforts in research and in social works (helping mothers and children to board jammed busses, cleaning up broken glass on public streets so as to prevent bicycle-tire punctures, many other stories).[103] Lo Jianfu, an electrical expert who was also a Party member, declined all salary increases and job promotions that were due him, took less good housing than his comrades at the same level, refused to use the "back door" to help his son and daughter enter universities, and even went abroad and to Hong Kong without ill effects.[104] (One of the most-mooted forms of spiritual pollution was *Gang feng*, the "Hong Kong breeze.")

The Spiritual Pollution Campaign had gradually eroded, by 1984, because its opponents could claim it was hurting China's modernization. As the campaign began to hamper rural efforts to decollectivize, it was stopped among peasants. Because the movement took industrial workers' time, it was then restricted to intellectuals. When it began clearly to reduce the productivity of technicians and professionals, it was limited to ideologues and artists.[105]

The Spiritual Pollution Campaign came to a halt in September 1984, when a meeting convened by Deng Liqun and Hu Qiaomu to rebut criticisms of this puritanism ended on a very opposite note: Deng Xiaoping, Hu Yaobang, and others called on the conference to criticize leftists instead. By December, at the 4th Congress of Chinese Writers and Artists, Hu Yaobang still called literary workers "engineers of the soul" (in the same way technicians are engineers, presumably). They were still supposed to educate the masses in socialism. But the upshot of the Congress, especially in its elections, confirmed a temporary trend toward more freedom for intellectuals. How far this will go, no one knows.[106]

CONCLUSION: OFFICIALS' UNCERTAINTY, INTELLECTUALS' HEALING

Some in China still appreciate the skeptical, open intellect, willing to try various values and use all styles of thought for the sake of really new understandings.[107] This kind of mind depends on personal and social forces outside the competence of the polity. Lenin, looking back at the revolution he had made, noticed just before his death that "defects . . . rooted in the past" could undo it.[108]

A similar uncertainty now bedevils even official propagandists in the PRC. Su Shaozhi, Director of the Institute of Marx-Leninism/ Mao Zedong Thought in the Chinese Academy of Social Sciences, co-authored in 1979 an article on "The Problem of Stages of Social Development After the Proletariat Obtains Power."[109] Su argues that China is not yet a socialist society. The country still needs small-scale production, more education, and generally a modern substructure to sustain real socialism:

We are still an undeveloped socialist society (*bu fada de shehuizhuyi shehui*), still in the transition to socialism. It cannot be said that our economic system is already evolved or complete socialism.

This article is partly designed to explain how the Cultural Revolution could have happened. The view is hardly liberal, but it sees the dangers of "feudal" bossism in small units, the inefficiencies of economic and political institutions that are centralized more than the evolution of infrastructure warrants, and the extent of popular gullibility that the PRC's educational system has produced. Such a view produces policy recommendations, especially for economic and administrative problems, that strongly resemble those that would come from a Chinese liberal.

Management decentralization, the encouragement of more diverse publishing and education to enliven intellectual life, more market-oriented pricing mechanisms, more policies taking a realistic view of the inherent "cellularity" of organization in an underdeveloped country—all these "tendencies of articulation"[110] could be based *either* on a neo-Marxist analysis of the sort Su presents *or* on a classic liberal one. Deng Xiaoping once said, "Whether it's a white cat or a black cat, it's a good cat if it catches mice."[111] Su expands on this: By showing Marxist grounds that can justify liberal policies, he implies there might be no practical reason to care about the color—even if cats came in red.

This has effects on Party legitimacy, because it suggests there is no need for the comrades to pretend exactness or cocksureness about actions, including repressive ones, that might bring progress. It implies that stubborn certainty about basic principles may hinder, rather than help, real-world effectiveness. Such an insight runs counter to some Chinese traditions—but it really destroys the moral certainty in historical action that Communists thought they had.

Hu Qiaomu, long associated with the Chinese Academy of Social Sciences, reportedly wanted a campaign to criticize Su Shaozhi. The fact that no witch hunt occurred says much about the state of mind of Party officials and intellectuals after the Cultural Revolution—they are no longer sure they can see the future perfectly. To a large extent, the Party legitimists' frustrations were vented later, in the 1981 criticisms of Bai Hua.[112] This diversion of the criticism might even aid future Bai Huas. Over time, the new diversity of opinions in China may help to free minds.

This will take many years. Campaigns still continue in China after Mao. No one, of any political stripe, expects future ones to be entirely non-repressive. As Vera Schwarcz has written:

An accurate reading of the mood of intellectuals remains elusive, as long as we fail to grasp the difference between the loud, official rehabilitation of intellectuals under way in China today and the quieter, more cautious self-healing that is being attempted by the intellectuals themselves.[113]

Thinkers have long stressed memory. "Self-healing" comes to their community partly in the revival of symbols that predate the revolution. Students now sometimes call their teachers "earlier born," *xiansheng*—a name more respectful than "comrade." At lunar New Year, they again may visit their mentors' homes (*bainian*). Old ideas like "integrity" (*qijie*) are somewhat back in style.[114] The Party might, of course, try to repress such symbols yet again. But it seems less certain than before of what it wants to do. It now runs on many conflicting, practical, ambiguous principles.

The overall conclusion is one of very muted optimism. Deng Xiaoping, even Hu Yaobang, may "in principle" be no different from Mao. To say this alone, though, without also evaluating the intellectuals' resources, would be to miss half the picture. Their policies toward government are as important as its toward them. If intellectuals think freely, the reason will not be just because the regime wishes this.

Intellectuals do not crucially oppose or support any government. That is not how their work influences most politics. If they support a regime, it lasts or falls mainly because of other constituencies. If they try to oppose it alone, they are regularly repressed. Their power is longer-term, more elusive, a matter of symbols. The social task of Chinese intellectuals is to see China clearly, and to say what they see.

CHAPTER TEN

Conclusion: New Trends Under Deng Xiaoping and His Successors

CAROL LEE HAMRIN*

Life for intellectuals in China has improved vastly in the past decade, in terms of both personal well-being and conditions conducive to creative work. These improvements have not occurred steadily, however; nor are the gains considered fully secure. As the foregoing chapters testify, state-intellectual relations continue to be characterized by much ambiguity and mistrust.[1] The activities of intellectuals—whether in management, teaching, researching or writing—are still subject to political criteria. The Party's policy toward intellectuals continues to be characterized by cycles of relative restriction and relative tolerance.[2]

---

*The following views are those of the author alone, not of any U.S. Government organization.

Since the structure and dynamics of the political system have changed little, despite changes in personnel and policy, intellectuals are still faced with a limited choice of three roles: ideological spokesmen explaining and enforcing regime policies, professionals and academics serving the regime's goals, and critical intellectuals lobbying for change. Anti-regime dissidents continue to find room only in the prisons and work camps. But, compared with the 1970s, when Maoist spokesmen terrorized their peers in the other two groups, things have changed greatly. Ideological spokesmen are on the defensive, their clubs laid aside, at least temporarily. Meanwhile, the professional-academic elite, which will include thousands of students now returning from study abroad, is mushrooming and has become an important constituency for economic reform. Once alienated from the Maoist regime of the 1960s and 1970s, these intellectuals are willing to become part of Deng Xiaoping's reformed establishment, but are more conscious of the need to speak up and take action in defense of their interests. Keeping them happy and productive is an important regime goal. A small, but influential, minority of scholars and professionals, young and old, have taken on the functional role of spokesmen for the interests of this elite, even though they do not explicitly portray themselves as such. Foremost among these interests are greater intellectual freedom and professional autonomy. Members of this group are not formally affiliated, but share similar views and webs of personal ties. They have chosen to retain a critical stance in the post-Mao era, pressing for further systemic reforms including political and ideological reform, arguing that this is necessary if economic reform is to be sustained and its fruits harvested. These intellectuals are not anti-establishment dissidents, however, since they have the backing of key leaders in the radical reform wing of the regime and consciously serve their political interests, both as advisors and propagandists. Following is a more detailed review of the changing nature of state-intellectual relations in the transition under Deng Xiaoping from Mao's era toward a post-revolutionary China.

INTELLECTUALS AND POLITICAL AUTHORITY

Emerging from the Cultural Revolution, the central political elite in China, including the intellectuals, is no longer willing to give total personal loyalty to a paternalistic leader; nor does it retain a blind faith in a Leninist "priesthood." With the shift of priorities from social transformation to economic growth and the transfer of authority from the handful of remaining revolutionaries to a younger modernizing elite that extends beyond the Party, new leaders must increasingly rely on current performance criteria and less on the Party's past glories as sources of legitimacy. The search for new grounds of legitimacy for the regime and a major redistribution of political authority has made the state's relationship with intellectuals particularly important in this period.[3]

The primary lesson of Mao's era is that state monopoly of power in politics, economics, and culture leads to stagnation. The incipient "retreat" of the state has resulted in a partial dispersal of authority from Party generalists to technicians, managers, and professionals in all fields. Intellectuals as a social group have regained some political influence, professional autonomy, and social status. The mad rush for diplomas in China is powerful testimony to this trend. Almost overnight, intellectuals have ceased to be a class of "untouchables" and are now the primary bearers of the next revolution—"the information revolution." Understandably, popular dissatisfaction and leadership controversy have accompanied this redistribution of social assets, as reflected first and foremost in inconsistencies in the treatment of intellectuals. The Party, like any good bureaucrat, knows instinctively that delegating authority may increase its immediate effectiveness, but may also weaken its control over future developments.

Policy affecting intellectual activities has also been the "barometer" of broader political controversy, because certain types of intellectuals, by the very nature of their work, are the articulators of the most basic political issues—the degree of legitimacy and authority of the regime, and the depth and nature of social disaffections. As in any system, nationally known literary figures and artists and generalists engaged in philosophy, history, economic theory, and the philosophy of science find it difficult to extricate themselves from politics. In a single-party system, where public opinion has few outlets for expression, the ideas voiced by such key intellectuals become the focal point for elite-mass tensions. This is especially so in periods like the current one in China, when the gap between state and society remains great. The hidden imperative driving all the policy changes, including economic reforms, is the Party's need to restore its legitimacy and authority in the eyes of the people and of the world.[4] Thus, discourse in theory and the arts that touches even indirectly on the need for limits on

Party authority in the name of the rights and interests of individuals and groups becomes highly sensitive. Work in the cinema and literature often receives the brunt of Party criticism because they have the most impact on youth and the general public.

There are also cultural attitudes that continue to hamper intellectual freedom. The "old guard" still running China is strongly influenced by a holistic, totalistic view of culture that regards intellectual ferment as a serious threat to the political system. This attitude has roots in traditional Chinese culture, which conflates politics, morality, and culture; in the May Fourth preoccupation with cultural change; and in the Marxist-Leninist emphasis on the importance of ideological control over the sources of information and expressions of ideas. In the Yan'an period, Mao captured the essence of these views when he insisted that literature and art must "serve politics," a dictum that has now been softened to "serve socialism and the people," but has not been abandoned. Anti-foreign and anti-imperialist prejudices have resurfaced perennially, most recently in controversy over the post-Mao opening to the outside world. As a result, there is still strong suspicion that the foreign professional ties of Chinese intellectuals are somehow unpatriotic.

THE DYNAMICS OF CULTURAL POLITICS

Focusing on these sources of tension in state-intellectual relations alone, however, may lead to misinterpreting the cycles of "loosening" and "tightening" in the state's treatment of intellectuals. These cycles, for example, are sometimes attributed to ambivalence on the part of top leaders, who know they need intellectuals to modernize and therefore woo them for a time, but then, feeling threatened politically by the way intellectuals use their new freedoms, clamp down again.[5] Or, it is argued, Deng Xiaoping personally "uses" the intellectuals for political purposes by allowing them to voice grievances whenever this serves to undermine his opponents, but, having gained the upper hand, he then turns against them.[6] Certainly, there is a large element of truth in both these perspectives. For, as Lynn White has indicated in the preceding chapter, recent policy toward intellectuals has been characterized by much experimental groping in the dark. Deng Xiaoping and most other top-level politicians take a fairly utilitarian stance toward intellectuals, assessing their activities in the light of nonartistic, nonprofessional criteria. No Chinese leader is above trading away intellectual freedoms for other goals.

And yet, to look at these two factors alone leads to false assumptions. The first view assumes that both the "leadership" and "intellectuals" are united groups with monolithic interests and values, thus focusing on the tension between the two and ignoring tensions inside each group as explanatory considerations. The second admits that the leadership may disagree about intellectual policy but still overstates Deng's strength and independence of action. By assuming that his statements about intellectuals always reflect his personal views, one ignores the possibility that he may be voicing a compromise position among alternative views that he must take into account. Both approaches fail to explore how trends in other issue areas may affect cultural policy.

A more accurate understanding of the dynamics of the tightening and loosening cycles in cultural policy can be gained by incorporating three additional factors: the shifting balance of power among leaders who have policy differences; the competition for influence among groups of intellectuals with different interests; and the linkage between cultural and other policy arenas.

Competing Politicians

During the transition period since Mao's death, considerable disagreement has arisen within the Chinese leadership. Divergent sources of political legitimacy, different policy preferences, and competing political constituencies have all contributed to the tensions. Three loose groupings have emerged, spread along a political continuum ranging from conservative aversion to change at one pole to reformist activism at the other pole. Cultural cycles have accompanied shifts in the balance of power from one pole to the other.[7]

The 1970s, including the period immediately following Mao's death, were dominated by those officials who tried to upgrade economic goals but still stressed the continuing importance of Maoist revolutionary ideals, social egalitarianism, tight central control, and economic self-reliance. Leaders like Hua Guofeng and Ye Jianying sought legitimacy in continuing Mao's legacy and found support in the military, security, and propaganda "control" bureaucracies that had been Mao's base of power. Thus, while they promised improvements for everyone, they did not place high priority on the concerns of intellectuals. As leaders tried to ensure political and social stability at a time of systemic crisis, they discouraged open questioning of the Maoist era in theoretical and literary work.

After 1978, however, large numbers of officials purged by Mao were brought back by Deng Xiaoping. This "old guard," including Chen Yun and Peng Zhen, sought to restore productivity and efficiency by relaxing economic restrictions on the market and resurrecting the bureaucratic system of the early 1960s, supervised by a disciplined Leninist Party. Their source of legitimacy derived from the Party's early successful efforts at development and organization in the 1950s. The treatment of intellectuals was upgraded so as to fill the need for technocrats in the renewed modernization effort. There was a corresponding necessity for a limited cultural relaxation, in order to allow social release and justify change from Maoist priorities. Public criticism was limited, however, to the dogmatism, arbitrary repression, and egalitarianism of the Great Leap and the Cultural Revolution. The previous practices of the Party and its leaders, including the "early Mao," remained sacrosanct; Marxist-Leninist orthodoxy and patriotic nationalism returned to favor. Those central Party, government, and military planners responsible for national-level development found their interests aligned with this group.

Although these two groups were at odds in the late 1970s, they gradually began to converge at the conservative end of the political spectrum in the early 1980s. Viewing the maintenance of Party hegemony and social stability as a prerequisite for economic progress, they prefer a moderate pace and limited scope for change. While accepting the need for incremental policy reform, they view fundamental systemic reform as dangerous. These "law-and-order" types argue that the Party's admission of past error must be quite limited and that criticism of the Party from the outside should be nipped in the bud in order to prevent exacerbation of the "crisis of confidence" in Party leadership and the socialist system as a whole. In their view, better discipline and moral training of Party cadre is a sufficient response to the problems of bureaucratism and corruption. Legal reform is valued as a means to regularize Party supervision over society, not as a protection for non-Party rights. Conservatives have attempted to "import" selective knowledge, funds, and technology from abroad while severely limiting non-socialist cultural influence. They remain quite suspicious of intellectuals and prefer to strengthen Party supervision over their work. They reached the height of their influence in 1981–1982.

By 1983, bolder reformers linked with Hu Yaobang and Zhao Ziyang began pressing for even greater intellectual relaxation to accompany systemic reforms far beyond anything previously tried in China. They have encouraged intellectuals not only to criticize Maoist excesses but also to question basic Marxist-Leninist dogma and the political-economic system imported from Moscow. This group has encouraged massive exposure of the Chinese elite and populace to non-socialist experiences and thinking through cultural exchange programs, training abroad, and looser media controls. They place a premium on education for Party membership and promotion of officials. This group of younger leaders have minimal revolutionary credentials; their legitimacy, authority, and bases of power depend heavily on Deng Xiaoping's support.

Their interests demand rapid political and socioeconomic change, despite the risks involved. They argue that a major reform of the Party—involving an overhaul of its structure, admission of past failures, a limitation of its role in society and a reshuffling of its personnel—is essential to improving economic efficiency, which in turn is the best route to rebuilding genuine esteem for the Party. They are willing to experiment with political procedures inside and outside the Party. The natural constituencies of this group are those that have been weakest in China under Mao—government and enterprise managers, technicians and professional writers, researchers, and educators at all levels. Party reformers attempt to strengthen ties with these groups by inducting them into the Party, granting them more responsibility and autonomy in their work, and allowing them more influence on policy. Reformers also try to expand their constituency by grooming urban youths who are potential power-holders.

Increasingly, reformers are confronting the linkage between economic modernization and cultural and social change. The more radical Party reformers have begun to stress the necessity of free exchanges of ideas at home and abroad, a more open political process, and freer lifestyles. These changes are described not as vague ideals to eventuate from economic progress but as prerequisites for genuine and thorough material and technological development.

Deng Xiaoping's role has become increasingly ambiguous through the past decade. His legitimacy stems from his membership in the tiny group of revolutionary founders, Mao's closest friends, and at the same time from his new-found role as the great reformer. He is an old-line Party man, and yet has approved the general "emancipation of the mind" underway in every field. As the reforms move farther from past policies, Deng is hard pressed to straddle the gap between conservatives and radical reformers and cover the distance with the cloak of continuity.

Divisions among Intellectuals

Of these competing leadership groups, the younger reformers speak most directly to the broad interests of the intellectuals as a social group. Yet, while systemic reform holds out the potential for greater influence and status for intellectuals inside and also outside the Party, this general perspective obscures cleavages among intellectuals. Many observers note that factionalism remains endemic within most institutions and groups, including intellectuals.

The interests of some members of the intellectual elite clearly lie with the conservatives, for example, because their jobs in central planning, Party research and education, and propaganda oversight are justified by a Leninist system of Party monopoly on power. Their own authority relies on unchallenged Party authority. Often, such cultural bureaucrats as Hu Qiaomu and Deng Liqun are veterans of the Revolution and largely self-educated.

Other Party intellectuals, usually those who are somewhat younger and better educated but not so well entrenched, make allies among non-Party scholars on the fringes of power—in government think tanks and the universities—to demand democratic reforms within the cultural sphere. They may want more professional autonomy, but they also want to move up in the political-intellectual hierarchy. The scope of their authority expands as that of the old guard at the highest level contracts. Such reform-minded intellectuals have included *People's Daily* official Wang Ruoshui and former "rightists" Bai Hua, a cultural official in the Wuhan Military Region, and Wang Meng, who has obtained a rare Central Committee membership. If major cultural reforms were to come about, these individuals would be among those promoted to administer the new policies. Wang

Meng's appointment as Minister of Culture in spring 1986 was a harbinger of renewed efforts to promote change.

Power competition, wrapped in intellectual and policy differences, can be observed between institutions as well as individuals. For example, intellectuals from the Central Party School, which formerly held a monopoly on matters of ideology and policy research, tend to have a more orthodox perspective than their competitors in the theory institutes of the Academy of Social Sciences. And reformist activism at *People's Daily* in recent years in part may reflect a desire to assert institutional autonomy vis-à-vis the Propaganda Department.

It is not too surprising that mundane concerns for political influence within the establishment often outweigh matters of principle. Thus, while reformist intellectuals have sometimes urged that official access be granted more widely to still younger intellectuals, no doubt to gain allies, they have equivocated when it came to supporting democratic demands for removal of Party control over intellectual activities altogether. For example, in an interview in summer 1985, Wang Ruoshui dismissed the Democracy Wall activists for "merely swearing at people. Is there anything justifiable in the abuse that a shrew shouts in the street?"[8] Since Wang was under considerable pressure at the time, he should not be *judged* by such statements. Nevertheless, it is significant that he parted from the activists over their *methods*, a response that conforms to Wang's general acceptance of the establishment rules of political activism despite his advocacy of freer expression of conflicting views, and use of legal rather than administrative means to arbitrate disputes.

In explaining Chinese cultural politics, these generational, institutional, and functional cleavages centered on competition for power and influence, are as significant as the Party-intellectual dichotomy, the broad distinction between "technocratic" and "humanistic" intellectuals, and professional subdivisions. Within every organization, alliances are built among those "in" power to conserve the "old" ideology-policy packages against the "outs" hoping to gain promotion by riding the coattails of the "new" reform program. This contributes to the politicization of even very technical work, and accounts for the existence of a loose "reform coalition" discernible across the spectrum of intellectual organizations.

Linkages and Cycles

The prominent reform-conservative cleavage among intellectuals clearly is an echo of the same cleavage in the leadership, stemming from the inseparable link in the Chinese system between cultural politics and politics in general. The link may seem loose at times, but it becomes a strong connection—that is, cultural matters become "politicized"—whenever leadership tensions arise. This is true for several reasons. Efforts by conservatives to tighten control and by reformers to relax control in cultural affairs can be viewed in part as direct bids for political support from competing groups of intellectuals.

A given intellectual policy also plays a more indirect role as an integral part of a larger "package" of policies or "political platform" offered by a political group in efforts to build a broad coalition. For example, reformist overtures to intellectuals are part and parcel of a comprehensive development strategy that also calls for the revival of the democratic parties, enticement of overseas Chinese financial and human investment, removal of ideological constraints on policy options, expansion of the market mechanism in industry as well as agriculture, expansion of foreign economic ties, and encouragement of negotiated reunification with Hong Kong and Taiwan. This is not to say that reform politicians don't periodically sacrifice the interests of intellectuals, particularly those in the humanities, in their power balancing. But a setback or a "step back" in any single policy area risks a lack of cohesion and loss of momentum in the others. Whatever the personal feelings of leaders about intellectuals, a broad range of vital political interests is at stake in each round of debate over the treatment of intellectuals, and, conversely, debates in other policy arenas reverberate in intellectual life.

The most important way in which cultural debates become linked with politics is in their effect on competition between politicians for control over the propaganda apparatus. Usually, one member of the Politburo and one member of the Secretariat have primary responsibility for shaping policy affecting intellectual-cultural-educational activities. The Party's Propaganda Department, in coordination with the State Council, oversees day-to-day execution of policy by lower-level units, including *People's Daily*, *Xinhua*, *Guangming Daily*, the Ministries of Culture and Education, the Academies of Sciences and

Social Sciences, and other "think tanks" of the Secretariat and State Council. The mandate given those at the apex of this hierarchy is quite wide-ranging, touching on ideological, research, and literary activities as well as public, moral, and technical education. Even theoretical aspects of foreign policy-making and of cultural work in the army come under their purview.

The degree of control over this hierarchy in turn affects politicians' abilities to control broader inner-Party debate and shape public opinion. Here, journalists, educators, and writers play an important role in manipulating (within limits) the nuances of media discussion, printing timely "leaks," raising sensitive issues, showcasing key leadership interviews or appearances, and so on. Journalists and researchers also play a hidden key role in influencing leadership decisions by providing internal briefing reports on policy issues, social trends, and public reactions to policy. Clearly, as long as the political process both allows and requires politicians to control the propaganda apparatus, and as long as intellectuals have no alternative sources of expression, career advancement, material well-being, and prestige, cultural affairs will be linked with politics.

TRENDS IN CULTURAL POLITICS UNDER DENG XIAOPING

Under Deng Xiaoping there has emerged a pattern whereby the reformist politicians seize the initiative on issues by drafting reformist documents or setting reformist agendas for scheduled meetings. Reform intellectuals hold supportive symposia or conferences, and write articles to shape elite opinion in their favor. Conservative opposition appears in the form of efforts to derail or reshape meeting agendas so as to focus attention on conservative concerns, criticize the contents or implementation of policy documents, or insist on representation on key oversight groups. Conservative intellectuals attack the "heretical" views of their more "liberal" peers. Periodic compromises are achieved through trading off both issues and appointments. These dynamics are reflected in reformist "surges" followed by conservative "backlashes," culminating in ambiguous compromise statements regarding policy. The length of the "lulls" between rounds varies, as reformers regain momentum for another surge. These patterns are evident throughout the post-Mao period.

Deng Xiaoping and Humanistic Intellectuals

During the three years following the summer of 1977, from the time of Deng's second rehabilitation up to the decision to replace Hua Guofeng as Party Chairman and Premier, Deng regained power by responding to widespread disaffection. As Deng Xiaoping's group redressed the grievances of a broad range of social groups that had lost out in the Mao era, it gained their loyalties. Former officials and intellectuals were the most politically influential of these. Hu Yaobang, first as Organization Department Director (December 1977–December 1978) and then as Secretary General of the Party (after December 1978), oversaw the rehabilitation of hundreds of thousands purged under Mao beginning in the mid-1950s. Cultural affairs, the stronghold for the "cultural revolutionaries" and the area of concern for intellectuals, naturally became a key arena of conflict. One of Deng's first moves was to criticize the dogma of continued class struggle and declare that intellectuals were to be considered equal in all respects to workers and peasants. His calls for non-discrimination against intellectuals correlated with his demand that education and expertise be given top priority in employment. These policies were justified and publicized through media campaigns against dogmatism orchestrated by the Party School, then under Hu Yaobang's leadership; *Guangming Daily*, the intellectuals' daily; and *People's Daily*, under its reform-minded editor, Hu Jiwei. Thus, the alliance between intellectuals and reformers was forged, and Hu Yaobang gained a reputation as a spokesman and protector for intellectuals.

The humanist moral critique of the holocaust of the Cultural Revolution was a powerful weapon in the effort to shift support to Deng's group. Wang Ruoshui's views on Marxist humanism emerged in 1979–1980 as part of a much larger outpouring of writing that explored the problem. The Cultural Revolution had been a personally degrading experience for hundreds of thousands of Chinese from all walks of life; family and work relationships and friendships alike were distorted by suspicion, betrayal, and mistrust. Many responded to the post-Mao loosening of strictures by joining the "consumer revolution." In a reaction to the Maoist imposition of public conformity, young people experimented with individual expressions of taste in hairstyle, clothing, reading matter, and leisure-time activities. Many avoided politics and sought new, private sources of meaning in personal and local community life. Themes of romantic and familial love, and human generosity, abounded in literature and film. Historians and philosophers began to resurrect the humanistic values of Confucianism. The startling expansion of numbers of believers in Christianity in the early 1980s, to an unofficial 15–30 million at least, had much to do with observable evidence of loving concern and mutual support within a community of believers.[9] Chinese who remained concerned about public political discourse, including the Democracy Wall activists, were clearly skeptical that socialism had the answers.

In this situation, Wang and other establishment intellectuals wrote about humanism in an effort to revitalize Chinese Marxism, as David Kelly has pointed out. In addressing their own intellectual questions at a time of authority crisis, they also served the establishment's need to renew its legitimacy. Wang's argument that politics should not be the sole means of "mediation" of people's interests, but that literature and even religion might be a more proper means of expressing and meeting *some* human needs, was a powerful challenge to the Maoist insistence on monopolizing culture. But, at the same time, it was an attempt to justify theoretically continued, albeit more limited, rule by the Party.

The humanist call for protection of the sanctity of the person represented the first real effort to set limits on the accumulation of wealth and power for the Chinese nation-state. Similarly, in the area of economic theory, attention focused on the need to recognize the material interests, not just of the collective and the nation, but also of the individual. Discussions appeared in the official press redefining socialism (as public ownership and distribution according to work, rather than egalitarianism) and clarifying its ultimate purpose (the people's well-being rather than economic growth for its own sake). These theoretical debates emanated from the Institute of Marxism-Leninism-Mao Zedong Thought, headed by Yu Guangyuan and Su Shaozhi. The Institute's very creation, in late 1979, was an affront to the orthodox-minded, who believed that doctrine was to be taught, not researched and debated. The emergence of this "intellectual revolution," involving some of China's most influential Party intellectuals, shows the depth of the authority crisis the Party faced with the total discrediting of radicalism. It has been easier, however, to identify what Party reformers are repudiating than what they are proposing to put in its place. The ambiguity in the reformist position comes through in a comparison of their views with those of Democracy-Wall activists. Lynn White has noted that non-dogmatic Marxists in the Party have espoused views that come surprisingly close to those of true liberals. The explanation for this seems to depend on the fact that both humanistic Marxists like Wang Ruoshui and liberals like Wei Jingsheng share a theoretical critique of the obstacles to progress posed by (1) patriarchal "feudal" thinking and behavior at all levels, reflected in the personality cult and the ethics of dependency and loyalty; (2) bureaucratism and special privilege within the elite; and (3) the oppressive, dehumanizing impact of such a political system on the rest of society.

Their practical prescriptions have differed greatly, however. Establishment Marxists like Wang Ruoshui look to systemic reform, but *from the top down*. As David Kelly has pointed out, this is fundamentally a moral solution, since it relies on a change of heart within officialdom spurred by reformers as the "conscience" of the Party. Liu Binyan's view that investigative journalists act as "scouts" for the Party leadership, as Rudolf Wagner points out, to keep them informed and keep them honest, falls into this category as well.

In contrast, the anti-establishment dissidents had little faith that the system would cleanse itself and called for genuine outside checks on the Party. The views of more moderate dissidents lay in a shady gray area in between; they spoke of reform within the system but their actions in organizing unofficial groups and creating unofficial means of public expression posed a challenge to the Party's hegemony.

David Kelly's study of Wang Ruoshui hints that, in fact, Wang's moral approach, which stops short of spelling out programmatic solutions to the problem of corrupt leadership, is merely a calculated "first step" toward a more liberal stance. Whether Wang and others like him would become less Leninist and more liberal under freer circumstances can be mere speculation. Nevertheless, there are powerful material attractions and traditional influences, as well as political pressures, that would lead establishment intellectuals to stop short of fundamental change in the status quo.

The ambiguous position of the critical intellectuals can be seen in their claim to speak on behalf of the people and to be responsible to the people, a theme that has suffused post-Mao literature. By this claim, intellectuals implicitly hold the Party accountable to a higher, universal moral criterion. At the same time, however, they implicitly justify a special role for intellectuals as mediators between the top ruler(s) and society, acting as the conscience of the sovereign and educators of the people. Such an approach, which assigns the populace a passive role, has its counterparts in Eastern Europe as well as deep roots in traditional Chinese political philosophy.[10]

The convergence of interests among reformers in the leadership and among the established intellectuals was most apparent when tension arose in the leadership in 1979–1980 over a number of sensitive issues, including the future of Hua and his supporters, the evaluation of the Mao era, and incipient linkages between Democracy-Movement activists and aggrieved social groups. In order to reforge a consensus within the leadership, Deng took steps to mute the criticism of Mao and draw the line on permissible political activity. Dissidents like Wei Jingsheng, who had gone beyond attacking Maoism to question Deng's own stance and the fundamentals of the one-party system, were jailed and Democracy Wall was closed. Establishment intellectuals offered little protest, which suggests that they, too, were intolerant of anti-establishment protest. Moreover, the Party was improving their economic situation and allowing official organizations, meetings, and journals for professionals to proliferate.

Thus, the immediate post-Mao period saw the triumph of the Leninist Party over anti-bureaucratic radicalism, whether Maoist or liberal in orientation. Deng built a winning coalition by addressing the interests of both mainstream intellectuals and Party veterans. The 8th Party Congress and its Hundred Flowers cultural policy of 1956 became the models for a return to normalcy and moderation, with an emphasis on collective leadership and social unity in the name of national development. These symbols of legitimacy buttressed the authority of Deng Xiaoping, since he had first risen to the top ranks as General Secretary of the 8th Central Committee.

The Old Guard and Cultural Bureaucrats

It proved more difficult, however, to resolve the problem of authority in practice. The fit between post-Cultural Revolution problems and twenty-year-old prescriptions was less than perfect. Younger reformers—both politicians and intellectuals—saw the need to move farther and faster, if economic development was to be sustained over the long term. Once the Maoists were defeated, divisions within Deng's unwieldly reform coalition began to emerge. The tensions reflected power interests as well as policy differences: Revolutionary veterans like Chen Yun and Peng Zhen were satisfied with the new status quo; they had regained authority as founders of the regime, and their supporters, experienced Party administrators, were in charge of a wide range of policy arenas, including economic planning. Cultural bureaucrats in charge of the propaganda apparatus, worked to strengthen its control. Younger leaders, like Hu Yaobang and Zhao Ziyang, however, could not build independent legitimacy upon the early successes of the Party, and they had yet to place their own like-minded supporters in key policy arenas. Thus, they kept pressing for change beyond the earlier model. Some of the reform intellectuals, especially those linked with *People's Daily,* continued to adopt a critical stance, turning their ire against Leninist as well as Maoist dogma.

As more orthodox party leaders like Chen Yun and Peng Zhen became increasingly concerned about the pace and scope of change, a new configuration of forces emerged, aligning the orthodox Leninist wing of Deng's reform coalition with the remaining neo-Maoists, many of them in the military. In late 1980, a major backlash occurred against the whole reform thrust, which greatly affected intellectual policy.

The linkage between politics and culture was most evident in the Bai Hua affair, which was not at all an isolated dispute over alleged "bourgeois" (anti-socialist) literary themes. Rather, the military establishment chose to exercise its prerogatives in disciplining one of its own (the writer Bai Hua worked in the Wuhan Military Region cultural apparatus) in order to register its dissent from broader political trends. This is reflected in the focus of military ire on the scenes in Bai's screenplay suggesting that Mao's rule was based more on feudal superstition than socialist principle and that, during his era, the CCP had damaged rather than served the national interest. Another focus of criticism was Ye Wenfu's poem depicting the degeneration of an Army general from a national hero to a self-serving bureaucrat. Such themes struck at the very heart of claims to legitimacy by the Party and the Army on the basis of the Revolution. Understandably, the Red Army was incensed. The literary inquisition of 1981 was led by the Army's left-leaning General Political Department through its subgroup in charge of culture, with the backing of military luminaries.

But this skirmish was not a matter of pure principle. It represented the indirect military refusal to accept Hu Yaobang's leadership, as recommended by Deng himself. Hu was known to be close to Bai Hua and he had encouraged the civilian press to ignore the complaints regarding Bai; when Deng (belatedly) stepped in to approve the criticism campaign, Hu's colleagues at *People's Daily* and *Wenyi bao* were forced to follow the Army's line. At the 6th plenum in June 1981, Hu became CCP Chairman, but Deng, not Hu, replaced Hua as head of the Military Commission; Hua Guofeng remained on the powerful standing committee of the Politburo.

Conservatives, especially in the military, stood to gain legitimacy and power through reestablishment of the discipline and orthodoxy symbolized by the Yan'an rectification campaign of 1942–1944. As David Kelly has noted, tensions were evident in the spring of 1982 during the celebration of the 40th anniversary of Mao's Yan'an Talks on Literature and Art. Conservative leaders and intellectuals stressed the continuing relevance of Mao's talks and "campaign" methods in cultural matters; reform politicians and critical intellectuals, intent on breaking away from the Yan'an model to disperse the exercise of authority and provide more indirect and regularized Party supervision, claimed the talks were outdated in all key aspects.

Deng's decision to side with the conservatives in the Bai Hua case was related in part to a shift in his political agenda and a corresponding change of tactics. Through 1980, he had been out in front pressing for reforms in the propaganda and cultural arena, the heart of the Maoist power base, in order to consolidate his own position as ultimate policy arbiter. He then turned in 1981 to the more difficult task of passing on authority to his younger successors. Facing opposition from the deeply conservative military and security apparatus, he needed the support of the Party veterans. Thus, even though Hu and Zhao pressed for more far-reaching economic and political reform to strengthen their own authority, Deng often stepped in to forge more illiberal compromises to keep the old guard on board, as evident in the Bai Hua affair. First Deng and then Hu reluctantly took a harder line with Bai, after failing to defuse the matter with milder actions. In 1981–1982, there was generally little headway regarding many aspects of reform, especially in cultural-intellectual policy.

In this period, several Deng allies, such as Party elder Chen Yun and ideological specialist Hu Qiaomu, enhanced their positions considerably by playing key roles in forging compromises between Party reformers and conservatives in the military. Chen had a hand in the relatively favorable assessment of Mao contained in a major Central Committee resolution on sixty years of Party history, 1921–1981. Hu Qiaomu oversaw the drafting of the Historical Resolution and the 12th Congress report. With his chief assistant, Deng Liqun, he also was responsible for the compilation of memoirs, speeches, and writings of respected Party veterans, including Deng Xiaoping and Chen Yun.

As Deng sought to rebuild consensus in the leadership, the reform intellectuals who chose to retain a critical stance were more a liability than an asset. Long-time propaganda administrators who excelled at enforcing unanimity of thought from the top down gained prominence. In early 1982, Deng Liqun took over the Propaganda Department, when Zhou Yang retired as its deputy. A major campaign was begun to publicize patriotic and Communist morality, in a transparent effort to strengthen faith in communism by equating it with nationalism. Religious-affairs functionaries were told to tighten control by cajoling or coercing Christian believers to register with the official church or cease meeting. At the 12th Congress, Hu Qiaomu joined the Politburo and Deng Liqun the Secretariat, respectively the member of each body in charge of culture and propaganda. Deng Liqun also took over management of the Secretariat's policy-research office. While the two men gave up active administration of the Academy of Social Sciences, they retained control there through their formal positions of oversight and through their close associates. Their preeminence reflected the Party's reassertion of tighter controls, especially on culture, and the temporary eclipse of calls for fundamental reform of the Party's role.

Deng's Successors and the Social Scientists

Beginning in late 1980, newly appointed Premier Zhao Ziyang began creating policy research organs to support his search for a new development strategy and concrete economic policies. By 1983–1984, several "think tanks" directly under the State Council and in key state commissions and ministries sought the advice of well-known social scientists, especially theoretical economists like Xue Muqiao and Yu Guangyuan, and hired younger researchers. Zhao's efforts to get researchers out of their ivory towers and to make their work useful for urgent policy needs included the appointment of his aide Ma Hong as President of the Academy of Social Sciences. Researchers were encouraged to "emancipate their thought" and explore new ideas and methodologies that could support the reform program.

These efforts were intended to buttress a new reform offensive launched by Hu Yaobang and Zhao just after the September 1982 12th Party Congress. Proclaiming 1983 a "year of reform," they stepped up the timetable for expanding rural agricultural and commercial reforms and experimenting with urban economic reform. In the cultural field, art troupes were encouraged to collect their own box-office receipts, foreshadowing the incursion of the market into intellectual pursuits. This venture may have been an appeal for intellectual support and part of a more general effort to cut back the state budget by limiting the dole. Conservatives, however, fearing loss of control, quickly nipped these blossoms. The new cultural reforms died a premature death in June 1983 amidst accusations that decadent content had crept into the repertoires of groups in search of *renminbi* (Chinese "dollars").

A similar "thrust and parry" was evident in theoretical matters. Hu Yaobang in March gave a remarkably iconoclastic speech on the occasion of the 100th anniversary of Marx's death.[11] The heart of Hu's message was to justify and strengthen a pro-intellectual policy. He stressed that intellectuals, with Marx as the premier example, have always been central to the success of revolutions, and he argued that China must adopt all "advanced" culture (socialist or not, by implication) in order to repair its backwardness. This was an effort in which the intellectuals naturally would play an important role. By staking out a controversial position on sensitive political issues, Hu was countering the vested interests of the older, uneducated "revolutionaries" and appealing to a younger, educated, and largely urban political constituency. This speech no doubt was intended to influence the drafting of the guidelines for the three-year Party rectification campaign to be launched in the autumn; the guidelines called for the retirement or purge of the first type of cadre in favor the latter. Hu's speech had several far-reaching implications for intellectuals. It promised to end anti-intellectual discrimination; suggested that more resources would be assigned to their areas of work; and loosened doctrinal strictures on the content of their work as well.

Hu's speech clearly reflected the influence of the intellectuals in his camp who had been fighting dogmatism in the name of "creative" Marxism. He emphasized the need to "develop" rather than "uphold" (the usual formula) Marxism. He praised Marx, Engels, and Lenin for their historic contributions, but omitted any reference to Stalin and gave short shrift to Mao. These hints of a renewed tolerance for unorthodox views were spelled out by reform intellectuals at a conference on Marxism at the time of the centennial in March. In his keynote address, Su Shaozhi, Director of the Marxism-Leninism-Mao Zedong Thought Institute, described widespread views abroad that "Marxism has become outmoded" and that "Marxism is now in crisis." Su refused to blame these attitudes solely on bourgeois bias, but instead faulted dogmatic Marxists worldwide for failing to

make exploration of, and give answers to, the many new phenomena in the development of modern capitalism, the many new problems in the contemporary practice of socialism, the many new achievements in present-day natural sciences, and the many newborn disciplines of present-day social sciences.[12]

Citing Daniel Bell, I. Prigogine, and other Western scholars, Su described the immense changes in "post-industrial" society wrought by the information revolution, all of which posed grave challenges to Marxist theory. He argued, for example, that Chinese theorists must begin to deal with the challenge posed to the Marxist labor theory of value by the fact that human intellectual creativity was replacing simple labor and capital as a source of value; to the Marxist theory of class by the fact that information was becoming a kind of commodity and education was assuming unprecedented importance; and to the Leninist theory of imperialism by the fact that the resilience of capitalism was seemingly demonstrated in its renewal through the new technological revolution.

Su laid out an ambitious and highly sensitive concrete agenda for Chinese Marxist theorists, including historical reevaluation of the failures of socialism, ranging from Stalinism to the Cultural Revolution to Pol Pot's regime; theoretical research into the relationship between the "early" and "late" Marx, the relative degree of ideology and science in Marxism, and the problems in the relationships of ruling Communist parties and their societies; and comparative studies of Soviet and East European reform attempts. Su Shaozhi implied that this agenda had encountered much opposition when he charged that current theoretical work in China was in a sorry state, focusing on outdated issues. "This provides a sanctuary and hotbed for 'left' ideology and offers an ideological ground on the basis of which exponents of such ideology can censure the current reforms"[13] Su's remarks were clearly aimed at both conservative politicians and the current overseers of cultural affairs, and they reflected the views of his like-minded associates such as Yu Guangyuan and Wang Ruoshui.

Su and a number of others at the conference, including Zhou Yang, touched on the theme of humanism and alienation. At one point, Su called for further study of Marx's theory of alienation and the need for thorough human emancipation, not just economic liberation. Su Shaozhi thus implied what he had said openly in the more relaxed atmosphere of 1979—that China was so far from achieving Marxian ideals that it should not be considered socialist.[14] According to later revelations, there was heated controversy at the centennial conference over the content of the speeches and also over their publication. Zhou, with Wang Ruoshui's support, insisted on publishing in *People's Daily* to give these views a high profile. This brought down on their heads the wrath of the propaganda czars. At the time, however, the struggle in the propaganda apparatus over ideas and influence was largely hidden from the public eye. As a result, six months later, the full-blown Campaign Against Spiritual Pollution, of which Zhou, Wang, and Su were prime targets, was a surprise to most, both inside and outside China.

THE CAMPAIGN AGAINST SPIRITUAL POLLUTION: LAST GASP OF LEFTISM?

Piecing together the sequence of events from later revelations, it appears that Deng Xiaoping, in his speech at the Party's plenary session in October 1983, was giving a green light to Deng Liqun and others responsible for propaganda work to tighten up discipline in their sphere of responsibility.[15] He spoke of "rightist" laxity among Party officials in dealing with "bourgeois liberal" trends in the arts. Although Deng no doubt was personally concerned about some of the issues involved, including pornography, he was also doing another political balancing act—throwing a bone to the conservatives in exchange for their acquiescence in launching a three-year rectification of the Party's rank and file. As one intellectual has put it, "It wouldn't matter if Deng were a liberal. He's a politician first." Nevertheless, the fact that the plenum communiqué primarily targeted leftists and set aside unspecified "ideological problems" for later consideration, without even mentioning the Anti-Spiritual Pollution Campaign, clearly revealed Deng's priorities.

Conservative leaders and propaganda officials immediately expanded the scope and heightened the urgency of the ideological campaign, however, both by hurling political charges of anti-Party activity against a wide range of intellectuals in the arts and social sciences and by discovering "spiritual pollution" in many other areas. By the end of October, Zhou Yang had been forced to make a self-criticism for his "irresponsible" handling of the humanism issue, and Hu Jiwei and Wang Ruoshui lost their posts at *People's Daily*. With these reform spokesmen out of the way, the press was flooded with articles and reports complaining about the reemergence of religious practices, degenerate lifestyles among youth and in the Army, "capitalist mentality" among peasants, and "worship of the West" among economic and scientific workers. By early November, the campaign had been "integrated" into the rectification campaign as one of its major elements, thus making free-thinking Party intellectuals more vulnerable to Party discipline and expulsion than they had been for many years.

By early December, after six short weeks, however, the campaign was being recapped. The Spiritual Pollution slogan was excluded from key areas—science and technology, economic reform policy, and practices in the countryside. A speech in October by Zhao Ziyang, calling for further research on the New Technological Revolution, is often mentioned by academics as a key turning point that saved social scientists from censure. This left primarily writers and artists still vulnerable for a time. And yet, even that classic ploy of splitting off the technocrats from the humanists failed. The "100-Day Cultural Revolution," as some have called it, sputtered to an embarrassing halt in the first half of 1984 in the face of foreign speculation over political instability in the leadership and concern among Chinese students and scholars abroad. Strong opposition to the campaign among Chinese intellectuals was expressed indirectly through requests for indefinite sick leave and refusals to join criticism sessions or submit new manuscipts. In internal study sessions on campaign documents, intellectuals pointedly offered their opinion that such leftist methods would not serve the cause of modernization.

The demise of the anti-intellectual campaign accompanied rumors that Hu Qili, a Secretariat member and chief aide to Hu Yaobang, had assumed the daily oversight of propaganda work and the rectification campaign as well. The leadership attempted to "save face" by dismissing rumors of disagreement in their ranks and retaining Deng Liqun as nominal Propaganda Department Director. They claimed that faulty communication alone was responsible for the raggedness of the campaign. But overwhelming evidence of high-level disagreement over the scope, targets, and methods of the campaign suggests strongly that, at its height, it represented a major conservative effort to challenge Deng's successors by discrediting bolder reform policies and weakening the rectification campaign by which the successors hoped to consolidate power.

Seeing the damage that could still be done to his program in the name of orthodoxy, Deng apparently lost patience with the conservatives and again weighed in heavily on the side of younger reformers. By mid-1984, he had refocused the rectification campaign to "thoroughly repudiate the Cultural Revolution," again shifting the target, but this time from "rightists" back to "leftists." This theme had special relevance in the PLA. Military units soon were reviewing critically the PLA's intervention "in support of the left" in 1967, which had previously been exempt from criticism. But the larger significance of this theme cannot be underestimated. Thorough discussion in China of the roots and effects of the Cultural Revolution is viewed by many intellectuals as essential if the intellectual and policy revolutions are to move beyond catharsis to fundamental change of the cultural and political sources of leftism.

Throughout late 1984 and 1985, leading up to the special Party conference in September, sparring over culture and ideology continued, with Hu Qiaomu and Deng Liqun under pressure to pass on leadership to more open-minded officials. First, a period of relaxation surrounded the convening of a National Congress of the Writers' Association in December-January. Hu Qili gave a major address promising Party support for "freedom of creativity" in artistic work. Perhaps more important, the prearranged slate of candidates for leadership in the association was modified in the process of discussion and balloting so as to include some younger reformers.[16] This was unprecedented. In such an atmosphere, there was a boom in submission and publication of works in new styles and themes, including experimental styles and apolitical themes in serious literature as well as much popular literature with martial-arts and detective plots, brimming with sex and violence. Media articles called for a more liberal publication law and academic freedom in all areas of intellectual life, not just the arts.

Conservative reaction was not long in coming. Early in the year, right on the heels of the Congress, came a recentralization of control in economic matters that typically presaged a tightening up in ideology and culture. Runaway local spending and inflationary prices triggered leadership concerns about social "unity and stability."[17] By the summer of 1985, there were "fierce debates" in the Party over the publication law, as was admitted in an interview by Hu Jiwei, now a National People's Congress official responsible for the drafting of such laws. He also indicated that there was controversy over a related speech on journalism given by Hu Yaobang, in which he bowed to conservatives by stressing the distinctions between freedoms to be accorded literary writers and much more circumscribed duties of journalists, who must act as the "mouthpiece" of the Party.[18]

These signs of continuing rivalry had implications far beyond the propaganda sphere. Hu Qili is Hu Yaobang's own chosen "successor," and whether the two of them can solidify control over this key area is a test of their power to control the succession. This question remained open after the September 1985 Party conference; Hu Qili and other supporters of Hu and Zhao were promoted, but Hu Qiaomu and Deng Liqun retained their top posts. This stalemate in power terms was also reflected in cultural policy. Deng Xiaoping's call at the Party's National Conference for a renewed nationwide effort to "study Marxism" produced a flood of articles, forums, and symposia in which conservatives figured prominently. In late October, a National Writers' Congress was convened to set straight the limits to "freedom of creation." Significantly, the key spokesman was Wang Meng, who had been one of a small handful of writers who criticized colleagues under attack during the Anti-Spiritual Pollution Campaign, virtually the only younger figure to do so. In October 1985, Wang's unwelcome, if not unexpected, message was that the "correct spirit" of Hu Qili's earlier speech was "freedom of creation *and* social responsibility." While Wang's tone was polite and persuasive rather than threatening, he was firm in insisting that the only legitimate literary works were those that somehow promoted the socialist cause. This was a necessary condition; criteria of quality could only be added, not substituted.[19] At the end of the year, a similar meeting of publishers was held to rein in apparently widespread sales of low-class popular literature by major publishing houses, journals, and newspapers in efforts to show profits on their ledgers. These moves of late 1985 seemed intended to get the reforms under control and address the problems they had engendered so as to defend them from conservative critics who would prefer a general rollback.

SOCIAL SCIENCE
AND GENERATIONAL DIFFERENCES

These continuing cycles of reform and counter-reform in the post-Mao period underscore how difficult it is to achieve policy stability, even in the best of times, given the basic weaknesses of the political system. But two sociological trends have emerged in this period that offer more hope for a gradual development of greater intellectual freedom and creativity—the growing strength of the social sciences and independent thinking in the younger generation. Social scientists are emerging as a strong force in Chinese intellectual and political life, resuming a trend that was evident only briefly in the 1960s, as discussed in Nina Halpern's chapter in this volume. For most of three decades, state-defined versions of Marxism monopolized research and teaching in social theory. This contributed to a lack of communication between "practical" scientists and engineers and intellectuals in the arts and humanities. In the early 1980s, however, both natural and social scientists in China began to catch up with trends in modern Western philosophy of science, with its emphasis on methodical skepticism and growing awareness of common methodological problems and analogues across disciplinary boundaries. Academic and government researchers, particularly those in CASS and the think tanks directed by Premier Zhao Ziyang's State Council, undertook a crash course in modern social theory. Simplistic hopes of modernizing by merely importing computers and machinery began to give way to new views on the relationship between cultural, technological, and economic factors in the modernization process.

Yu Guangyuan, a "jack of all trades" who is a key advisor on science, economic, and ideological matters, has been a primary booster of this shift in thinking. He constructed and promoted the idea that China needs a new cultural-development strategy, arguing in early

1986, for example, that "China's economic development gives impetus to, and conditions, its cultural development. [But] this is just one facet of the relationship between an economy and a culture. Another facet of this relationship is the impetus given to economic development by cultural development . . . However, [people] rarely study or publicize this."[20] Yu went on to argue that China must study the questions of cultural management and cultural economics and develop reforms in this arena. Stripped of their transparent "scientific" terminology, Yu's arguments have amounted to a clarion call for political reforms. His efforts were to pay off handsomely in May 1986, when a Shanghai forum on cultural development strategy engendered an outpouring of discussions in the press of the need for a "breakthrough" to totally new ideological concepts and major political and legal reforms to guarantee intellectual freedoms. This new upsurge of reform activism, as usual, had the back-stage support of political reformers such as Hu Qili and the new Director of the Propaganda Department, Zhu Houze, as part of an effort to gain yet more ground at the expense of the conservatives.

Such writings implicitly repudiate the technological determinism of conservatives who insist that democracy must await material prosperity. Yan Jiaqi, at 45 the youngest director of a CASS institute—the controversial new Institute of Political Science—has played a key role in raising this issue. In the summer of 1986, taking advantage of the celebration of the 30th anniversary of the Hundred Flowers policy, Yan wrote articles, gave interviews, and organized symposia to promote the concept that reform of the political structure must be carried out simultaneously with reform of the economic structure. For example, a gathering in June of "young social scientists" to discuss these issues, sponsored by the journals of CASS and of Yan's institute, openly called for participation of all citizens in political activities and decision-making, the introduction of checks and balances to protect against errors in political leadership, and strong legislative and judicial oversight of administration.[21]

Such explicit discussions are extremely rare. For the most part, reformers are rather vague about what they mean by democracy. At a minimum, they desire a democratization of information to provide accurate feedback for development planning and policy implementation. They also recognize that the social milieu of creativity and dynamism necessary for modernization requires the freedom to discuss and explore a diversity of ideas. Whether they harbor a non-utilitarian desire for some sort of political pluralism composed of genuine autonomy from Party control for institutions, backed by law, is hard to say, since this topic is still largely taboo. Very few writers have analyzed the existing conflicts of social interests in China, much less explored how to legitimize them and provide institutional means for their articulation—the process at the heart of a liberal democratic system. And yet, as long as there are no effective constraints on state power, individual freedom and democratic processes can be sacrificed in the name of the national interest.

The incipient discussions of political reform in 1986 suggest there may be important differences between generations of Chinese intellectuals and officials in their attitudes toward the delicate issue of state-individual relations. The founding generation of revolutionaries, largely self-educated, well over the age of 60, is still preoccupied with the goal of "national salvation," which requires individuals, especially intellectuals, to remold their thinking along orthodox lines and prove their loyalty by submitting their interests and endeavors to central direction by the Leninist Party "priesthood." Their societal ideal remains the original Yan'an model of "unity and stability" among the populace through emulation of a disciplined Party. On the other hand, those in their sixties seem more flexible, willing to admit to the diversity of social interests and needs. To accommodate them, they are willing to revise Marxist theory and create a more limited role for the Party. They are better educated than their elders, often with training in Western-style schools and in the humanities and social sciences. Yet, like their elders of the May Fourth generation, they demand a strong sense of individual responsibility to work directly for national socio-political goals and tend to seek moral as much as institutional solutions to abuses of state power. For this generation, the experiences of Eastern Europe appear attractive as inspiration for a "benevolent-tutor" model of government, in which social-science and planning elites could provide a functional substitute for representational democracy in mediating between state and society.

Intellectuals in their fifties join with their mentors in devotion to "building a new China." But they appear more desirous and capable of separating their work and life from political-moral themes, perhaps because more of them have a technical, often an engineering, training. They exhibit a complacency about politics so long as they have improved livelihoods and work conditions. The true devotees of a down-to-earth Four Modernizations program, they admire Western and

Japanese technology and methods but are comfortable with benevolent authoritarianism. Averse to grand visions, they will nevertheless accept a flexible, pragmatic, and rather vague "Marxism" as a national ideology. Practitioners of old-fashioned personal virtues, they worry about trends among young people.

The generation of Chinese thinkers in their thirties and early forties, most of whom spent their formative years in the countryside, tend to be skeptical and questioning about all Party programs and programming, including the reforms. They often are bitter about the past, but eschew radical activism as a "middle-school exercise" that leads to a dead end. As survivors, they feel "lucky" for still having a future, somewhat resigned to working within the system, and wistfully hope for a genuine breakthrough from past political cycles. They are drawn especially to American political values and material and technical dynamism, but are ambivalent about much of American culture and personal lifestyles. A "flight from politics" is quite noticeable among this age group. Some young writers for the first time explicitly view themselves as departing from the moral-political orientation of their elders, eschewing social commentary for experiments in folk art and self-expression.[22] Those budding social scientists who still retain a strong sense of social commitment seem to suffer great inner conflict as they view their own future and the prospects for state-society relations in China. Knowing they are expected to use their new knowledge as policy advisors to the state, they feel quite ambivalent about accepting the honor and danger accruing to such posts. For the most part, they genuinely do not see the need or the prospects for a multi-party political system, but rather hope that historical necessity and social pressures for an open economy (indirectly expressed) will eventually prove the guarantee for an open society still under the umbrella of the CCP. They would probably prefer a quiet life of professional autonomy and scholarly success. Yet, they feel drawn to political activity to add their weight to the balance in favor of reform.

PROSPECTS FOR INTELLECTUAL FREEDOM

For most intellectuals, the post-Mao era meant the end of harsh repression. Once again, intellectuals had their homes, families, and jobs, and officials called for an end to discrimination. But the chief source of past political oppression—the system of control over intellectual activities, adapted from tradition and the Soviet Union, had been revived, regularized, and strengthened. So long as control over intellectuals is a chief asset in political competition, intellectual activities will be linked with politics. So long as the state maintains monopoly control over the incomes, housing, employment, and publishing opportunities of intellectuals, the parameters for the content of their work will always narrow or widen at the whim of current Party policy. Moreover, there will continue to be divisions among officials and intellectuals based on different types of training, personal jealousies over scarce resources like foreign training or visits, and bureaucratic competition, all of which provide the breeding grounds for factional fighting.

Yet, to predict a bleak future for Chinese intellectual life, under the heavy hand of a bureaucratic state or caught up in political turmoil, would be too pessimistic. Granted, the emergence of an urban middle class able to provide both the demand and the funds for independent intellectual writing, research, and consulting, and even for semi-official *dangwai* (outside-the-Party) political lobbying such as has developed in Taiwan, would require considerable time and consistent change. In the meantime, a kind of "consultative authoritarianism," whereby the views and interests of intellectuals are taken into account, is emerging. The proliferation of professional organizations and meetings provides official sanction for horizontal ties based on common interests and the public expression of group views. Reaction to the Cultural Revolution era has not yet run its course and the flood of new ideas and experiences during the transitional period following Mao's death has only begun to be absorbed and reflected in systemic change. As one graduate student in the United States commented, "Before I came here, I thought that the Chinese people were among the most free in the world. Now I know they are among the least free." By mid-1986, there were many new Party administrators for culture, including new leadership of the Propaganda Department, the Ministry of Culture, the Federation of Writers and Artists, and key institutes in the Academy of Social Sciences. Reforms were just unfolding in the educational system and in the management and financing of research. As these changes (such as greater control by better-qualified university presidents as well as peer review and commercial contracting for research and consulting) begin to have their effect, professional autonomy may well increase. There are seeds now being sown that could ensure that the intellectual revolution may outlive those who would stifle it. As the introduction to this volume suggests, today's intellectuals appear more aware of the necessity and efficacy of solidarity and resistance in enlarging the sphere of autonomy. The Cultural Revolution taught them there is no "safe area" and no exception to attacks once they begin. For its part, the Party leadership seems painfully aware of the limits of its authority and the fragility of domestic and foreign confidence, as reflected in the ignominious ending of the 1983 Campaign Against Spiritual Pollution.

Overall, the current regime, compared to its predecessors, is more committed to development goals and is more convinced of the importance of individual initiative and creativity and the need for an appropriate cultural environment to achieve those goals. This augurs well for intellectuals. In the short run, Deng, Hu, and Zhao are trying to woo the younger generation into the party and press for the promotion of educated reform loyalists to official posts, while discouraging any activities that question or undermine the one-party "socialist" system and thus make them politically vulnerable. In a sense, there is a race underway in which the Party hopes to recoup its losses in terms of direct administrative control through its gains in legitimacy from resulting economic progress. Thus far, the reformers have proved quite adept at resolving mini-crises, both economic and social, and resuming the momentum toward cultural relaxation and diversification. However, the economic reforms underway since 1984, which require the Party to give up its monopoly on decision-making in exchange for "mere" hegemony in setting policy directions, will bring increasing pressures for similar changes in the rest of society. There will be many testing points along the way when the imperatives of economic efficiency will be pitted against the imperatives of power.

Willing or not, intellectuals will become more important and more involved in these contests than ever before. As the younger generations gain influence, they will exhibit more independence of thought and action, and the bargaining between the state and intellectuals will become more open, more direct, and more central to the very nature of the regime.

Notes
Index

Introduction: Uncertain Change,
by Merle Goldman and Timothy Cheek

1. We should like to acknowledge the insightful comments of the participants of the 5 May 1984 New England China Seminar from which this book has developed. In particular we should like to thank those who kindly offered specific criticisms and suggestions for this introduction: Joshua Fogel, Carol Hamrin, Philip Kuhn, Kyna Rubin, Rudolf Wagner, and Benjamin Schwartz.
2. "The Price of Autonomy: Intellectuals in Ming and Ch'ing Politics," *Daedalus* 1972.2:78.
3. Edward Shils, "Intellectuals," in *International Encyclopedia of the Social Sciences,* Vol. VII, ed. David Sills (New York, Macmillan, 1968), pp. 413–414.
4. See, Merle Goldman, ed., *Modern Chinese Literature in the May Fourth Era* (Cambridge, Harvard University Press, 1977).
5. These themes and the place of intellectuals whose formative years were touched by the May Fourth experience are placed in context of other significant generations of Chinese intellectuals in the past century by Li Zehou and Vera Schwarcz, "Six Generations of Modern Chinese Intellectuals," *Chinese Studies in History* 17:2:42–56 (Winter 1983–1984).
6. Although Ai Siqi prospered and died a natural death in 1966 before the Cultural Revolution, the case of Zhou Yang, the ideological spokesman in literary affairs from the 1930s, shows the perils for even the extreme conformist.

For available details, see Merle Goldman, *China's Intellectuals: Advise and Dissent* (Cambridge, Harvard Unversity Press, 1981).

7. John Dardess, *Confucianism and Autocracy: Professional Elites and the Founding of the Ming Dynasty* (Berkeley, University of California Press, 1983).

8. See Joanna Handlin's review of Dardess's book in the *Journal of Asian Studies* 44.3:583–585 (1985).

9. Benjamin Elman, *From Philosophy to Philology: Intellectual and Social Aspects of Change in Late Imperial China* (Cambridge, Council on East Asian Studies, Harvard University, 1984).

10. See Charles Hayford, "Professions in Republican China," paper given at the Southwest Association of Asian Studies, 1984.

11. John Israel, "The Liberal Style of Southwest University: A Failed Model?" paper given at "Chinese Intellectuals and the CCP: The Search for a New Relationship," The New England China Seminar, Harvard, 5 May 1984. These views will be incorporated in his forthcoming monograph on Southwestern University.

12. Suzanne Pepper, "Socialism, Democracy, and Chinese Communism: A Problem of Choice for the Intelligentsia, 1945–49," in Chalmers Johnson, ed., *Ideology and Politics in Contemporary China* (Seattle, University of Washington Press, 1973), pp. 161–218.

13. Joanna Handlin, *Action in Late Ming Thought: The Reorientation of Lü Kun and Other Scholar-Officials* (Berkeley, University of California Press, 1983), p. 103.

14. Kjeld Brodsgaard, "The Democracy Movement in China, 1978–79: Opposition Movements, Wall Poster Campaigns, and Underground Journals," *Asian Survey* 21.7:747–774 (July 1981).

15. Leo Ou-fan Lee, "The Politics of Technique: Perspectives of Literary Dissidents in Contemporary Chinese Fiction," in Jeffrey Kinkley, ed., *After Mao: Chinese Literature and Society 1978–1981* (Cambridge, Council on East Asian Studies, Harvard University, 1985).

16. Chiang Yung-chen, "Professional Service Through The Social Sciences: Serving the People Through Sociology in the 1930s and 1940s," New England China Seminar, 5 May 1985.

17. A moving personal account of one such intellectual's participation in the anti-Rightist campaign and her own later purge, is given in Yue Daiyun and Carolyn Wakeman, *To The Storm: The Odyssey of a Revolutionary Chinese Woman* (Berkeley, University of California Press, 1985), pp. 1–53.

18. Michael Duke, *Blooming and Contending* (Bloomington, Indiana University Press, 1985), p. 143.

19. Ibid., p. 144.

20. Liu Binyan, quoted in Howard Goldblatt, ed., *Chinese Literature in the 1980s* (Armonk, M. E. Sharpe, 1982), pp. 105–106.

21. George Konrád and Ivan Szelényi, *Intellectuals on the Road to Class Power* (New York, Harcourt, Brace, Jovanovich, 1979).

22. Li Honglin, "Socialism and Opening to the Outside World," *People's Daily*, 15 October 1984, p. 5.

23. Ba Jin, *Random Thoughts* (Hong Kong, 1984), p. xvi.
24. Ibid., p. 76.
25. *People's Daily,* 14 April 1985, p. 1.
26. *People's Daily* (overseas edition), 4 August 1985.
27. As in the past hundred years, true dissidents from the government in China have sought refuge outside China and have pushed their views in emigré publications. Currently this is the case with the "China Spring" group located in Canada.

1. Ai Siqi, by Joshua A. Fogel

1. Recent work by Japanese Sinologists has shown that certain intellectuals did drop out of society in the Later Han dynasty out of disgust for the salacious politics of the central government, only to assume positions of local prestige because of the moral righteousness of their stance. Ultimately, they formed the basis of the Six Dynasties aristocracy. From the late Tang, and especially with the spread of the examination system in the Song, the relationship of intellectuals to the state underwent a radical transformation. The very definition of scholar-official (or gentry) no longer required the intermediacy of local society. There were endemic conflicts between *shengyuan* (those who had passed the lowest level of the examinations) and local officials, but these were usually the result of an insufficient number of government posts for them. The late Ming example of the Donglin faction provides another extraordinary example of intellectuals at odds with the state. Liu Zongzhou's self-imposed starvation and the refusal of his student Huang Zongxi to serve the alien Qing were, in neither case, a rejection of the state's *appropriate* role in the creation and maintenance of an ethos. What it really signified, as Ono Kazuko and Mizoguchi Yūzō have demonstrated, was an early attempt to demarcate where the state's authority extended and where the local gentry elites wanted to retain control. See, respectively, Tanigawa Michio, *Chūgoku chūsei shakai ron josetsu* (An introduction to a theory of medieval Chinese society), in *Chūgoku chūsei shakai to kyōdōtai* (Medieval Chinese society and the "local community"; Tokyo, Kokusho kankōkai, 1976), pp. 1–116; Kawakatsu Yoshio, *Gi Shin Nambokuchō: Sōdai na bunretsu jidai* (Wei, Chin, Northern and Southern Dynasties: An era of great disunity; Tokyo, Kōdansha, 1974); Mori Masao, "Sōdai igo no shitaifu to chiiki shakai: Mondaiten no mosaku"; (*Shidafu* [Literati] and local society from the Song dynasty on: In search of the issues), in *Chūgoku shitaifu kaikyū to chiiki shakai to no kankei ni tsuite no sōgō teki kenkyū* (Studies on the relationship between the literati class and local society in China), ed. Tanigawa Michio (Kyoto, Kyoto University, 1983), pp. 95–103; Joshua A. Fogel, "A New Direction in Japanese Sinology," *Harvard Journal of Asiatic Studies* 44.1:225–247 (June 1984); Ono Kazuko, *Kō Sōgi* (Huang Zongxi; Tokyo, Jimbutsu ōraisha, 1967; Ono Kazuko, "Minmatsu Shinsho ni okeru chishikijin no seiji kōdō" (Political behavior among intellectuals in the late Ming and early Qing), in *Sekai no rekishi 11: Yuragu Chūgoku teikoku* (History of the world, Vol. XI: The

trembling Chinese empire; Tokyo, Chikuma shobō, pp. 81–110; and Mizoguchi Yūzō, "Iwayuru Tōrinha jinshi no shisō: Zenkindai ki ni okeru Chūgoku shisō no tenkai" (The thought of scholars in the "Donglin faction":
The development of Chinese thought in the pre-modern era), *Tōyō bunka
kenkyūjo kiyō* 75:111–341 (March 1979).

2. Wu Boxiao, "Wo so zhidao de lao Ai tongzhi" (The Comrade Ai that I knew),
Shehui kexue zhanxian 1978.7:12–15; Yi Wenho, "Jiaxiang renmin de huainian" (Reminiscences of hometown folk), in *Yige zhexuejia de daolu, huiyi Ai
Siqi tongzhi* (One philosopher's path, remembrances of Comrade Ai Siqi,
hereafter, *Yige;* Kunming, Yunnan renmin chuban she, 1981), p. 123; Li
Shengmian and Li Xianzhen, "Yi erge qingshaonian shidai" (Remembering
our second brother in his youth), in *Yige,* pp. 5–6; Chu Tunan, "Xuesheng,
zhanyou, tongzhi" (Student, fighting friend, comrade), in *Yige,* p. 10; Zhang
Kecheng, "Ai Siqi tongzhi zai Kunming Yizhong" (Comrade Ai Siqi at Number One Middle School in Kunming), in *Yige,* pp. 18–20; Zhang Tian-fang,
"Qinfen de xuezhe, chianren de zhanshi" (Struggling scholar, stubborn war-
rior), in *Yige,* pp. 14–15; Liu Huizhi, "Yi Siqi tongzhi" (Remembering Comrade Siqi), in *Yige,* pp. 67–68; and Lu Guoying and Ye Zuoying, "*Ai Siqi wenji*
diyizhuan bianji gongzuo yijing wancheng" (Editorial work on the first volume of the writings of Ai Siqi has been completed), *Zhexue yanjiu* 1979.12:75.

3. Huang Luofeng, "Sixiang zhanxian shang de zhuoyue zhanshi" (Spectacular
fighter on the intellectual front), in *Yige,* p. 53; Ye Zuoying, "Ai Siqi zhuyao
chuyi nianpu" (Chronological biography of Ai Siqi's major writings and
translations), *Xueshu yanjiu* 1983.1:48–49; Xu Dixin, "Lao Ai zai Shanghai"
(Old Ai in Shanghai), in *Yige,* pp. 34–35. Many of Ai's philosophical essays
from these years can be found in *Ai Siqi wenji* (The writings of Ai Siqi), Vol.
I (Beijing, Jenmin chuban she, 1979). On the debate between Ye Qing and
Ai, see O. Brière, S. J., "L'Effort de la philosophie marxiste en Chine," *Bulletin de l'Université d'Aurore,* Series 3, 8.3:309–347 (1947).

4. O. Brière, *Fifty Years of Chinese Philosophy 1898–1949* (New York, Praeger,
1965), p. 78. I have used the third edition of Ai's popular work, *Zhexue
jianghua* (Shanghai, Tushu shenghuo she, 1936); however, I have had occasion
to look over six editions of the book.

5. Ai Siqi, "Yizhe xu" (Translator's introduction, 26 June 1936), in *Xin zhexue
dagang* (Beijing, Sanlian shudian, 4th edition, 1950), p. 1; Karl A. Wittfogel,
"Some Remarks on Mao's Handling of Concepts and Problems of Dialectics," *Studies in Soviet Thought* 3.4:262 (December 1963); quotation from
Gustav A. Wetter, *Dialectical Materialism: A Historical and Systematic Survey
of Philosophy in the Soviet Union* (New York, Praeger, 1958), p. 176; Ye
Zuoying, pp. 52–53.

6. Wang Danyi, "Guanyu Mao zhuxi gei Ai Siqi tongzhi xin de jidian huiyi"
(Reminiscences concerning certain points in Chairman Mao's letter to Comrade Ai Siqi), *Zhongguo zhexue* 1979.1:41; and Wu Liping, "Mao zhuxi
guanxin *Fan Dulin lun* de fanyi" (Chairman Mao's concern with the translation of [Engels's] *Anti-Dühring*), *Zhongguo zhexue* 1979.1:44.

7. Wang Zuye, "Xuexi Mao zhuxi renzhen dushu buchixiawen de jingshen"

Beijing, Renmin chuban she, 1977); and *Pipan Liang Shuming de zhexue sixiang* (Beijing, Renmin chuban she, 1956). In 1977, this last collection and the essays of his short *Hu Shi yongshizhuyi pipan* (A critique of Hu Shi's pragmatism) were posthumously reissued in Beijing as part of the advertisement campaign for the debut of Volume V of the *Selected Works of Mao Zedong.* See also Guy Alitto, *The Last Confucian: Liang Shu-ming and the Chinese Dilemma of Modernity* (Berkeley, University of California Press, 1979), pp. 328–329; and Jerome B. Grieder, *Hu Shih and the Chinese Renaissance* (Cambridge, Harvard University Press, 1970), pp. 363–364.

29. Ai Siqi, *Bianzheng weiwuzhuyi jiangke tigang* (Outline of lectures on dialectical materialism; Beijing, Renmin chuban she, 1957). This work was translated in full into Japanese: Gai Shiki, *Benshōhō teki yuibutsuron* (On dialectical materialism), tr. Yamamura Kenzō (Tokyo, Shin Nihon shuppan-sha, 1959). See Yamamura's introduction (pp. 5–6) for some extremely interesting details.

30. Wang Chunwu, "He Ai Siqi tongzhi iqi canjia tugai" (Participating in land reform with Comrade Ai Siqi), in *Yige,* p. 101; Liang Hanping et al., "Ai Siqi tongzhi zai Tianjin" (Comrade Ai Siqi in Tianjin), in *Yige,* p. 105. See also Zhang Lei, "Ma Lie zhuyi Mao Zedong sixiang de reqing xuanchuanzhe" (Enthusiastic propagandist for Marxism-Leninism-Mao Zedong Thought), in *Yige,* p. 135.

31. Wang Danyi, Lu Guoying, and Ye Zuoying, "Ai Siqi nianpu" (Chronological biography of Ai Siqi), in *Ai Siqi wenji* (The writings of Ai Siqi; Beijing, Renmin chuban she, 1983) II, 909.

32. Zhang Lei, p. 138; Wu Bingyuan, p. 153; Ge Li, "Huainian Ai Siqi tongzhi" (Reminiscences of Comrade Ai Siqi), in *Yige,* p. 148. Lu Guoying argues that the attack on Ai in 1958 involved the debate on the "unity of thought and existence," but he says nothing further, in Lu, "Xuezhe ho zhanshi" (Scholar and fighter), in *Yige,* p. 179.

33. Han Shuying, "Ai Siqi tongzhi zai Henan Tengfeng" (Comrade Ai Siqi in Tengfeng county, Henan), in *Yige,* p. 125; Zhang Lei, p. 138; and Wu Bingyuan, pp. 153–154.

34. Ai, "Surreptitious Substitution of Theory of Reconciliation of Contradictions and Classes for Revolutionary Dialectics Must Not Be Permitted," from *People's Daily,* 20 May 1965, as translated in *Survey of the China Mainland Press* 3475:1–11 (11 June 1965). See also the chapter by Carol Hamrin in this volume.

35. Stuart Schram, ed., *Chairman Mao Talks to the People* (New York, Pantheon Books, 1974), p. 226. The careful reader will note that what Mao actually says here is utter gibberish.

36. See Carol Hamrin, "Yang Xianzhen: Upholding Orthodox Leninist Theory," in *China's Establishment Intellectuals,* ed. Timothy Cheek and Carol Hamrin (Armonk, M. E. Sharpe, 1986).

37. Lu Guoying, p. 177. Lu later quotes (p. 178) Ai: "A worker in philosophical theory must deeply take part in practice to advance his investigative research. For me, land reform, being sent down, and the Anti-Rightist Campaign will reform my thought, clarify reality, and help me immensely." Wang, Lu, and Ye, "Ai Siqi nianpu," pp. 911. The Sakata essay in question was published on

1 June 1965 in *Red Flag,* and the editorial board of *Red Flag* asked Ai to attend a symposium on Sakata's essay later that year. Ai's speech on that occasion, "Weiwu bianzhengfa shi tansuo ziranjie mimi te lilun wuqi" (Dialectical materialism is the secret theoretical weapon to search for truth in the natural realm), was subsequently published in *Red Flag* (No. 9).

38. Wu Boxiao, p. 12.
39. "Mao Zedong tongzhi gei Ai Siqi tongzhi de xin ho Ai zhu *Zhexue yu shenghuo* zhailu" (Comrade Mao Zedong's letter to Comrade Ai Siqi and excerpts from Ai's book *Zhexue yu shenghuo*), *Zhongguo zhexue* 1979.1:3, 4; *Xinhua yuebao* 1980.2:1; and in Ai Siqi, *Dazhong zhexue* (Kunming, Yunnan renmin chuban she, 1979), as cited in Ye Zuoying, part II, p. 53.
40. Wang Danyi, pp. 42–43.
41. Wang Zuye, pp. 38–39.
42. Guo Huajuo, "Mao zhuxi kangzhan," p. 5.
43. Liu Baiyu, "Xu" (Introduction), in *Yige,* p. 1.
44. Liang Hanping et al., p. 108.
45. Wu Liping, "Zhongcheng zhengzhi de geming zhexuejia," pp. 81–82.
46. Guo Huajuo, "Mao zhuxi kangzhan," p. 6. The section on formal logic and dialectics missing from the later edition has been translated by Nick Knight, "Mao Zedong's *On Contradiction* and *On Practice:* Pre-Liberation Texts," *China Quarterly* 84:661–668 (December 1980).
47. Zheng Yili, "Ai Siqi he ta de *Dazhong zhexue*" (Ai Siqi and his *Philosophy for the Masses*), in *Yige,* p. 48.
48. Guo Huajuo, "Mao zhuxi kangzhan," p. 6.
49. Li Shengmian and Li Xianzhen, p. 9; Zhang Kecheng, p. 19; Su Ying, "Zhexuejia Ai Siqi de wenhua yishu huodong" (The cultural and artistic activities of philosopher Ai Siqi), *Xin wenxue shiliao* 20.3:117 (1983); Lu Wanmei, "Huiyi Ai Siqi tongzhi zai *Yunnan minzhong ribao* pianduan" (Scattered memories of Comrade Ai Siqi at the *Yunnan minzhong ribao*), in *Yige,* p. 24; and Ye Zuoying, part I, pp. 49, 51.
50. Leszek Kolakowski, *Main Currents of Marxism, Vol. III: The Breakdown* (New York, Oxford University Press, 1982), pp. 494, 495.
51. "Mitin, Mark Borisovich," *Bol'shaia Sovetskaia Entsiklopediia* (Moscow, "Sovietskaia Entsiklopediia," 1974) XVI, 335; "Mitin, Mark Borisovich," *Encyclopaedia Judaica* (Jerusalem, Keter Publishing House, 1972) XII, col. 160–161; and "Miding zhuanlüe" (Short biography of Mitin), in *Xin zhexue dagang,* frontispiece. No bibliography of the works of M. B. Mitin should lack the following select titles: *Filosofiia i sovremennost'* (Philosophy and the present time; Moscow, Akademiia nauk SSSR, 1960), *Gegel' i teoriia materialisticheskoi dialektiki* (Hegel and the theory of materialist dialectics; Moscow, 1932); *Za materialisticheskuiu biologicheskuiu nauku* (Toward a science of materialist biology; Moscow, Akademiia nauk SSSR, 1949); *Sionizm, raznovidnost' shovinizma i rasizma* (Zionism, a variety of chauvinism and racism; Moscow, Obshchestvo "Znanie" RSFSR, 1972); and the 5-volume work he edited, *Istoriia filosofii* (History of philosophy; Moscow, 1957–1961).

52. I have been able to locate 10 books (in a total of at least 18 editions) and 2 articles by Mitin in Chinese translation; I presume that there are more.

2. Economists and Economic Policy-Making, by Nina Halpern

I should like to thank Merle Goldman and Christine Wong for helpful comments on earlier drafts of this chapter.

1. As a recent article put it: "Beginning with the 2nd Five-Year Plan, the whole country smelted iron and steel on a large scale, industry blossomed everywhere, and the necessary regional plan for rationally arranging the local economic structure was in practice negated." Chen Jiyuan, "Diqu jingji jiegou" (Local economic structure), in Ma Hong and Sun Shangqing, eds., *Zhongguo jingji jiegou wenti yanjiu* (Research on China's economic structure; Beijing, Renmin chuban she, 1981) II, 657.
2. The most comprehensive statement of this sort was made by Chen Zhenhan et al., "Women duiyu dangqian jingji kexue gongzuode yixie yijian" (Some opinions on current work in economic science), in *Jingji yanjiu* 1957.10:123–133.
3. *Jingjixue dongtai,* May 1978, p. 2; June 1978, p. 11. The Institute's access to economic information was also enhanced in another way: It was assigned two "test point" counties, Fengrun and Changli in Hebei province, where it could study the implementation of agricultural policies. In this way it could gather first-hand information on the results of economic policy, and supply feedback and policy suggestions to policy-makers. See Sun Yefang, "Fight for the Defense of Marxist Political Economy," *People's Daily,* 16 March 1978, p. 3, in *JPRS* #71002, p. 4.
4. Nina P. Halpern, "Economic Specialists and the Making of China's Economic Policy, 1955–1983" (PhD dissertation, University of Michigan, 1985), Chapter 3.
5. Zhu Banshi, "1960 nian 7 yue zhi 1965 nian youguan guomin jingji tiaozheng gongzuode dashi jiyao" (Summary of the major events from July 1960 to 1965 in the work of readjusting the national economy), in Liu Suinian et al., *Liushi niandai guomin jingji tiaozhengde huigu* (Review of the readjustment of the national economy in the 1960s; Beijing, Zhongguo caizheng jingji chuban she, 1982), p. 184.
6. In January, a decision was made to adjust the industrial management system so that, for the next two to three years, major decisions on production, construction, purchasing, finance, etc., would be made by the central authorities. See Zhu Banshi, p. 186. Correspondingly, in the same month a decision was made to lower the percentage of enterprise-retained profits from an average of 13.2% to 6.9%. See Wu Qungan, "Guanyu 'da yuejin' he tiaozhengde qingkuang he jingyan," (The circumstances and experiences of the 'Great Leap Forward' and readjustment) in Liu Suinian et al., p. 42.

7. Beijing diyi jichuangchang diaochazu (Beijing First Machine Tools Plant Investigation Group), *Beijing diyi jichuangchang diaocha* (Investigation of the Beijing First Machine Tools Plant; Beijing, Shehui kexue chuban she, 1980), p. 3.

8. Gui Shiyong, "Tentative Discussion of Sun Yefang's Thinking on Reforming the Economic System," *Guangming Daily*, 9 October 1983, p. 3, in *JPRS* #84762, *Economic Affairs* 400:69 (16 November 1983).

9. Sun Yefang, *Shehuizhuyi jingjide ruogan lilun wenti (xuji)* (Some theoretical problems regarding the socialist economy [sequel]; Beijing, Renmin chuban she, 1981), p. 12.

10. Available in Sun Yefang, *Shehuizhuyi jingjide ruogan lilun wenti* (Some theoretical problems regarding the socialist economy; Beijing, Renmin chuban she, 1979), pp. 138–151.

11. This discussion is based on Beijing diyi jichuangchang diaochazu (Beijing First Machine Tools Plant Investigation Group), "Xuyan" (Afterword) and "Chuban shuoming" (Publication explanation).

12. I include the member of the Central Party School among the "academics" (as opposed to considering him primarily a Party figure) because Chinese discussions of the social-science research network generally include high-level Party schools as a component part. (See, for example, Chou Hsun, "The Present State and Future Outlook for Social Science Research in Communist China," *Ch'i-shih nien-tai*, No. 107, December 1978, tr. Alexander DeAngelis, in *Chinese Law and Government* 12.4: 93 (Winter 1979–1980). These schools had research sections, although it is not known whether the particular individual included in the 9-man team, Gao Jiangyang, was a member of such a research section.

13. Beijing diyi jichuangchang (Beijing First Machine Tools Plant Investigation Group), "Xuyan" (Afterword), p. 7.

14. Wu Qungan, p. 48.

15. *Beijing diyi jichuangchang diaocha* (Investigation of the Beijing First Machine Tools Plant) is a slightly shortened and revised version of the report. Unfortunately, it is the only version available. However, the foreword says that the basic contents and viewpoint of the original document had been retained to "maintain the original features of these historical materials." The Seventy Points is available in Zhongguo Shehui Kexueyuan Gongye Jingji Yanjiusuo Qiye Guanlishi (Chinese Academy of Social Sciences, Institute of Industrial Economics, Office of Enterprise Management), ed., *Zhongguo gongye guanli bufen tiaolie huibian* (Compilation of some regulations on Chinese industrial management; Beijing, Dizhi chuban she, 1980), pp. 216–243.

16. The book has recently been published. It is *Zhongguo shehuizhuyi guoying qiye guanli* (Management of China's socialist state-run enterprises), Vols. I and II (Beijing, Renmin chuban she, 1981). The description of its preparation is in Vol. I, "Jidian shuoming" (Some explanations).

17. Zhu Banshi, p. 180.

18. Ibid., pp. 182–183; and Wang Ping, "'Da yuejin' he tiaozhengde qingkuang

he jingyan" (The circumstances and experiences of the Great Leap Forward and readjustment), in Liu Suinian et al., p. 170.

19. Deng Liqun, *Xiang Chen Yun tongzhi xuexi zuo jingji gongzuo* (Learn how to do economic work from comrade Chen Yun; Beijing, Zhonggong Zhongyang Dangxiao chuban she, 1981), p. 8.

20. See Byung-joon Ahn, *Chinese Politics and the Cultural Revolution* (Seattle and London, University of Washington Press, 1976), p. 55, for details.

21. Ibid., p. 55.

22. *Red Flag* 24:2–3 (16 December 1982) in *FBIS*, 11 January 1983, pp. K7–8.

23. Byung-joon Ahn, p. 54.

24. Its head, Deng Zihui, had been sent by Liu Shaoqi to do rural investigations during the summer of 1960. After visiting Shanxi province and Wuxi county, Deng had drafted 40 articles on the internal affairs (*neiwu*) of the communes. Mao praised these articles at the March 1961 work conference that drafted the Sixty Points; it seems quite likely that Deng's articles served as one basis for the latter. See Jiang Boying et al., "Deng Zihui," in Zhonggong Dangshi Renwu Yanjiuhui, ed., *Zhonggong dangshi renwu zhuan* (Biographies of CCP historical figures; Shanxi, Shanxi Renmin chuban she, 1983) VII, 372–373.

25. MacFarquhar, *The Origins of the Cultural Revolution* (New York, Columbia University Press, 1974) I, 28.

26. Mao Tsetung, *On the Ten Major Relationships* (Bejing, Foreign Language Press, 1977), p. 1.

27. Nina Halpern, "Economic Specialists," Chapter 2.

28. MacFarquhar, p. 59.

29. For example, Sun Yefang describes how, in 1956, Li Fuchun made a point of inviting some academic specialists to participate in bureaucratic discussions on the theory and method of national income and statistics at a time when academics were rarely consulted. See *Renmin shouce*, 1958, p. 170.

30. Between April and July 1962, three researchers at the Institute of Economics are said to have carried out rural investigations which led them to advocate expanding the scope of rural markets and fixing output quotas at the household level (i.e., *baochandaohu*), liberalizing measures that went beyond the Sixty Points but were already prevalent at that time. The three were Luo Gengmo, Zhang Wentian, and an unnamed "young researcher." (See Jin Sanzhi, "Luo Gengmo is a Fanatic Advocate of 'Fixing Output Quotas at the Household Level,'" *Guangming Daily*, 20 January 1967, in *Survey of China Mainland Press* 3895:22 (9 March 1967); "Resolutely Strike Down the Anti-Party Element Chang Wen-ti'en," *Ch'in-chun pao* 22–23:8 (31 May 1967) in *JPRS* #41, 898, 20 July 1967, p. 8; and Xiang Qiyuan, "Sun Yefang tongzhi shi zenmeyang zai jingji yanjiusuo guanche 'shuang bai' fangzhende" (How comrade Sun Yefang upheld the policy of the "2 100s" in the Institute of Economics, *Jingji yanjiu*, March 1983, p. 37.) Zhang Wentian was a prominent Party figure who was sent to the Institute of Economics in 1960 after his political fall resulting from being linked with Peng Dehuai at the Lushan Conference. I include him here not as an economist per se, but

because various sources indicate that he was participating in the regular work of the Institute at the time, so that his activities are indicative of the tasks performed by Institute researchers. This activity might have been initiated by the Institute itself, but, since members of the Institute are only known to have conducted rural investigations during these three months, it seems more likely that they were responding to some signal from the top. A meeting of the Secretariat was held during the summer of 1962 to review the policy of individual farming (see Kenneth Lieberthal, *A Research Guide to Central Party and Government Meetings in China, 1949–1975,* White Plains, International Arts and Sciences Press, 1976, p. 188); conceivably, the Institute might have been asked to prepare materials and advice for this review.

31. Barry Naughton, "Sun Yefang," in Carol Hamrin and Timothy Cheek, eds., *China's Establishment Intellectuals* (Armonk, M. E. Sharpe, 1986), is a good biography of Sun.

32. Sun Yefang, *Shehuizhuyi jingjide ruogan lilun wenti (xuji)* (Some theoretical problems regarding the socialist economy [sequel]), p. 13.

33. It is possible that this was simply the proper bureaucratic channel, i.e., that reports from the Institute of Economics traveled first to the State Planning Commission, and then on to the "Center" (probably meaning the Party Secretariat), but Sun's comment suggests otherwise.

34. This was titled "Some Opinions on the Question of Accumulation," and is in Sun Yefang, *Shehuizhuyi jingjide ruogan lilun wenti (xuji)* (Some problems regarding the socialist economy [sequel]), pp. 289–292. Sun's discussion of why he wrote the report is in his *Shehuizhuyi jingjide ruogan lilun wenti* (Some theoretical problems regarding the socialist economy), "Qianyan" (foreword), pp. 5–6.

35. Sun Yefang, *Shehuizhuyi jingjide ruogan lilun wenti,* "Qianyan," p. 6.

36. Sun's report is in Sun Yefang, *Shehuizhuyi jingjide ruogan lilun wenti,* pp. 192–201. It seems very likely that Chen's report was presented at the July-August Beidaihe planning conference. Chen is known to have presented a report on this subject at the conference (see Lieberthal, p. 189), and, since Sun's response was written in late August, it seems almost certain that he was responding to Chen's Beidaihe report.

37. Sun Yefang, *Shehuizhuyi jingjide ruogan lilun wenti,* p. 192.

38. In a December 1982 interview in Beijing, Dong Fureng, a Deputy Director of the Institute of Economics, explained to me that, although minor policy matters could be openly discussed, discussions of important policies must be carried out internally because public questioning of such policies might lead cadres to cease implementing them.

3. The Politics of Historiography, by Clifford Edmunds

The author is grateful to Lyman Miller and Joseph Fewsmith for their helpful comments.

1. The first public signs of Jian's impending rehabilitation appeared in wall posters at Beijing University in April 1978. See the Agence France-Presse report by George Biannic, 28 April 1978, *FBIS:PRC,* 28 April 1978, pp. E

11–12. On 15 September 1978, the party newspaper *People's Daily* published excerpts from an article in the September issue of *Lishi yanjiu* containing Jian's official rehabilitation. See *FBIS:PRC,* 20 September 1978, pp. E 19–20, for translated excerpts of a New China News Agency summary of the article.

2. The criticism campaign against Jian during the Cultural Revolution extended from March to December 1966, including more than 40 scathing attacks in a dozen different newspapers and journals. Jian was attacked as an anti-socialist, anti-Party bourgeois "academic authority" who sought to lay the ideological foundation for the restoration of capitalism. See the two articles by Qi Benyu, Lin Jie, and Yan Changgui, "Jian Bozan tongzhi de lishi guandian ying dang pipan" (The historical viewpoint of Comrade Jian Bozan ought to be criticized), *Red Flag* 1966.4:19–30, translated in *Survey of China Mainland Press,* (Hong Kong, U.S. Consulate General) 521:28–44 (25 April 1966); and "Fangong zhishi fenzi Jian Bozan de zhen mianmu" (The true face of anti-communist intellectual Jian Bozan), *Red Flag* 1966.15:25–35, translated in ibid. 556:1–14 (28 December 1966). The suicide of Jian and his wife, long discussed in Beijing rumor mills, was officially acknowledged, and dated 16 December 1968, by NCNA on 22 February 1979. The report is excerpted in *FBIS:PRC,* 26 February 1979, pp. E 8–9.

3. See Arif Dirlik, "Mirror to Revolution: Early Marxist Images of Chinese History," *Journal of Asian Studies* 1974.33:193–223, and *Revolution and History: Origins of Marxist Historiography, 1919–1937* (Berkeley, University of California Press, 1978) for an analysis of these debates and their meaning in Chinese social history.

4. Jian Bozan *Zhongguo shigang (An outline of Chinese history;* Shanghai, 1946–1947). Other historians, such as Fan Wenlan, Lu Zhenyu, and Bai Shouyi, who played a prominent role in academic history in the PRC after 1949, wrote similar general histories.

5. Jian Bozan, *Lishi zhexue jiao cheng (Course on the philosophy of history,* 2nd ed; Shanghai and Chongqing, 1939), and "Zenyang yanjiu zhongguo lishi" (How to study Chinese history), a 1950 essay reprinted in Jian's *Lishi wenti luncong* (Essays on historical questions, rev. ed.; Beijing, Renmin chuban she 1962), pp. 79–91.

6. Jian Bozan, "Ji Baili qingnian Hanxuejia huiyi" (An account of the Paris Congress of Junior Sinologues), *People's Daily,* 31 October 1956.

7. Jian Bozan, *Zhongguo shilunji* (Essays on Chinese history; Chongqing, 1944).

8. Albert Feuerwerker, "China's History in Marxian Dress," *American Historical Review* 1961.66:323–353.

9. The five official topics for research on Chinese history marked out in 1951 were: periodization, the role of individuals, peasant rebellions, nationality relations, and the origins of capitalism.

10. The criticism campaign against the liberal scholar and historian Hu Shi in the mid-1950s was not directed against historiography but against philosophical pragmatism, which was uncomfortably similar to Maoism in its epistemology. See the analysis by Chan Lien, "Chinese Communism versus Pragmatism: The Criticism of Hu Shi's Philosophy, 1950–1958," *Journal of Asian Studies* 1968.27:551–570.

11. The literal translation of the Chinese term for "historicism," (*lishi zhuyi*), is "historyism." The term is problematic because of the various connotations associated with it in Western scholarly parlance. This chapter will focus on Jian's interpretation of the concept, and will not concern itself with comparisons with Western usage.

12. Yue Shi, "Yi ge fan Makesi Zhuyi de shixue gangling" (An anti-Marxist historiographical framework), *Guangming Daily*, 3 April 1966.

13. This follows the usage of Arif Dirlik, "The Problems of Class Viewpoint versus Historicism in Chinese Historiography," *Modern China* 1977.3:465–488.

14. For the peasant-rebellion issue, see James O. Harrison, "Communist Interpretations of the Chinese Peasant Wars," *China Quarterly* 1965.23:92, and *The Communists and Chinese Peasant Rebellions* (New York, Atheneum, 1969). The reevaluation movement began with a debate over the role of Cao Cao: *Cao Cao lunji* (Essays on Cao Cao; Peking, Sanlian shudian, 1962). Evidently Shang Yue's thesis that the "sprouts," or origins, of capitalism could be traced to the Ming dynasty was too politically sensitive even for Jian, who joined in the criticism of Shang. Shang's thesis raised questions about the timing of the CCP's rise to power, and its role in modern Chinese history, and hence about its legitimacy.

15. Merle Goldman, "The Role of History in Party Struggle," *China Quarterly* 1972.51:500–519; Dirlik, "Class Viewpoint," and Jian Bozan, "'Xin mao chulai' de shixue tixi, hai shi 'jiu de chuantong shixue tixi' de fanpan?" (A "recently emerged" historical system or a new version of "an old traditional historical system"?), *Lishi yanjiu* 1960.3:107.

16. Jian Bozan, "Dui chuli ruogan lishi wenti de chubu yijian (Initial opinions on handling various historical questions), *Guangming Daily*, 22 December 1961.

17. Jian Bozan, "Lishi kexue zhanxian shang liangtiao luxian duozheng" (The struggle of two lines on the historical science front), *People's Daily*, 15 July 1958.

18. Jian Bozan, "Guanyu dapo wangchao tixi wenti" (On the question of smashing the dynastic system), *Xinjianshe* 1959.9:17–19. See also Jian, "Muqian lishi jiaoxue zhong de jige wenti" (Several problems in the recent teaching of history), *Red Flag* 1959.10:21–31.

19. The term *anonymous history* is borrowed from Feuerwerker, "China's History."

20. Jian, "Guanyu dapo" and "Dui chuli."

21. Jian, "Dui chuli."

22. See note 18.

23. Jian Bozan, "Muqian shixue yanjiu zhong cuncai de jige wenti" (Several questions in current historical research), *Jianghai xuekan*, June 1962. For a more accessible reprint, see *Wenhui bao*, 28 March 1966.

24. Jian, "Muqian lishi jiaoxue."

25. Ibid.

26. Jian, "Dui chuli."

27. Ibid.
28. Ibid.
29. Jian Bozan, "Yinggai ti Cao Cao huifu mingyu" (We ought to restore Cao Cao's good name), *Guangming Daily,* 19 February 1959.
30. Jian, "Dui chuli."
31. Jian, "Guanyu dapo."
32. Jian, "Muqian shixue yanjiu."
33. Ibid.
34. Jian substituted the character *dai* (代), "replace," for its homophone *dai* (帶) "lead," in the formula *yi lun dai shi.*
35. Ibid.
36. Qi Benyu et al., "Jian Bozan tongzhi de lishi guandian."
37. Ibid.
38. Jian, "Muqian shixue yanjiu."
39. See note 1. The posters on Jian preceded a purge of the Beijing University History Department's Cultural Revolution leadership. These events are discussed in Robin Munro, "Settling Accounts with the Cultural Revolution at Beijing University, 1977–78," *The China Quarterly* 1980.82:329–330.
40. Li Honglin, "Jian Bozan tongzhi shinian ji–bo Qi Benyu dui Jian Bozan de wuxian" (A decennial memorial to Comrade Jian Bozan–A refutation of Qi Benyu's frame-up), *Lishi yenjiu* 1978.9:27–37, abridged in *People's Daily,* 13 September 1978, p. 3. Excerpts of an NCNA summary of the article can be found in *FBIS:PRC,* 20 September 1978, pp. E 19–20.
41. *FBIS:PRC,* 21 September 1978, p. E 13.
42. Li Xuekun, "Esha lishi kexue de eba xingjing–zai bo Qi Benyu dui Jian Bozan tongzhi de wu xian" (Throttle the despotic act in historical science–Another refutation of Qi Benyu's frame-up of Comrade Jian Bozan), *Lishi yanjiu* 1978.10:27–42.
43. Excerpted in *FBIS:PRC,* 26 February 1979, pp. E 8–9. The memorial service was held on 22 February. Writing in 1985, Li Honglin acknowledged that he had first hesitated to write his 1978 *Lishi yanjiu* memorial essay because the proposal to hold a memorial service for Jian was controversial. Li further revealed that some of his views on Jian's historiography, and his criticism of Qi Benyu, one of Jian's persecutors during the Cultural Revolution, were criticized after the memorial essay was published. See Li's "Wo weishenmo xie 'Jian Bozan shinian ji'" (Why I wrote "A memorial to Jian Bozan"), in Li's collection of essays, *Lilun fengyu* (Beijing, Sanlian she, 1985), pp. 485–488.
44. A commemorative conference held at Beijing University on 17 and 18 November 1982, however, did receive attention in the official Party press. Reported first on the front page of the intellectuals' newspaper, *Guangming Daily,* on 18 November, the event was carried on page 4 of *People's Daily* the next day. Several essays presented at the conference were published in the university's journal, *Beijing daxue xuebao* 3 (1983), in June.
45. Jian Siping, "Kunnan de licheng–huiyi wo fuqin Jian Bozan tongzhi de zhishi daolu" (A difficult course–In memory of my beloved father Comrade Jian Bozan's road to the mastery of history), *Lishi zhishi* 1982.5:12.

46. As reported in *Guangming Daily*, 27 October 1979, p. 1, under the title "Lishi yanjiu bixu tichang zhenshixing he kexuexing" (Historical research must promote truthfulness and scientific character), *FBIS:PRC*, 9 November 1979, pp. L 16–18. The late 1950s controversy over the radicals' slogan "Lead history with theory" had reopened by the early 1980s. The weight of authoritative opinion appears to support Jian's view that the slogan "Theory emerges from history" is a more fitting guide for historical scholarship. For a review of the controversy, see the article by Li Xin of the Central Committee's Party History Research Department, in *Lishi yanjiu* 1984.4:3–6. Li rejects "Lead history with theory" as contrary to Marxism-Leninism and Mao Zedong Thought, and calls for serious debate on this question, which, he says, "has not been resolved after 30 years."

47. Xu Xudian, "The 1980 Conference on the History of the Boxer Movement," *Modern China* 1981.7:384.

48. A selection of Jian's essays were republished under the title *Lishi lunwen xuanji* (Selected essays on history; Beijing 1980).

49. David D. Buck, "Appraising the Revival of Historical Studies in China," *China Quarterly* 105:131–142 (March 1986), provides an excellent brief summary of both the new professionalism in history circles and the political context that shapes it. For a very useful and interesting comparative essay on Party historiography under Mao and under Deng, see Susanne Weigelin-Schwiedrzik, "Party Historiography in the People's Republic of China," unpublished paper, 1985. Li Honglin, whose 1978 memorial essay served as the basis for Jian's rehabilitation, also wrote a key article in the movement to rethink Party historiography. The article, "Dapo dangshi jinqu" (Smash the forbidden zones in Party history), originally published in 1978, is reprinted with an explanatory note in Li's *Lilun fengyu*, pp. 39–41 and 58–78.

50. *Guangming Daily*, "Historical Research Must Promote Truthfulness."

51. Shi Wen, "Tan Makesi zhuyi zhidao xia de xueshu ziyou wenti" (On academic freedom under the guidance of Marxism), *Guangming Daily*, 20 March 1985, p. 3, *FBIS:PRC*, 26 March 1985, pp. K 13–14.

52. Hu Sheng, "Guanyu jiaqiang shehui kexue yanjiu de jige wenti" (Several questions concerning the strengthening of the study of social sciences), *Red Flag*, No. 9, 1 May 1986, pp. 3–10, *FBIS:PRC*, 28 May 1986, pp. K 11–22.

53. Su Shuangbi, "Guanyu kaizhan 'baijia zhengning' de jige wenti" (Several questions concerning the promotion of "A Hundred Schools of Thought Contend"), *Guangming Daily*, 30 April 1986, p. 3, *FBIS:PRC*, 19 May 1986, pp. K 4–12.

54. Li Kan, "Shuangbai fangzhen de xingqing yu lishi xue de rongku" (The rise and fall of the double-hundred policy and the flourishing and withering of historical study), *People's Daily*, 2 June 1986, p. 5, *FBIS:PRC*, 4 June 1986, pp. K 7–11.

55. The following review of the Qinshihuang allegory is drawn from a paper on the subject by Lyman Miller, "Deng Xiaoping and Qinshihuang: Politics and History in Post-Mao China," presented to the China Colloquium, University of Washington, 28 April 1980. Miller brilliantly demonstrates the

connection between the discussion of Qinshihuang among historians and the reassessment of Mao and the Cultural Revolution being carried out in inner-Party circles, and the connection between both of these and Deng Xiaoping's political fortunes.

56. Miller, "Deng Xiaoping and Qinshihuang." The political target of the slogan "Practice is the sole criterion of truth" was the "two-whatever" doctrine espoused by Hua Guofeng to tie his legitimacy to Mao. The slogan's pragmatic criterion of truth, however, implied that all other ideas and policies of Mao were also open to question, and would be retained only if they measured up to this test. In similar fashion, cadres could be evaluated against this pragmatic standard and removed if judged deficient. For a perceptive analysis of Deng's strategy of reinterpreting Mao and legitimizing political reform, see Tsou Tang, "The Historic Change in Direction and Continuity with the Past," *China Quarterly* 98: 226–232 (June 1984).

57. For an excellent analysis of the historiographical issues addressed in the peasant-war debates, see Kwang-ching Liu, "Worldview and Peasant Rebellion: Reflections on Post-Mao Historiography," *Journal of Asian Studies* 1981.40:295–326. While Profesor Liu calls attention to the fact that debates on class struggle in the Party press paralleled the history controversy, he does not mention the concurrent Dengist effort to redefine the Party's political line or the modifying effect of the dissident trials on this effort. For these insights I am indebted to Lyman Miller.

58. The 23 December 1978 and 21 June 1979 NCNA reports on the 3rd Plenum Communiqué and Hua Guofeng's NPC speech are found in *FBIS:PRC*, 26 December 1978, p. E 6, and 22 June 1979, pp. L 5–7, respectively. On 15 April 1980, *Guangming Daily* called a halt to the discussion of motive forces that it had been carrying on its "history supplement" page. The debate reemerged in 1981, possibly in conjunction with the trials that spring of dissidents Wei Xizhe and Xu Wenlu, and Deng Xiaoping's criticism of Bai Hua and other critical writers.

59. Kong Xiangji, "Bairi weixin shibai yuanyin xinlun" (A new theory on the causes of the failure of the hundred-day reform), *People's Daily*, 21 October 1985, p. 5, *FBIS:PRC*, 5 November 1985, pp. K 1–7. This analysis of Kong's essay is, of course, tentative. While the essay appears transparently allegorical, the ambiguities of theme and symbolism in such treatments of sensitive political issues make precise interpretation of their meaning very difficult. Attempts to identify historical characters with specific individuals on the current political scene, in particular, may distort the thematic parallels intended by the allegorist. In Kong's essay, especially, the same historical actors appear to represent different present-day figures or groups as the context shifts.

Kong, a young history professor at People's University in Beijing, appears to be a Dengist. His previous articles on the 1898 reforms, both in academic publications and the Party press, have consistently praised the radical reformers for attempting the sweeping changes necessary for China's survival. Although he has dealt with political intrigue and factional infighting at the Qing court in earlier articles, none of these has been as suggestive of current PRC politics as the October 1985 article under discussion here.

60. The regime has similarly blurred the line between scholarship and politics in its "patriotic history" campaign, a continuous effort over the past several years to use history as a didactic tool for regenerating Chinese national pride. The Campaign Against Spiritual Pollution in late 1983, however, was the most serious threat to the new-found autonomy and professionalism of historians and other scholars.

The agrarian-socialism debate emerged in *Nanjing daxue xuebao,* Spring 1980. I am indebted to Lyman Miller for calling this material to my attention and suggesting an interpretation.

4. Law and Legal Professionalism, by James V. Feinerman

1. Sybil van der Sprenkel, *Legal Institutions in Manchu China* (London, Athlone, 1962), p. 69. See also Derk Bodde and Clarence Morris, *Law in Imperial China* (Cambridge, Harvard University Press, 1967), particularly p. 189, describing "litigation tricksters" who "for a price [stirred] up disputes and [corrupted] simple country folk."

2. Shao-chuan Leng, *Justice in Communist China* (New York, Oceana, 1967), pp. xiii–xiv; see also Jean Escarra, *Le Droit Chinois* (Peking, H. Vetch, 1936) and Franz Michael, "The Role of Law in Traditional, Nationalist and Communist China," *China Quarterly* 9:134 (January–March 1962).

3. Ch'ien Tuan-sheng, *The Government and Politics of China* (Cambridge, Harvard University Press, 1950), especially pp. 247–261.

4. Leng, note 2, Chapter 1 "Pre-1949 Development of the Communist Chinese System of Justice," pp. 1–26.

5. Ibid., p. 9; Leng also cites Ma's dictum, p. 19, that "three old peasants are equal to a local judge." (Citing a 1944 "Order concerning the execution of the Resolution for the Improvement of the Judicial System.")

6. Ibid. Chapter 7, "The People's Lawyer," pp. 127–146.

7. See, e.g., Beverly G. Baker, "Chinese Law in the Eighties: the Lawyer and the Criminal Process," *Albany Law Review* 46:751 (1982); Jerome Cohen, "China's New Lawyer's Law," *American Bar Association Journal* 1980.66: 1533; Ernest Gellhorn, "The Developing Role of Law and Lawyers in China: Introduction," *Albany Law Review* 1982.46:687; Tao-tai Hsia and Charlotte Hambly, "The Lawyer's Law: An Introduction," *China Law Reporter* 1981.1:213; Lamont-Brown, "Lawyers and the Bamboo Curtain," *Solicitors Journal* 1980.124:95.

8. Entitled "Provisional Regulations for Lawyers of the People's Republic of China," adopted by the 15th Session of the 5th National People's Congress, 26 August 1980, effective 1 January 1982 (hereafter, Provisional Regulations).

9. The reestablishment of a formal legal system in the PRC begins with this event—an historical turning point which announced a reversal of Cultural Revolution political attitudes and the adoption of modernizing policies under the direction of Deng Xiaoping. The Communiqué of the 3rd

Plenary Session of the 11th Central Committee of the Communist Party (18 and 22 December 1978) stated:

In order to safeguard the people's democracy, it is imperative to strengthen the socialist legal system so that democracy is systematized and written into law in such a way as to ensure the stability, continuity, and full authority of this democratic system and these laws; *there must be laws for people to follow, these laws must be observed, their enforcement must be strict, and law-breakers must be dealt with.* (emphasis added)

"Quarterly Chronicle and Documention (October–December 1978)," *China Quarterly* 77:172 (March 1979).

10. For an official statement about the background to these laws, see Peng Zhen, "Explanation on Seven Laws," *Beijing Review*, 22.28:8–16 (20 July 1979), particularly pp. 11–13, for the criminal law and criminal-procedure law. The other laws passed were the Organic Law of the Local People's Congresses and the Local People's Governments, the Electoral Law for the National People's Congress and the Local People's Congresses, the Organic Law of the People's Courts and the Organic Law of the People's Procuratorates, and the Law on Joint Ventures with Chinese and Foreign Investment.

11. For a comprehensive analysis of this period, see Hungdah Chiu, *Socialist Legalism: Reform and Continuity in Post-Mao People's Republic of China* (Baltimore Occasional Papers/Reprints Series in Contemporary Asian Studies, 1982), especially pp. 3–14 and Jerome Cohen, *The Criminal Process in the People's Republic of China, 1949–1963* (Cambridge, Harvard University Press, 1968), pp. 468 ff. ("The Antirightist Movement Ends the Constitutional Experiment").

12. Jerome Cohen, "Notes on Legal Education in China," *Journal of the Law Association for Asia and the Western Pacific* 4:205 (June 1979); Timothy A. Gelatt and Frederick E. Snyder, "Legal Education in China: Training for a New Era," *China Law Reporter* 1980.1:41; Richard H. Herman, "The Education of China's Lawyers," *Albany Law Review* 1982.46:789; John F. Murphy, "Legal Education in China: Some Impressions," *China Law Reporter* 1982.2:50.

13. Hungdah Chiu, note 11, p. 31.

14. See Gelatt, "China Makes Lawyers Legitimate," *Asian Wall Street Journal Weekly*, 6 October 1980, p. 11. Also see Jerome Cohen, "China's New Lawyer's Law," note 7.

15. Gelatt and Snyder, note 12, p. 58.

16. See also De-pei Han and Stephen Kanter, "Legal Education in China," *American Journal of Comparative Law* 1984.32:543.

17. Wu Yuehui, "Taking the Rule of Law Seriously," *PRC Quarterly*, October 1984, p. 18, notes:

In big cities, professionals and law students often provide free legal advice to people in need. Because of the shortage of lawyers, this service is very well recieved [*sic*].

18. Beijing *Xinhua* Domestic Service in Chinese, 1329 GMT, 11 March 1985, monitored in *FBIS Daily Report: China, FBIS-CHI*-85-053 (19 March 1985), p. K 34.
19. For example, an article entitled "Nobody is above Constitution and law," appearing in the *China Daily* analyzed both the 1982 State Constitution and the new Party Constitution adopted by the 12th National Congress of the Chinese Communist Party to conclude:

    All the activities of any Party organization and Party members must not go against the Constitution and the law. This is the attitude of the Party.

    China Daily, 25 January 1983, p. 3.
20. *People's Daily,* 25 April 1984, p. 4.
21. Gelatt and Snyder, note 12, p. 53:

    As an article in one of China's legal journals recently pointed out, since the People's Republic has graduated only a few thousand students from its institutions of formal legal education in its thirty-year history, the tradition has always been for the majority of "cadres," or officials, of judicial institutions, to "learn to fight in the course of the war." In fact, less than six percent of current members of the court system in China have received formal legal education.

22. A trenchant criticism of this pervasive problem is presented by Andrew Walder, "Organized Dependence and Cultures of Authority in Chinese Industry," *Journal of Asian Studies* 43:51 (November 1983). Walder's study emphasizes the importance of informal, interpersonal relationships in the Chinese workplace but describes a pattern replicated elsewhere in Chinese society.
23. Some university law departments in China reflect these areas of specialization; the Peking University Law Faculty, for example, has three specializations: basic law (including criminal and constitutional law), economic law, and international law. The Provisional Regulations (Art. 14) also anticipated the establishment of specialized Legal Advisory Offices to develop greater expertise for areas demanding certain skills (e.g., foreign-language capability) and experience.
24. *China Daily,* 24 December 1982, p. 2.
25. See e.g., Hungdah Chiu, note 11, pp. 29–32.
26. The 15th Session of the Standing Committee of the 5th National People's Congress devoted itself to passing legislation implementing the joint-venture law; detailed rules and regulations for implementing the tax provisions thereunder were promulgated by the Ministry of Finance shortly afterwards. Not much progress was made in promulgating domestic law until 1982.
27. The Criminal Law of the People's Republic of China and The Criminal Procedure Law of the People's Republic of China, adopted by the 2nd Session of the 5th National People's Congress, 1 July 1979.
28. Criminal Procedure Law, Articles 26–30. According to Article 26, the defender does not have to be a trained lawyer but may also be a relative, guardian, or other citizen recommended by the defendant's work unit or the court.

29. Provisional Regulations, Article 2(c):

> (c) To be entrusted by defendants in criminal cases or appointed by people's courts to act as advocates. . . .

30. The indictment and the highlights of the trial are described in the book *A Great Trial in Chinese History* (Peking, New World Press, 1981). As an official account prepared by the government of the PRC for foreign consumption, its objectivity and accuracy are somewhat doubtful.

31. Ibid. p. 26. Counsel included several distinguished professors of law, researchers at the Institute of Law of the Chinese Academy of Social Science, and lawyers from the Beijing and Shanghai Lawyers' (Bar) Associations.

32. Ibid. Jiang Qing interviewed counsel recommended to her by the special court, but she reportedly rejected their assistance when informed that the lawyers could not completely speak for her in court, answering questions in her stead.

33. The Economic Contract Law of the People's Republic of China, adopted at the 4th Session of the 5th National People's Congress, 13 December 1980, to become effective 1 July 1982.

34. On 13 April 1982, the State Council promulgated "Provisional Regulations for Notarization of the People's Republic of China." Article 4(a) of these regulations makes the certification of contracts one of the tasks of a notary in China. Article 59 of the Civil Procedure Law of the People's Republic of China, approved by the 22nd Session of the Standing Committee of the 5th National People's Congress on 8 March 1982 for trial implementation beginning 1 October 1982, requires the people's courts to recognize the validity of legal acts and documents that have been notarized.

35. See, e.g., "Lawyers Help Solve Business Disputes," *China Daily,* 7 April 1983, p. 3, stating that 70 major enterprises in Shanghai, China's largest city, have formally engaged legal counsel.

36. For example, legal advice given to Chinese purchasers of steel-mill equipment from foreign suppliers caused major embarrassment when Japanese and West German parties to the purchase contracts insisted upon penalty payments when China reneged on the purchases. See Tony Walker, "China's Cancellation of Foreign Contracts Damages Its Image," *Los Angeles Daily Journal,* 2 March 1981, p. 5; also "Some Cancelled Western Contracts May Be Restored," *East Asian Executive Reports* 3.12:5 (1981).

37. See Gelatt, "The People's Republic of China and the Presumption of Innocence," *Journal of Criminal Law and Criminology* 73:135 (1982). Article 11, ¶1, of the International Declaration of Human Rights incorporates the provision thus:

> Everyone charged with a penal offense has the right to be presumed innocent until proven guilty according to law in a public trial at which he has had all the guarantees necessary for his defense.

38. Ibid. See also Zhang Zipei, "An Analysis of the Principle of 'Presumption of Innocence,'" *Faxue yanjiu* (Studies in law) 1980.3:33.

39. See, e.g., Jerome Cohen, *The Criminal Process in the People's Republic of China, 1949–1965*, note 11, pp. 445–460. Cohen notes (p. 460) that, in Japan also, "the closing argument of the defense is generally aimed mainly at the reduction of the sentence suggested by the procurator."

40. The willingness of Chinese entities to operate without legal advice is perhaps best illustrated by the title and contents of V. Li, *Law Without Lawyers* (Stanford, Stanford Alumni Association, 1977).

41. "Legal Aid Offices Grow in Rural Areas," *China Daily*, 29 January 1985, p. 1, quoting a report in *People's Daily*.

42. Provisional Regulations, Article 1.

43. Ibid., Article 2.

44. Ibid., Articles 3, 5.

45. Ibid., Articles 4, 5.

46. Ibid., Article 8.

47. Ibid.

48. E.g., Article 79 of the Criminal Law, which contains an analogy provision:

Those who commit acts not explicitly defined in the specific parts of the criminal law may be convicted and sentenced after obtaining the approval of the Supreme People's Court, according to the most similar article in the law.

49. In fact, only the first alternative requires any formal training in law, suggesting that legal education still lags far behind China's needs.

50. Provisional Regulations, Article 9.

51. Ibid., Article 11; the period of probation is for two years, after which the graduate lawyer is allowed to take the examination provided for in Article 9. Those who fail this examination may have their periods of probation extended.

52. Ibid., Article 12. These regulations contain no definition of "grossly incompetent."

53. Ibid., Chapter 3, Articles 13–19.

54. Ibid., Article 13. The 1950s lawyers' organizations are described in "Provisional Measures of the People's Republic of China for Receipt of Fees by Lawyers," approved by the 19th Plenary Meeting of the State Council, 25 May 1945; promulgated by the Ministry of Justice, 20 July 1956, *Fagui huibian* 1956.4:235–238, translated in Jerome Cohen, *The Criminal Process in the People's Republic of China, 1949–1963*, note 11, pp. 436–437.

55. Provisional Regulations, Article 14:

Legal Advisory offices are not affiliated to each other.

56. Ibid., Article 16. A deputy chief is elected "where necessary."

57. Ibid., Article 17.

58. Ibid., Article 19.

59. These have increased greatly in recent years and may provide another basis

for new self-confidence among Chinese lawyers. Concerned friends belonging to foreign bars may provide some assurance that the Chinese government will not treat its lawyers as cavalierly in the future as it did from 1957 to 1978. See, e.g., *Australian International Law News,* September 1984, p. 620, detailing a broad agreement of July 1984 for exchanges of legal personnel from a range of legal institutions (judges, government legal officers, academics, etc.) between the Australian Attorney General and the Chinese Minister of Justice.

60. Specialized firms have begun to appear. The China Council for the Promotion of International Trade, to give just one example, has organized a "China Global Law Office" and published its "statutes" or articles of association. The aim of this organization is "to promote economic, trade, and financial exchanges between China and foreign countries." Article 2, Statutes of the China Global Law Office (hereafter, China Global Statutes), *China Economic News,* No. 50, 31 December 1984.

61. China Global Statutes, Article 1, states that the office provides various legal services to "enterprises, economic, trade, and financial organizations, or individuals, both Chinese and foreign, as well as those in Hong Kong and Macao. . . ."

62. These Chinese lawyers, when requested, will provide opinions as to the validity of an agreement under Chinese law or as to the due incorporation and existence of an entity according to Chinese law.

63. China Global Statutes, Article 9, provides that the office "charges reasonable fees for its services."

64. Provisional Regulations, Article 8.

65. A ranking member of the Central Secretariat of the Communist Party, Xi Zhongxun, said that this would be a "new test of the reform of the legal work system." *Zhongguo fazhibao* (China legal news), 13 February 1985, p. 1.

66. See note 39, above and accompanying text.

67. Criminal Procedure Law, Articles 26–30, note 28 above.

68. See Jerome Cohen, *The Criminal Process in the People's Republic of China, 1949–1963,* note 11, Chapter 2, "Informal Adjustment and Sanctioning" and Chapter 3, "Security Administration Punishment Act."

69. See Decisions of the Standing Committee approved by the 19th Session of the Standing Committee of the 5th National People's Congress, 10 June 1981, on Death Sentences (approval of the Supreme People's Court no longer required for various classes of offenses) and on Escapees and Recidivists (extending terms of reeducation through labor or reform through labor beyond statutory maximums for escapees and recidivists); see also Decisions of the Standing Committee on Severely Punishing Criminals Who Gravely Endanger Public Security (stipulating application of severest penalty permissible and making crimes punishable by death which had not previously carried such severe penalties) and on the Procedure to Try Swiftly Criminals Who Seriously Jeopardize Public Security (eliminating time limits for delivery of indictments and subpoenas; lengthening time for appeals and

requests for retrial by the procuratorate), adopted at the 2nd Session of the Standing Committee of the 6th National People's Congress, 2 September 1983.

70. Zhou Jianren, "A Random Talk on Law and Social Order," *People's Daily,* 18 January 1984, cited in *FBIS Daily Report: China, FBIS-CHI*-85-015 (23 January 1984), p. K 7.

71. *People's Daily,* 18 February 1985, p. 4.

72. *People's Daily,* 1 March 1985, p. 4; *China Daily,* 2 March 1985, p. 3. I am indebted to Prof. William Alford, of the UCLA Law School, for calling my attention to these reports.

73. *People's Daily,* 1 March 1985, p. 4.

74. See notes 35 and 41 above and accompanying text.

75. "Communiqué of the 3rd Plenary Session of the 12th Central Committee of the Communist Party of China," 20 October 1984, translated in *FBIS Daily Report: China, FBIS-CHI*-84-204 (22 October 1984), p. K 12:

> More and more, norms guiding economic relations and activities will have to be framed in the form of law in the restructuring of the economy and national economic development. State legislative bodies must produce economic legislation faster, the courts should make greater efforts to try economic cases, the procuratorates should strengthen their work in dealing with economic crimes and the judicial departments should offer active services for economic construction.

76. John Hazard, *Managing Change in the U.S.S.R.: The Politico-Legal Role of the Soviet Jurist* (Cambridge and London, Cambridge University Press, 1983).

77. Ibid., p. 54.

78. "Xi Zhongxun Addresses China Law Firm Reception," Beijing *Xinhua* Domestic Service in Chinese 1434 GMT 12 February 85, as monitored by *FBIS Daily Report: China, FBIS-CHI*-85-031 (14 February 1985), p. K 4:

> The establishment of the China Law Firm is a fresh attempt to restore the lawyers' system. [Xi] expressed the conviction that constant and in-depth reform is bound rapidly to develop the work on lawyers [*sic*]. In his speech, Zou Yu, Minister of Justice, hoped that the company will [*sic*] contribute to reforming the economic system and promoting economic development in China.

79. Provincial-level commitment to these developments is reflected in a broadcast, "Zhejiang Urges Strong Economic Legal System," Hangzhou Zhejiang Provincial Service 0400 GMT 28 October 84, monitored by *FBIS Daily Report: China, FBIS-CHI*-84-210 (29 October 1984), p. O 4, transmitting the provincial Economic Law Research Center's views on strengthening the economic legal system.

80. See description of a broken-contract case handled by the First Secretary of the Henan Province Communist Party Central Committee, Liu Jie, Zhongzhou Henan Provincial Service 1030 GMT 21 March 1984, monitored in *FBIS Daily Report: China, FBIS-CHI*-84-060 (23 March 1984) p. P 1. The First

Secretary ordered local officials who had arbitrarily torn up a contract with a specialized household running a brick kiln to carry out the contract's terms, following a court verdict issued by the county-level people's court. Liu's intervention was sought after jealous county leaders and production-team members tried to impose new terms on a specialized household that had profited handsomely from a production-responsibility contract to run the brick kiln.

5. *China's Scientists and Technologists in the Post-Mao Era,* *by Denis Fred Simon*

1. Zhao Ziyang, "Report on the Work of the Government," *Beijing Review,* 4 July 1983.
2. F. H. Harbison and C. A. Myers, *Education, Manpower and Economic Growth* (New York, McGraw Hill, 1964).
3. Gunnar Myrdal, *Asian Drama: An Inquiry into the Poverty of Nations, Volumes I–III* (New York, Pantheon Books, 1968). See also Mark Blaugh, ed., *The Economics of Education, Volumes I and II* (Middlesex, Penguin Books, 1969).
4. *Guangming Daily,* 17 October 1984, pp. 1, 4. See also *Beijing Review,* 14 February 1983, p. 16.
5. Richard P. Suttmeier, *Research and Revolution: Science Policy and Societal Change in China* (Lexington, Mass., Lexington Books, 1974). In 1956, as part of the effort to promote more rapid industrial progress, an elaborate 12-year science and technology development plan (1956–1967) was formulated.
6. "Party's Experience Shows Key Role of Intellectuals," *China Daily,* 24 November 1982. See also Suttmeier, *Research and Revolution.* According to Zhou's own words, the meeting was designed "to find a correct solution for the question of intellectuals, to mobilize them more efficiently, and to make fuller use of their abililties."
7. Cheng Chu-yuan, *Scientific and Engineering Manpower in Communist China, 1949–1963,* #NSF 65–14 (Washington, National Science Foundation, 1965), p. 257.
8. P. 108.
9. *Red Flag* 1958.9:8. For an overview of Nie Rongzhen's views regarding China's intellectuals, see Dong Kegong et al., "Comrade Nie Rongzhen and Intellectuals," *Guangming Daily,* 4 October 1982 translated in *JPRS* 82237, 16 November 1982, pp. 132–139.
10. This theme about the importance of basic research is articulated by Xu Liangying and Fan Dainian in the volume edited by Pierre Perrolle entitled *Science and Socialist Construction in China* (Beijing, People's Publishing House, 1957). In the book, the authors reflect on the requirements for rapid scientific and technical advance in China. Unfortunately, the Anti-Rightist Campaign of 1957 emerged, shelving the hopes of the scientific community.
11. The "demolition" of the CAS occurred in spite of the efforts of Zhou Enlai, who in 1956 made an important address of the need to improve

the treatment of scientists and give science its due place in the country's affairs.

12. John Lindbeck, "The Organization and Development of Science," in Sidney Gould, ed., *Sciences in Communist China* (Washington, American Association for the Advancement of Science, 1961), pp. 3–58.

13. Orleans, p. 106.

14. See L. V. Filatov, *An Economic Appraisal of Soviet Scientific and Technical Assistance to China, 1949–1966* (Moscow, Nauka Publishing House, 1980), translated by the Foreign Technology Division, US Air Force, Wright Patterson Air Force Base, Dayton, Ohio.

15. For a discussion of the treatment of intellectuals during the mid-1950s, see Roderick MacFarquhar, *The Origins of the Cultural Revolution: Contradictions Among the People, 1956–57* (New York, Columbia University Press, 1974).

16. An important event in this regard was the Guangzhou conference on science and technology planning held in 1962. The conference, which was chaired by Nie Rongzhen, saw the formulation of a second long-term program for S&T development (1963–1972)—a program that was eventually disrupted by the Cultural Revolution. See Yan Jici, "Development of the Natural Sciences Over the Past 30 Years," in Ma Feihai, ed., *Thirty Years' Review of China's Science and Technology, 1949–79* (Singapore, World Scientific Publishing Company, 1981), pp. 1–9.

17. See Chu-yuan Cheng, *Scientific and Engineering Manpower in Communist China, 1949–63* (Washington, National Science Foundation, 1965), pp. 31–33.

18. Pierre Perrolle, ed. *Science and Socialist Construction in China.*

19. See Rudi Volti, *Technology, Politics, and Society in China* (Boulder, Westview Press, 1982), pp. 59–113.

20. John Lindbeck, "The Organization and Development of Science," in Roderick MacFarquhar, ed., *China Under Mao: Politics Takes Command* (Cambridge, MIT Press, 1966), p. 362.

21. Merle Goldman, *China's Intellectuals: Advise and Dissent* (Cambridge, Harvard University Press, 1981), pp. 89–155.

22. Jerome B. Grieder, *Intellectuals and the State in Modern China* (New York, Free Press, 1981). Grieder also shows that Chinese intellectuals have furthermore had a difficult time sorting out their own role and place in society.

23. Roger Revelle, "The Scientist and the Politician," *Science,* 21 March 1975, pp. 1100–1105.

24. For example, see Robert Miller, "The Scientific-Technical Revolution and the Soviet Administrative Debate," in Paul Cocks, et al., *The Dynamics of Soviet Politics* (Cambridge, Harvard University Press, 1976), pp. 137–155.

25. See Denis Fred Simon, "Implementation of S&T Reforms in China's Modernization," in David Michael Lampton, ed., *Policy Implementation in Post-Mao China* (Berkeley, University of California Press, forthcoming).

26. For a discussion of China's views regarding bureaucratic organization during the Maoist period, see Harry Harding, *Organizing China: The Problem of Bureaucracy, 1949–76* (Stanford, Stanford University Press, 1981).

27. For some preliminary speculation on this issue, see Peter R. Moody, Jr., *Chinese Politics After Mao: Development and Liberalization, 1976–1983* (New York, Praeger, 1983).
28. For an analysis of the backdrop to the March 1978 meeting, see Chung Ko, "The Struggle Around the Outline Report on Science and Technology," *Beijing Review*, 28 October 1977, pp. 5–8. Also see Chung Ko, "Scientific Research Speeds Up," *Beijing Review*, 22 July 1977, pp. 5–12.
29. Richard P. Suttmeier, *Science, Technology, and China's Drive for Modernization* (Stanford, Hoover Institution Press, 1980).
30. See Deng Xiaoping's speech at a science and education work conference on 8 August 1977 for the background to the March 1978 meeting. Deng Xiaoping, "Several Opinions Concerning Science and Education Work," translated in *FBIS-PRC*, 11 July 1983, pp. K1–K9.
31. Deng Xiaoping, "Speech at the Opening Ceremony of the National Science Conference," *Beijing Review*, No. 12, 24 March 1978, pp. 9–18.
32. Suttmeier, *Science, Technology and China's Drive for Modernization*, p. 6.
33. Leo Orleans, ed. *Science in Contemporary China* (Stanford, Stanford University Press, 1981).
34. For a discussion of these problems by Chinese authors, see the special issue entitled *China Examines Science Policy*, No. 2, 83240, 12 April 1983, especially pp. 121–206.
35. "Deng Xiaoping Calls for Mobilizing Scientists," *FBIS*, 1 December 1982, p. K1.
36. Nathan Kaplan, "Some Organizational Factors Affecting Creativity," *IRE Transactions on Engineering Management*, EM-7, No. 1, 1960, pp. 24–30.
37. See assorted articles in Ina Spiegel-Rosing and Derek de Solla Price, eds., *Science, Technology and Society: A Cross-Disciplinary Perspective* (Beverly Hills, Sage Publications, 1977).
38. Xia Yulong and Liu Ji, "It Is Also Necessary to Eliminate Erroneous 'Leftist' Influence on the Science and Technology Front," *Jiefang ribao*, 2 June 1983 translated in *FBIS-PRC, China Report*, 11 June 1981, pp. K8–12.
39. "The Entire Party Should Accord the Proper Importance to Science and Technology," *Guangming ribao*, 18 April 1981, translated in *JPRS 78147*, 22 May 1981, pp. 1–5.
40. "Science and Technology Must Be Developed in Coordination with the National Economy in the Course of Readjustment," *Guangming Daily*, 15 January 1981, translated in *China Examines Science Policy* (Springfield, FBIS, January 1982), pp. 3–5.
41. "Further Clarify the Policy for the Development of Science and Technology," *People's Daily*, 7 April 1981, translated in *China Examines Science Policy*, pp. 16–19.
42. Jia Weiwen, "Combine the Plans for the Development of Science and Technology with the Plans for Development of the Economy and Society," *People's Daily*, 5 July 1981, p. 3, translated in *China Examines Science Policy* (Washington, FBIS, January 1982). See also R. P. Suttmeier, *Science, Technology, and China's Drive for Modernization*.
43. For a description of the development of nuclear weapons in China,

see "China's Atomic Weapon Story Told," *New York Times,* 5 May 1985, p. 34.

44. It was also in 1982 that a new constitution was adopted. Within the framework of this new constitution, the role of science and technology was acknowledged and the legitimate rights of scientific and technical personnel were spelled out. See Jurgen Domes, *Government and Politics in the PRC: A Time of Transition* (Boulder, Westview Press, 1985). See also Foreign Languages Press, *Politics: China Handbook Series* (Beijing, 1985).

45. See Zhao Ziyang, "A Strategic Question on Invigorating the Economy," *Beijing Review,* 15 November 1982, pp. 13–20. See also "Leaders Attend Science Awards Meeting," *Xinhua,* 23 October 1982, translated in *FBIS-PRC,* 25 October 1982, pp. K3–12.

46. "Zhao Ziyang To Head New Scientific Work Group," *FBIS-PRC,* 31 January 1983, p. K8.

47. In many cases, the directives provided the basis for setting up experimental sites to try out the new policies. See Denis Fred Simon, "Rethinking R&D," *China Business Review,* July–August 1983, pp. 25–31.

48. Denis Fred Simon, "Rethinking R&D," pp. 25–31.

49. For example, in mid-1982, two engineers were named deputy governors of Liaoning province. *Beijing Review,* 17 May 1982, pp. 5–6.

50. In May 1981, there were 283 members added to the Scientific Council through a series of examinations and voting by the original members. According to Fang Yi's comments, this made the council both authoritative and representative. See "Leaders Attend Academy of Sciences Session," *Xinhua,* translated in *China Examines Science Policy,* p. 146.

51. Of course, this meant added administrative burdens for many of the scientists, particularly Lu Jiaxi, who, during a trip to the United States in late 1984, complained about having little time for actual research.

52. These moves, while generally welcomed by the scientific community, also met with some criticism from some of the scientists who felt that their new administrative responsibilities imposed excessive time constraints on their ability to conduct research. For example, the newly appointed director of the Institute of Chemical Metallurgy under the CAS complained that he was tied up by endless meetings, in which he spent almost 30% of his time. See "Give Our Specialists a Free Hand," *China Daily,* 6 April 1984.

53. Suttmeier argues that this fund was introduced to further depoliticize the research environment and to attack such emerging problems as fraud in scientific research. See R. P. Suttmeier, "New Conflicts in the Research Environment," *Bulletin of the Atomic Scientists,* October 1984, pp. 7S–11S.

54. "Chief Engineer Becomes Tianjin's New Vice-Mayor," *China Daily,* 12 April 1983.

55. "State Council Issues Scientists Work Regulations," *Xinhua,* translated in *FBIS-PRC,* 25 March 1982, pp. K8–9.

56. "Scientific Consulting Services Expanded," *Xinhua,* translated in *FBIS-PRC,* 20 January 1983, pp. K6–7. The first consulting corporation, which operated under the Ministry of Aeronautics Industry, was formed in September 1983.

See "First Science and Technology Consultancy Set Up," *Xinhua*, translated in *FBIS-PRC*, 13 September 1983, p. K5.

57. "University Faculty & Staff Receive Bonus for Consulting Work," *China Daily*, 10 February 1983, p. 3.

58. See Leo Orleans, "The Training and Utilization of Scientific and Engineering Manpower in the People's Republic of China," Congressional Research Service, Committee on Science and Technology, US House of Representatives, October 1983.

59. "Bu He on Shortage of Engineers in Nei Monggol," *Xinhua*, translated in *FBIS-PRC*, 17 August 1983, p. R7.

60. Tao Kai and Geng Qing, "On the Question of Directional Flow of Scientific and Technical Personnel," *Guangming Daily*, 12 July 1982, translated in *JPRS* 83240, 12 April 1983, p. 246.

61. "Overcoming the Phenomenon of Inbreeding in the Training of Qualified Personnel," *People's Daily*, 19 September 1983, translated in *JPRS* 83240, 12 April 1983, pp. 243–244.

62. Gu Jiuguang, "Views of Research Personnel on the Current Reform of Scientific Research," *Kexuexue yu kexue jishu guanli* (Scientology and the management of science and technology), No. 8, 1983, translated in *JPRS-CST-84-011*, 17 April 1984, pp. 155–163.

63. According to a report in *Jingji Daily*, among those S&T personnel with professional titles of high rank, those 61 years or older account for 30.5%, those 56 years or over account for 53%, and those 45 or younger account for 2%. See "Problems of the Present State and Existence of China's Science and Technology Contingent," *Jingji Daily*, 4 January 1984, translated in *JPRS-CST-84-011*, 17 April 1984, pp. 139–140.

64. See Orleans, "The Training and Utilization of Scientific and Engineering Manpower in the PRC."

65. For example, according to a survey conducted in late 1984 by the Talent Resources Survey Committee of Shanghai, an extreme shortage of S&T specialists aged 25–35 may severely hamper the city's development ten years from now. See "Shanghai Faces Talent Shortage," *China Daily*, 24 November 1984.

66. "Decision of the Central Committee of the Communist Party of China on Reform of the Economic Structure," 3rd Plenary Session of the 12th Central Committee, 20 October 1984, p. xiv.

67. "Mobility of Scientists Advocated," *China Daily*, 19 July 1983, p. 4.

68. Zhao Ziyang, "Revamping China's Research System," *Beijing Review*, 8 April 1985, pp. 15–21.

69. "A Strategic Task in Building the Party," *People's Daily*, 20 November 1984, translated in *FBIS-PRC*, 23 November 1984, p. K6.

70. "More Intellectuals Should Be Admitted As Party Members," *China Daily*, 16 January 1985, p. 4.

71. "Absorb Large Numbers of Outstanding Intellectuals Into the Party," *Liaowang*, 26 November 1984, translated in *FBIS-PRC*, 19 December 1984, pp. K5–6.

72. Wang Xuezhen, "We Must Take Further Steps to Solve the Problems Intellectuals Face in Joining the Party," *Zhongguo jiaoyu bao,* 25 December 1984, translated in *JPRS-CPS*-85-024, 13 March 1985, pp. 98–100.
73. For Yunnan, see "Problem of Intellectuals' Difficulties in Becoming Party Members Can Be Resolved Through Conscientious Work," *Yunnan Daily,* 2 July 1984 translated in *JPRS-CPS*-84-068, 15 October 1984, pp. 143–145. For Liaoning, see "Conscientiously Solve Intellectuals' Problems in Joining the Party," translated in *FBIS-PRC,* 26 November 1984, pp. S3–4.
74. "Earnestly Solve the Problems Faced by Intellectuals in Joining the CPC," *People's Daily,* 4 July 1983, translated in *FBIS-PRC,* 7 July 1983, pp. K11–14.
75. Zhu He, "Intellectuals Bitterly Disappointed By Inability to Join the Party," *Shanxi Daily,* 7 May 1984, translated in *JPRS-CPS*-84-055, 15 August 1984, pp. 102–103.
76. "Seven Examples of How Difficult It Is For Intellectuals to Join the Party," *People's Daily,* 10 July 1984, p. 5.
77. "Clarify the Muddleheaded Understanding in the Recruitment of Party Members," *People's Daily,* 21 November 1984, translated in *FBIS-PRC,* 21 November 1984, pp. K9–11.
78. "Hu Qiaomu Addresses Party Member Scientists," *FBIS-PRC,* 6 July 1983, pp. K29–30.
79. "University Graduates To Go To PLA Units," *Xinhua,* translated in *FBIS-PRC,* 26 May 1983, p. K3.
80. "Defense S&T Cadres Study Technical Subjects on the Job," *Guangming Daily,* 12 May 1983, translated in *JPRS* 84245, 2 September 1983, pp. 21–22.
81. Shi Jinchang, "Party Committee of Nanjing Forest Chemicals Research Institute Vigorously Develops Intellectuals Into Party Members," *Xinhua Daily* (Nanjing), 31 May 1984, translated in *JPRS-CPS*-84-056, 16 August 1984, pp. 37–38.
82. "Cadre Protects Intellectuals," *China Daily,* 25 July 1984, p. 4.
83. Peng Ziqiang, "After the Professor Enters Into Politics," *People's Daily,* 7 December 1984, translated in *JPRS-CPS*-85-013, 11 February 1985, pp. 50–53.
84. Yue Ping, "Combat Ignorance To Advance S&T Development," *Guangming Daily,* 21 April 1984, translated in *JPRS-CST*-84-040, 6 December 1984, pp. 41–43.
85. Sun Jian and Zhu Weiqun, "What Is The Current Situation in Implementing Policies on Intellectuals?" *People's Daily,* 8 July 1984, translated in *FBIS-PRC,* 9 July 1984, pp. K8–10.
86. Li Jie, et al., "The Problem Is Already Obvious, the Obstruction Still Awaits Removal," *People's Daily,* 8 June 1984, translated in *JPRS-CPS*-84-056, 16 August 1984, pp. 59–61.
87. "Returned Scientists Feeling Stifled," *China Daily,* 31 August 1984, p. 4.
88. "Boom Years for Studying Abroad," *China Daily,* 26 November 1984.
89. "Cadres Dismissed for Persecuting Intellectuals," *Xinhua,* 2 November 1984, translated in *FBIS-PRC,* 5 November 1984, pp. K12–14.
90. "Ministry To Probe Bullying of Intellectuals," *China Daily,* 28 March 1984.

91. Naturally, however, it must be assumed that those engaged in such investigations are not just going through the motions and are fully committed to seeing the policy toward intellectuals carried out. In certain instances, some investigation teams have not been as thorough as they might have been in making an accurate evaluation of particular situations.

92. "Guanxi Reports on Persecution of Engineer," *FBIS-PRC*, 20 July 1984, p. P3.

93. "Award for Factory Hero Is Disputed," *China Daily*, 26 September 1984, p. 3.

94. "Science Awards Cut To Ribbons," *China Daily*, 19 February 1983, p. 3.

95. "Inventor Wins Award After Three Year Delay," *China Daily*, 10 August 1983, p. 3.

96. "State Plan To Improve the Flow of Scientists," *China Daily*, 23 July 1984, p. 1. The other features of the plan include creation of a national exchange center for science and technology personnel, establishment of post-doctoral intermediate work assignments, improvements in the work assignments for those who have returned from overseas training, and the empowering of local S&T commissions to intervene in those situations where S&T personnel are not being used properly.

97. "Scientists Given Right to Select Work Units," *China Daily*, 24 July 1986, p. 4.

98. "Scientists in Big Jobs Shake-up," *China Daily*, 18 October 1984.

99. "Graduates Assignment Revamped," *China Daily*, 6 March 1985, p. 3.

100. "Meeting on Technical Personnel Transfer Ends," *Xinhua*, 30 March 1984, translated in *FBIS-PRC*, 3 April 1984, pp. K18–19.

101. "Doing Away with "Departmental Ownership of Talents," *People's Daily*, 17 December 1984, translated in *JPRS-CPS*-85-021, 7 March 1985, p. 60.

102. "Flow of Talent Held Up by Personnel System," *China Daily*, 17 August 1984, p. 4.

103. "Indigenous Policy Hampers Talent Exchange," *Xinhua*, 4 December 1984, translated in *FBIS-PRC*, 5 December 1984, pp. K8–9.

104. David Holloway, "Scientific Truth and Political Authority in the Soviet Union," in Leonard Shapiro, ed., *Political Opposition in One-Party States* (London, Macmillan, 1972), pp. 152–178.

6. *The Emergence of Humanism, by David A. Kelly*

1. Until his downfall in the Cultural Revolution, the leading Party spokesman on ideology and culture. Since 1978, Chairman of the All-China Federation of Literature and Art Circles and a Vice-President of the Chinese Academy of Social Sciences; 1980–1982 Deputy Director of the Propaganda Department.

2. This expression derives from the work of Peter C. Ludz and is discussed in detail below. Zhou Yang, "Inquiry into some Theoretical Problems of Marxism," *People's Daily*, 16 March 1983, pp. 4–5. See analyses of the campaign by Stuart Schram, "'Economics in Command?' Ideology and Policy since the Third Plenum," *China Quarterly* 99:417–461 (September 1984); Thomas

Gold, "'Just in Time!' China Battles Spiritual Pollution on the Eve of 1984," *Asian Survey* 24.9:941–974 (September 1984).

3. In 1972, Wang led the effort to brand the Lin Biao-Chen Boda group "ultra-leftist," and to carry out a systematic critique of ultra-leftism. When Lin's crime was redefined as "left in form and right in essence," he had to make a self-criticism. But, after the Shanghai group (later known as the Gang of Four) intensified what Wang had come clearly to see as ultra-left abuses, Wang promised himself that he would never again make such a self-criticism. Wang's account in "The Pain Brought About by Wisdom" appeared in *Qingnian luntan* (Youth forum), March 1985. Xu Wen, "Reassessment of Mao Zedong is Being carried Out Quietly," *Zheng ming* 92:22–23 (June 1985), tr. in *JPRS CPS-85-067*, 3 July 1985, pp. 92–96. See also two articles criticizing Chen Boda, which Wang states were written in May and June of 1971: "Pipan Chen Boda de 'Guofang zhexue'" (Criticize Chen Boda's 'philosophy of national defense'), *Shehui kexue zhanxian* 1:32–34 (May 1978).

4. Interview with PRC General Secretary Hu Yaobang conducted in Beijing on 10 May, *Bai xing* (HK) 97:3–16 (1 June 1985), tr. in *FBIS*, Hong Kong, 2 June 1985. It was around this time that Wang began to publish his views openly once again: "On Revolutionary Humanism," *Gongren Daily*, 20 June 1985, in *SWB/FE/7987/BII/4–5*, 26 June 1985.

5. Timothy Cheek, "Interview with Wang Ruoshui, Fuzhou, 14 May 1986" (unpublished). See also "Wang Ruoshui today," *Ta kung pao* (Hong Kong), Thursday, 8 May 1986, p. 14.

6. "I was at Beida in 1948 and soon met Deng Tuo in the Hebei countryside. Soon after that I worked under Deng in the Beiping Political Research Office. At the end of 1950, around December, I entered *People's Daily* as a junior editor. Later I was moved to the Commentary Department (*pinglun bu*)." (Cheek, "Interview," p. 3.) A brief biography is given in *Zhongguo zhexue nianjian, 1983*, ed. CASS Institute of Philosophy, "Zhongguo Baike Quanshu" Publishing House, Shanghai, 1983, p. 345, tr. in D. A. Kelly, ed., "Wang Ruoshui: Writings on Humanism, Alienation and Philosophy," *Chinese Studies in Philosophy*, Spring 1985. ("WR" in subsequent references).

7. See Carol Lee Hamrin, "Alternatives within Chinese Marxism 1955–1965: Yang Hsien-chen's Theory of Dialectics," PhD dissertation, University of Wisconsin, 1975, especially Chapter 6; and "Yang Xianzhen: Upholding Orthodox Leninist Theory," in *China's Establishment Intellectuals*, ed. Carol Lee Hamrin and Timothy Cheek (Armonk, M. E. Sharpe, 1986).

8. See "The destiny of dialectics", *Shehui kexue zhanxian* 1981.3:1–19; "Did German Classical Philosophy Simply 'End'?" *Guangming Daily*, 24 May 1982, p. 3, "WR," pp. 94–102; Yang Xianzhen's riposte, "The destiny of materialism," *Shehui kexue zhanxian* 1982.1:7–25, brought a further response from Wang: "The destiny that materialism and dialectics are obliged to share," *Xueshu yuekan* 1982.6:1–12, repr. in *Zhexue yuanli* (Chinese People's University photocopy series) 1982.13:19–31.

9. "Deng and I were reasonably close. Later I wrote editorials for him"; Cheek,

"Interview," p. 3. Luo Bing, "Criticism of Zhou Yang and the Party Press Earthquake," *Zheng Ming* 74:10 (December 1983).

10. "The Greatest Lesson of the Cultural Revolution is that the Personality Cult Should be Opposed," speech at conference on theoretical work of the CCP Central Committee, 13 February 1979; *Ming bao yuekan* (HK) 2:2–15 (February 1980), tr. in *JPRS* 75291, 12 March 1980.

11. Tang Tsou, "Back from the Brink of Revolutionary-'Feudal' Totalitarianism,'" in *State and Society in Contemporary China*, ed. Victor Nee and David Mozingo (Ithaca, Cornell University Press, 1983), pp. 58–88, quotation from p. 65.

12. Ding Wang, "On 'the Alienation of Man'–Survey of the Intellectual Emancipation Movement in the PRC, Part 2," *Ming bao yuekan* 17.1:57 (December 1982). In his more recent "From 'Blindness to Humanity' to the Return to Human Nature–a Study of the Theory of Socialist Alienation," ibid. 19.1: 29–36 (January 1984), Ding drops "alienation school" in favor of "representatives" of the theory in question.

13. Peter C. Ludz, *The Changing Party Elite in East Germany* (Cambridge, MIT Press, 1972), p. 62.

14. This term is used advisedly. Hamrin has described the Chinese political system in terms of "cycles or rounds of competition in which the leaders of smaller factions and geographic and professional interest groups form alliances"; Carol Lee Hamrin, "Competing 'Policy Packages' in Post-Mao China," *Asian Survey* 24.5:487–518 (May 1984), p. 488. Cotton makes a similar analysis, drawing on the work of Merle Goldman, and distinguishes the "scientific and technological stratum" from those in literary and artistic fields, with social scientists occupying a grey middle area; James Cotton, "Intellectuals as a Group in the Chinese Political Process," in David S. G. Goodman, ed., *Groups and Politics in the People's Republic of China* (Armonk, M. .E. Sharpe, 1984), pp. 175–195. Such distinctions are capable of much further refinement.

15. Tang Tsou, "The Middle Course in Changing the State-Society Relationship and in Reforming the Political Structure in China" (conference paper, University of Chicago, 1982; cited by permission). Tsou's "Back from the Brink" analyzes in depth the leadership's "self-examination." I am indebted to Professor Tsou for valuable criticism and comment.

16. Writing in 1968, Ludz perceived that Marx's "definitely ambiguous" attitude toward technology and the technical world differed radically from the optimistic, uni-dimensional technological utopias then being propagated in Soviet and East European "revisionist" circles. Important sections of Ludz's work deal with "revisionist" attempts to integrate the concept of alienation within ideological dogma: "The outlooks of revisionist philosophers coincide in their basic recognition of alienation even in a 'socialist society' leading to a commitment to achieving the liberation of the individual and a call for a rationalized bureaucracy and system of planning." Marxists have been unable to preserve Marx's concept of alienation in a convincing form: "They

have not been able to revive the transcendental point of reference which has disappeared over the hundred years of Marxist thought." Many interpretations of alienation, notably the Yugoslavian variety, are in Ludz's view intended to revive the universal and utopian character of Marxism. Contradictory emphases emerge, on the one hand on ethical purism, on the other on modernization of the social system. The philosophies of Wolfgang Heise and Georg Klaus display this contrast. Klaus reduces alienation under socialism to a technical phenomenon. Technical progress, a new order of rationality based on cybernetics will abolish it. In the case of Heise, the critical and utopian concept does not lead to any systematically elaborated, positive theory of society that could point to the future path of development of a dynamic industrial society. This is a measure, says Ludz, of the dogmatic cast of this type of thinking. "Such puristic, utopian thinking can hardly be reconciled with the institutionalization of this revisionist position"; Ludz, *Party Elite* pp. 341 ff, 351 ff, quotation from p. 351.

17. D. A. Kelly, "Chinese Controversies on the 'Guiding Role' of Philosophy over Science," *Australian Journal of Chinese Affairs*, 14:21–35 (July 1985).

18. Ru Xin, "New Tasks Facing Marxist Philosophy," *People's Daily*, 20 July 1983, p. 5. CASS itself, and particularly its Institute of Philosophy (in which Wang himself holds the senior rank of Research Fellow), plays a part in this account. It was hived off in 1978 from the Academy of Sciences (where it had formed the Department of Philosophy and Social Science), to form a massive new organization of quasi-ministerial status. This change had symbolic as well as practical meaning. The Academy, under the presidency of Mao's long-time political secretary, Hu Qiaomu, reaffirmed the role of intellectuals in general, as essential to the modernizing state, and as custodians in their own right of intellectual and spiritual values. But, while CASS provided a model for intellectual activity within a privileged, delimited arena, its tendency has been strongly toward technology-driven models of social change. See D. A. Kelly, "At Last, An Arena: Current policies in Chinese Social Science," *Australian Journal of Chinese Affairs* 2:135–126 (July 1979); Merle Goldman, *China's Intellectuals: Advise and Dissent* (Cambridge, Harvard University Press), pp. 241–243.

19. Ru Xin,, "Is Humanism Just Revisionism—Rethinking Humanism," *People's Daily*, 15 August 1980; *RRWT*, p. 20.

20. Ru Xin, "Criticize the Philosophical Basis of Zhou Gucheng's Views on Art," *Red Flag* 1964.15:32–42, p. 40; quoted by D. W. Fokkema, "Chinese Criticism of Humanism: Campaigns Against the Intellectuals 1964–65," *China Quarterly* 26:74–76 (April–June 1966).

21. Goldman, *China's Intellectuals*, p. 77. Zhou in his "Firstly to Maintain, Secondly to Develop" of 1982 (see below, note 42), drew attention to a passage in the 1963 address, "So it should be acknowledged, alienation is a universal phenomenon of the natural world and human society, and it takes many forms," as a correct principle which he would still uphold. Hence his present views were to be taken as continuous with those of 1963.

22. Gajo Petrovic, s.v., "Alienation," in Tom Bottomore et al., eds., *A Dictionary*

of Marxist Thought (Cambridge, Harvard University Press, 1983), pp. 9–10; David Schweitzer, "Alienation Theory and Research: Trends, Issues and Priorities," *International Social Science Journal* 33.3: 523–556 (1981), esp. pp. 524ff. On the interpretation of the concept in China, see Donald J. Munro, "The Chinese View of 'Alientation,'" *China Quarterly* 59: 580–583, and Cheng Hsueh-chia, "The 'Thoughts of Marx Disturb Maoists," *Inside China Mainland,* 1–3 (June 1983).

23. "Guanyu 'yihua' de gainian—cong Heige'er dao Makesi" (On the concept of 'alienation'–from Hegel to Marx), *Waiguo zhexue yanjiu jikan* (Collected studies in foreign philosophy; Shanghai, 1978), p. 1; "WR" pp. 39–70. The group's task was to produce an anti-Soviet "Critique of Humanism"; Ru Xin and Xing Fensi were also members. Zhou's position was destablized shortly afterward, and publication of the pamphlet was blocked. Wang completed chapters on human nature and alienation which finally appeared in 1978–1980 as "Guanyu renxing wenti" (On human nature), ZZZS pp. 444–467, and "Guanyu 'yihua' de gainian" (Wang Ruoshui, personal correspondence, December 1986).

24. Wang Ruoshui, "Concept," p. 29; "WR," p. 65.

25. Ibid., p. 30; "WR," p. 66.

26. Wang Ruoshui, "Concept," p. 33; "WR," p. 69. My translation follows Karl Marx and Frederick Engels, *Collected Works* (London, 1976) V, 78.

27. Wang Ruoshui, "Makesizhuyi he sixiang jiefang," *Xin shiqi* 1980.4:2–3; "WR," pp. 89–93. "Tantan yihua wenti," *Xinwen zhanxian* 9 (1980), reprinted in *RRWT,* pp. 383–393; "WR," pp. 25–38. In this group also belongs "Zhenli biaozhun yu lilun yanjiu" (The criterion of truth and theoretical research), *Xinhua yuebao* 1980.3:11–15; "WR," pp. 12–24.

28. See below, note 40.

29. Wang Ruoshui, "Makesizhuyi," p. 3; "WR," p. 92.

30. My expression. The terminology of necessary and sufficient conditions is well known in Soviet and Eastern European literature on "socialist alienation." Joachim Israel, *Alienation: from Marx to Modern Sociology,* p. 239, poses the problem as one of the conditions for the *existence* rather than the *elimination* of alienation. His entire Chapter 8, "Alienation in Socialist Societies," where this discussion occurs, has been made available in China in excerpted form. See Yin Jizuo, "Research on the Theory of Alienation by Foreign Scholars," *Xueshu yanjiu* 1981.1:37–41, and especially p. 39.

31. *RRWT,* p. 387.

32. Kostas Axelos suggests this is endemic in certain Marxist tradition: *Alienation, Praxis and Techne in the Thought of Karl Marx,* tr. R. Bruzina from French ed. of 1969 (Austin, University of Texas Press, 1976), p. 305.

33. Wang Ruoshui, "Wenyi yu ren de yihua wenti," *Wenhui bao,* 25 September 1980, p. 3; originally in *Shanghai wenxue,* No. 3 (1980). Discussed in Kelly, "Truthfulness and the Chinese Writer: The Emotions of Skilled Workers," *Westerly* 3:111 (September 1981), and Huai Bing, "Chinese Communist Literature and Alienation," *Zheng ming* 75:62–63 (January 1984).

34. E.g. Xing Fensi, who, during the Spiritual Pollution Campaign, made indirect

reference to the opinions of Wang Ruoshui, associating him with the view that the expression of alienation should be the main theme of the arts; "The alienation issue and spiritual pollution," *People's Daily*, 5 November 1980.

35. Wang Ruoshui, "Wenyi–zhengzhi–renmin," *People's Daily*, 28 April 1982, p. 5.

36. "Ren shi Makesizhuyide chufadian," *RRWT*, p. 48. First appeared as title essay of *RSMC*; tr. in BBC *Summary of World Broadcasts*, 21 March 1984. "Wei ren daozhuyi bianhu," *Wenhui bao*, 17 January 1983, p. 3; "WR."

37. Hu Qiaomu, "On Humanism," p. 13.

38. Mu Fu, "Yihualun," p. 59, speaks of the "self-alienation of the literary Czar." Tao Jun, "Movement Attacks Alien Thought," *Zheng ming* 74:54–55 (December 1983); Xu Xing, "Alienation of the CPC," ibid., pp. 49–50.

39. Tang Tsou, "The Middle Course," p. 20. Zhou admitted "our responsibility in not conducting timely and accurate criticism."

40. "Uphold Seeking the Truth from Facts and Setting Out in All Matters from Actuality," *People's Daily*, 31 July 1978, p. 2.

41. "Our Lessons and Tasks Ahead," *Beijing Review*, No. 50 (15 December 1979); discussed in Kelly, "Truthfulness," pp. 107–108.

42. "Firstly to Maintain, Secondly to Develop," *People's Daily*, 23 June 1982, p. 5. Lin Mohan, "On Humanism and Other Things," *Guangming Daily*, 25 December 1983. See comment in Luo Bing, "Reverberations," p. 8.

43. Leszek Kolakowski, *Main Currents of Marxism* (Oxford, Oxford University Press, 1978) I, 57. Also Istvan Meszaros, *Marx's Theory of Alienation*, (New York, Saifer, 1972): "*Aufhebung* necessarily implies not only the supersession of any given form of alienation but also the preservation of some of its aspects."

44. Ru Xin, "Criticize Bourgeois Humanism," Part 2: "In the past, I said that Marxism could not be subsumed under humanism. Obviously this is incorrect, for it confuses the principal demarcation between the two."

45. Zhou Yang, "Inquiry into some Theoretical Problems of Marxism."

46. Tang Tsou, "Reflections on the Formation and Foundation of the Communist Party-State in China," unpublished paper, University of Chicago, 4 May 1983, p. 109.

47. Wang Ruoshui, "Concept." Ru Xin, "Social and Political Thought of the Young Hegel," *Waiguo zhexueshi jikan* 1:178–253 (Shanghai, 1978); "The young Hegel's ideas on alienated labor: inquiry into the problem of alienation, I," *Zhexue yanjiu* 1978.8:44–52, also in *RRWT*, pp. 349–367. "Diderot: Outstanding Representative of Aesthetic Thought in the French Enlightenment," *Waiguo zhexueshi yanjiu jikan* 3:175–210 (Shanghai, 1980). See entry on Ru Xin in *Zhongguo zhexue nianjian–1983*, pp. 355–356.

48. Ding Wang, "Alienation of Man," p. 59.

49. The excerpts are in *Zhongguo zhexue nianjian–1983*, pp. 95–98. My references will be to the original sources. Yuan Yayu, "The Theoretical and Practical Significance of the Concept of Alienation," *Shehui kexue yanjiu* 1982.4: 73–75; quotation from p. 73.

50. Xu Ming, "Man's Material Productive Activity is the Starting Point of

Marxism," *Xueshu yuekan* 1982.4:15–20; Xu (p. 20) admits that "man" is the goal of communism. Meng Jinshan, "Man Advances through the Unceasing Conquest of Alienation," *Shehui kexue jikan* 1982.2:25–30. Meng concludes (p. 30) that "alienation is everlasting."

51. Tong Xing, "Concretely Analyze the Theories of Alienation of Marx's Earlier and Later Periods," *Jiang-Han luntan* 1982.7:8–13. Tong concludes (p. 13) that it is baseless to hold that alienation is inherently humanistic or idealistic.

52. Chen Xianda, "Two Transitions in the Formation of Marx's Theory of Alienation," *Zhongguo shehui kexue,* No. 2 (1982), tr. in *Social Sciences in China* 1982.2:97–113.

53. Chen Xianda, "Two Transitions," English ed., p. 111.

54. Wu Yue, "The Sublation of Alienation and the Abolition of Class," *Guonei zhexue dongtai* 1980.12:22–24.

55. Liu Pen, "The Cult of Power and Its Origins," *Xueshu yuekan* No. 6 (1981); *RRWT,* pp. 412–421.

56. Jiang Guozhu, "Preliminary Investigation of Alienated Thought in Ancient China," *Shehui kexue jikan* 1981.4:17–23, p. 23. On alienation of civilization, see Weng Qiyin, "On Alienation From and Return To Civilization," *Shehui kexue (Gansu)*1980.1:29–33.

57. *People's Daily,* 13 October 1983, p. 1, and 16 November 1983, p. 1.

58. Luo Bin, "Zhongnan Hai li yichang edou" (A vicious fight in the Zhongnan Hai), *Zheng ming* 77:8–10 (February 1984).

59. *People's Daily,* 9, 10, 11 January 1984, p. 5, tr. in *FBIS,* 1 February 1984 (K1–6), 2 February (K2–7), 3 February (K1–6).

60. Karl Marx, "Theses on Feuerbach," in Karl Marx and Frederick Engels, *Selected Works* 2 vols (Moscow, 1949) II, 366.

61. Ru Xin, "Criticize Bourgeois Humanism," Part 2.

62. *People's Daily,* 27 January 1984, pp. 1–5, reprinted in *Red Flag* 2:2–28 (26 January 1984), and in book form. The translation in *China Report/Red Flag* (19 March 1984), pp. 1–42, is more reliable than that in *FBIS* (7 February 1984), K1–33. Subsequent references will be to the *Red Flag* version.

63. Hu Qiaomu, "On Humanism," pp. 11, 12.

64. Zhou Yang, "Inquiry into Some Theoretical Problems of Marxism," p. 5.

65. I deviate here from the version in *FBIS,* 7 February 1984, K24.

66. Zhou Yang, "Fighting Tasks of Workers in Philosophy and the Social Sciences," speech to the Department of Philosophy and Social Sciences, Chinese Academy of Sciences, 26 October 1963, *Red Flag* 24:1–30 (December 1963). Here are the relevant passages in translation:

Zhou (1963): "At a certain stage of development the subject divides off its own opposite, which changes into an external, alien force." (p. 17)

Wang (1978) (see note 22 above): "'Alienation' . . . , put simply, is when in its process of development the subject by its own activity creates something that is its opposite, and which then becomes an external, alien force, turning around and opposing or controlling the subject itself"; cf. "WR," p. 39.

Zhou (1983): "'Alienation' is when in its process of development . . ." (remainder as for the previous).

67. Hu, "On Humanism," p. 23.

68. Ibid., p. 26.

69. Li Yizhe (*Li* Zhentian, Chen *Yi*yang and Wang Xi*zhe*), "On Socialist Democracy and Legal System," *Chinese Law and Government* 10:3:15–61 (Fall 1977). A marked similarity is perception of the "strongly religious coloring and aura of the Cultural Revolution" (p. 22). Mu Fu, "Theory of Alienation," p. 59, notes the dangerous closeness of Wang Ruoshui's position to the "criminal political criticisms" of Wang Xizhe.

70. It is instructive to compare the alienation school with the anti-fascist resistance in mid-century Europe as described by James Wilkinson, *The Intellectual Resistance in Europe* (Cambridge, Harvard University Press, 1981). In France, "The intellectual *résistants* believed they had found the solution to the problem of (the meaning of) 'man' at first hand; it had ceased to be abstract for them, and took on the shape of the friendship, sacrifices, daring and fulfilment of the underground" (p. 265). In Germany, resistance had been more a matter of "inner migration," a struggle to keep oneself in a secret haven of fascist-proof culture. At the end of the war, these intellectuals were confronted with a society stained with complicity in the fascist state. German intellectuals attempted to confront and thereby expiate the group guilt. A similar impulse runs through the writings of Wang Ruoshui and his school.

71. "Wang Ruoshui Today," *Ta kung pao*, Thursday, 8 May 1986, p. 14.

7. The Chinese Writer in His Own Mirror, by Rudolf G. Wagner

Research for this study was conducted at various times with the generous support of the Society for the Humanities, Cornell University in 1981–1982, the John K. Fairbank Center for East Asian Research, Harvard University, in early 1984, and the Center for Chinese Studies, University of California, Berkeley, in late 1984. My sincere thanks go to all three institutions and to my colleagues there for their support, encouragement, and criticisms.

1. Liu, E, *Laocan youji* (Taibei, Lianjing chuban, 1976). A translation by Harold Shadick, *The Travels of Lao Ts'an* (Ithaca, Cornell University Press, 1952).

2. Zeng Pu, *Niehai hua* (Shanghai, Shanghai guji chuban she, 1979); Wu Jianren (= Wu Woyao), *Ershi nian mudu zhi guaixianzhuang* (Shanghai, Shanghai guangzhi shuju, 1907–1908).

3. Guo Moruo, *Qu Yuan* (Beijing, Renmin chuban she, 1954). A translation by Yang Hsien-yi and Gladys Yang is *Chu Yuan* (Peking, Foreign Languages Press, 1953).

4. Laurence A. Schneider, *A Madman of Ch'u, The Chinese Myth of Loyalty and Dissent* (Berkeley, University of California Press, 1980).

5. Cf. David Hawkes, *Ch'u Tz'u, the Songs of the South* (Oxford, Clarendon Press, 1959), Introduction.

6. Cf. Schneider, pp. 112 ff.

7. Ezra Vogel, "The Unlikely Heroes: The Social Role of the May Fourth Writers," in Merle Goldman, ed., *Modern Chinese Literature in the May Fourth Era* (Cambridge, Harvard University Press, 1977), pp. 145 ff.

8. Li Oufan (Leo Ou-fan Lee), "Wusi wenren de langman jingshen" (The romantic stand of the May Fourth Writers), in Zhou Cezong, ed., *Wusi yu zhongguo* (Taibei, Shibao wenhua, 1979), pp. 295 ff.

9. Yi-tsi M. Feuerwerker, "The Changing Relationship between Literature and Life: Aspects of the Writer's Role in Ding Ling," in Goldman, ed., *Modern Chinese Literature,* pp. 283, 303.

10. Huang Zhongmo, *Guo Moruo lishiju "Qu Yuan" shihu* (Chengdu, Sichuan renmin, 1981), pp. 1 ff.

11. Guo Moruo, "Wo zenyang xie wunu shiju 'Qu Yuan'," in Guo Moruo, *Qu Yuan,* p. 118.

12. Guo Moruo, *Qu Yuan,* p. 3.

13. Ibid., p. 103; cf. p. 116 in the translation.

14. Ibid., pp. 96 ff. The Dongting Lake, Yangtze, and Eastern Sea refer to Qu's own poetry; the Queen had earlier provided the clue to this line by saying: "Your poems are not as simple as those of the average poets, you have depth and width, you are the Dongting Lake, you are the Yangtze, you are the Eastern Sea" (p. 30).

15. "Fangwen Gong Xiaogang tongzhi di tanhua jilu" (A protocol of an interview with Comrade Gong Xiaogang), in Huang Zhongmo, p. 133.

16. Zhou Libo, *Baofeng zouyu* (Tianjin, 1949); cf. for more detailed analysis my "Der Moderne Chinesische Untersuchungsroman," in Jost Hermand, ed., *Neues Handbuch der Literaturwissenschaft, Literatur nach 1945 I* (Wiesbaden, Athenaeum Verlag, 1981), pp. 375 ff.

17. Egon Erwin Kisch, *Secret China* (London 1935). A Chinese translation by Zhou Libo: *Mimi de zhongguo* (Shanghai 1936).

18. Ai Qing, *Heiman* (Beijing, Zuojia chuban she, 1955). A translation is *Black Eel* (Beijing, Foreign Languages Press, 1982).

19. Zhou Yang, "Jianshe shehuizhuyi wenxue de renwu" (The task of building a socialist literature), in *Wenyi bao,* 1956 5/6, p. 15.

20. Ai Qing returned to the theme in an allegorical piece, "The Gardener's Dream," in Eugene Chen Eoyang, ed., *Selected Poems by Ai Qing* (Bloomington, Indiana University Press, 1982), p. 456; a translation is on pp. 268 ff.

21. Wang Meng, "Zuzhibu xinlai de qingnianren" (The newcomer in the Organization Department), in *Renmin wenxue* 1956.9; Wang Meng's original text can be gathered from his article in *People's Daily,* 9 May 1957. For a more detailed analysis of Wang Meng's and Liu Binyan's works at the time, see my "The Cog and the Scout: Functional Concepts of Literature in Socialist Political Culture: the Chinese Debate in the Mid-Fifties," in Wolfgang Kubin, R. Wagner, eds., *Essays in Modern Chinese Literature and Literary Criticism* (Bochum, Brockmeyer, 1982).

22. Galina Nikolayeva, (Chinese ed.) "Tuolajizhan zhanzhang he zongnong yishi," in *Zhongguo qingnian* 1955:23–24.

23. Wang Ruowang, *Xiang Nastya xuexi* (Beijing 1956).

24. Liu Binyan, "Zai qiaoliang gongdi shang" in *Renmin wenxue* 1956.4.

25. Fang Ji, "Laifangzhe," in *Shouhuo* 1958.3. The story was attacked by Yao Wenyuan and Kong Luosun for distorting socialist reality.

26. In October 1957, Fang Ji spelled out the basic charges contained in "The Visitor" in a personal attack on Liu Binyan. Fang Ji, "Liu Binyan chuangzuo-zhong sanbu shenme dusuo" (What kind of poison is spread in Liu Binyans' works), in *Zhongguo qingnianbao*, 29 July, 1957, p. 3.

27. Zhongguo juxie geming caofan tuan, "Chedi chanchu Tian Han de daducao *Guan Hanqing*" (Radically tear out Tian Han's great poisonous weed, *Guan Hanqing*), in *Xiju zhanbao* 7 June 1967.

28. For a more detailed analysis of this play, see my "A Guide for the Perplexed and a Call to the Wavering: Tian Han's *Guan Hanqing*," in Rudolf G. Wagner, *The Contemporary Chinese Historical Drama: Four Studies* (University of California Press, forthcoming.)

29. Guo Moruo, *Cai wenji* (Beijing 1959).

30. Liu Xinwu, "Banzhuren," in *Renmin wenxue* 1977.11: "Suanlaiba, didi," in *Zhongguo qingnian* 1978.2; "Zheli you huangjin," in *Shanghai wenxue* 1979.11.

31. Wang Meng, "Youyou cuncaoxin," in *Shanghai wenxue*, September 1979. For a more extensive analysis, see my "A Lonely Barber in China's Literary Shop: Wang Meng's 'Youyou cuncaoxin'" (forthcoming).

32. Liu Binyan, "Diwuge chen dayi de ren," in *Beijing wenyi* 1979.11. A translation by John S. Rohsenow with Perry Link, "The Fifth Man in the Overcoat," in Liu Binyan, *People or Monsters*, ed. Perry Link (Bloomington, Indiana University Press, 1983). Liu Binyan, "Renyao zhi jian," in *Renmin wenxue* 1979.9. An English translation by James V. Feinerman with Perry Link in Liu Binyan, *People or Monsters*. For a more extensive analysis of both texts, see my "Liu Binyan oder der Autor als wandelnde Nische," in W. Kubin, ed., *Moderne Chinesische Literatur* (Frankfurt, Suhrkamp, 1985).

33. Zheng Yi, "Feng," in *Wenhui bao*, 11 February 1979. English translation in P. Link, ed., *Stubborn Weeds* (Bloomington, Indiana University Press, 1983).

34. Bai Hua, Peng Ning, "Kulian," in *Shiyue* 1979.3. An English translation in T. C. Chang, S. Y. Chen, Y. T. Lin, eds. *Pai Hua's Cinematic Script "Unrequited Love" with related introductory materials* (Institute of Current China Studies, Taipei) 1981.

35. Cf. Xi Long, "Liangtiao zhanxian douzheng yu 'ge da wushi daban'" (The struggle between two political lines and giving 50 strokes to each one), in *Zuopin yu zhengming* 1983.11, p. 29; Hu Yaobang's speech at a conference on problems at the ideological front in early August 1981 was not published. A short summary is in *Xinhua yuebao* 1981.8:6.

36. Ke Yunlu, Xue Ke, "Lishi jiang zhengming," in *Zuopin yu zhengming* 1983. 11, 12. I am grateful to Helmut Martin, Ruhr-University, Bochum, for drawing my attention to this piece. See his paper "The Drama 'Tragic Song of Our Time' and the Limits of Literary Discourse in China," presented at the International Workshop on Contemporary Chinese Drama and Theatre, SUNY Buffalo, October 1984.

37. Cf. Xi Long, p. 29.
38. Ke/Xue, p. 13.
39. Ibid., p. 7.
40. Ibid., p. 14.
41. Ibid., p. 7.
42. Ibid., p. 10.
43. Ibid., p. 16.
44. Ibid., p. 20.
45. For a literature lobbying in this fashion, see my "Lobby Literature: The Archaeology and Present Functions of Science Fiction in China," in Jeffrey C. Kinkley, ed., *After Mao: Chinese Literature and Society 1978–1981* (Cambridge, Council on East Asian Studies, Harvard University, 1985).
46. Lev Kassil, "The Tale of the Three Master Craftsmen," in Patricia Blake, Max Hayward, eds., *Dissonant Voices in Soviet Literature* (New York, Pantheon, 1961).
47. Dina Spechler, *Permitted Dissent in the USSR, Nowy Mir and the Soviet Regime* (New York, Praeger, 1982).
48. Abram Tertz, *The Trial Begins* & *On Socialist Realism* (New York, Vintage Books, 1960).
49. Heinar Kipphardt, *Stücke I* (Frankfurt, Suhrkamp, 1973).
50. Stefan Heym, *The King David Report* (London, Hodder and Stoughton, 1973).
51. Christa Wolf, *Kassandra* (Darmstadt, Luchterhand, 1982) and Christa Wolf, *Voraussetzungen einer Erzählung: Kassandra* (Darmstadt, Luchterhand, 1982). English translation of both texts: Ch. Wolf, *Cassandra: a Novel and Four Essays* (New York, Farrar, Strauss, Giroux, 1984).
52. T. Konwicki, *A Minor Apokalypse* (New York, Farrar, Straus, Giroux, 1983).
53. M. Kundera, *The Joke* (New York, Harper and Row, 1982).
54. George Konrád, *The Loser* (San Diego, Farrar, Straus, Giroux, 1982); see also his brilliant sociological study with Ivan Szelenyi, *The Intellectuals on the Way to Class Power* (New York, Harcourt, Brace, Jovanovich, 1979).
55. Stefan Heym, *Collin* (Munich, Bertelsmann Verlag, 1979).

8. *Keeper of the Flame, by Kyna Rubin*

Wang Ruowang has not reviewed this article and bears no responsibility for its content.

1. Unpublished translation by Timothy Cheek, July 1982. "Statesmen and Artists" (Zhengzhijia, yishujia) has been partially translated by Gregor Benton as "Politicians, Artists" in G. Benton, ed., *Wild Lilies: Poisonous Weeds: Dissident Voices from People's China* (London, Pluto Press, 1982), pp. 175–178. I prefer the translation by Cheek. For the original Chinese text, see the reprint in *Wenxue yundong shiliao xuan* (Selected historical materials of literary movements; Shanghai jiaoyu chuban she, 1979), IV 594–597. The article first appeared 15 March 1942 in *Guyu* 1.4.

2. "Wenyi yu zhengzhi bushi congshu guanxi" (Literature and art are not subordinate to politics), *Wenyi yanjiu* 1980.1:65.
3. "Tan wenyi de 'wuwei er zhi'" (On the "governing through inaction" of literature and art), *Red Flag* 1979.9:48.
4. "Wild Lily" (Ye baihehua), translated by G. Benton in Benton, p. 180. Benton's translation first appeared appended to his article, "The Yan'an 'Literary Opposition,'" *New Left Review* 92:96–102 (July–August 1975). A reprint of the original Chinese is in *Wenxue yundong shiliao xuan* IV, 586–593. The article was first printed in two parts in *Jiefang ribao*, 13 and 23 March 1942, p. 4.
5. "'Ducao' bian," *Mangzhong* 1979.1:30.
6. For an excellent and detailed discussion of the Wang Shiwei case, see Timothy Cheek, "The Fading of Wild Lilies: Wang Shiwei and Mao Zedong's 'Yan'an Talks' in the First CPC Rectification Movement," *Australian Journal of Chinese Affairs* No. 11 (January 1984). See also Guilhem Fabre, "L'affaire Wang Shiwei: genese de l'opposition en Chine populaire, Yan'an 1942" (Thèse de 3eme cycle, Paris VII, 1980). Mr. Fabre is revising his thesis for book publication.
7. K. Rubin, "Literary Problems During the War of Resistance against Japan as Viewed from Yan'an: A Study of the Literature Page of *Jiefang ribao* from May 16, 1941 to August 31, 1942" (unpublished MA thesis, University of British Columbia, August 1979). For a study of one debate between writers and Zhou Yang months before the *zawen* of spring 1942, see Rubin, "Writers' Discontent and Party Response before 'Wild Lily': the Manchurian Writers and Zhou Yang," *Modern Chinese Literature* 1984.1:1.

See also Merle Goldman, *Literary Dissent in Communist China* (New York, Atheneum, 1971), pp. 18–50; Tsi-an Hsia, *The Gate of Darkness: Studies on the Leftist Literary Movement in China* (Seattle, University of Washington Press, 1968), particularly pp. 239–256.

For an analysis of the "Yan'an Talks," see Bonnie McDougall, *Mao Zedong's 'Talks at the Yan'an Conference on Literature and Art': A Translation of the 1943 Text with Comments* (Ann Arbor, Michigan Papers in Chinese Studies, No. 33, 1980); and David Holm, "The Literary Rectification in Yan'an" in *Essays in Modern Chinese Literature and Literary Criticism, Papers of the Berlin Conference 1978*, ed. Wolfgang Kubin and Rudolph G. Wagner (Bochum, Studienverlag Brockmayer, 1982), pp. 272–308.
8. To my knowledge, very little open information on the suppression of particular writers during this most recent of government efforts to control artistic freedom is available. Friends within China serve as my sources here. The official press has printed a vast number of general articles urging writers to accentuate the positive in their writing and to keep away from "bourgeois" influences. See *Guangming Daily*, 12 and 19 November 1983, p. 3; and *Red Flag* 1983.22:17–19.
9. K. Rubin, "An Interview with Mr. Wang Ruowang," *China Quarterly* 87:504–505 (September 1981), and author's talks with Wang in May 1986. Wang is also Secretary of the Chinese and Shanghai Writers Associations,

and Dean of the Chinese Amateur Arts School, a private institution set up in 1984.

10. Ibid., p. 509; and Ding Ling, "Yan'an wenyi zuotanhui de qianqian houhou" (Before and after the Yan'an talks on literature and art), *Xinwenxue shiliao* 1982.2:43; also Tsia-an Hsia, p. 254, where Mr. Hsia has translated the reminiscences of a writer in Yan'an who recalls a "poem-in-prose" in *Qingqidui* that "ridiculed the old cadres" in a "malicious" way. Hsia has translated *Qingqidui* as The Light Brigade.

11. Ding Ling, p. 43. Ding Ling's "Wenyi" section in *Jiefang ribao* started on 16 September 1941.

12. Rubin, p. 509; Ding Ling, p. 43.

13. Rubin, p. 509.

14. Rubin, pp. 510–511.

15. Rubin, p. 508.

16. "Tan wenyi de 'wuwei er zhi,'" *Red Flag* 1979.9:49.

17. He Qifang, in particular, presents Xiao Jun as haughty and overbearing in "Mao Zedong sixiang de yangguang zhaoyaozhe women: huiyi Yan'an wenyi zuotanhui," *Wenyi lucong* 1979.1:15.

18. Conversations on this subject with Chinese intellectuals both in and outside China confirm this.

19. Interviews with Wang by the author, May 1986.

20. These remarks are based on notes from the author's meetings with Wang in the fall of 1983 and May 1986. As of May 1986, Wang had written 450,000 characters of his autobiography, up to the time of his release from the Guomindang prison in 1937. He plans to end his narrative in 1977, because he believes that discussing the 1980s requires distance and could be politically damaging at this time.

21. See, for example, "Wei 'chuantongju' bian" (In defense of traditional opera), *Shanghai wenxue* 1979.6; and "Daonian Wei Jinzhi tongzhi" (In remembrance of Comrade Wei Jinzhi), *Wenhui bao*, 14 March 1979, p. 4. A good example of his thoughts on love and marriage is "Zhenzheng de aiqing shi zhengqulaide" (True love is obtained through struggle) *Jiating* (Guangdong) 12:18–20.

22. "Wang Ruowang da wenxue qingnian wen" (Wang Ruowang responds to questions from literary youth), *Zuojia shenghuo bao*, 8 June 1985, p. 4.

23. Ibid.

24. Rubin, pp. 506–507.

25. "Bubu shefang" (Creating barriers step by step), *Wenhui bao*, 26 April 1957; "Yiban zhi ge" (A partition apart), *Xinwen ribao*, 7 May 1957, p. 4; "Bu duitou" (Something amiss) was a letter sent to a friend at *Jiefang ribao* that was never intended for publication. It was used at a meeting to criticize Wang. Rubin, p. 506.

26. "Yiban zhi ge," p. 4.

27. "Shi 'luohou fenzi,'" *Wenhui bao*, 27 May 1957.

28. Ibid.

29. Xu Hui (Zhang Chunqiao), "Wang Ruowang shi shei jia de xianghua?"

(Whose fragrant flower is Wang Ruowang?), *People's Daily,* 30 July 1957. In the preface to a handwritten collection of some of the attacks against Wang in 1957 and the *zawen* for which he was criticized, Wang groups Yao Wenyuan with Zhang Chunqiao as "self-appointed 'Anti-Rightist heroes'" who selected Wang as their first victim in 1957. The collection, compiled by Wang, was given to the author in 1980. As far as I know it has not been published in its present form, although the individual articles, of course, appeared in the official press in 1957.

It is ironic that, after the fall of Yao Wenyuan, two articles attacked him on the pretext of his having sympathized with the views expressed by Wang Ruowang in his 1957 "rightist" *zawen*. See "Ping fangeming liangmianpai Yao Wenyuan," *People's Daily,* 31 March 1977; and Tang Tiehai, "Yige youde zai buneng you de jiyoupai," *Wenhui bao,* 22 June 1977, p. 3.

30. *Shanghai wenxue* 1962.7.
31. Wang Ruowang, *Yanbuzhu de guangmang* (The inextinguishable light; Beijing, Renmin wenxue chuban she, 1983), pp. 6–8.
32. "Ke Qingshi and I once had an unpleasant dispute in Yan'an . . . which is rather complicated to explain," Wang remarked to this author in 1986. Rumors point to competition for a woman, but, in any event, this is an example of how vendettas in China can be played out years later.
33. *Yanbuzhu de guangmang,* p. 10.
34. Rubin, p. 507.
35. Ibid.
36. "Literature of the wounded" derived its name from a short story written in 1978 by then Fudan University student Lu Xinhua, "The Wounded" (Shanghen). The story was one of the first sentimental but powerful indictments of the Gang of Four (i.e., Cultural Revolution). See *Wenhui bao,* 11 August 1978; translated by Bennett Lee in *The Wounded: New Stories of the Cultural Revolution 77–88* (Hong Kong, Joint Publishing Co., 1978), pp. 9–24.
37. "Wang Ruowang tongzhi zuopin" (Writings of Comrade Wang Ruowang), unpublished bibliography of Wang Ruowang's writings. Between 1979 and spring 1986, he had published some 240 separate pieces, mainly *zawen,* 10 works of fiction (short stories, novellas, reportage), literary critiques, and some 20 articles on love and marriage.
38. Ibid.
39. "Xiyan bu keyi wei 'fa'" (The "law" is no joking matter), *Minzhu yu fazhi* 1980.1:25–27.
40. "'Wu bu pa' xiao yi" (A small discussion on the "five things not to fear"), *Minzhu yu fazhi* 1979.2:24–26; reprinted in *Xinhua yuebao* 1980.1:39–40.
41. Conversations with Wang in spring 1980 and autumn 1983.
42. *Hebei wenyi* 1979.6:5–6. This article is mentioned in passing by Perry Link in his Introduction to Link, ed., *Stubborn Weeds: Popular and Controversial Chinese Literature after the Cultural Revolution* (Bloomington, Indiana University Press, 1983), p. 11.
43. Ibid., p. 5.
44. *Guangming Daily,* 20 July 1979, p. 3. For mention of this article, see Kam

Louie, "Between Paradise and Hell: Literary Double-Think in Post-Mao China," *The Australian Journal of Chinese Affairs* 1983.10:4–5.
45. "Tan wenyi de 'wuwei er zhi,'" *Red Flag* 1979.9:47–49.
46. Ibid., p. 48.
47. Ibid., pp. 47, 49.
48. See "Yiju taici de boxi," *Yuhua* 1980.2:57, where Wang refers to the reaction to his essay "Tan wenyi de 'wuwei er zhi.'" See also Yu Yiding, "On Liberating Thought and Bourgeois Liberalism" *Red Flag* 1981.13: in *JPRS* 80998, 7 June 1982. In 1981 the controversial article was brought up in the context of the Bai Hua affair in which Wang was implicated. In late 1983, Wang's opponents dragged it out again as a target of criticism during the "Anti-Spiritual Pollution" Campaign. Wang asserts that Ba Jin has been a supporter of the idea of *wuwei er zhi* in the literary world. For a discussion and defense of this article by Wang, see *Zhengming* 1982.3:51–53.

It is interesting that Deng Tuo, in 1957, advocated *wuwei er zhi* in the same manner as Wang in 1979. See Timothy Cheek's translation in *Chinese Law and Government*, 1984, Spring/Summer, of "Feiqi 'yongren de zhengzhi,'" *People's Daily*, 11 May 1957, p. 8, translated as "Discard the 'Politics of Simpletons.'"
49. "Yiju taici de boxi" (Analysis of a stage line), pp. 57–58.
50. Ibid., p. 57.
51. Ibid., p. 58.
52. Ibid.
53. "Wenyi yu zhengzhi bu shi congshu guanxi," *Wenyi yanjiu* 1980.1:61–65.
54. Ibid., p. 61.
55. Ibid., p. 63.
56. Ibid., p. 62.
57. Ibid., p. 65.
58. See, for example, Wei 'chuantongju' bian"; and "Gei Yang Silang huifu mingyu" (Restore Yang Silang's good name), *Shanghai xiju* 1979.5:23–25.
59. "Jiaru wo shi zhende" (If I were real), reprinted in *Qishi niandai* 1980.1. It was written by Sha Yexin, Li Shoucheng, and Yao Mingde. See English translation by Edward M. Gunn, "If I Really Were" in Link, *Stubborn Weeds*, pp. 198–250.
60. Rubin, p. 515.
61. Wang's idea of intellectual freedom is on both a political and personal level. In the political realm, he sees freedom of expression as the freedom to reveal to politicians through public exposure and debate the folly of Party policies that harm fellow citizens of the state. His 1957 series of *zawen* admonishing the Party for alienating those outside it, particularly intellectuals, is but one illustration of his exercising this freedom. On a personal level, his notion of intellectual freedom is the right of citizens to pursue intellectual interests such as writing without the constraints of having to speak out for any one particular faction in power at the time; freedom is also the right of the intellectual to retreat from bureaucratic and ceremonial obligations in order to pursue his creative work. See "Tang Zeng banji he 'ma tai xiaoying'" (Tang

Zeng and the "Mathew effect"), *Wenhui bao,* 12 January 1983, p. 4, for this latter point.

62. "'Shangxingou' daixu" originally appeared in *Shanghai wenxue* 1980.6:36–43, 52. It has been reprinted in Wang Ruowang, *Yanbuzhu de guangmang,* pp. 223–245. English translation by Rubin in Mason Y. H. Wang, ed., *Perspectives in Contemporary Chinese literature,* pp. 137–168.

63. "Renyao zhijian" was first published in *Renmin wenxue* 1979.9. For English translation by James Feinerman, see "People or Monsters?" in P. Link, *People or Monsters? And Other Stories and Reportage from China after Mao,* pp. 11–68.

64. Wang Ruowang, *Shanghai wenxue* 1980.6:42.

65. Ibid., p. 52.

66. *Ji'e san buqu,* originally published in *Shouhuo* 1980.1:116–173; reprinted in *Yanbuzhu de guangmang,* pp. 78–222.

67. *Yanbuzhu de guangmang,* p. 154.

68. Ibid., p. 157.

69. Ibid., pp. 151–152.

70. Ibid., p. 159.

71. Ibid., p. 164.

72. Wang uses the word *counterfeit* (*jia*) to describe the Party throughout Part 3 of *Hunger Trilogy.*

73. Ibid., p. 168.

74. Ibid., p. 167.

75. Ibid., p. 159.

76. Ibid., p. 208.

77. *Kulian* first appeared in *Shiyue* 1979.3. For a discussion of the Bai Hua affair, see Leo Ou-fan Lee, "Literary Policy in the People's Republic of China: A Position Paper," in *Mainland China, Taiwan, and U.S. Policy,* (Cambridge, Oelgeschlager, Gunn, and Hain, 1983), pp. 103–114.

78. Yu Yiding, *Red Flag,* No. 13 (1981), which criticized Wang Ruowang though not by name; *Zhengming* 1982.6:23–24; Leo Ou-fan Lee, above; direct talks with Wang himself confirm this.

79. Information from Wang Ruowang. See "Gongchen hu? zuifan hu? ji hongdong Jiaxing diqu de yi zhuang gong'an" (Heroine or criminal? Record of a case that shook the Jiaxing region), *Minzhu yu fazhi* 1984.2:21–24, in which Wang defends a woman he feels was unjustly sentenced for corruption in running her own factory. Wang holds local factional politics and corruption responsible for her unjust three-year sentence. An editorial note following the author's exposé reveals that journal editors sent the piece to Zhejiang and Jiaxing political and legal units for comment and then sent reporters to investigate the case. It seems that the defendant, Tang Lijuan, appealed to the higher court several times. Her case was repeatedly bounced back and forth between the Jiaxing Municipal People's Court and the Jiaxing Regional Intermediate People's Court. At the time of publication (March 1984), despite the hard work of her lawyers, Tang was still being held in prison, made to wait past the legal limit of time for appeals decisions. The *Minzu yu fazhi* editors praise the persistence of her lawyers in seeking to secure her freedom.

This exposé writing by Wang can be compared in intent (if not effect) to Liu Binyan's "Between Man and Monster" ("Renyao zhijian"), note 63 above.

"To plead for the people" (*weimin qingming*) is a set term meaning to represent the cause of the people, a very conscious mission of Wang and Liu Binyan.

80. The 1983 collection, *Yanbuzhu de guangmang,* sold out immediately in bookstores in China.

81. According to Wang, he was accused of being a dissident because of his writing, and one high-level leader asked rhetorically at a meeting, "Does this person deserve to be a member of the CCP?" Wang's articles in question were reviewed by a Party investigation and eventually cleared, enabling him to publish again in spring 1986. He was not expelled from the Party as rumors assumed. (Notes from this author's May 1986 talks with Wang.)

82. "Xiaoxiao shinian," *Haixia* 1982.6:183–214, 225.

9. *Thought Workers in Deng's Time, by Lynn T. White III*

The author wishes to thank the Joint Committee on Contemporary China and Princeton University for generous financial assistance—and for general intellectual assistance he thanks Professor Merle Goldman, Dr. Wu Anchia of the Center of International Relations, and Mr. Huan Guocang of Princeton.

1. The phrase *loyal opposition* comes from the anthropologist Fei Xiaotong. See Suzanne Pepper, *Civil War in China: The Political Struggle, 1945–49* (Berkeley, University of California Press, 1978), esp. Chapter 6, "The Intelligentsia's Critique of the Chinese Communists."

2. See "Changing Concepts of Corruption in Communist China" (unpublished paper by Lynn White) for many examples of this effort.

3. There is neither space nor need here to reproduce the information in Merle Goldman's indispensable books: *Literary Dissent in Communist China* (Cambridge, Harvard University Press, 1967) and *China's Intellectuals: Advise and Dissent* (Cambridge, Harvard University Press, 1981).

4. More attention is paid here to teachers and scientists than to writers and artists, partly because the former groups are large and partly because they are less well treated in most of the literature cited above. On high intellectuals, see also Hsuan Mo, "Peiping's Current Policy toward Literature and Art," paper at the 11th Sino-American Conference on Mainland China.

5. Deng's speech is in *Red Flag,* Peking, 1978.4:9–18.

6. *People's Daily,* 2 January 1969.

7. *People's Daily,* 13 January 1979.

8. *People's Daily,* 5 April 1982.

9. It would be safe to assume that not all intellectuals in the sample received better housing, i.e. that the total was greater than 2,300—probably much greater. Even if the sample were only that size, the article would imply that only about 10 percent of these Peking intellectuals were Party members. This compares interestingly with a statement in *Red Flag* 1979.2:32, that 36% of all intellectuals in the country are Party members. The conclusion: A

large majority of intellectuals in the Party are probably teachers outside big cities. The portion of all "high intellectuals" in the Party may be well below 10%.

10. *People's Daily,* 14 July 1979.

11. This information comes from an interview, in the United States during March 1984. Local CCP officials did *not* have to sign the absolving resolution—an act that would have been embarrassing for those who had classed intellectuals as rightists. They could merely seal a resolution with the local unit's chop.

12. The prominent dissident of 1957, Lin Xiling, moved to Paris in 1983 and was quoted as saying, "Les cadres réhabilités se sont servis pour vivre dans le luxe, et surtout pour y faire vivre leurs enfants." See "Les vents mauvais qui soufflent sur la Chine," *L'Esprit,* December 1983, p. 73. The present author also spoke with Lin Xiling in Princeton, New Jersey, 28 February 1984.

13. *Guangming Daily,* Peking, 21 January 1980, especially the twelfth and last recommendation in this Xinhua article.

14. *People's Daily,* 19 February 1981.

15. *People's Daily,* 14 October 1982.

16. *People's Daily,* 25 July 1980.

17. Dissident Lin Xiling guesses that Hu Yaobang may be more pro-intellectual than other leaders such as Ye Jianying. See note 12 above.

18. The title of an article in *Red Flag* 1980.22:15–18.

19. The outline of an article in *Guangming Daily,* 3 October 1980.

20. *People's Daily,* 22 September 1981.

21. Mary Louise O'Callaghan, "China's Educated Class Struggles for End to Harassment," *Christian Science Monitor,* 21 July 1983, p. 13.

22. *Guangming Daily,* 22 July 1982.

23. *Red Flag* 1982.12.

24. *Guangming Daily,* 24 July 1982.

25. *People's Daily,* 26 July 1982.

26. See Robert Taylor, *China's Intellectual Dilemma: Politics and University Enrollment, 1949–1978* (Vancouver, University of British Columbia Press, 1981), and Suzanne Pepper, *China's Universities* (Ann Arbor, University of Michigan Center for Chinese Studies, 1984).

27. This information comes from an interview at Princeton in 1984, with a source who knew much about such matters.

28. *People's Daily,* 14 February 1980. A commentary by the Education Minister on the new regulations is also included.

29. *People's Daily,* 13 June 1981.

30. *People's Daily,* 28 May 1982. The names, specialties, universities, and professorial advisors of the 18 new PhDs were provided on the next day.

31. *People's Daily,* 30 December 1979.

32. *People's Daily,* 28 December 1979.

33. *People's Daily,* 4 August 1980.

34. *People's Daily,* 13 January 1982.

35. Reported in the *New York Times,* 4 March 1984.

36. Quoted in *Christian Science Monitor,* 21 July 1983, p. 13.
37. *Red Flag* 1979.2:32.
38. See note 9 above.
39. *Guangming Daily,* 19 September 1977. See also *Red Flag* 1977.4 for another report.
40. See Vice-Premier Bo Yibo's interview with the *Beijing keji bao* (Peking science and technology news), reproduced in *People's Daily,* 19 February 1981. Also *Red Flag* 1979.2:34–35.
41. A recent film, *Neighbors* by Zheng Dongtian and Xu Juming, is a scathing attack on China's housing shortage.
42. *People's Daily,* 14 July 1982.
43. Richard Curt Kraus, *Class Conflict in Chinese Socialism* (New York, Columbia University Press, 1981), p. 167. See also Richard P. Suttmeier, *Science, Technology, and China's Drive for Modernization* (Stanford, Hoover Institution Press, 1981), p. 39.
44. *Liaowang* (Lookout), Shanghai, 7 (July) 1982.
45. *Wenhui bao* (Literary news), Shanghai, 15 January 1983.
46. *People's Daily,* 4 March 1984.
47. *People's Daily,* 19 January and 16 August 1982.
48. *Red Flag* 1980.21. The high number of cross appointments among institute heads and deputy heads shows the scarcity of intellectuals whom the Party thought it could trust.
49. For a few examples, see *Jiefang ribao* (Liberation daily), Shanghai, 6 August 1956. Or on housing, *Qingnian bao* (Youth news), 21 December 1956. Or from the "sit-and-talk" sessions of 1957, *Xinwen ribao* (News daily), Shanghai, 4 May, 15 May, and 21 July especially.
50. Martin Whyte and William Parish suggest this in *Urban Life in Contemporary China* (Chicago, University of Chicago Press, 1984), p. 166.
51. On Shanghai-to-Northwest rustication in general, see Lynn White, "The Road to Urumchi," *China Quarterly,* September 1979, pp. 481–510. Although not all the Jiaotong staff were finally shifted to Xian, a sufficient number went to form a second Jiaotong in that city.
52. *People's Daily,* 22 May 1982, based on Xinhua report of 21 May.
53. *Xinhua* (New China News Agency), 30 April 1983.
54. On a move of scientists to Anhwei to make recommendations for the development of industry and agriculture, see *People's Daily,* 27 November 1980.
55. On an early move from Fudan University to northern Anhwei, for example, see *Jiefang ribao* (Liberation daily), Shanghai, 24 September 1951.
56. Ibid., but a different article.
57. *People's Daily,* 29 February 1984.
58. See Martin Whyte and William Parish, *Urban Life,* for much material on the significance of the refusers' future income and livelihood. The information here also comes from an interview in Princeton.
59. *People's Daily,* 3 March 1984, p. 3, for this fascinating "letter from a correspondent" (*jizhe laixin*).
60. *People's Daily,* 9 January 1981.

61. Ibid.
62. See *Guangming Daily,* 27 April 1983.
63. *People's Daily,* 24 March 1982.
64. *Guangming Daily,* 23 May 1982.
65. A larger problem, of course, was that the bureaucrats in a shifted expert's new unit might have developed an aversion to experts in general.
66. *Beijing ribao* (Peking daily), 4 August 1979. This refers to the previous PRC Constitution. The new Constitution, promulgated on 4 December 1982, provides in Article 1 that "sabotage of the socialist system by any organization or individual is prohibited." *Fifth Session of the Fifth National People's Congress* (Beijing, Foreign Languages Press, 1983), p. 9. The reference to freedom of speech is in Article 35, p. 22. Article 47 (p. 27) cites "freedom to engage in scientific research, literary and artistic creation, and other cultural pursuits"–subject, presumably, to the stricture about socialism in Article 1.
67. This is a classical expression; *xin sheng* is a bit like the French *cri de coeur.*
68. *Red Flag* 1975.5; the commentary is on pp. 11–15, but the main point is in the first paragraph.
69. Here and for occasional reference elsewhere: Wolfgang Bartke, *Who's Who in the People's Republic of China* (Armonk, Sharpe, 1981).
70. Lin Mohan, "Suowei jinqu wenti" (So-called forbidden questions), *Zuopin* (Works), Canton 1979.4:71.
71. See the article by Ying Guoqing and Xiao Wanquan, "Zuozhe de 'jiashuo' quan," (An author's rights of hypothesis), *Shanghai kexue* (Shanghai science), No. 6 (June 1980).
72. *Red Flag* 1980.3, e.g., p. 37. Some prescriptions for reform in China, at this time, were written entirely as *descriptions* of common practices abroad. For example, see an article about the legal meaning of "intellectual patents" in *Shehui kexue* (Social science), No. 6 (1980).
73. *Guangming Daily,* 28 March 1982.
74. *People's Daily,* 26 February 1982.
75. *People's Daily,* 7 March 1984.
76. *Resolution on CPC History (1949–81)* (Beijing, Foreign Languages Press, 1981), p. 8.
77. Ibid., pp. 22, 27.
78. Ibid., p. 29. This statement is hard to verify independently.
79. Ibid., p. 30.
80. Ibid., pp. 34–35.
81. Ibid., p. 43.
82. An example of the first view is in Liang Heng and Judith Shapiro, *Son of the Revolution* (New York, Knopf, 1983). The more ambiguous second position is well illustrated by "Dai Xiaoai," and it became the main thesis of an article drawn from his experiences, by Ronald N. Montaperto, "From Revolutionary Successors to Revolutionaries: Chinese Youth in the Early Stages of the Cultural Revolution," in Robert A. Scalapino, ed., *Elites in the People's Republic of China* (Seattle, University of Washington Press, 1972), pp. 540 ff.

83. *Resolution on CPC History (1949–81),* pp. 44–45.
84. The footnote is hardly needed by now, but it is offered just in case anybody has not yet read Chalmers A. Johnson, *Peasant Nationalism and Communist Power: The Emergence of Revolutionary China, 1937–1945* (Stanford, Stanford University Press, 1962).
85. *Resolution on CPC History (1949–81),* pp. 46, 47.
86. Ibid., p. 51.
87. Ibid., p. 74.
88. See *China Update,* No. 12 (March 1984), p. 1.
89. For background, see the fine paper of Hsuan Mo cited above. For recent material in English, see the series of cover articles in the *Far Eastern Economic Review* of 9 February 1984, by Ian Findlay, David Bonavia, Michel Masson, and Robert Delfts.
90. Critiques of "humanism" have also featured in this campaign – partly because its prime movers found less resistance to attacking people in cultural circles, notably writers, than to attacking those in fields related to the economy.
91. *People's Daily,* 24 December 1983. Ba Jin, during a famous speech published in *Shanghai wenxue* No. 5 (6 May 1962), used a similar word, *kuang* – with a wood radical rather than a bamboo radical as in the 1983 citation above – to denote the "end of a coffin" into which radicals like Yao Wenyuan tried to put writers. See also Lynn White, "Leadership in Shanghai, 1955–69," in Robert A. Scalapino, ed., *Elites,* pp. 334–335.
92. For example, Gong Yuzhi's article in *Red Flag* 1983.19:10–17 – which is translated without credit in *Beijing Review* 27.12:16–20 (19 March 1984).
93. *People's Daily,* 28 January 1983.
94. See *People's Daily,* 26 March 1983; also 21 October 1982.
95. *Guangming Daily,* 18 July and 1 September 1982.
96. *People's Daily,* 22 August 1982.
97. For paeans to thinkers from Chen Peixian and Liu Da, see *Red Flag* 1978.6:41–46, and 1980.1:36–38.
98. See Lin Xiling, "Les vents mauvais," cited above, for an especially juicy anecdote about Ye Jianying's use of position to protect his malfeasant son.
99. *Liaowang* (Lookout), No. 3 (March 1983).
100. Just a few examples, among literally hundreds of similar articles are in *Guangming Daily,* 8 January and 12 March 1983; or *Red Flag* 1979.2:31 ff, or 1980.1:39 ff., or 1982.5:34 ff.; or *People's Daily,* 28 November 1979, or 13 June or 4 June 1982.
101. *Wenhui bao* (Literary news), 18 April 1983.
102. *People's Daily,* 22 January 1984.
103. *Guangming Daily,* 10 October 1982.
104. *Gongren ribao* (Workers' daily), Peking, 5 November 1982.
105. This follows Merle Goldman, "Culture," in Steven M. Goldstein, ed., *China Briefing, 1984* (Boulder, Westview Press, 1985), p. 22.
106. Ibid., pp. 26–29.
107. A striking example, quoted from *Jiaoyu yanjiu* (Educational research) 1981.16:24–39 is in John Israel, "The Ideal of Liberal Education in China,"

in Ronald A. Morse, ed., *The Limits of Reform in China* (Boulder, Westview, 1983), p. 107.

108. This is from *Pravda*, 4 March 1923, tr. in Robert C. Tucker, ed., *The Lenin Anthology* (New York, Norton, 1975), pp. 735–736.

109. Su Shaozhi and Feng Lanrui, in *Jingji yanjiu* (Economic research) 1979.5. Feng is an economist—and her husband, Li Chang, is a member of the Central Committee, a Yenan cadre, and a leading science administrator. Su's identification is confirmed by the name roster, *Zhongguo Shehui Kexue Yuan* (The Chinese Academy of Social Sciences; Peking, CASS, 1983), p. 15.

110. The term is from Franklyn Griffiths, "A Tendency Analysis in Soviet Policy-Making," in H. Gordon Skilling and Franklyn Griffiths, *Interest Groups in Soviet Politics* (Princeton, Princeton University Press, 1971), pp. 335 ff.

111. "*Bai mao, hei mao—jua haozi de jiu shi hao mao.*"

112. Bai Hua's filmscript could be more easily accused of anti-socialism, because it was not so burdened by Marxist jargon. See the articles by the Minister of Culture Zhou Weishi, *Wenyi bao* (Arts news), Peking, No. 19, 1981, and by Tang En and Tang Dacheng (the 'Two Tangs' are pseudonyms for people in the Ministry of Culture) in the same issue.

113. "Reflections on the Intellectual Climate of China," in Morse, p. 121.

114. Ibid., p. 128.

10. New Trends under Deng Xiaoping and His Successors, by Carol Lee Hamrin

1. For a good overview of this period, see Liang Heng and Judith Shapiro, *Intellectual Freedom in China After Mao* (New York, The Fund for Free Expression, 1984), and *Intellectual Freedom in China: An Update* (New York, The Fund for Free Expression Asia Watch Committee, 1985).

2. Perry Link, ed., *Stubborn Weeds: Popular and Controversial Chinese Literature after the Cultural Revolution* (Bloomington, Indiana University Press, 1983), Introduction, pp. 1–30, provides a good discussion of the definition and mechanics of these cycles.

3. Frederick C. Teiwes, *Leadership, Legitimacy, and Conflict in China: From a Charismatic Mao to the Politics of Succession* (Armonk, Sharpe, 1984), pp. 49, 67. Chapter 2, pp. 43–76, is a creative application of Weberian concepts of authority and legitimacy to the Chinese situation. I agree with Teiwes's general interpretation of the post-Mao problem of authority and, in this chapter, explore its impact on state-intellectual relations.

4. Harry Harding, "Marx, Mao, and Markets," *The New Republic*, 7 October 1985, pp. 32–41, also makes the point that "the causes of Chinese reform are to be found, therefore, less in the economic sphere than in the realm of politics" (p. 34), and points to the "crisis of confidence" as a central problem.

5. This is the primary interpretation suggested by Link, p. 10, who attributes "warm winds" to the desire of the "top leadership" to win support of intellectuals at the beginning of a modernization drive, or to encourage complaints about former leaders, or to lure dissenting opinion into the open. "Cold winds" reflect a renewed "burst of faith" in orthodoxy or desire

for social control. He implies that disagreement in the leadership is largely unknowable and (therefore?) secondary.

6. Kjeld Erik Brodsgaard, "The Democracy Movement in China, 1978–1979: Opposition Movements, Wall Poster Campaigns, and Underground Journals," *Asian Survey* 21.7:747–773 (July 1981), reaches this more cynical conclusion. His discussion of vertical and horizontal cleavages at play is quite illuminating, but I think he overlooks the complexity of interests both within the leadership and among intellectuals.

7. Carol Lee Hamrin, "Competing 'Policy Packages' in Post-Mao China," *Asian Survey* 24.5:487–518 (May 1984).

8. Lu Keng, "A Meeting with Wang Ruoshui in Beijing," Hong Kong *Pai Hsing* 103:18–21 (1 September 1985), pp. 18–21, in *FBIS*, 10 September 1985, pp. W1–9.

9. Personal conversations with former PRC citizens, both Christian and non-Christian. Officially, the regime admits to only 6 million Christians in China; privately, an official with the Institute of World Religions at the Academy of Social Sciences volunteered the 15-million number. Informed Chinese Christian leaders in Hong Kong believe the number may be much higher. While Christianity is still the faith of just a small minority of the total population, episodes in the Spiritual Pollution Campaign indicated that it is viewed as a threat to the Party in competition for the loyalty of youth. Two possible reasons come to mind: Christianity increasingly is seen as a religion compatible with or even causally connected to modernity in the West; and its membership in China has a higher level of commitment than the bloated, cynical Party rank and file.

10. George Konrád and Ivan Szelenyi, *The Intellectuals on the Road to Class Power* (New York, Harcourt Brace, 1979), in a rich discussion of the privileged position accorded intellectuals, especially as planners, in Leninist systems in Eastern Europe, makes the perceptive comment that Liu Shaoqi's program in the early 1960s was a "class program for the intellectuals." The revised version of that program today similarly offers much to intellectuals. For an excellent discussion of traditional attitudes that retain salience, see Andrew J. Nathan, *Chinese Democracy* (New York, Knopf, 1985).

11. Hu Yaobang, "The Radiance of the Great Truth of Marxism Lights Our Way Forward," speech at the meeting in commemoration of the centenary of the death of Karl Marx, *Xinhua*, 13 March 1983, in *FBIS*, 14 March 1983, pp. K1–17.

12. Su Shaozhi, "Develop Marxism Under Contemporary Conditions: in Commemoration of the Centenary of the Death of Karl Marx," *Selected Writings on Studies of Marxism*, No. 2, 1983 (Beijing, Institute of Marxism-Leninism-Mao Zedong Thought, CASS), p. 6.

13. Ibid., p. 32.

14. In personal conversation, a theoretician familiar with the dispute confirmed that criticism of this concept in Politburo member Wang Zhen's October 1983 public criticism of literary "modernism" and three "heretical" theories was aimed directly at Su.

15. Thomas B. Gold, "'Just in Time!' China Battles Spiritual Pollution on the

Eve of 1984," *Asian Survey* 24.9:947–974 (September 1984), provides an excellent summary of the campaign, noting that it must be analyzed "as primarily an elite power struggle," and linking it with the fundamental authority problem of defining the acceptable limit of social autonomy in China.

16. On the congress, see: Hu Qili, congratulatory speech at the 4th National Congress of the Chinese Writers Asociation, 29 December 1984, in *Xinhua*, same date, in *FBIS*, 31 December 1984, pp. K4–6; and Chen Chi-sun, "Reorganization of the Writers Association on China's Mainland as seen from the Namelist of its Directors," Hong Kong *Pai Hsing*, No. 90, 16 February 1985, pp. 18–19, in *FBIS*, 5 March 1985, pp. W1–3.

17. In separate conversations, several intellectuals from different organizations have stressed this linkage in early 1985.

18. See note 8 above and Hu Yaobang, "On the Party's Journalism Work," speech at a meeting of the CCP Secretariat on 8 February 1985, in *FBIS*, 15 April 1985, pp. K1–14.

19. Wang Meng, comments to a work meeting of the China Writers' Association, *Xinhua*, 5 November 1985, in *FBIS*, 6 November 1985, pp. K3–5.

20. Yu Guangyuan, "Have a Clear Idea of the Place of Cultural Development in Social Development," *Guangming Daily*, 13 January 1986, p. 2, in *FBIS*, 31 January 1986, pp. K18–20.

21. See reports on the symposium by Huang Qing in *China Daily*, 9 June 1986, p. 4, in *FBIS*, 11 June 1986, pp. K11–12, and by Chen Lebo in *World Economic Herald*, 26 May 1986, pp. 1–2, in *FBIS*, 13 June 1986, pp. R1–2.

22. Liang and Shapiro, *Update*, p. 53.

INDEX

a new class, 219; new power of, 222, 224
International law. *See* Foreign investment
law
Israel, John, 4–5

Japan: influence on professionalism, 4; in
Guo Muruo's play, 187
Jian Bozan, 5; rehabilitation of, 65, 93–94,
95–96; career of, 66; on history, 67–68;
relation to CCP, 68, 71; and cultural na-
tionalism movement, 71–73, 75; the
Great Leap mobilization, 73–75, 90; on
historicism, 75–88; and bureaucratic
authority, 88–90; quest for limited pro-
fessional autonomy, 91–92, 105; republi-
cation of, 96. *See also* Historicism
Jian Siping, 94
Jiang Qing, 14, 115, 210, 221
Jiang Zhuying, 271
Jiaotong University, 261; re-assignment of
personnel by 262
Jiaru woshi zhende (If I were real; Sha Yexin),
224, 244
Jiefang ribao (Liberation daily), 27, 30, 138,
235, 236
Jingji yanjiu, 58
Joint-Venture law, 113, 122
Journalists: protection demanded, 17; as
channels of communication, 199, 200,
288; propaganda role of, 285, 298
Journey to the West, 243
Justice, Ministry of, on admission to the
bar, 120

Kang Sheng, 33–34, 236
Kang Youwei, 103–104
Kaplan, Nathan, 138, 149
Kassil, Lev, 228
Ke Ling, 17
Ke Yunlu, 221
Keats, John, 39
Kelly, David, 8, 9, 12, 287, 288, 291
Kexue lishiguan jiaocheng (Textbook on the
scientific view of history; Ai Siqi and
Wu Liping), 30
Khrushchev, Nikita, 32, 197, 200
Kipphardt, Heinar, 228
Kisch, Egon Erwin, 193
Kolakowski, Leszek, 40
Komakadamiia, textbooks for, 28
Konrád, George, 14–15, 228, 229, 230
Konwicki, Tadeucz, 228, 230
Korean War, 253
Krasnaia zvezda (Red star; Bogdanov), 39
Kublai Khan, 206, 207, 208, 227

Kulian (film), 219, 226, 248; banned, 220;
and "History Will Prove," 221–224
Kundera, Milan, 228, 229
Kunikida Doppo, 39

Land reform, *The Hurrican* on, 193–194
Lao Can's Travels (Liu E), 185, 226, 227
Lawyers: post-Mao training of, 110, 112;
status of, 110–111, 116–117; fields of,
113–115; regulation of, 117–121; qualifications of, 118–120, 122–123; role in defense, 123–125. *See also* Legal profession
"Lawyers' Law," 109
Lee, Leo Ou-fan, 10, 186
Legal Advisory Offices (LAOs), 120–121
Legal profession: in West vs. China, 107; in
Qing dynasty, 108–109; during post-
Mao era, 109–111, 280; residual problems of, 111–112; emergence of new system, 112–115; foreign-investment law,
113–114, 116, 122–123; criminal law,
114–115, 123–125; domestic economic
regulation, 115, 117, 125–126; CCP's reg-
ulation of, 117–121; future prospects of,
121–126; Wang Ruowang on, 241; re-
forms urged, 300
Leiyu (Cao Yu), 244
Lenin, Nikolai, 80, 83, 272, 294; on func-
tion of writers, 192
Leninism: and control of intellectuals, 19,
184; in post-Mao era, 289, 290
Li Da, 38
Li Dazhao, 24
Li Fuchun, 49–50, 58; and report on indus-
try, 51, 54, 56; on specialists, 57; and Sun
Yefang, 58, 59, 60, 61
Li Honglin, 15; on historicism, 95
Li Huiniang, 208
Li Kan, 99–100
Li Shengmian, 38
Li Xiannian, 270
Li Yizhe, 181
Liang Shuming, 160, 164; Ai Siqi in cam-
paign against, 32
Liaoning, 146
Liaowang, 146
Lin Biao, 14, 94, 101, 115, 164, 167
Lin-Jiang clique, 115
Lin Mohan, 31, 172, 264
Lin Mu, 263
Lindbeck, John, 133, 134
"Lishi jiang zhengming" (History will
prove; Ke Yunlu), 221, 230; in *Kulian*
case, 221–224
Lishi yanjiu, 93; legitimation of historicism